BLUE PERIOD

TSUBASA YAMAGUCHI

11

No one wears anything different when they make art outside

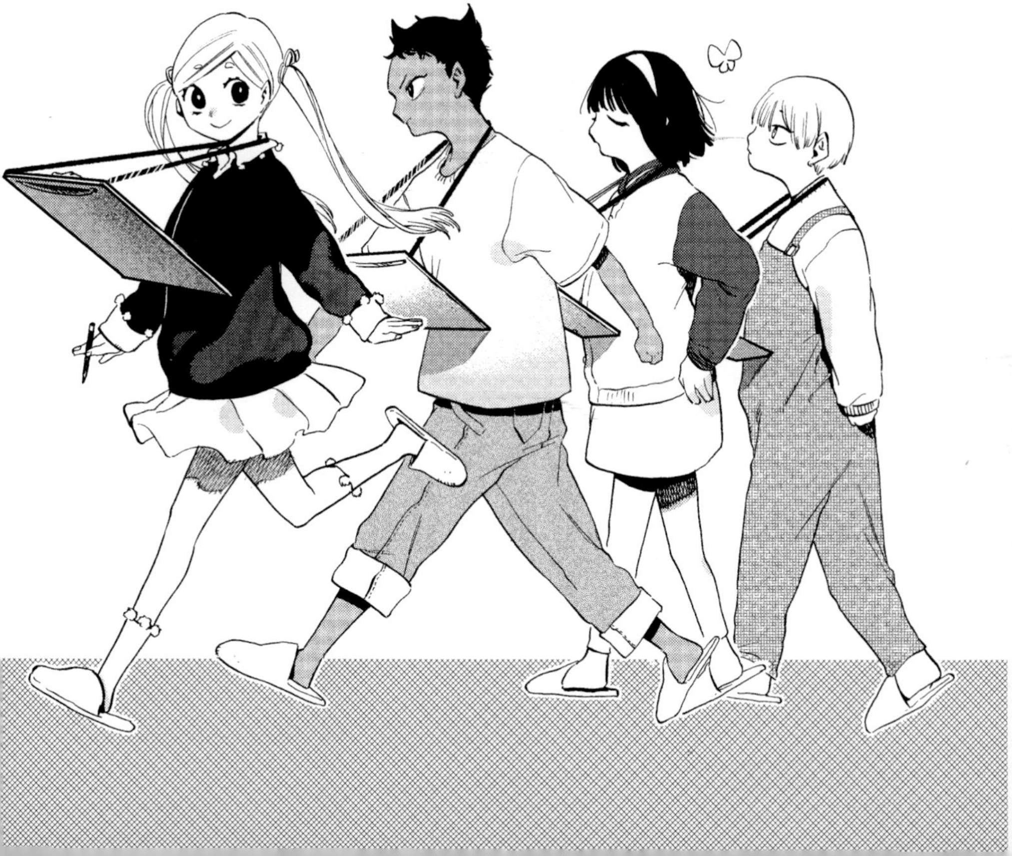

CHARACTERS

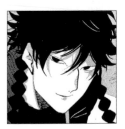

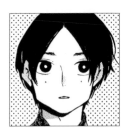

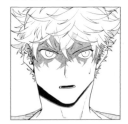

Yatora Yaguchi
After getting hooked on the joy of making art, he studied to get into Tokyo University of the Arts, the most competitive of all Japanese art colleges, and passed on his first attempt. He's a hardworking normie.

Yotasuke Takahashi
He studied on his own and passed TUA's exams on his first attempt. His talent, skills, and unsociable character inspire Yatora to be a better artist.

Haruka Hashida
He used to attend the same prep school as Yatora. He's currently a first-year at Tama Art University.

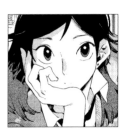

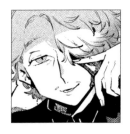

Masako Saeki
Yatora's former art teacher. She's a high school art teacher and the advisor for her school's Art Club.

Maki Kuwana
She used to attend the same prep school as Yatora. She aimed for TUA but failed to get in and is now studying for next year's exam.

TABLE OF CONTENTS

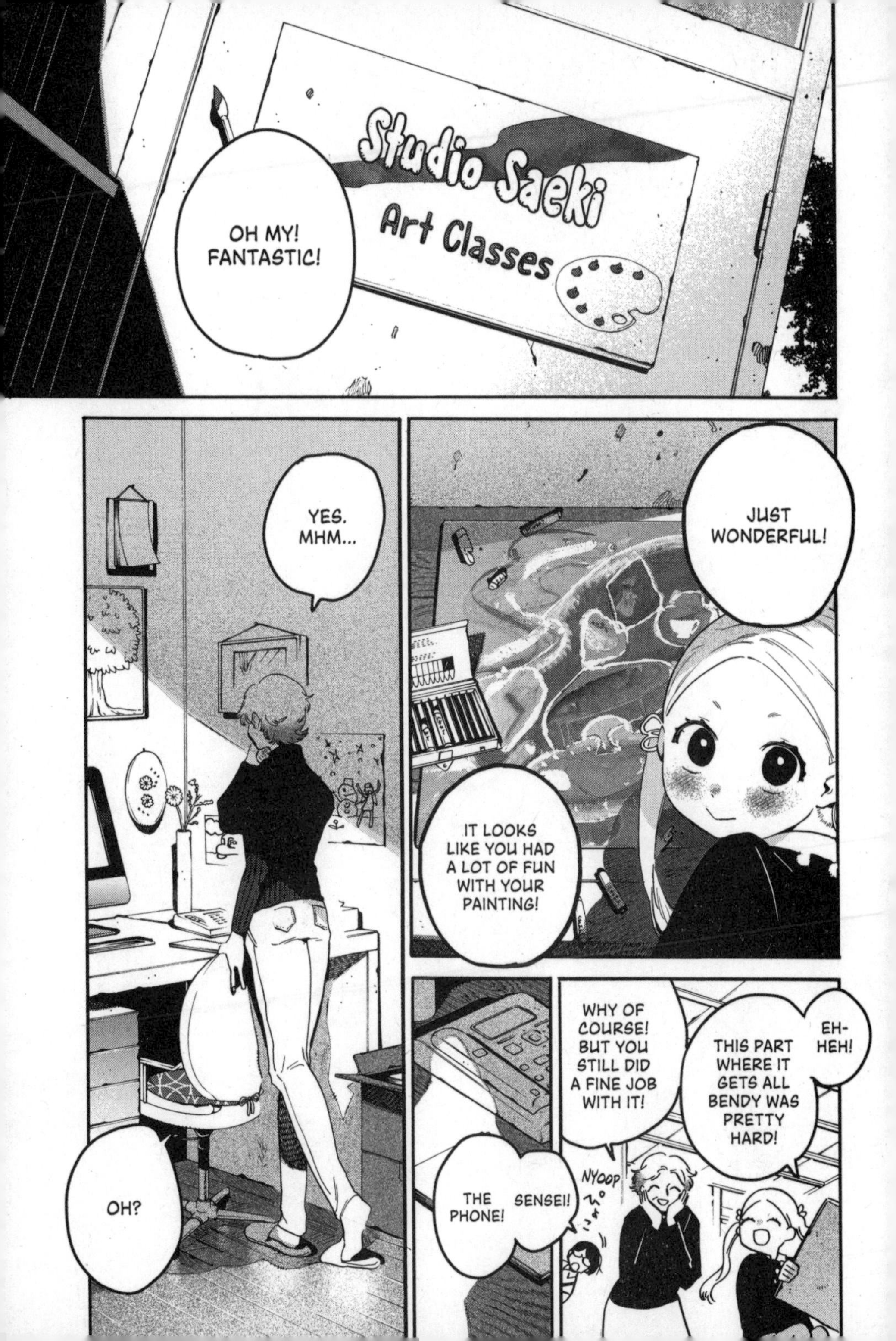
Studio Saeki
Art Classes
OH MY! FANTASTIC!
JUST WONDERFUL!
IT LOOKS LIKE YOU HAD A LOT OF FUN WITH YOUR PAINTING!
EH-HEH!
THIS PART WHERE IT GETS ALL BENDY WAS PRETTY HARD!
WHY OF COURSE! BUT YOU STILL DID A FINE JOB WITH IT!
NYOOP
SENSEI! THE PHONE!
YES. MHM...
OH?

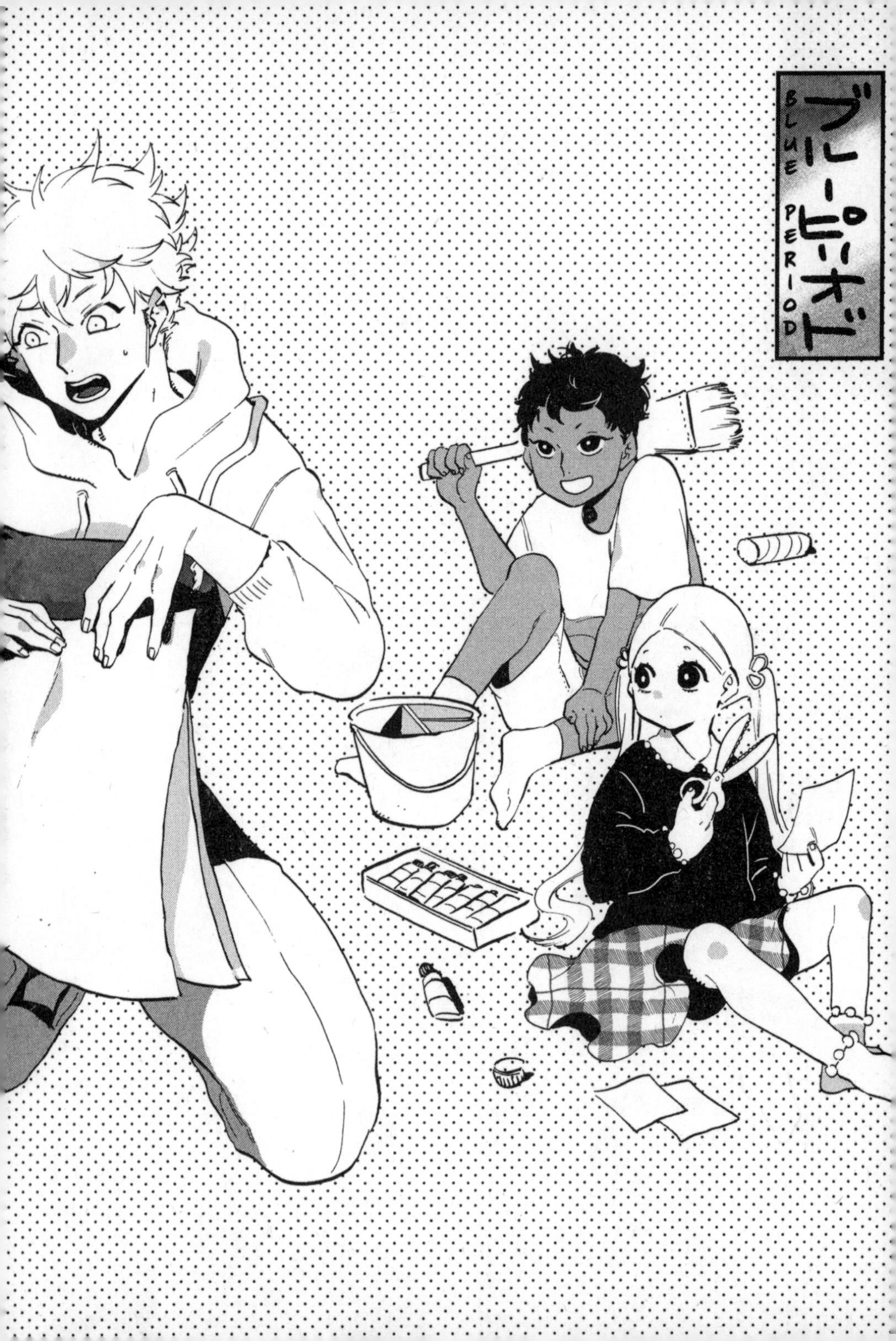
ブルーピリオド
BLUE PERIOD

STROKE 43

WHY, WHY, WHY

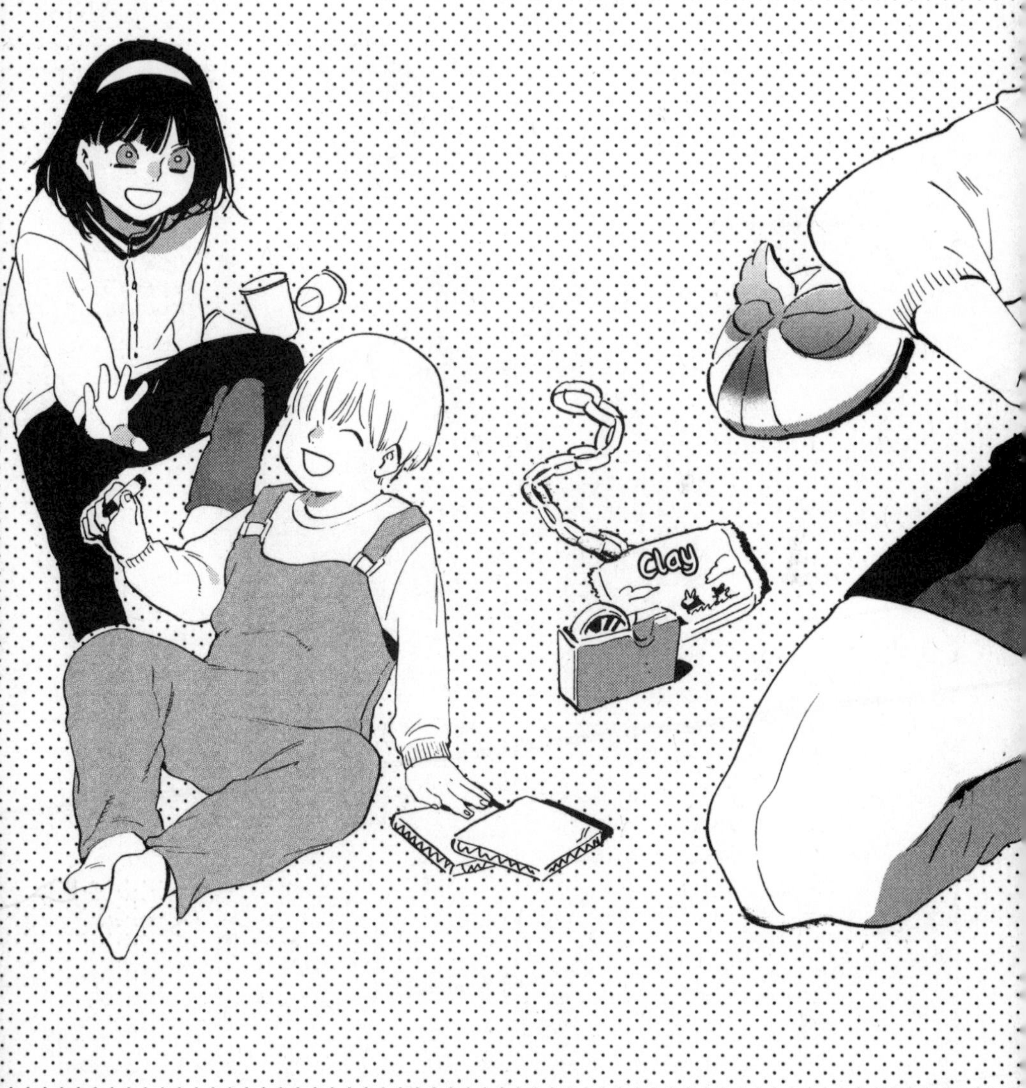
Clay

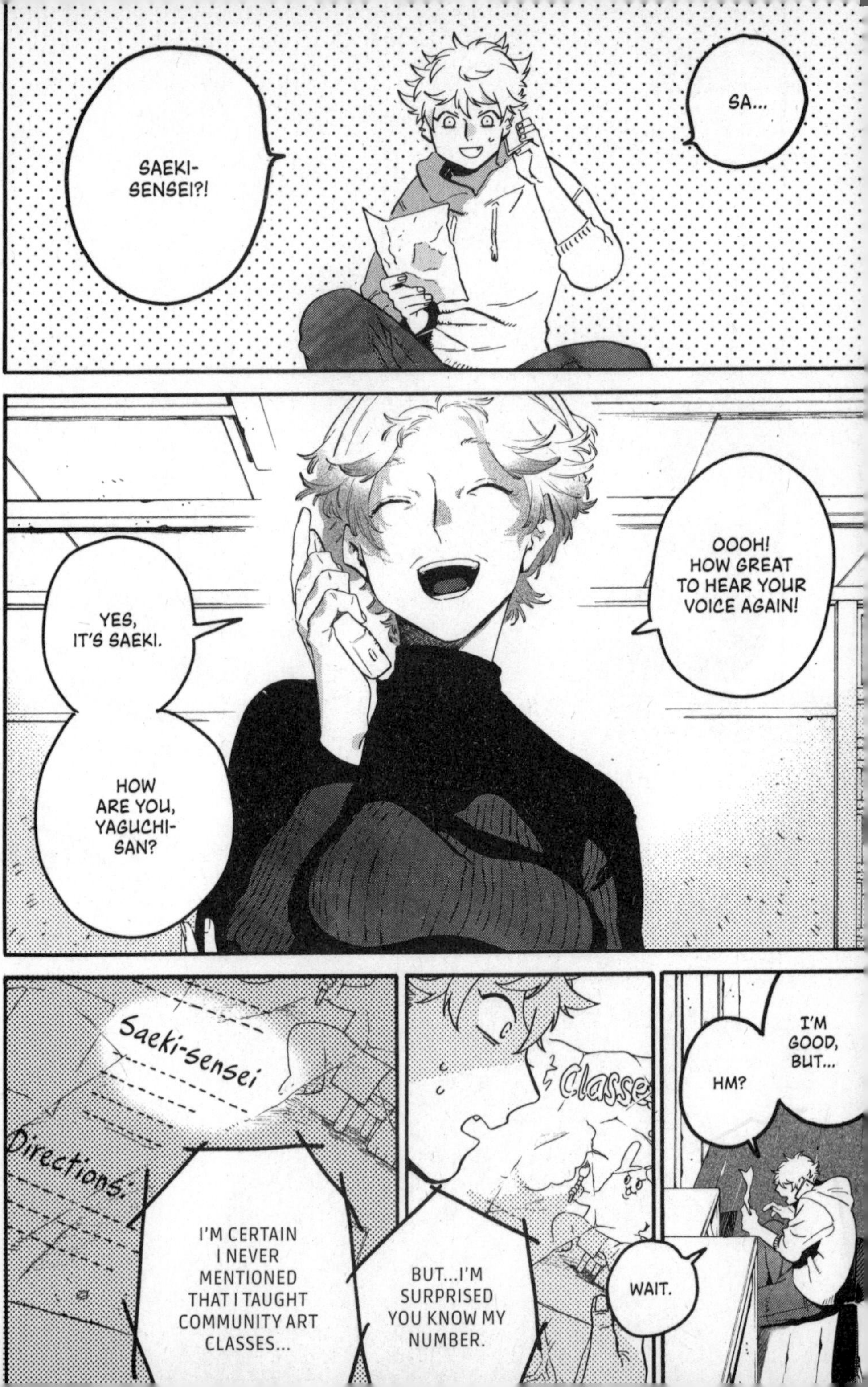
SA...
SAEKI-SENSEI?!
OOOH! HOW GREAT TO HEAR YOUR VOICE AGAIN!
YES, IT'S SAEKI.
HOW ARE YOU, YAGUCHI-SAN?
I'M GOOD, BUT...
HM?
WAIT.
Classes
BUT...I'M SURPRISED YOU KNOW MY NUMBER.
Saeki-sensei
Directions:
I'M CERTAIN I NEVER MENTIONED THAT I TAUGHT COMMUNITY ART CLASSES...

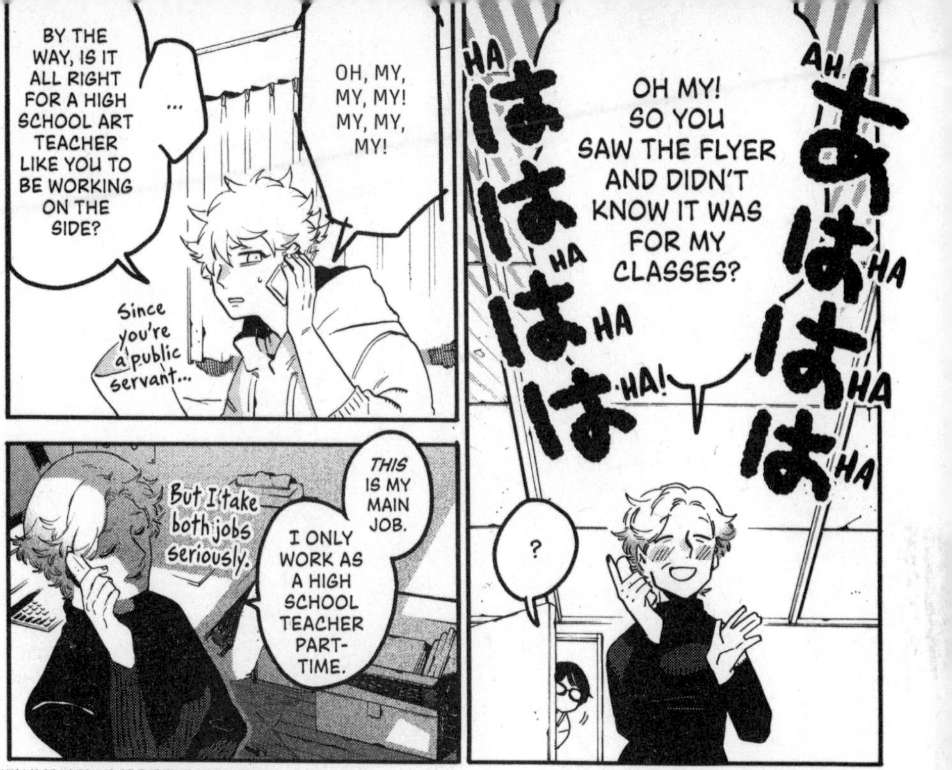
AH
あははは
HA HA HA HA
HA
ははは
HA HA HA!
OH MY! SO YOU SAW THE FLYER AND DIDN'T KNOW IT WAS FOR MY CLASSES?
?
OH, MY, MY, MY! MY, MY, MY!
...
BY THE WAY, IS IT ALL RIGHT FOR A HIGH SCHOOL ART TEACHER LIKE YOU TO BE WORKING ON THE SIDE?
Since you're a public servant...
THIS IS MY MAIN JOB.
I ONLY WORK AS A HIGH SCHOOL TEACHER PART-TIME.
But I take both jobs seriously.

*THE MINIMUM WAGE IN TOKYO AT THE TIME OF PRINTING.

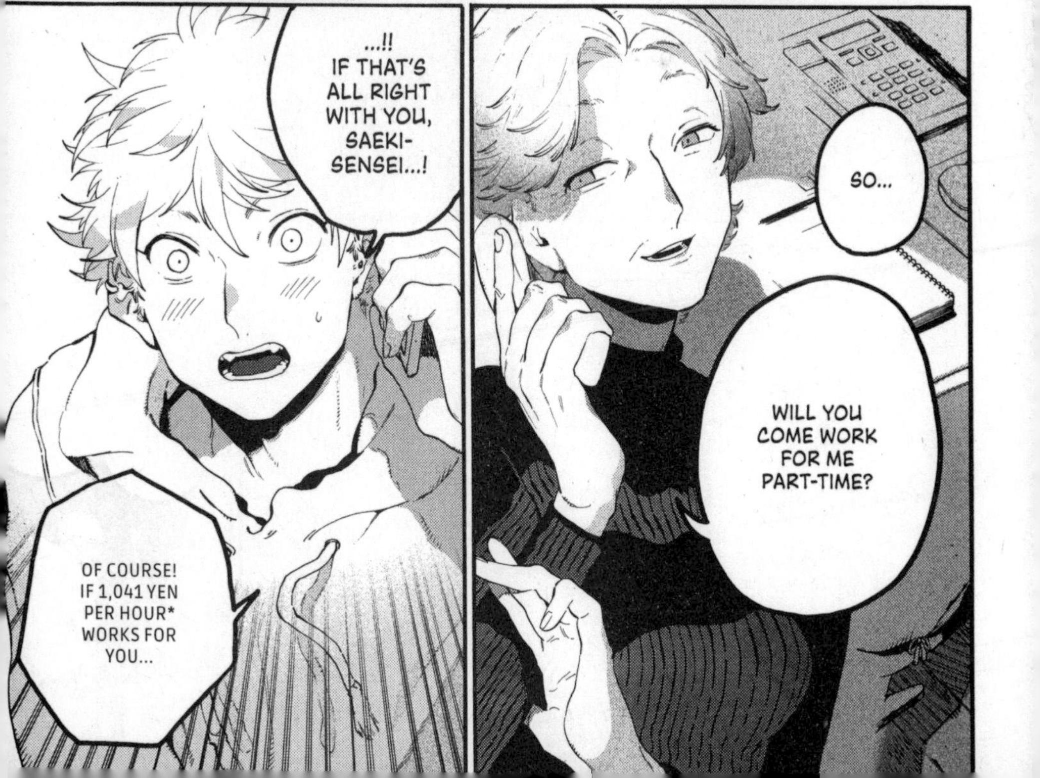
SO...
WILL YOU COME WORK FOR ME PART-TIME?
...!! IF THAT'S ALL RIGHT WITH YOU, SAEKI-SENSEI...!
OF COURSE! IF 1,041 YEN PER HOUR* WORKS FOR YOU...

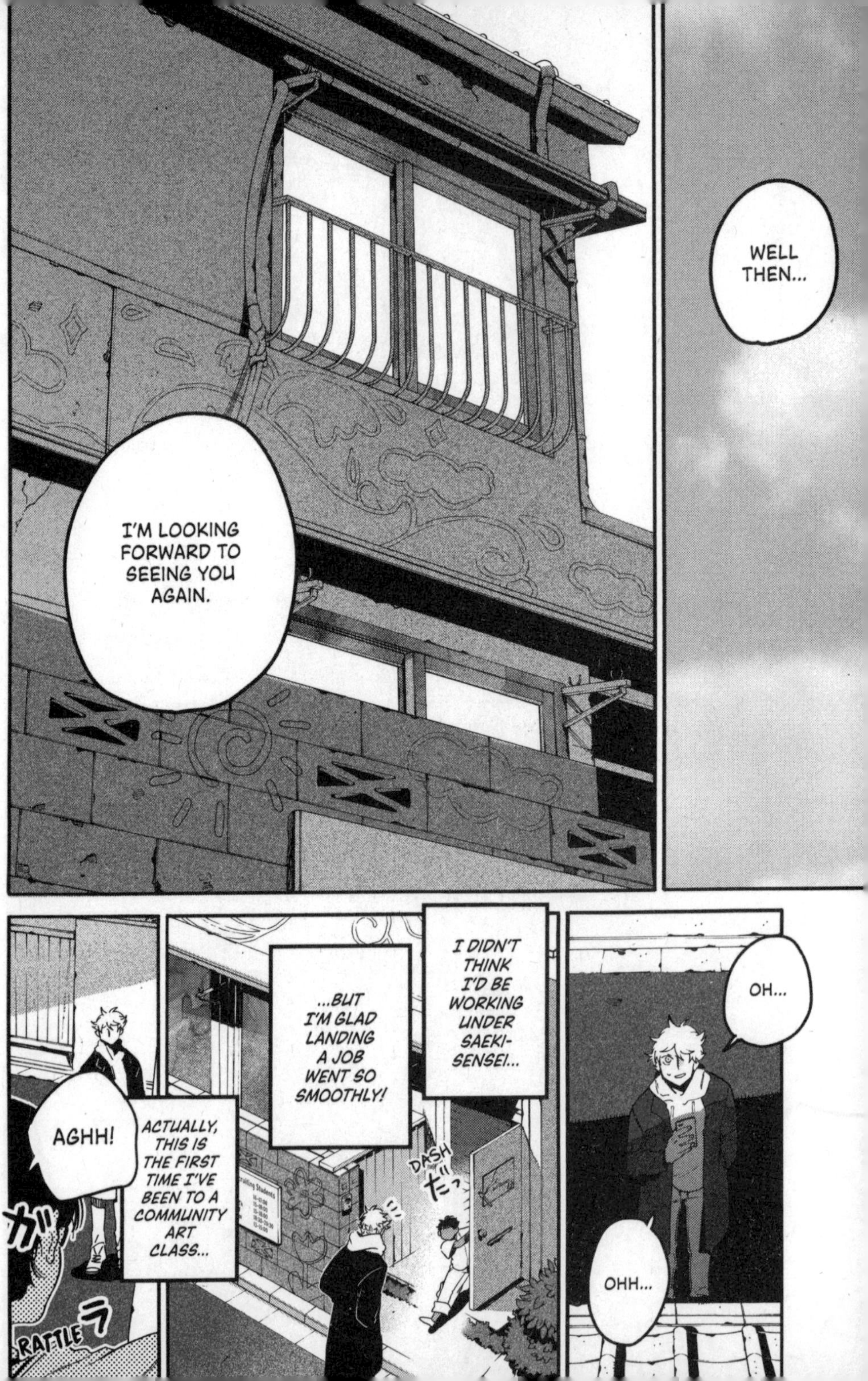
WELL THEN...
I'M LOOKING FORWARD TO SEEING YOU AGAIN.
OH...
OHH...
I DIDN'T THINK I'D BE WORKING UNDER SAEKI-SENSEI...
...BUT I'M GLAD LANDING A JOB WENT SO SMOOTHLY!
DASH だっ
ACTUALLY, THIS IS THE FIRST TIME I'VE BEEN TO A COMMUNITY ART CLASS...
AGHH!
ガ
RATTLE ラ

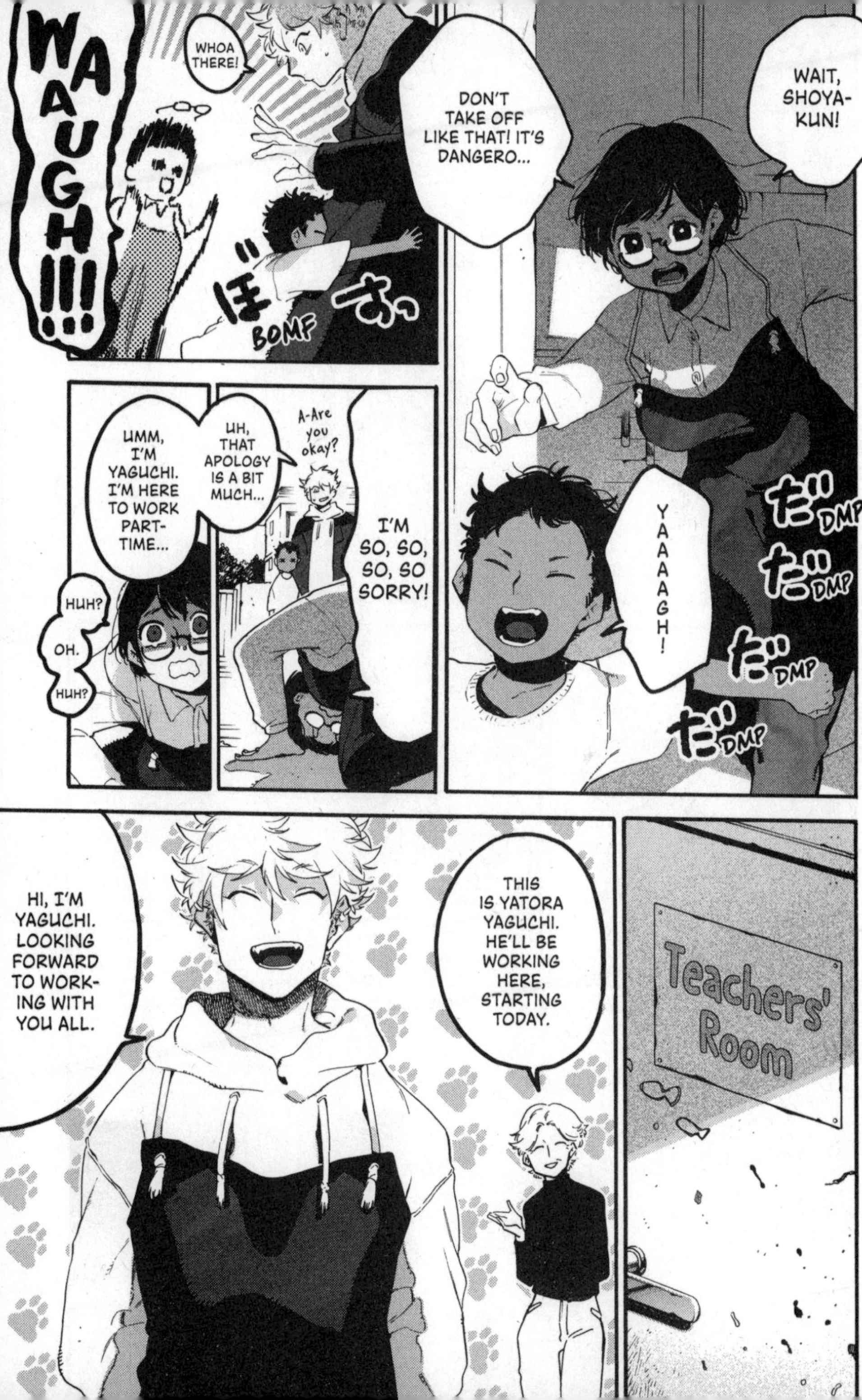
WAIT, SHOYA-KUN!
YAAAAAGH!
DMP
DMP
DMP
DMP
DON'T TAKE OFF LIKE THAT! IT'S DANGERO...
WHOA THERE!
WAAUGH!!!
BOMF
I'M SO, SO, SO, SO SORRY!
A-Are you okay?
UH, THAT APOLOGY IS A BIT MUCH...
UMM, I'M YAGUCHI. I'M HERE TO WORK PART-TIME...
HUH?
OH.
HUH?
Teachers' Room
THIS IS YATORA YAGUCHI. HE'LL BE WORKING HERE, STARTING TODAY.
HI, I'M YAGUCHI. LOOKING FORWARD TO WORKING WITH YOU ALL.

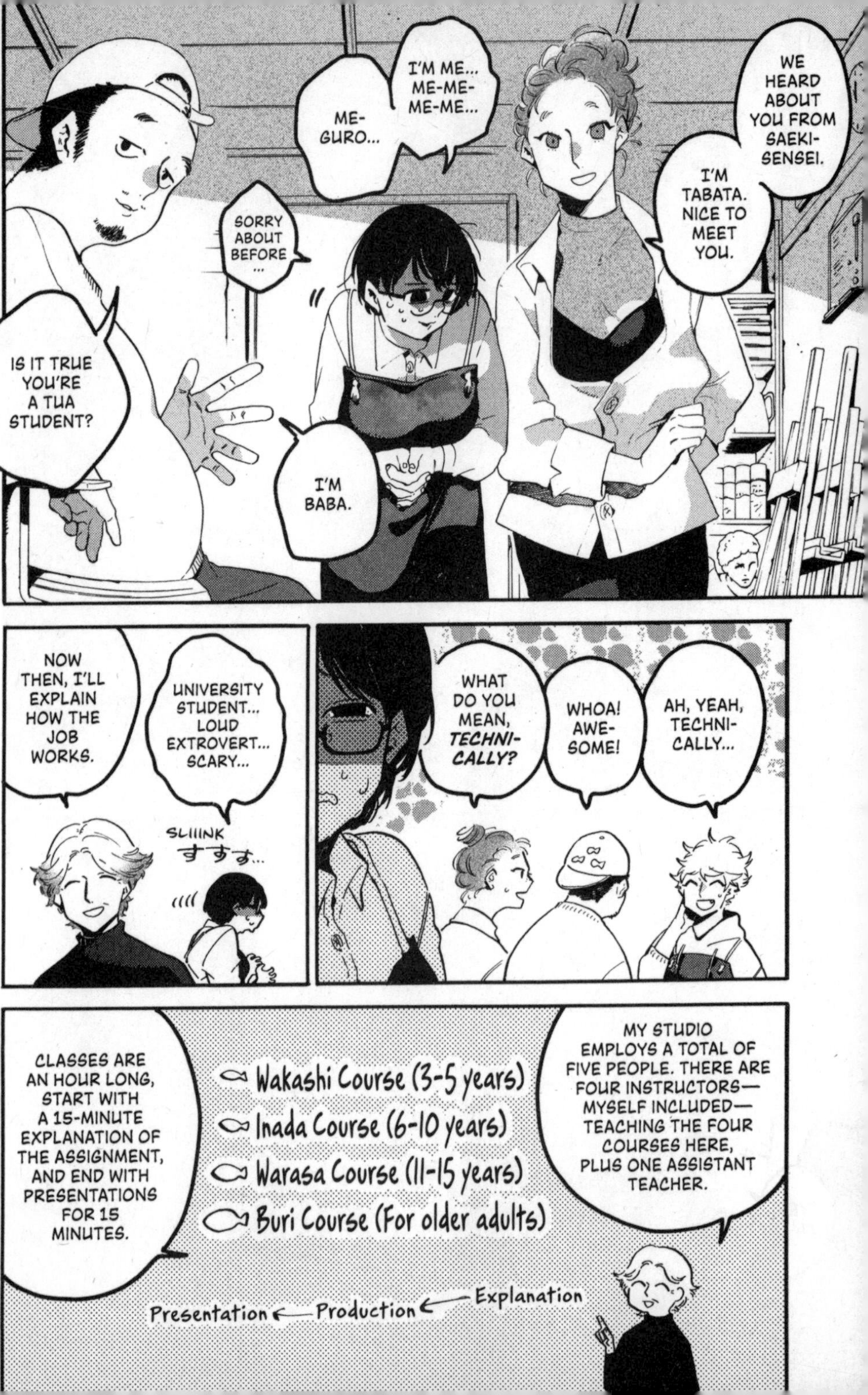
WE HEARD ABOUT YOU FROM SAEKI-SENSEI.
I'M TABATA. NICE TO MEET YOU.
I'M ME... ME-ME-ME-ME...
ME-GURO...
SORRY ABOUT BEFORE...
IS IT TRUE YOU'RE A TUA STUDENT?
I'M BABA.
AH, YEAH, TECHNICALLY...
WHOA! AWESOME!
WHAT DO YOU MEAN, *TECHNICALLY?*
UNIVERSITY STUDENT... LOUD EXTROVERT... SCARY...
NOW THEN, I'LL EXPLAIN HOW THE JOB WORKS.
SLIIINK
すすす...
MY STUDIO EMPLOYS A TOTAL OF FIVE PEOPLE. THERE ARE FOUR INSTRUCTORS—MYSELF INCLUDED—TEACHING THE FOUR COURSES HERE, PLUS ONE ASSISTANT TEACHER.
Wakashi Course (3-5 years)
Inada Course (6-10 years)
Warasa Course (11-15 years)
Buri Course (For older adults)
CLASSES ARE AN HOUR LONG, START WITH A 15-MINUTE EXPLANATION OF THE ASSIGNMENT, AND END WITH PRESENTATIONS FOR 15 MINUTES.
Explanation
Production
Presentation

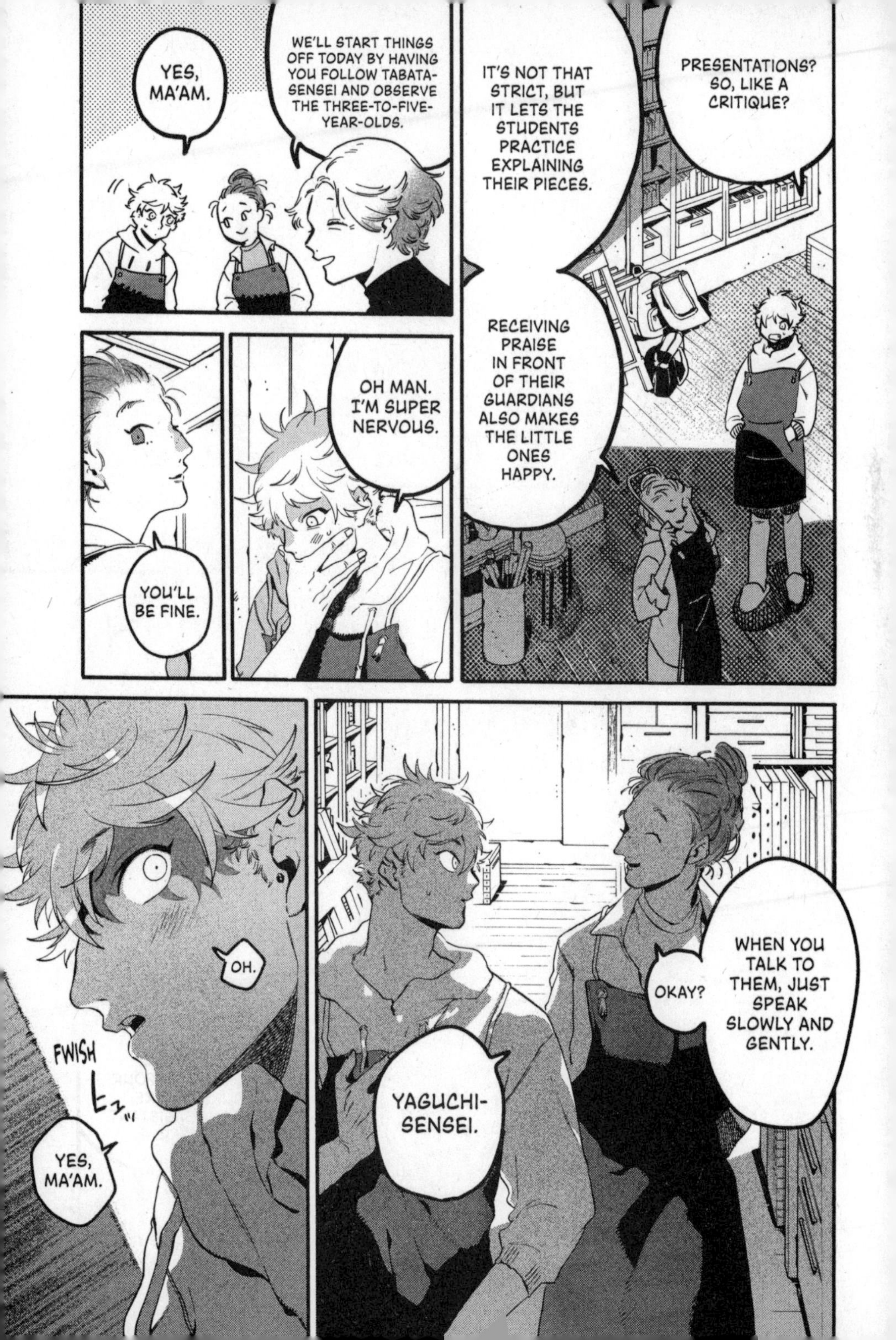
PRESENTATIONS? SO, LIKE A CRITIQUE?
IT'S NOT THAT STRICT, BUT IT LETS THE STUDENTS PRACTICE EXPLAINING THEIR PIECES.
RECEIVING PRAISE IN FRONT OF THEIR GUARDIANS ALSO MAKES THE LITTLE ONES HAPPY.
WE'LL START THINGS OFF TODAY BY HAVING YOU FOLLOW TABATA-SENSEI AND OBSERVE THE THREE-TO-FIVE-YEAR-OLDS.
YES, MA'AM.
OH MAN. I'M SUPER NERVOUS.
YOU'LL BE FINE.
WHEN YOU TALK TO THEM, JUST SPEAK SLOWLY AND GENTLY.
OKAY?
YAGUCHI-SENSEI.
OH.
FWISH
YES, MA'AM.

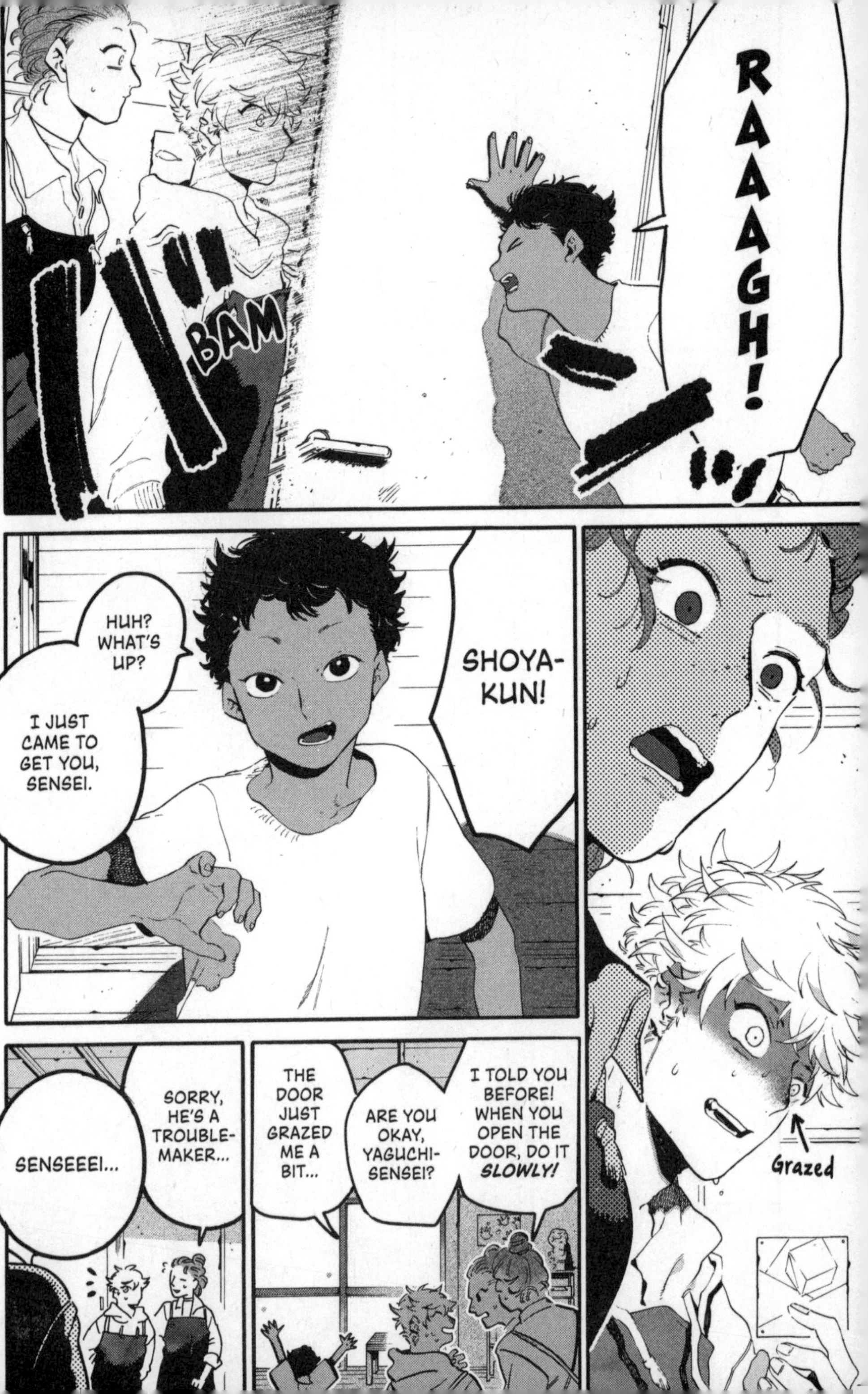
RAAAGH!
BAM
Grazed
SHOYA-KUN!
HUH? WHAT'S UP?
I JUST CAME TO GET YOU, SENSEI.
I TOLD YOU BEFORE! WHEN YOU OPEN THE DOOR, DO IT *SLOWLY!*
ARE YOU OKAY, YAGUCHI-SENSEI?
THE DOOR JUST GRAZED ME A BIT...
SORRY, HE'S A TROUBLE-MAKER...
SENSEEEI...

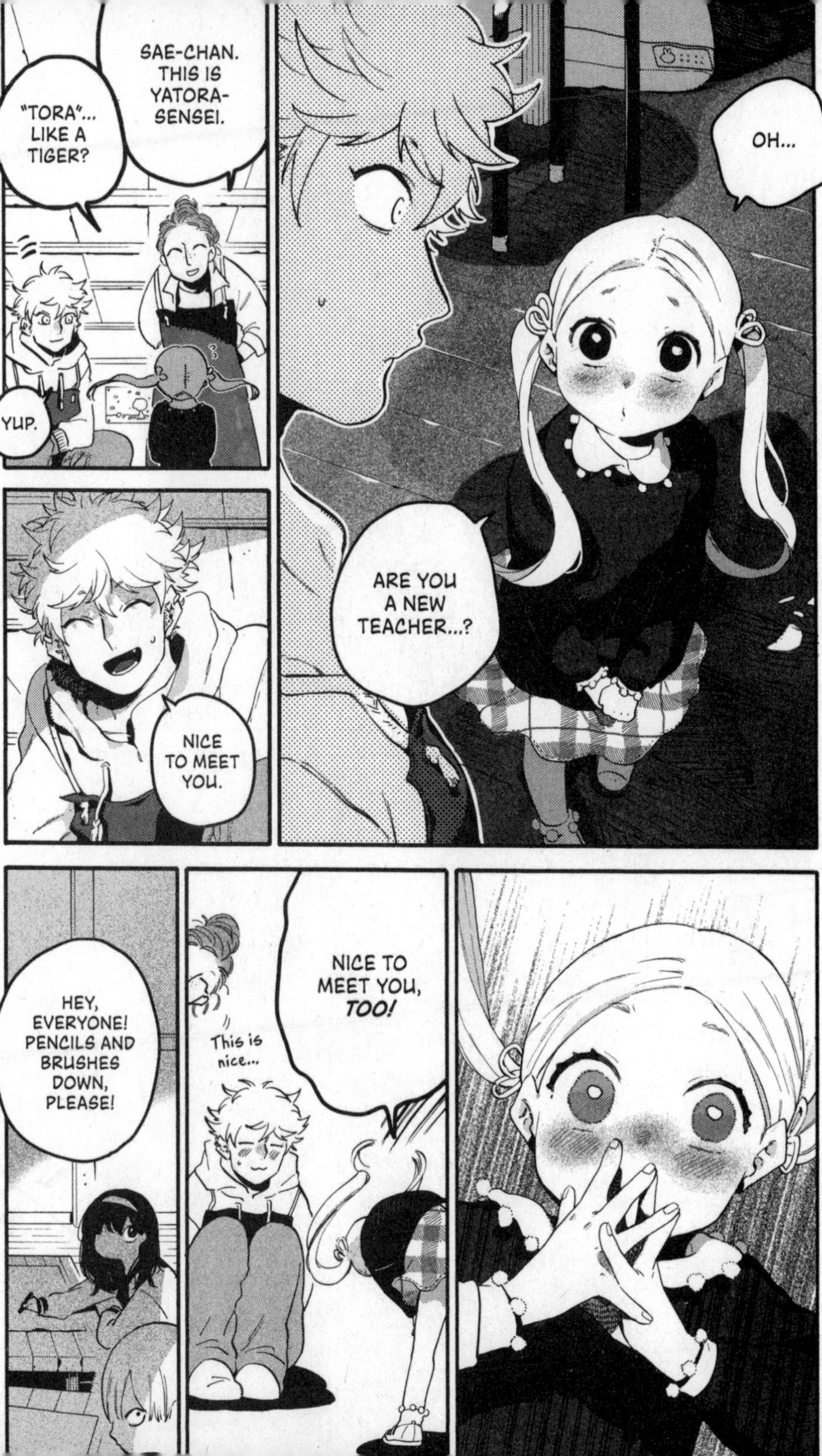
OH...
ARE YOU A NEW TEACHER...?
SAE-CHAN. THIS IS YATORA-SENSEI.
"TORA"... LIKE A TIGER?
YUP.
NICE TO MEET YOU.
NICE TO MEET YOU, *TOO!*
This is nice...
HEY, EVERYONE! PENCILS AND BRUSHES DOWN, PLEASE!

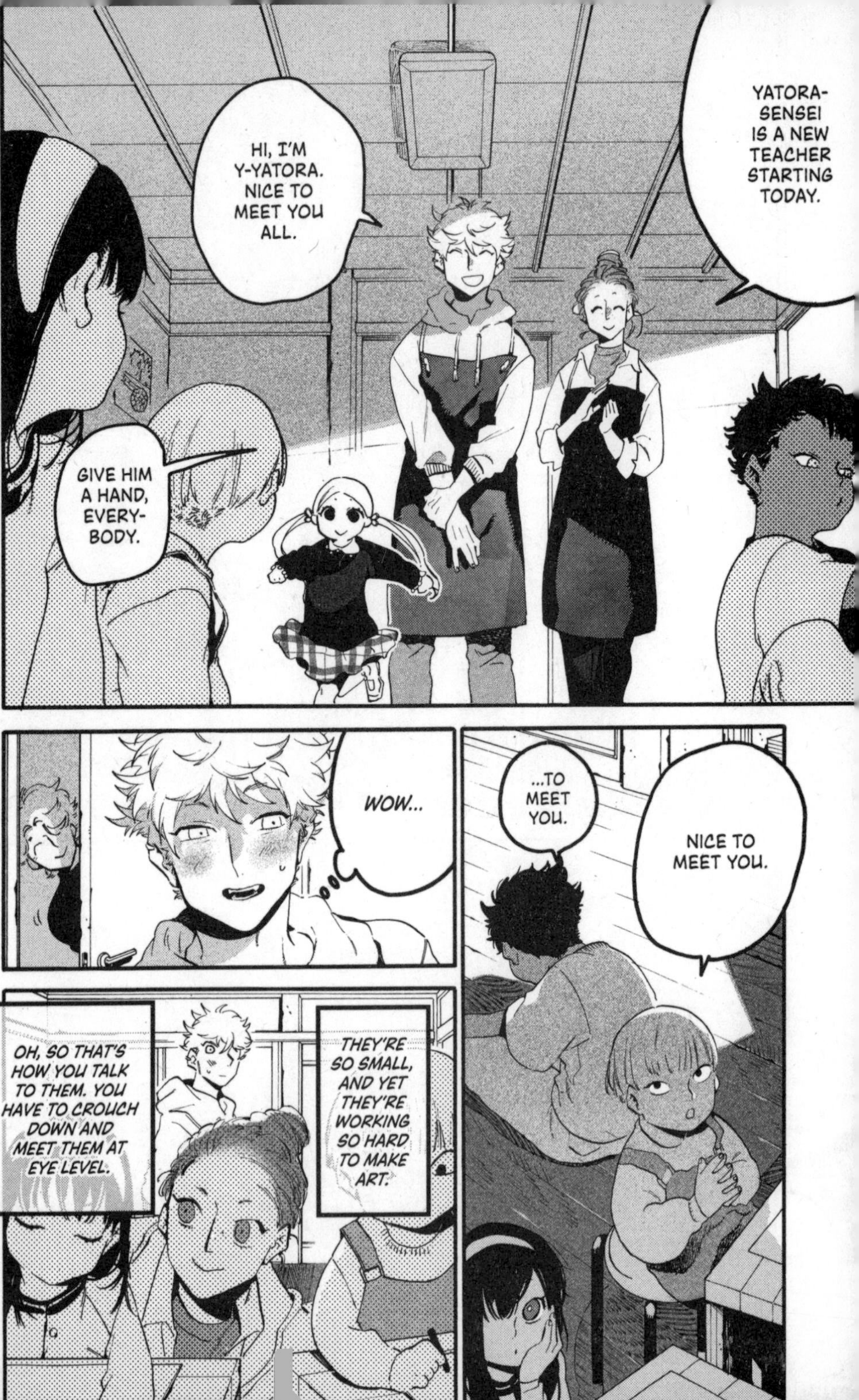
YATORA-SENSEI IS A NEW TEACHER STARTING TODAY.
HI, I'M Y-YATORA. NICE TO MEET YOU ALL.
GIVE HIM A HAND, EVERY-BODY.
NICE TO MEET YOU.
...TO MEET YOU.
WOW...
THEY'RE SO SMALL, AND YET THEY'RE WORKING SO HARD TO MAKE ART.
OH, SO THAT'S HOW YOU TALK TO THEM. YOU HAVE TO CROUCH DOWN AND MEET THEM AT EYE LEVEL.

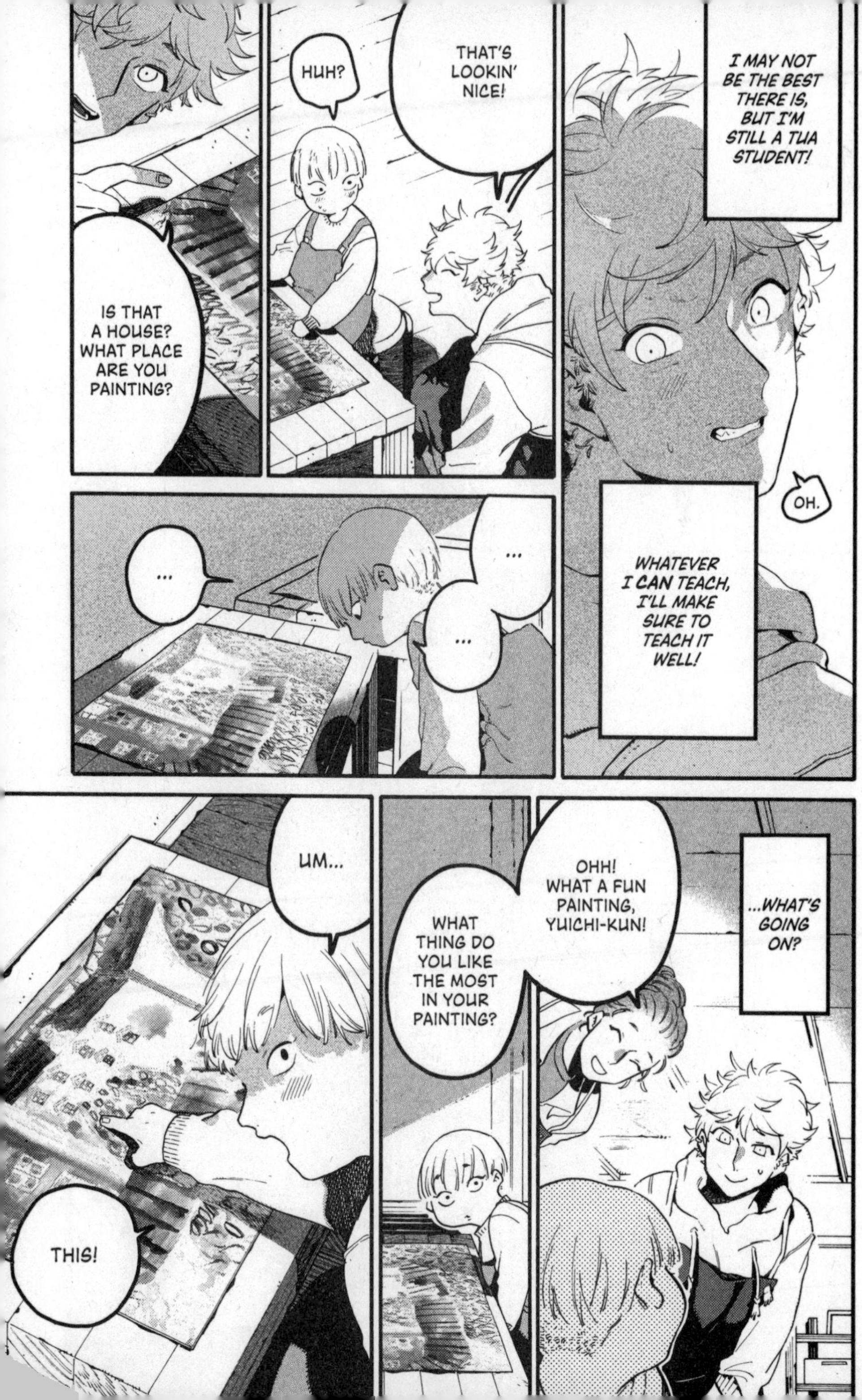

I MAY NOT BE THE BEST THERE IS, BUT I'M STILL A TUA STUDENT!
OH.
WHATEVER I CAN TEACH, I'LL MAKE SURE TO TEACH IT WELL!
THAT'S LOOKIN' NICE!
HUH?
IS THAT A HOUSE? WHAT PLACE ARE YOU PAINTING?
...
...
...
...WHAT'S GOING ON?
OHH! WHAT A FUN PAINTING, YUICHI-KUN!
WHAT THING DO YOU LIKE THE MOST IN YOUR PAINTING?
UM...
THIS!

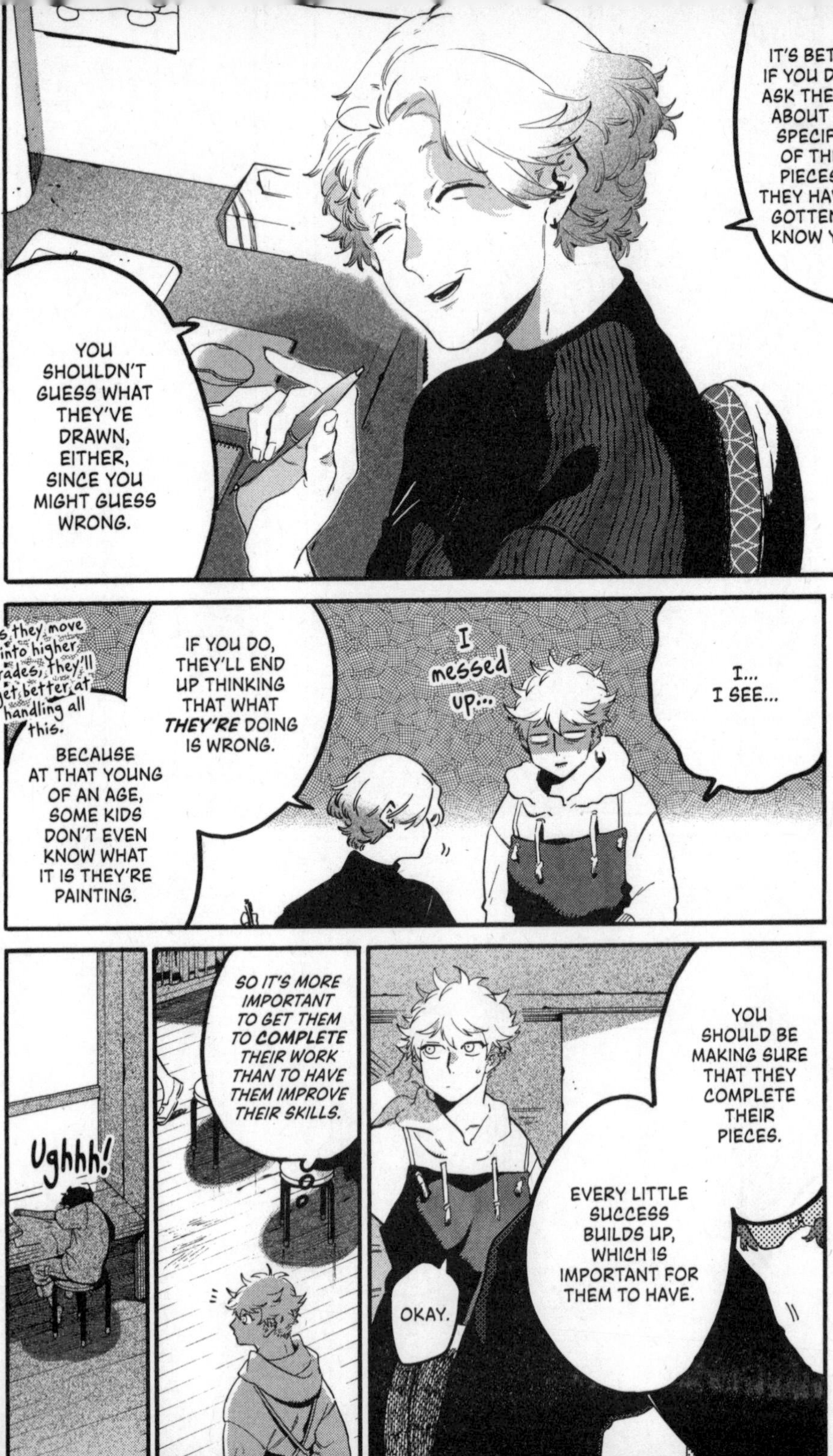
IT'S BETTER IF YOU DON'T ASK THE KIDS ABOUT THE SPECIFICS OF THEIR PIECES IF THEY HAVEN'T GOTTEN TO KNOW YOU.
YOU SHOULDN'T GUESS WHAT THEY'VE DRAWN, EITHER, SINCE YOU MIGHT GUESS WRONG.
I... I SEE...
I messed up...
IF YOU DO, THEY'LL END UP THINKING THAT WHAT THEY'RE DOING IS WRONG.
BECAUSE AT THAT YOUNG OF AN AGE, SOME KIDS DON'T EVEN KNOW WHAT IT IS THEY'RE PAINTING.
As they move into higher grades, they'll get better at handling all this.
YOU SHOULD BE MAKING SURE THAT THEY COMPLETE THEIR PIECES.
EVERY LITTLE SUCCESS BUILDS UP, WHICH IS IMPORTANT FOR THEM TO HAVE.
OKAY.
SO IT'S MORE IMPORTANT TO GET THEM TO COMPLETE THEIR WORK THAN TO HAVE THEM IMPROVE THEIR SKILLS.
Ughhh!

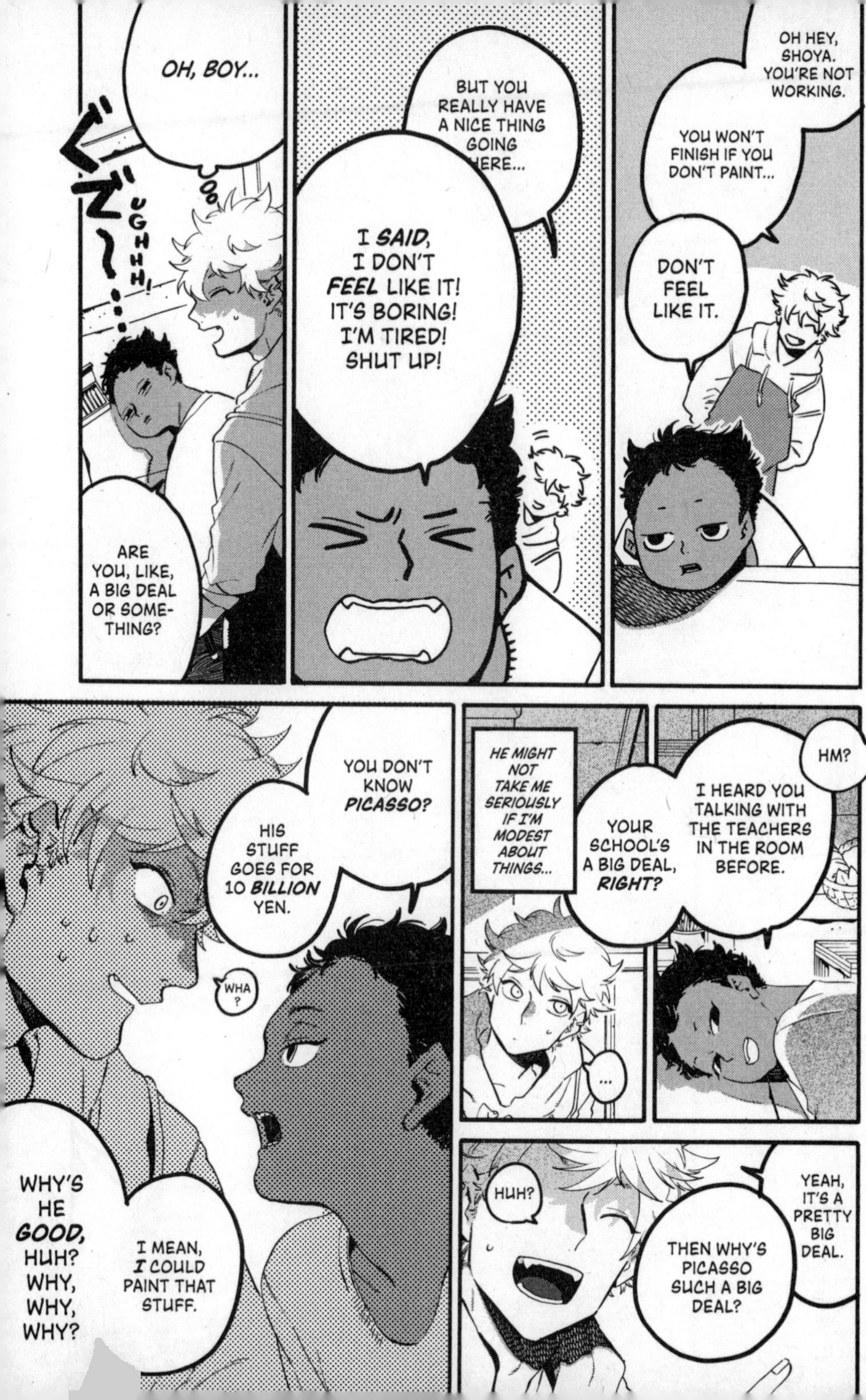
OH HEY, SHOYA. YOU'RE NOT WORKING.
YOU WON'T FINISH IF YOU DON'T PAINT...
DON'T FEEL LIKE IT.
BUT YOU REALLY HAVE A NICE THING GOING HERE...
I SAID, I DON'T FEEL LIKE IT! IT'S BORING! I'M TIRED! SHUT UP!
OH, BOY...
UGHHH!
ARE YOU, LIKE, A BIG DEAL OR SOME-THING?
HM?
I HEARD YOU TALKING WITH THE TEACHERS IN THE ROOM BEFORE.
YOUR SCHOOL'S A BIG DEAL, RIGHT?
HE MIGHT NOT TAKE ME SERIOUSLY IF I'M MODEST ABOUT THINGS...
...
YEAH, IT'S A PRETTY BIG DEAL.
THEN WHY'S PICASSO SUCH A BIG DEAL?
HUH?
YOU DON'T KNOW PICASSO?
HIS STUFF GOES FOR 10 BILLION YEN.
WHA?
I MEAN, I COULD PAINT THAT STUFF.
WHY'S HE GOOD, HUH? WHY, WHY, WHY?

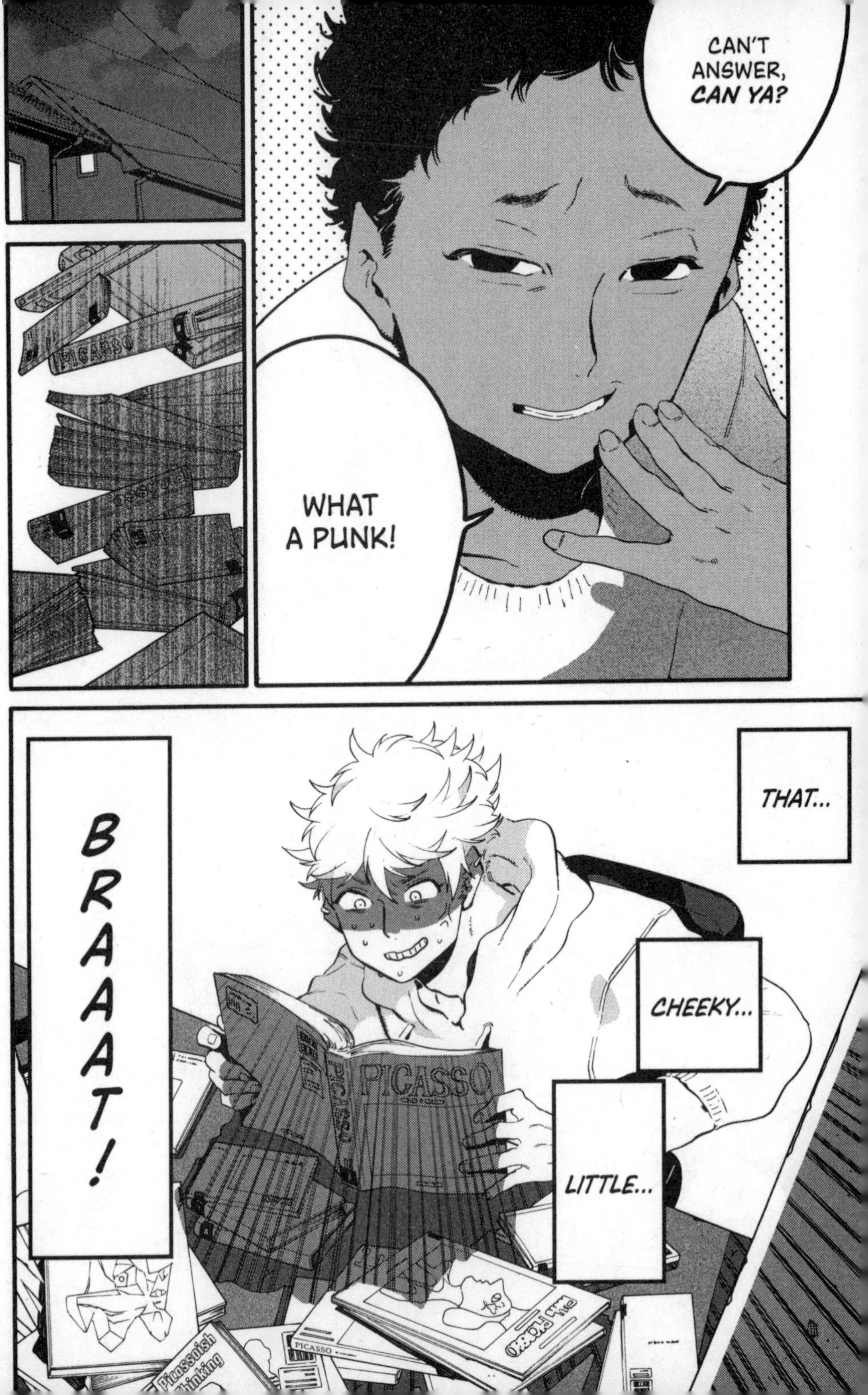
CAN'T ANSWER, CAN YA?
WHAT A PUNK!
THAT...
CHEEKY...
LITTLE...
BRAAAAT!

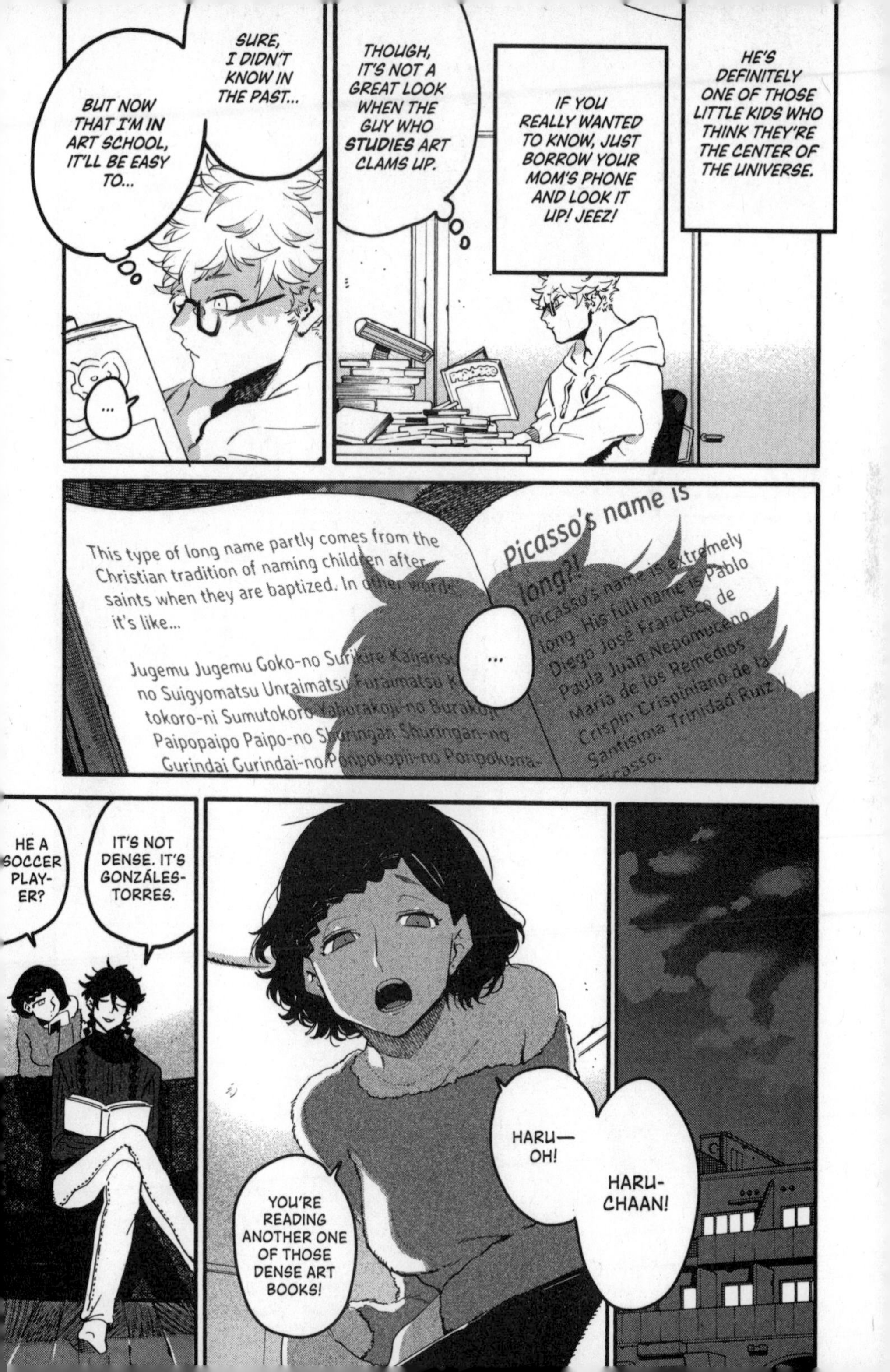
HE'S DEFINITELY ONE OF THOSE LITTLE KIDS WHO THINK THEY'RE THE CENTER OF THE UNIVERSE.
IF YOU REALLY WANTED TO KNOW, JUST BORROW YOUR MOM'S PHONE AND LOOK IT UP! JEEZ!
THOUGH, IT'S NOT A GREAT LOOK WHEN THE GUY WHO STUDIES ART CLAMS UP.
SURE, I DIDN'T KNOW IN THE PAST...
BUT NOW THAT I'M IN ART SCHOOL, IT'LL BE EASY TO...
...
Picasso's name is long?!
Picasso's name is extremely long. His full name is Pablo Diego José Francisco de Paula Juan Nepomuceno María de los Remedios Crispín Crispiniano de la Santísima Trinidad Ruiz
Picasso.
This type of long name partly comes from the Christian tradition of naming children after saints when they are baptized. In other words, it's like...
Jugemu Jugemu Goko-no Surikire Kaijari
no Suigyomatsu Unraimatsu Furaimatsu
tokoro-ni Sumutokoro Yaburakoji-no Burakoji
Paipopaipo Paipo-no Shuringan Shuringan-no
Gurindai Gurindai-no Ponpokopii-no Ponpokona-
...
HARU—OH!
HARU-CHAAN!
YOU'RE READING ANOTHER ONE OF THOSE DENSE ART BOOKS!
IT'S NOT DENSE. IT'S GONZÁLES-TORRES.
HE A SOCCER PLAYER?

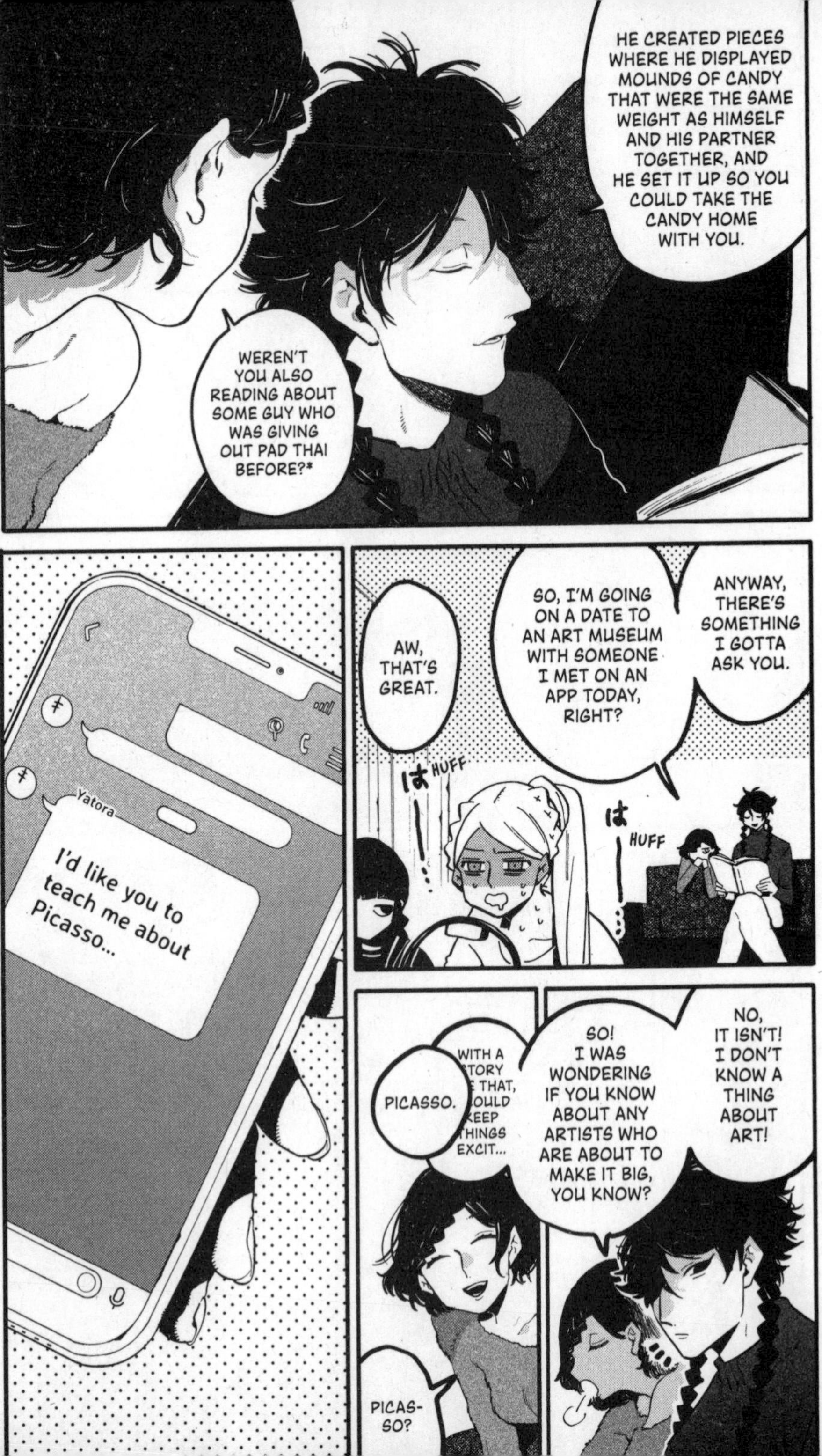
HE CREATED PIECES WHERE HE DISPLAYED MOUNDS OF CANDY THAT WERE THE SAME WEIGHT AS HIMSELF AND HIS PARTNER TOGETHER, AND HE SET IT UP SO YOU COULD TAKE THE CANDY HOME WITH YOU.
WEREN'T YOU ALSO READING ABOUT SOME GUY WHO WAS GIVING OUT PAD THAI BEFORE?*
ANYWAY, THERE'S SOMETHING I GOTTA ASK YOU.
SO, I'M GOING ON A DATE TO AN ART MUSEUM WITH SOMEONE I MET ON AN APP TODAY, RIGHT?
AW, THAT'S GREAT.
は HUFF
は HUFF
NO, IT ISN'T! I DON'T KNOW A THING ABOUT ART!
SO! I WAS WONDERING IF YOU KNOW ABOUT ANY ARTISTS WHO ARE ABOUT TO MAKE IT BIG, YOU KNOW?
WITH A TORY E THAT, OULD KEEP HINGS EXCIT...
PICASSO.
PICAS-SO?
Yatora
I'd like you to teach me about Picasso...

*RIRKRIT TIRAVANIJA

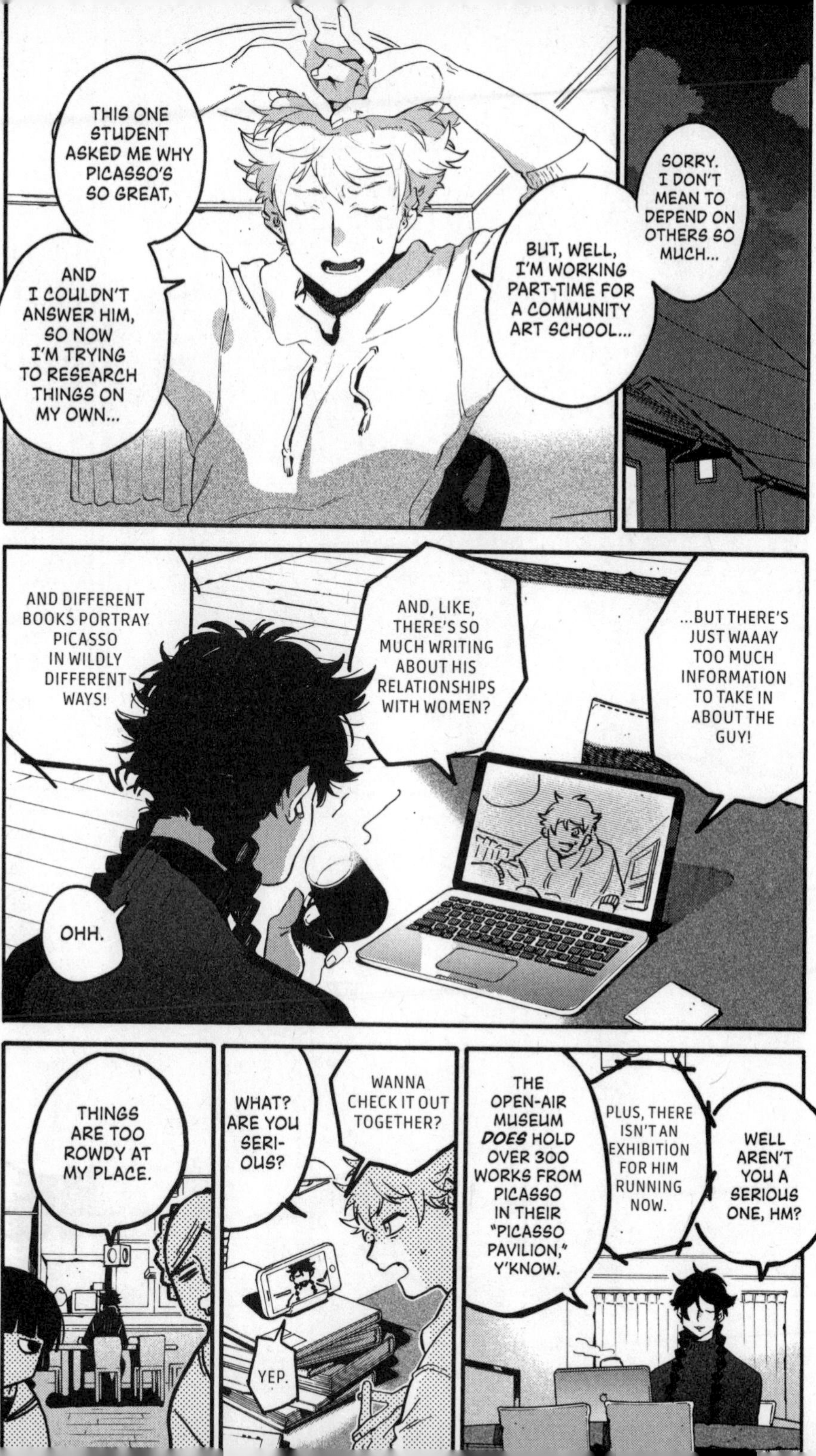
SORRY. I DON'T MEAN TO DEPEND ON OTHERS SO MUCH...
BUT, WELL, I'M WORKING PART-TIME FOR A COMMUNITY ART SCHOOL...
THIS ONE STUDENT ASKED ME WHY PICASSO'S SO GREAT,
AND I COULDN'T ANSWER HIM, SO NOW I'M TRYING TO RESEARCH THINGS ON MY OWN...
...BUT THERE'S JUST WAAAY TOO MUCH INFORMATION TO TAKE IN ABOUT THE GUY!
AND, LIKE, THERE'S SO MUCH WRITING ABOUT HIS RELATIONSHIPS WITH WOMEN?
AND DIFFERENT BOOKS PORTRAY PICASSO IN WILDLY DIFFERENT WAYS!
OHH.
WELL AREN'T YOU A SERIOUS ONE, HM?
PLUS, THERE ISN'T AN EXHIBITION FOR HIM RUNNING NOW.
THE OPEN-AIR MUSEUM *DOES* HOLD OVER 300 WORKS FROM PICASSO IN THEIR "PICASSO PAVILION," Y'KNOW.
WANNA CHECK IT OUT TOGETHER?
WHAT? ARE YOU SERI-OUS?
YEP.
THINGS ARE TOO ROWDY AT MY PLACE.

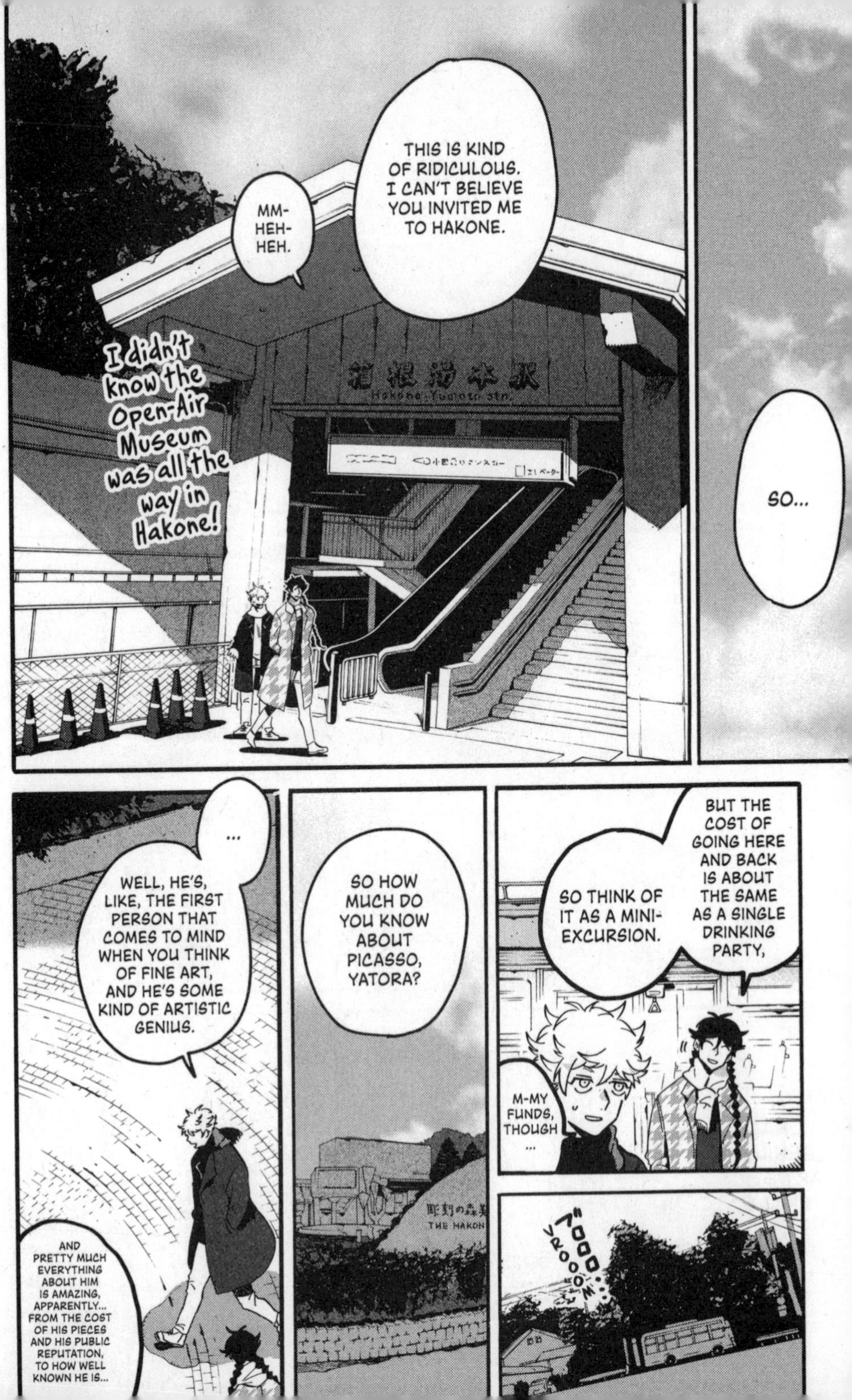
SO...
THIS IS KIND OF RIDICULOUS. I CAN'T BELIEVE YOU INVITED ME TO HAKONE.
MM-HEH-HEH.
Hakone-Yumoto stn.
I didn't know the Open-Air Museum was all the way in Hakone!
BUT THE COST OF GOING HERE AND BACK IS ABOUT THE SAME AS A SINGLE DRINKING PARTY,
SO THINK OF IT AS A MINI-EXCURSION.
M-MY FUNDS, THOUGH...
VROOOOM...
SO HOW MUCH DO YOU KNOW ABOUT PICASSO, YATORA?
THE HAKON
...
WELL, HE'S, LIKE, THE FIRST PERSON THAT COMES TO MIND WHEN YOU THINK OF FINE ART, AND HE'S SOME KIND OF ARTISTIC GENIUS.
AND PRETTY MUCH EVERYTHING ABOUT HIM IS AMAZING, APPARENTLY... FROM THE COST OF HIS PIECES AND HIS PUBLIC REPUTATION, TO HOW WELL KNOWN HE IS...

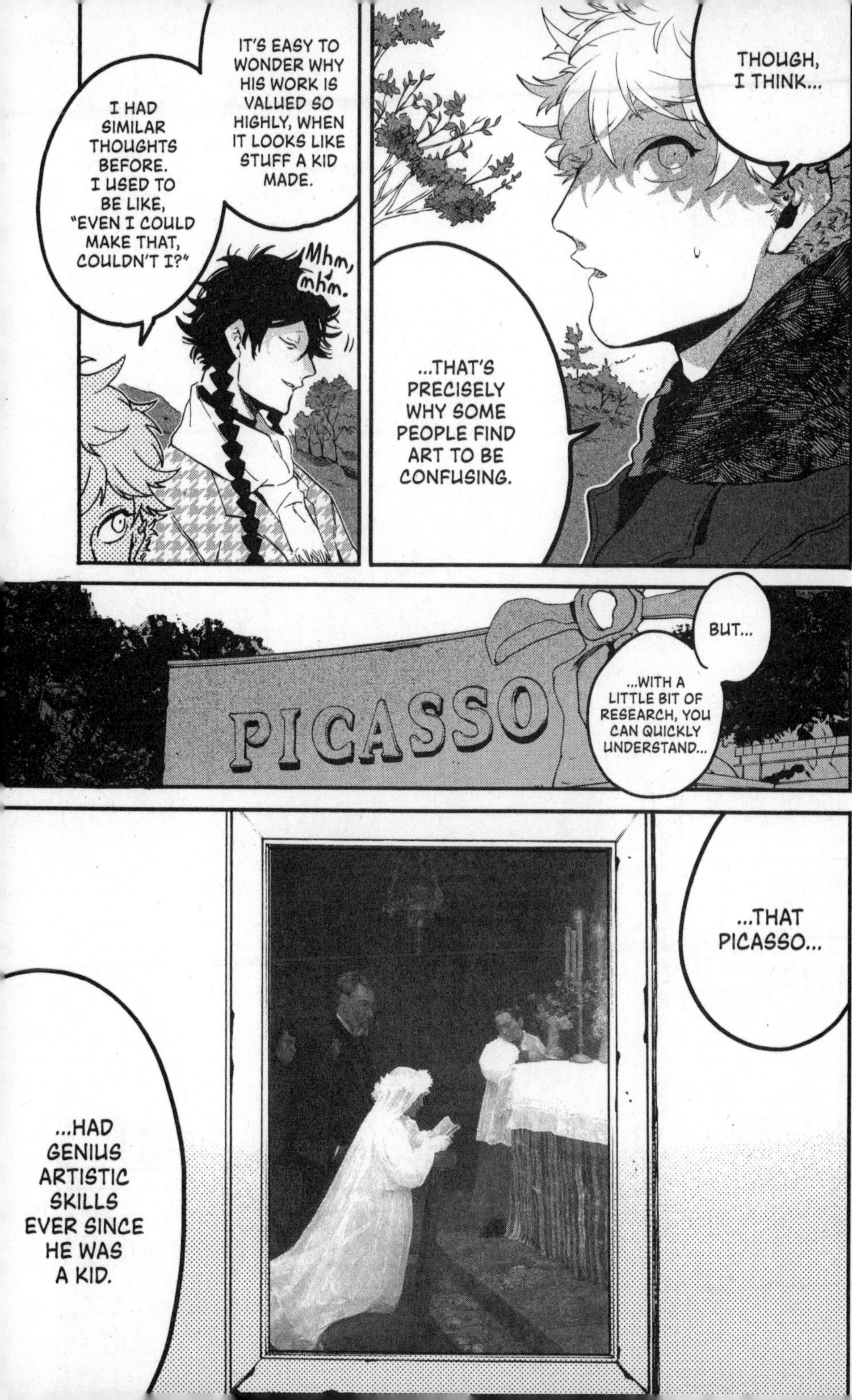
THOUGH, I THINK...
...THAT'S PRECISELY WHY SOME PEOPLE FIND ART TO BE CONFUSING.
IT'S EASY TO WONDER WHY HIS WORK IS VALUED SO HIGHLY, WHEN IT LOOKS LIKE STUFF A KID MADE.
I HAD SIMILAR THOUGHTS BEFORE. I USED TO BE LIKE, "EVEN I COULD MAKE THAT, COULDN'T I?"
Mhm, mhm.
BUT...
...WITH A LITTLE BIT OF RESEARCH, YOU CAN QUICKLY UNDERSTAND...
PICASSO
...THAT PICASSO...
...HAD GENIUS ARTISTIC SKILLS EVER SINCE HE WAS A KID.

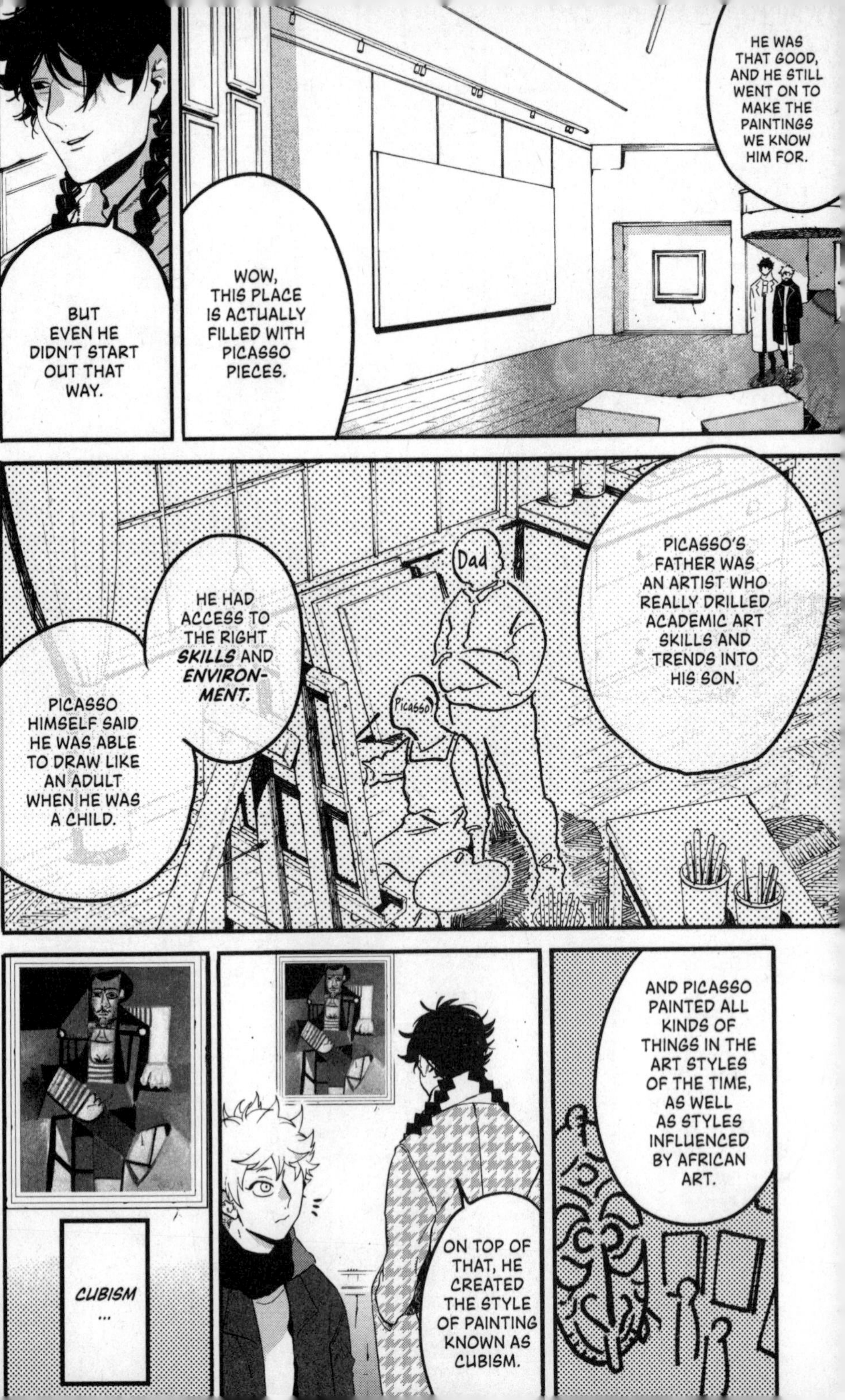
HE WAS THAT GOOD, AND HE STILL WENT ON TO MAKE THE PAINTINGS WE KNOW HIM FOR.
WOW, THIS PLACE IS ACTUALLY FILLED WITH PICASSO PIECES.
BUT EVEN HE DIDN'T START OUT THAT WAY.
PICASSO'S FATHER WAS AN ARTIST WHO REALLY DRILLED ACADEMIC ART SKILLS AND TRENDS INTO HIS SON.
Dad
HE HAD ACCESS TO THE RIGHT SKILLS AND ENVIRON-MENT.
Picasso
PICASSO HIMSELF SAID HE WAS ABLE TO DRAW LIKE AN ADULT WHEN HE WAS A CHILD.
AND PICASSO PAINTED ALL KINDS OF THINGS IN THE ART STYLES OF THE TIME, AS WELL AS STYLES INFLUENCED BY AFRICAN ART.
ON TOP OF THAT, HE CREATED THE STYLE OF PAINTING KNOWN AS CUBISM.
CUBISM ...

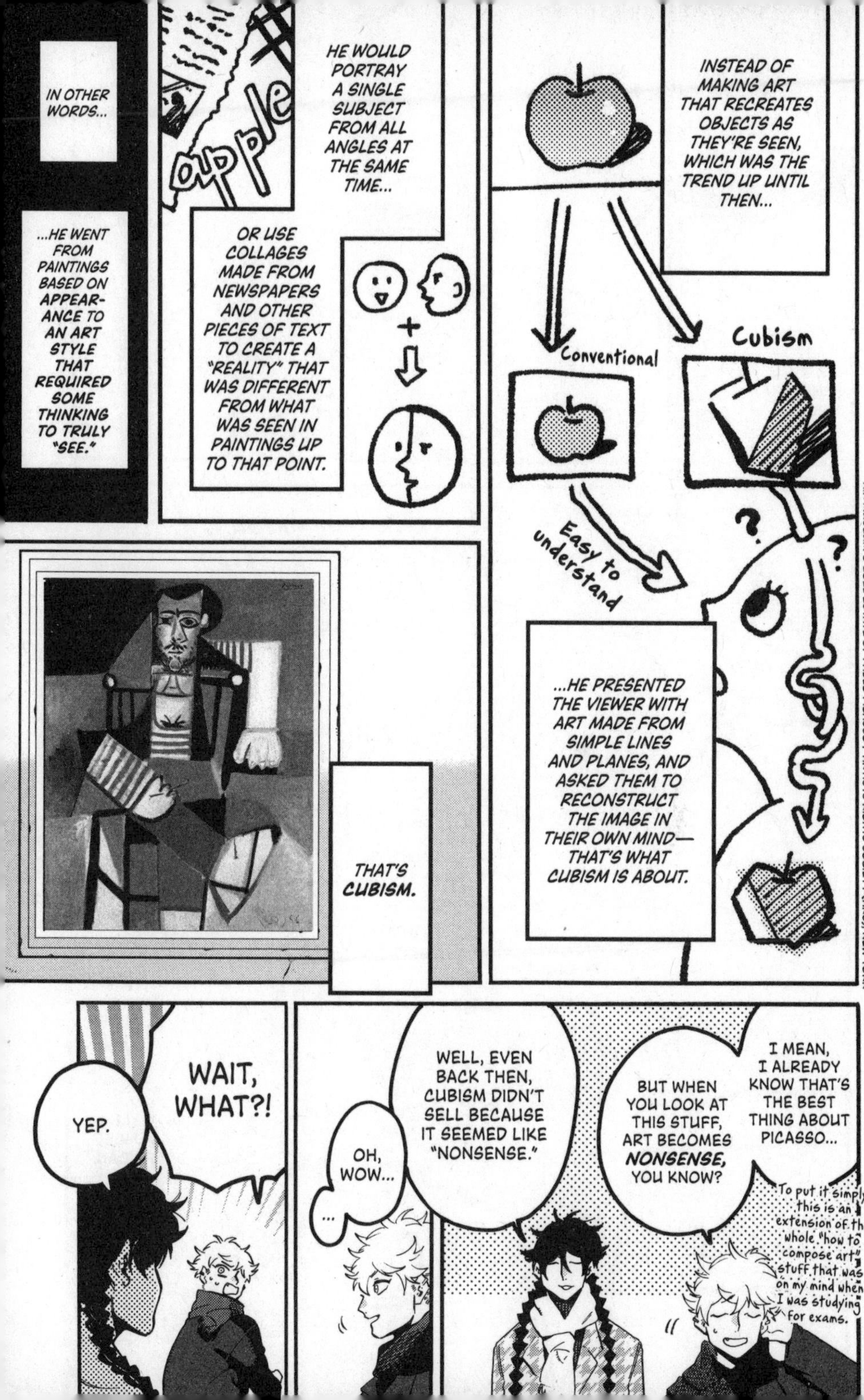

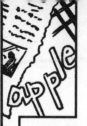

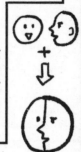

INSTEAD OF MAKING ART THAT RECREATES OBJECTS AS THEY'RE SEEN, WHICH WAS THE TREND UP UNTIL THEN...
Cubism
Conventional
Easy to understand
...HE PRESENTED THE VIEWER WITH ART MADE FROM SIMPLE LINES AND PLANES, AND ASKED THEM TO RECONSTRUCT THE IMAGE IN THEIR OWN MIND—THAT'S WHAT CUBISM IS ABOUT.
HE WOULD PORTRAY A SINGLE SUBJECT FROM ALL ANGLES AT THE SAME TIME...
apple
OR USE COLLAGES MADE FROM NEWSPAPERS AND OTHER PIECES OF TEXT TO CREATE A "REALITY" THAT WAS DIFFERENT FROM WHAT WAS SEEN IN PAINTINGS UP TO THAT POINT.
IN OTHER WORDS...
...HE WENT FROM PAINTINGS BASED ON APPEAR-ANCE TO AN ART STYLE THAT REQUIRED SOME THINKING TO TRULY "SEE."
THAT'S CUBISM.
I MEAN, I ALREADY KNOW THAT'S THE BEST THING ABOUT PICASSO...
To put it simply, this is an extension of the whole "how to compose art" stuff that was on my mind when I was studying for exams.
BUT WHEN YOU LOOK AT THIS STUFF, ART BECOMES NONSENSE, YOU KNOW?
WELL, EVEN BACK THEN, CUBISM DIDN'T SELL BECAUSE IT SEEMED LIKE "NONSENSE."
OH, WOW...
...
WAIT, WHAT?!
YEP.

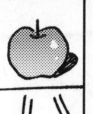

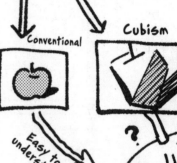

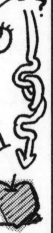

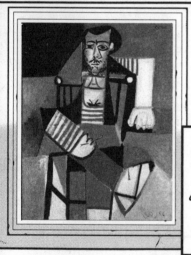

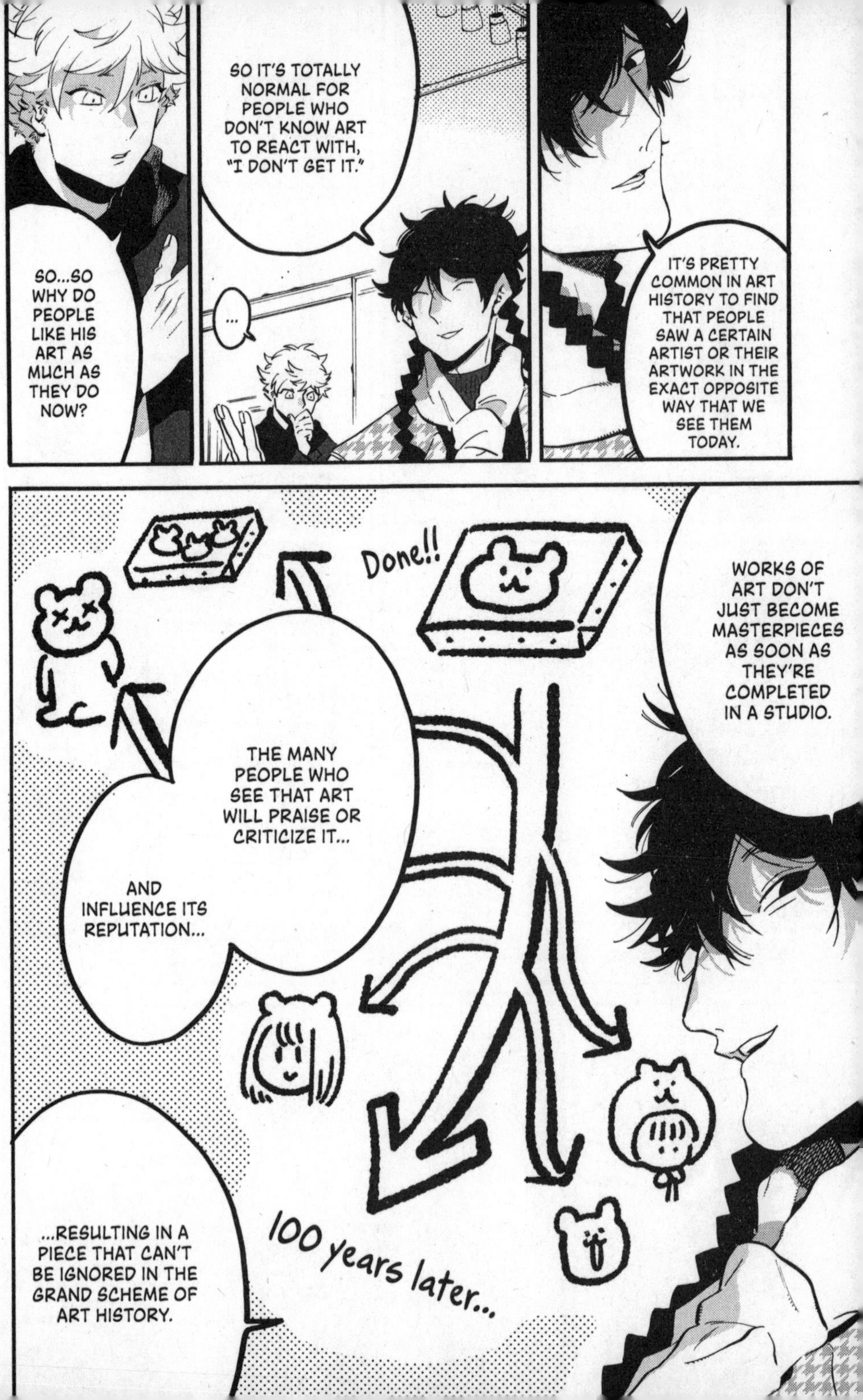
IT'S PRETTY COMMON IN ART HISTORY TO FIND THAT PEOPLE SAW A CERTAIN ARTIST OR THEIR ARTWORK IN THE EXACT OPPOSITE WAY THAT WE SEE THEM TODAY.
SO IT'S TOTALLY NORMAL FOR PEOPLE WHO DON'T KNOW ART TO REACT WITH, "I DON'T GET IT."
...
SO...SO WHY DO PEOPLE LIKE HIS ART AS MUCH AS THEY DO NOW?
WORKS OF ART DON'T JUST BECOME MASTERPIECES AS SOON AS THEY'RE COMPLETED IN A STUDIO.
Done!!
THE MANY PEOPLE WHO SEE THAT ART WILL PRAISE OR CRITICIZE IT...
AND INFLUENCE ITS REPUTATION...
100 years later...
...RESULTING IN A PIECE THAT CAN'T BE IGNORED IN THE GRAND SCHEME OF ART HISTORY.

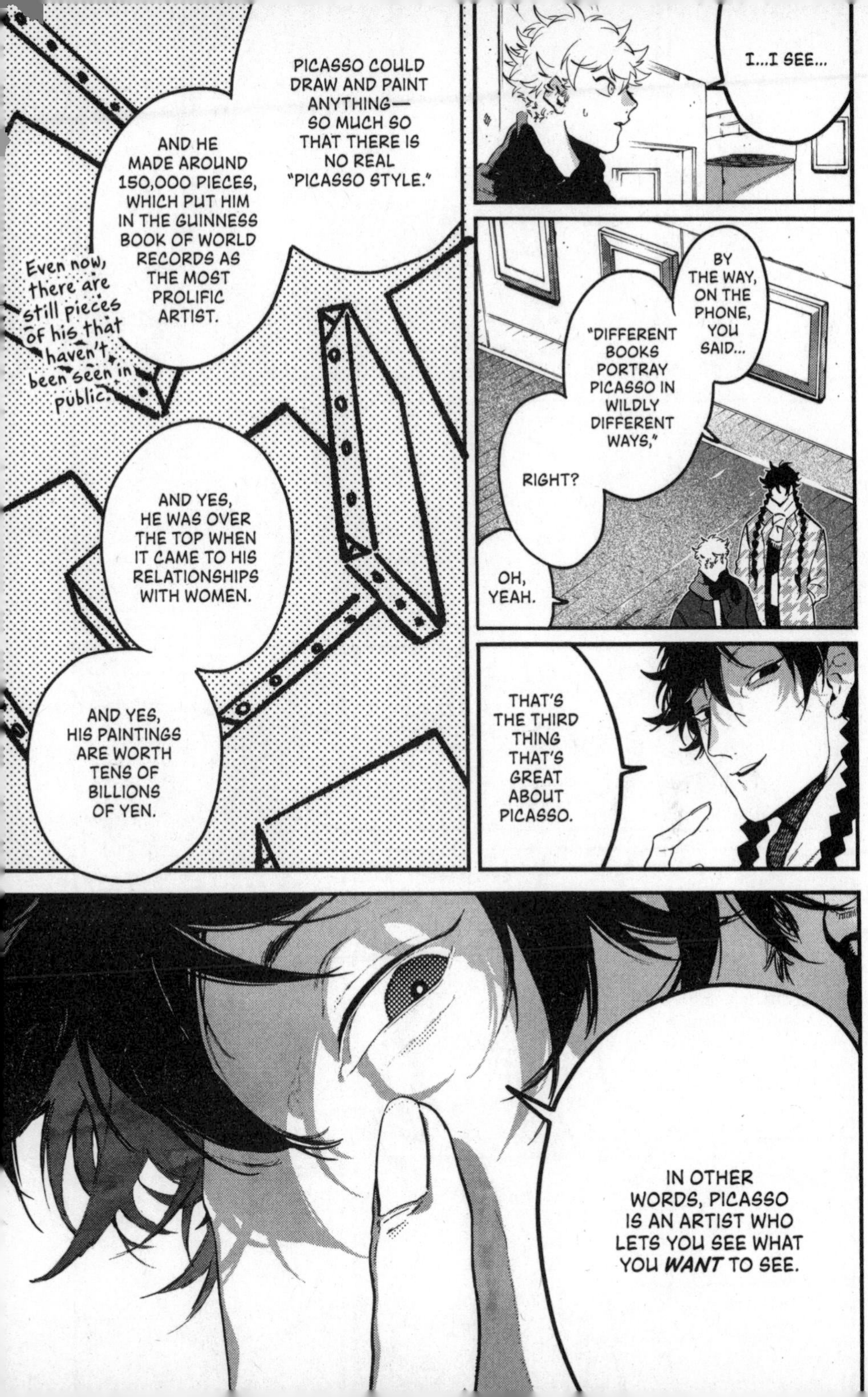
I...I SEE...
BY THE WAY, ON THE PHONE, YOU SAID...
"DIFFERENT BOOKS PORTRAY PICASSO IN WILDLY DIFFERENT WAYS,"
RIGHT?
OH, YEAH.
THAT'S THE THIRD THING THAT'S GREAT ABOUT PICASSO.
PICASSO COULD DRAW AND PAINT ANYTHING—SO MUCH SO THAT THERE IS NO REAL "PICASSO STYLE."
AND HE MADE AROUND 150,000 PIECES, WHICH PUT HIM IN THE GUINNESS BOOK OF WORLD RECORDS AS THE MOST PROLIFIC ARTIST.
Even now, there are still pieces of his that haven't been seen in public.
AND YES, HE WAS OVER THE TOP WHEN IT CAME TO HIS RELATIONSHIPS WITH WOMEN.
AND YES, HIS PAINTINGS ARE WORTH TENS OF BILLIONS OF YEN.
IN OTHER WORDS, PICASSO IS AN ARTIST WHO LETS YOU SEE WHAT YOU *WANT* TO SEE.

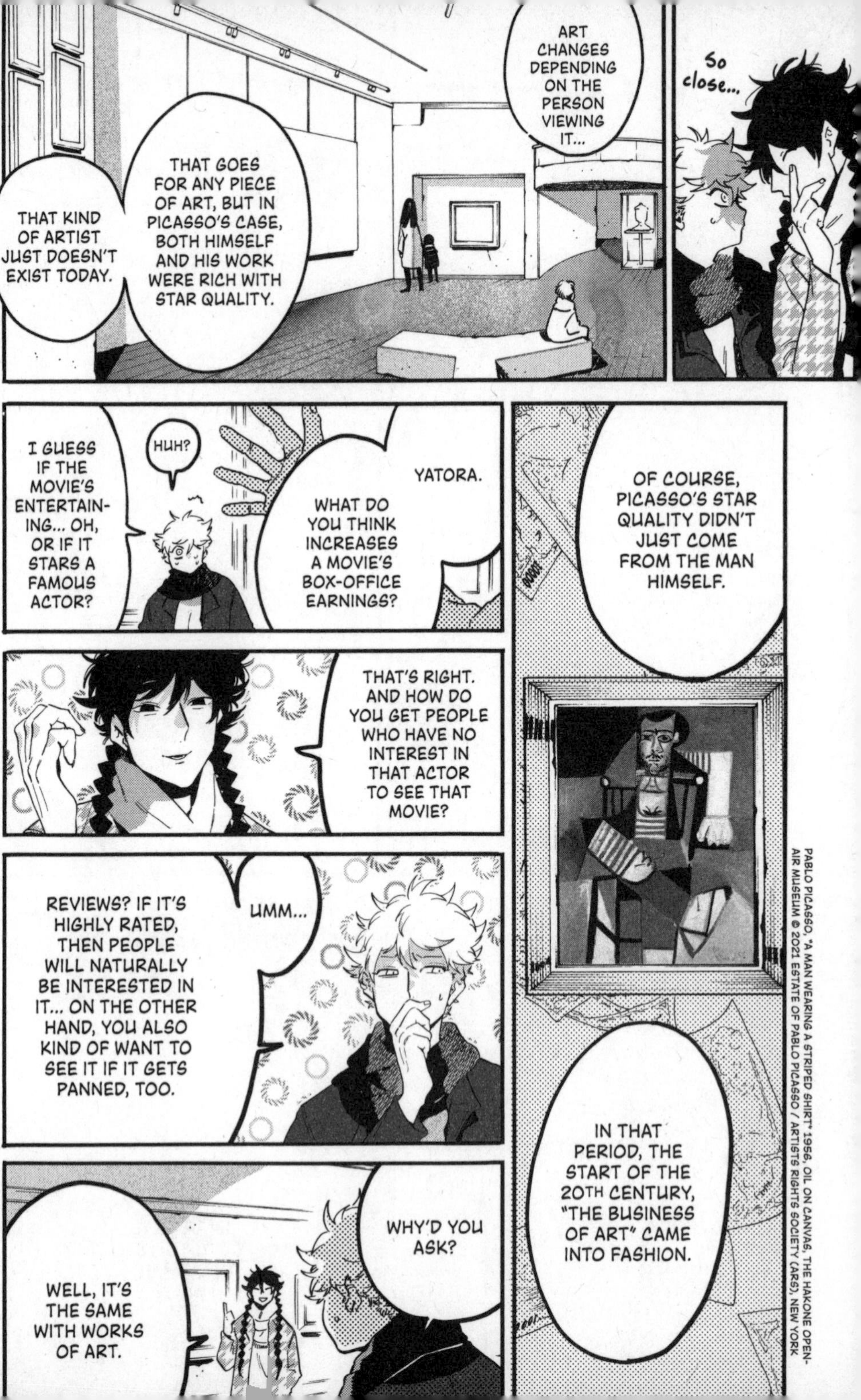
So close...
ART CHANGES DEPENDING ON THE PERSON VIEWING IT...
THAT GOES FOR ANY PIECE OF ART, BUT IN PICASSO'S CASE, BOTH HIMSELF AND HIS WORK WERE RICH WITH STAR QUALITY.
THAT KIND OF ARTIST JUST DOESN'T EXIST TODAY.
OF COURSE, PICASSO'S STAR QUALITY DIDN'T JUST COME FROM THE MAN HIMSELF.
IN THAT PERIOD, THE START OF THE 20TH CENTURY, "THE BUSINESS OF ART" CAME INTO FASHION.
YATORA.
WHAT DO YOU THINK INCREASES A MOVIE'S BOX-OFFICE EARNINGS?
HUH?
I GUESS IF THE MOVIE'S ENTERTAIN-ING... OH, OR IF IT STARS A FAMOUS ACTOR?
THAT'S RIGHT. AND HOW DO YOU GET PEOPLE WHO HAVE NO INTEREST IN THAT ACTOR TO SEE THAT MOVIE?
UMM...
REVIEWS? IF IT'S HIGHLY RATED, THEN PEOPLE WILL NATURALLY BE INTERESTED IN IT... ON THE OTHER HAND, YOU ALSO KIND OF WANT TO SEE IT IF IT GETS PANNED, TOO.
WHY'D YOU ASK?
WELL, IT'S THE SAME WITH WORKS OF ART.
PABLO PICASSO, "A MAN WEARING A STRIPED SHIRT" 1956, OIL ON CANVAS, THE HAKONE OPEN-AIR MUSEUM © 2021 ESTATE OF PABLO PICASSO / ARTISTS RIGHTS SOCIETY (ARS), NEW YORK

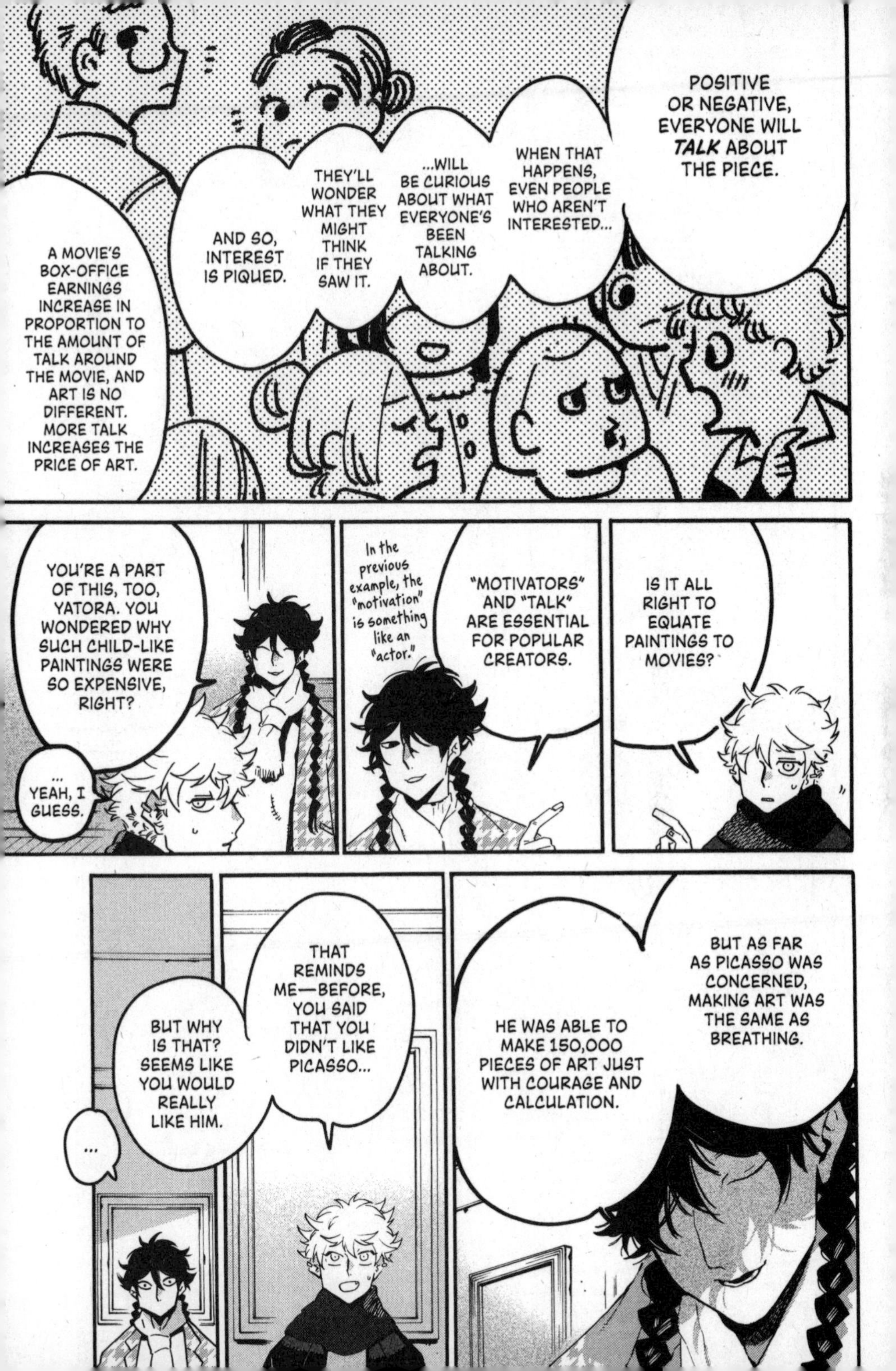
POSITIVE OR NEGATIVE, EVERYONE WILL *TALK* ABOUT THE PIECE.
WHEN THAT HAPPENS, EVEN PEOPLE WHO AREN'T INTERESTED...
...WILL BE CURIOUS ABOUT WHAT EVERYONE'S BEEN TALKING ABOUT.
THEY'LL WONDER WHAT THEY MIGHT THINK IF THEY SAW IT.
AND SO, INTEREST IS PIQUED.
A MOVIE'S BOX-OFFICE EARNINGS INCREASE IN PROPORTION TO THE AMOUNT OF TALK AROUND THE MOVIE, AND ART IS NO DIFFERENT. MORE TALK INCREASES THE PRICE OF ART.
IS IT ALL RIGHT TO EQUATE PAINTINGS TO MOVIES?
"MOTIVATORS" AND "TALK" ARE ESSENTIAL FOR POPULAR CREATORS.
In the previous example, the "motivation" is something like an "actor."
YOU'RE A PART OF THIS, TOO, YATORA. YOU WONDERED WHY SUCH CHILD-LIKE PAINTINGS WERE SO EXPENSIVE, RIGHT?
... YEAH, I GUESS.
BUT AS FAR AS PICASSO WAS CONCERNED, MAKING ART WAS THE SAME AS BREATHING.
HE WAS ABLE TO MAKE 150,000 PIECES OF ART JUST WITH COURAGE AND CALCULATION.
THAT REMINDS ME—BEFORE, YOU SAID THAT YOU DIDN'T LIKE PICASSO...
BUT WHY IS THAT? SEEMS LIKE YOU WOULD REALLY LIKE HIM.
...

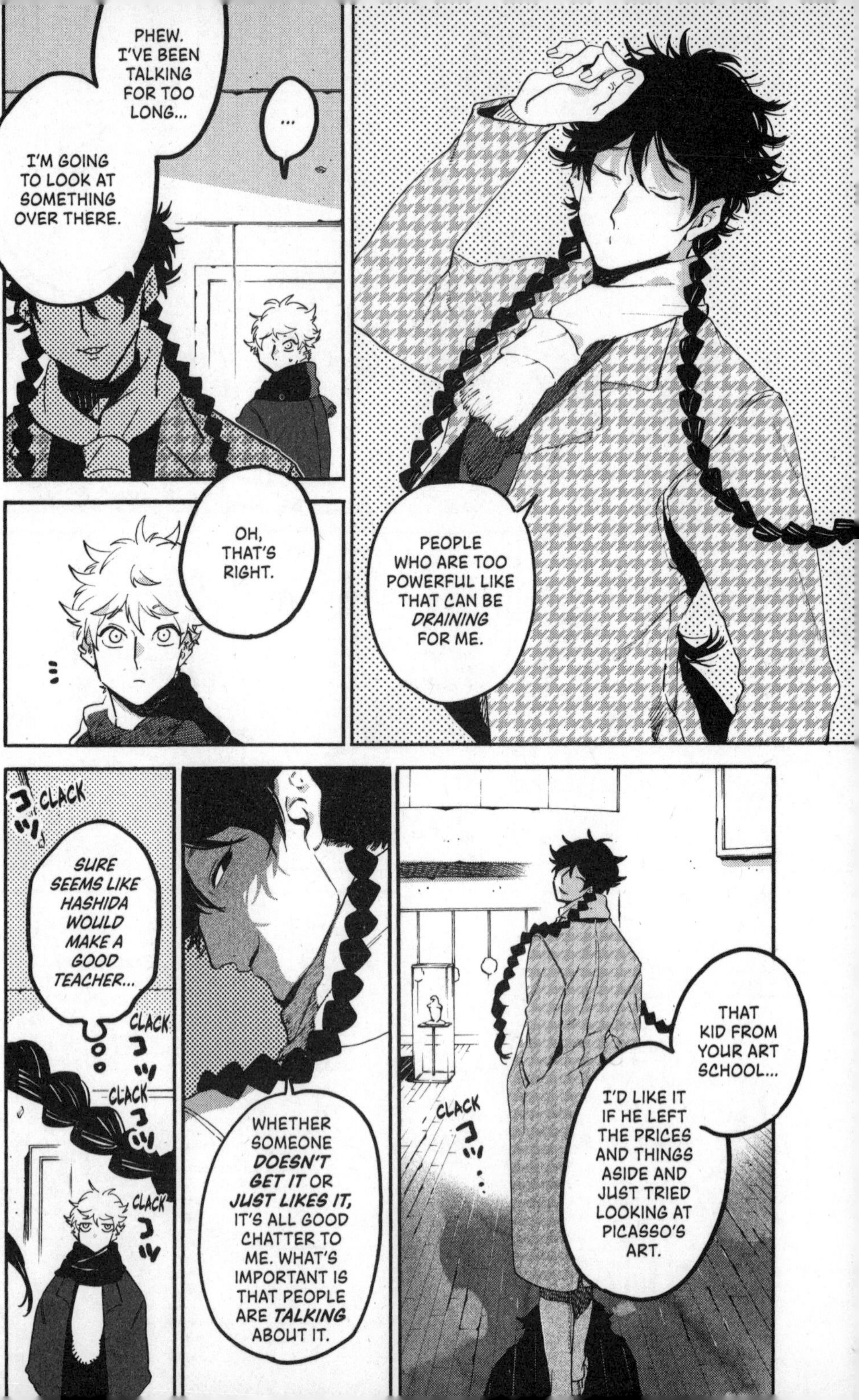
PEOPLE WHO ARE TOO POWERFUL LIKE THAT CAN BE *DRAINING* FOR ME.
PHEW. I'VE BEEN TALKING FOR TOO LONG...
...
I'M GOING TO LOOK AT SOMETHING OVER THERE.
OH, THAT'S RIGHT.
THAT KID FROM YOUR ART SCHOOL...
I'D LIKE IT IF HE LEFT THE PRICES AND THINGS ASIDE AND JUST TRIED LOOKING AT PICASSO'S ART.
CLACK
WHETHER SOMEONE ***DOESN'T GET IT*** OR ***JUST LIKES IT,*** IT'S ALL GOOD CHATTER TO ME. WHAT'S IMPORTANT IS THAT PEOPLE ARE ***TALKING*** ABOUT IT.
CLACK
SURE SEEMS LIKE HASHIDA WOULD MAKE A GOOD TEACHER...
CLACK
CLACK
CLACK

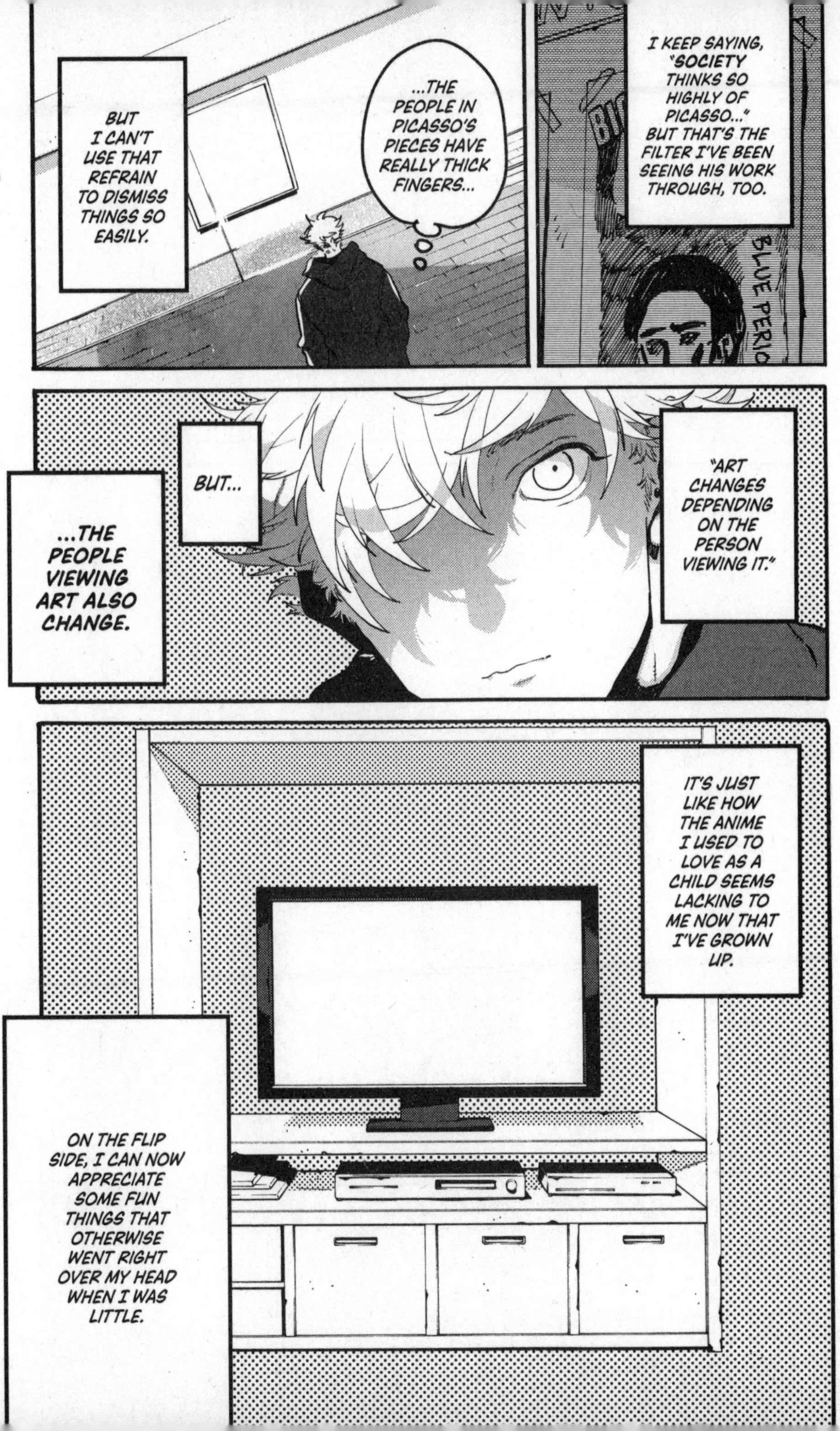
I KEEP SAYING, "SOCIETY THINKS SO HIGHLY OF PICASSO..." BUT THAT'S THE FILTER I'VE BEEN SEEING HIS WORK THROUGH, TOO.
BLUE PERIO
...THE PEOPLE IN PICASSO'S PIECES HAVE REALLY THICK FINGERS...
BUT I CAN'T USE THAT REFRAIN TO DISMISS THINGS SO EASILY.
"ART CHANGES DEPENDING ON THE PERSON VIEWING IT."
BUT...
...THE PEOPLE VIEWING ART ALSO CHANGE.
IT'S JUST LIKE HOW THE ANIME I USED TO LOVE AS A CHILD SEEMS LACKING TO ME NOW THAT I'VE GROWN UP.
ON THE FLIP SIDE, I CAN NOW APPRECIATE SOME FUN THINGS THAT OTHERWISE WENT RIGHT OVER MY HEAD WHEN I WAS LITTLE.

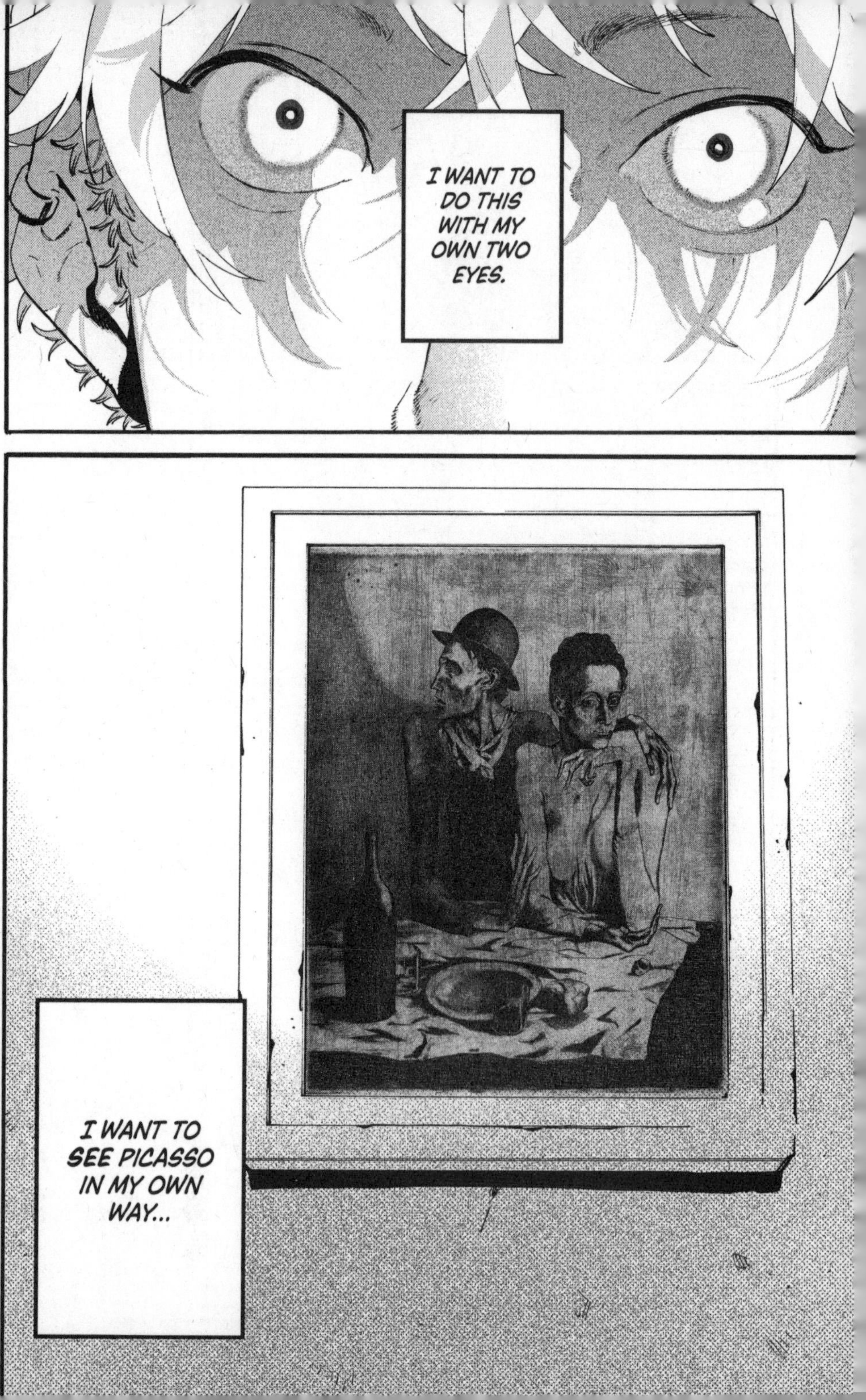
I WANT TO DO THIS WITH MY OWN TWO EYES.
I WANT TO SEE PICASSO IN MY OWN WAY...

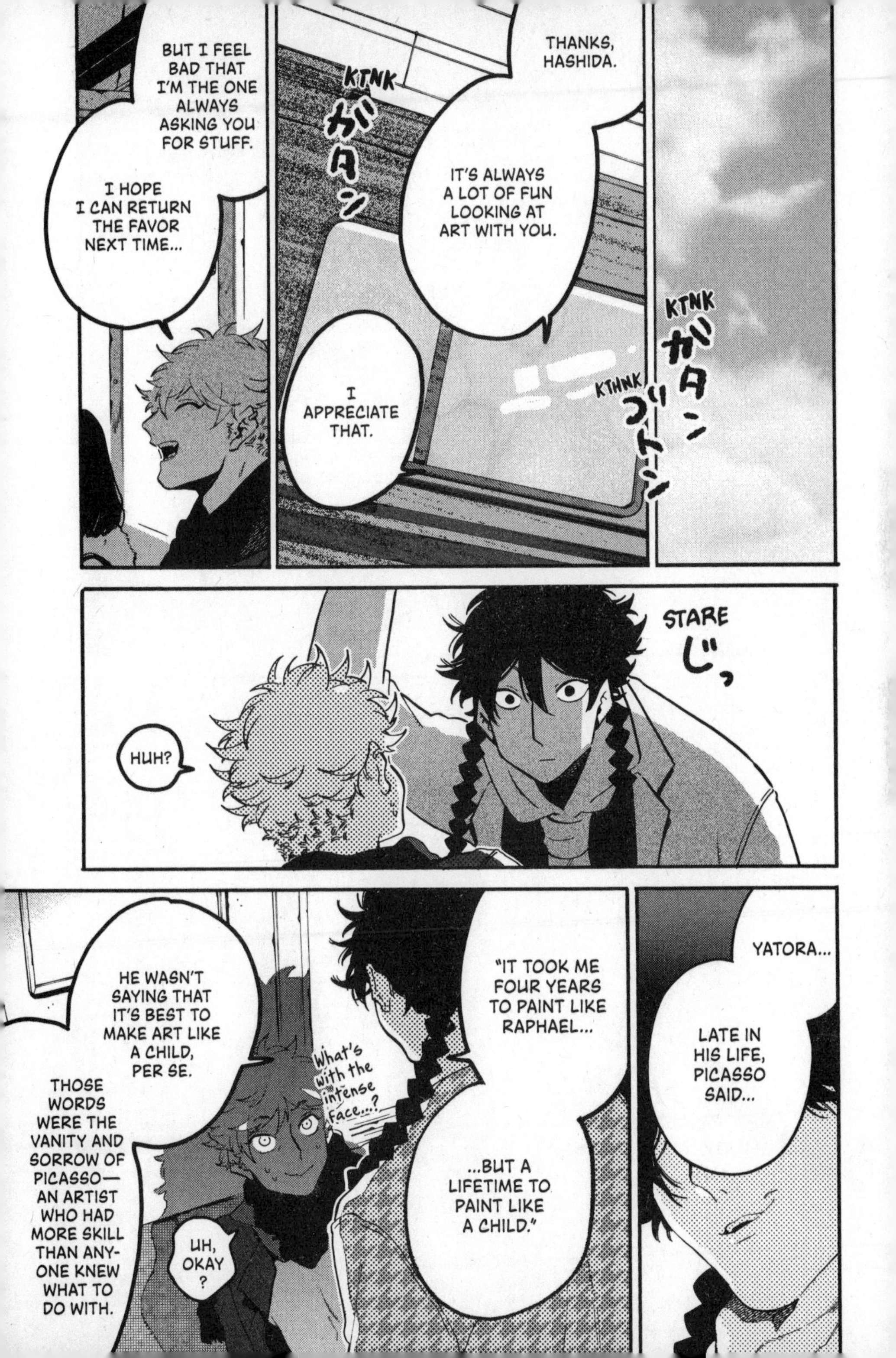
KTNK
ガタン
KTHNK
ゴトン
THANKS, HASHIDA.
KTNK
ガタン
IT'S ALWAYS A LOT OF FUN LOOKING AT ART WITH YOU.
I APPRECIATE THAT.
BUT I FEEL BAD THAT I'M THE ONE ALWAYS ASKING YOU FOR STUFF.
I HOPE I CAN RETURN THE FAVOR NEXT TIME...
STARE
じっ
HUH?
YATORA...
LATE IN HIS LIFE, PICASSO SAID...
"IT TOOK ME FOUR YEARS TO PAINT LIKE RAPHAEL...
...BUT A LIFETIME TO PAINT LIKE A CHILD."
HE WASN'T SAYING THAT IT'S BEST TO MAKE ART LIKE A CHILD, PER SE.
What's with the intense face...?
THOSE WORDS WERE THE VANITY AND SORROW OF PICASSO—AN ARTIST WHO HAD MORE SKILL THAN ANYONE KNEW WHAT TO DO WITH.
UH, OKAY?

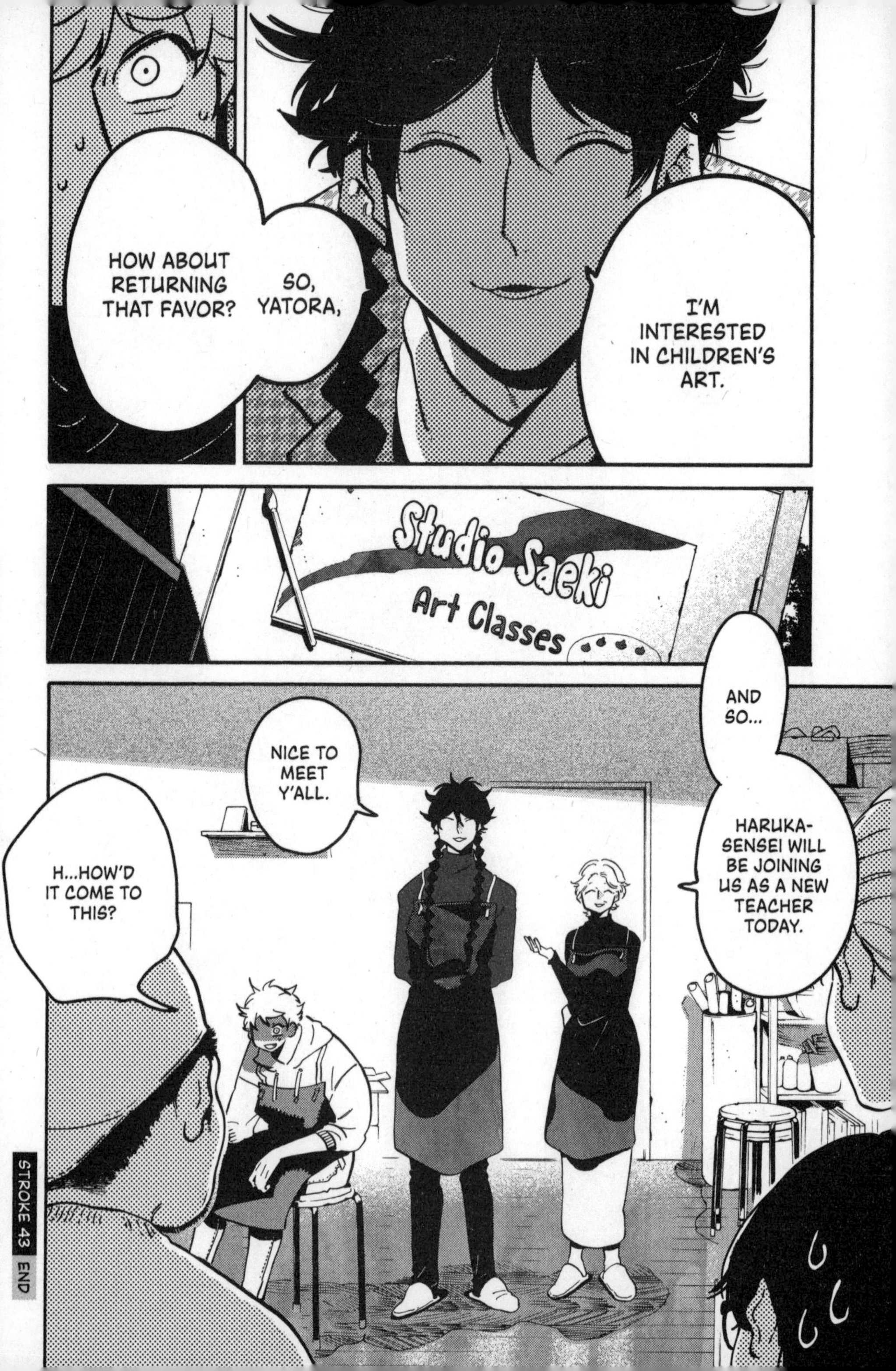
I'M INTERESTED IN CHILDREN'S ART.
SO, YATORA,
HOW ABOUT RETURNING THAT FAVOR?
Studio Saeki
Art Classes
AND SO...
HARUKA-SENSEI WILL BE JOINING US AS A NEW TEACHER TODAY.
NICE TO MEET Y'ALL.
H...HOW'D IT COME TO THIS?
STROKE 43 END

YATORA'S UNPOPULAR WITH KIDS

So then, like...
The other day...
And then...
...
YUICHI-KUN ISN'T REALLY REACTING... I'LL LISTEN TO HER!
OH, WOW. THAT'S SO FUNNY.
I WASN'T TALKING TO *YOU*, YATORA-KUN...

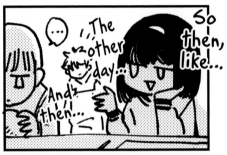

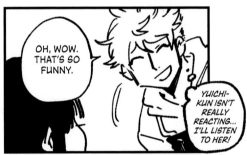

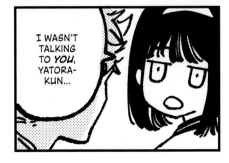

BLUE PERIOD

STROKE 44

IS IT ALL RIGHT IF I REEXAMINE MYSELF FOR NOW

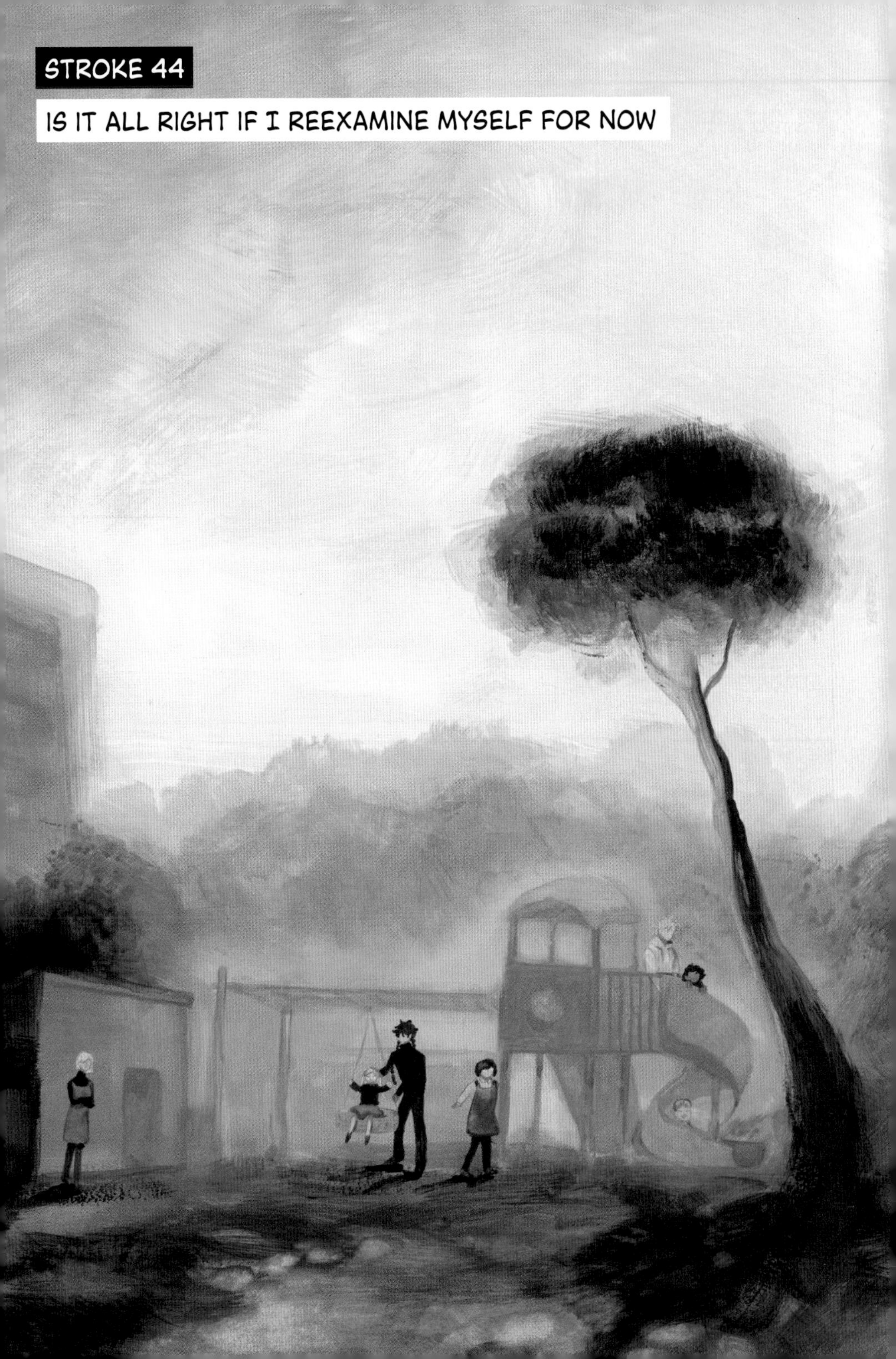

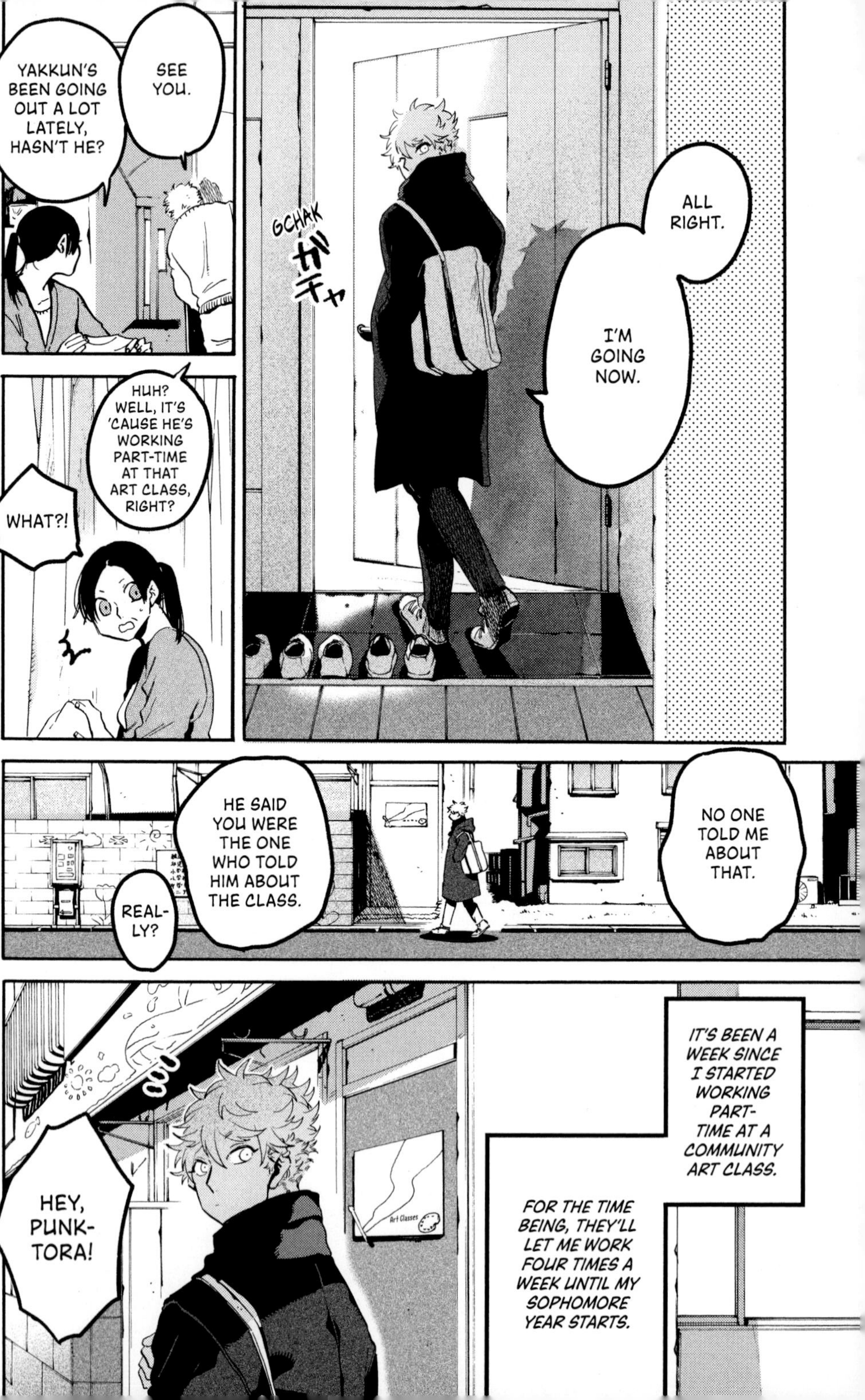
ALL RIGHT.
I'M GOING NOW.
GCHAK
SEE YOU.
YAKKUN'S BEEN GOING OUT A LOT LATELY, HASN'T HE?
HUH? WELL, IT'S 'CAUSE HE'S WORKING PART-TIME AT THAT ART CLASS, RIGHT?
WHAT?!
NO ONE TOLD ME ABOUT THAT.
HE SAID YOU WERE THE ONE WHO TOLD HIM ABOUT THE CLASS.
REAL-LY?
IT'S BEEN A WEEK SINCE I STARTED WORKING PART-TIME AT A COMMUNITY ART CLASS.
FOR THE TIME BEING, THEY'LL LET ME WORK FOUR TIMES A WEEK UNTIL MY SOPHOMORE YEAR STARTS.
Art Classes
HEY, PUNK-TORA!

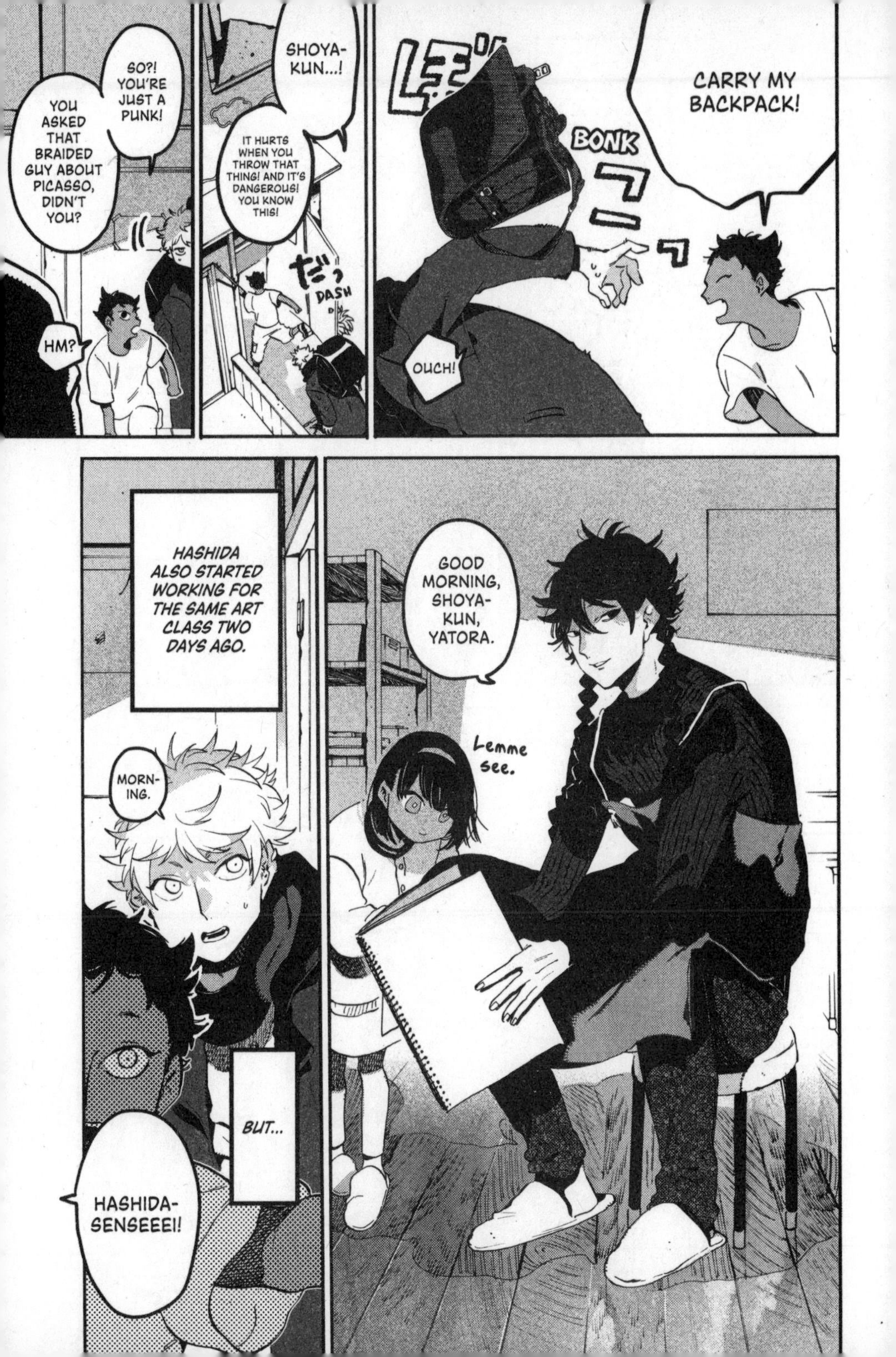
CARRY MY BACKPACK!
BONK
OUCH!
SHOYA-KUN...!
IT HURTS WHEN YOU THROW THAT THING! AND IT'S DANGEROUS! YOU KNOW THIS!
だっ
DASH
SO?! YOU'RE JUST A PUNK!
YOU ASKED THAT BRAIDED GUY ABOUT PICASSO, DIDN'T YOU?
HM?
GOOD MORNING, SHOYA-KUN, YATORA.
Lemme see.
HASHIDA ALSO STARTED WORKING FOR THE SAME ART CLASS TWO DAYS AGO.
MORNING.
BUT...
HASHIDA-SENSEEEI!

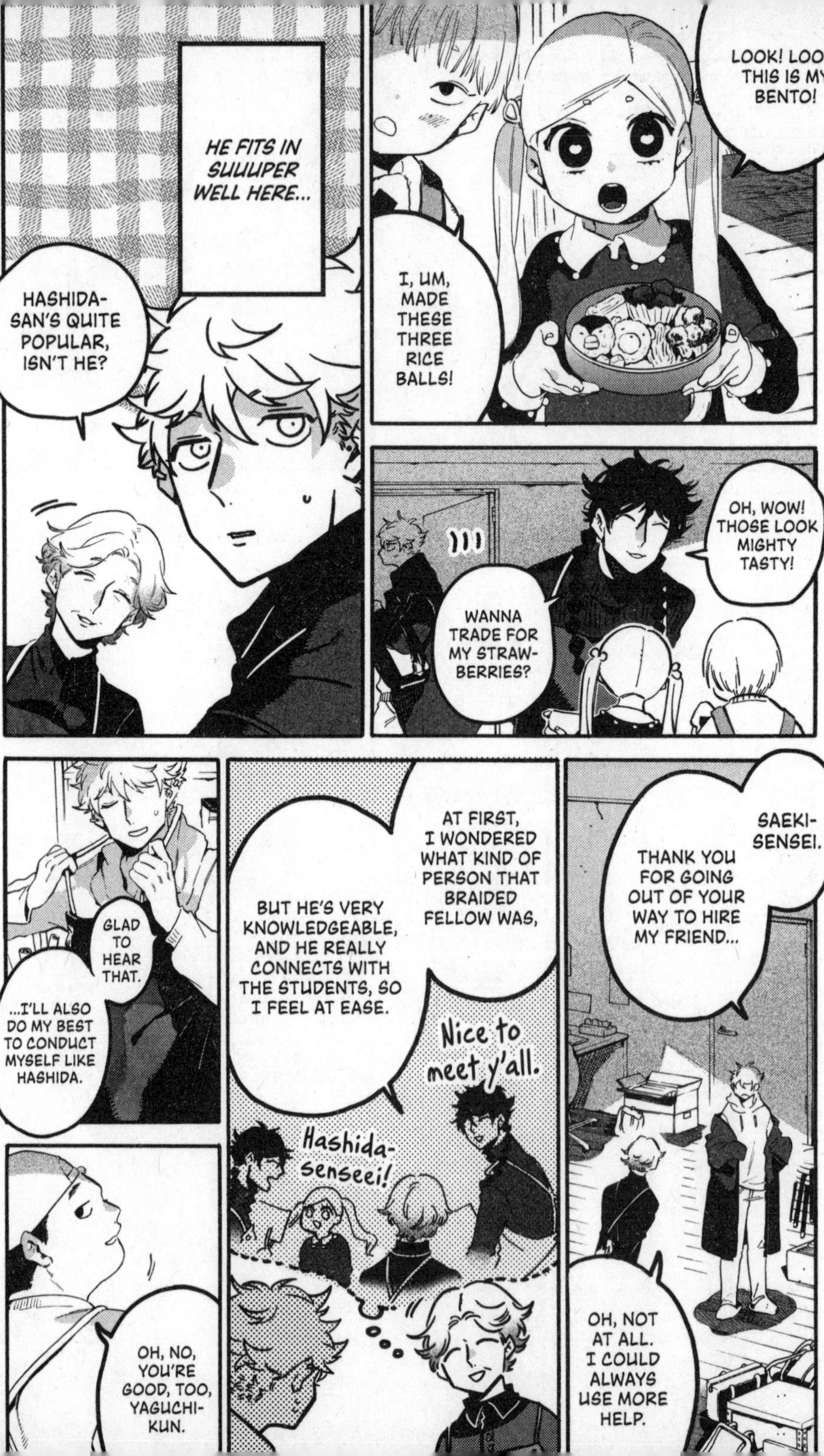
LOOK! LOOK! THIS IS MY BENTO!
I, UM, MADE THESE THREE RICE BALLS!
OH, WOW! THOSE LOOK MIGHTY TASTY!
WANNA TRADE FOR MY STRAWBERRIES?
HE FITS IN SUUUPER WELL HERE...
HASHIDA-SAN'S QUITE POPULAR, ISN'T HE?
SAEKI-SENSEI.
THANK YOU FOR GOING OUT OF YOUR WAY TO HIRE MY FRIEND...
OH, NOT AT ALL. I COULD ALWAYS USE MORE HELP.
AT FIRST, I WONDERED WHAT KIND OF PERSON THAT BRAIDED FELLOW WAS,
BUT HE'S VERY KNOWLEDGEABLE, AND HE REALLY CONNECTS WITH THE STUDENTS, SO I FEEL AT EASE.
Nice to meet y'all.
Hashida-senseei!
GLAD TO HEAR THAT.
...I'LL ALSO DO MY BEST TO CONDUCT MYSELF LIKE HASHIDA.
OH, NO, YOU'RE GOOD, TOO, YAGUCHI-KUN.

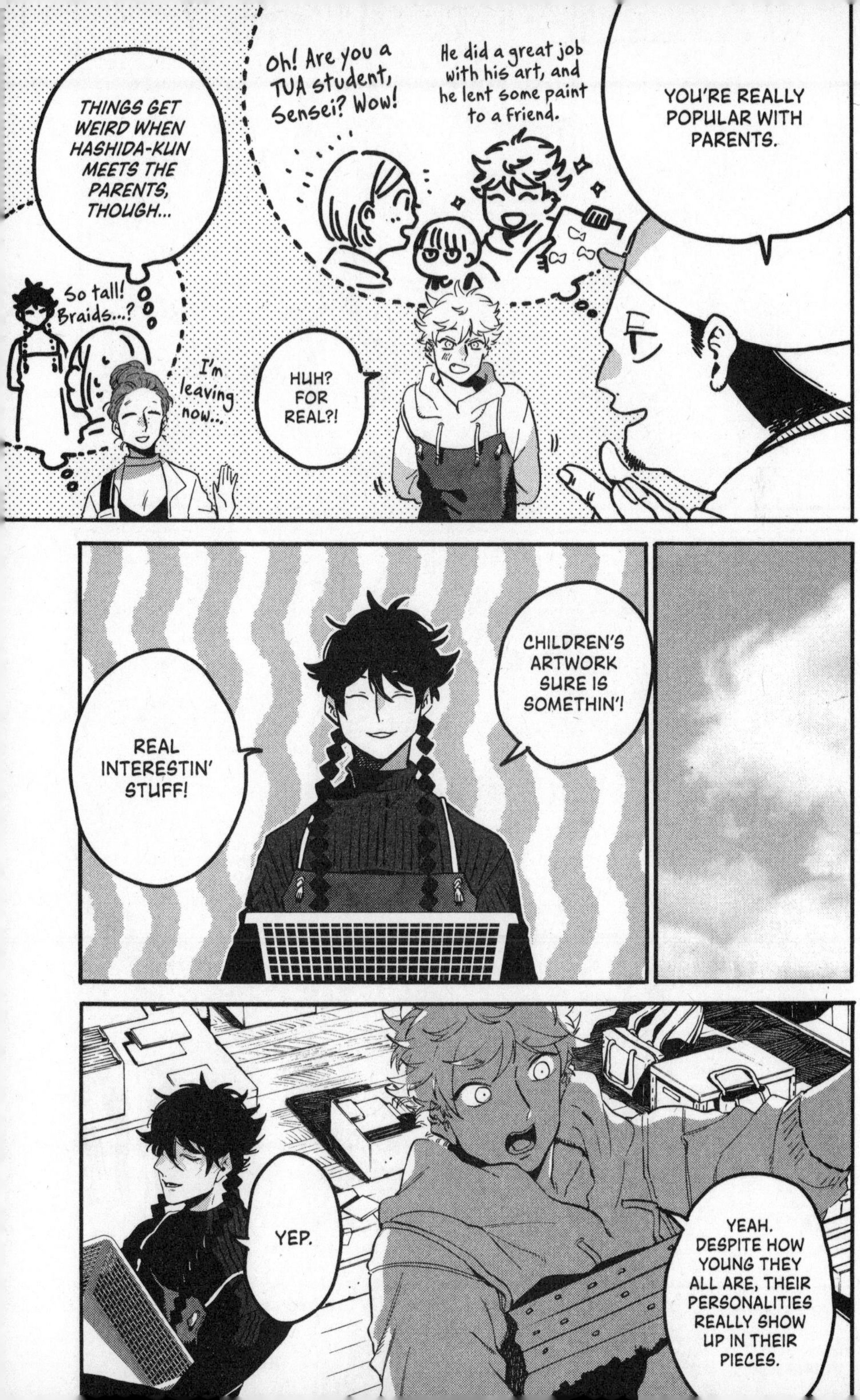
YOU'RE REALLY POPULAR WITH PARENTS.
He did a great job with his art, and he lent some paint to a friend.
Oh! Are you a TUA student, Sensei? Wow!
THINGS GET WEIRD WHEN HASHIDA-KUN MEETS THE PARENTS, THOUGH...
HUH? FOR REAL?!
So tall! Braids...?
I'm leaving now...
CHILDREN'S ARTWORK SURE IS SOMETHIN'!
REAL INTERESTIN' STUFF!
YEAH. DESPITE HOW YOUNG THEY ALL ARE, THEIR PERSONALITIES REALLY SHOW UP IN THEIR PIECES.
YEP.

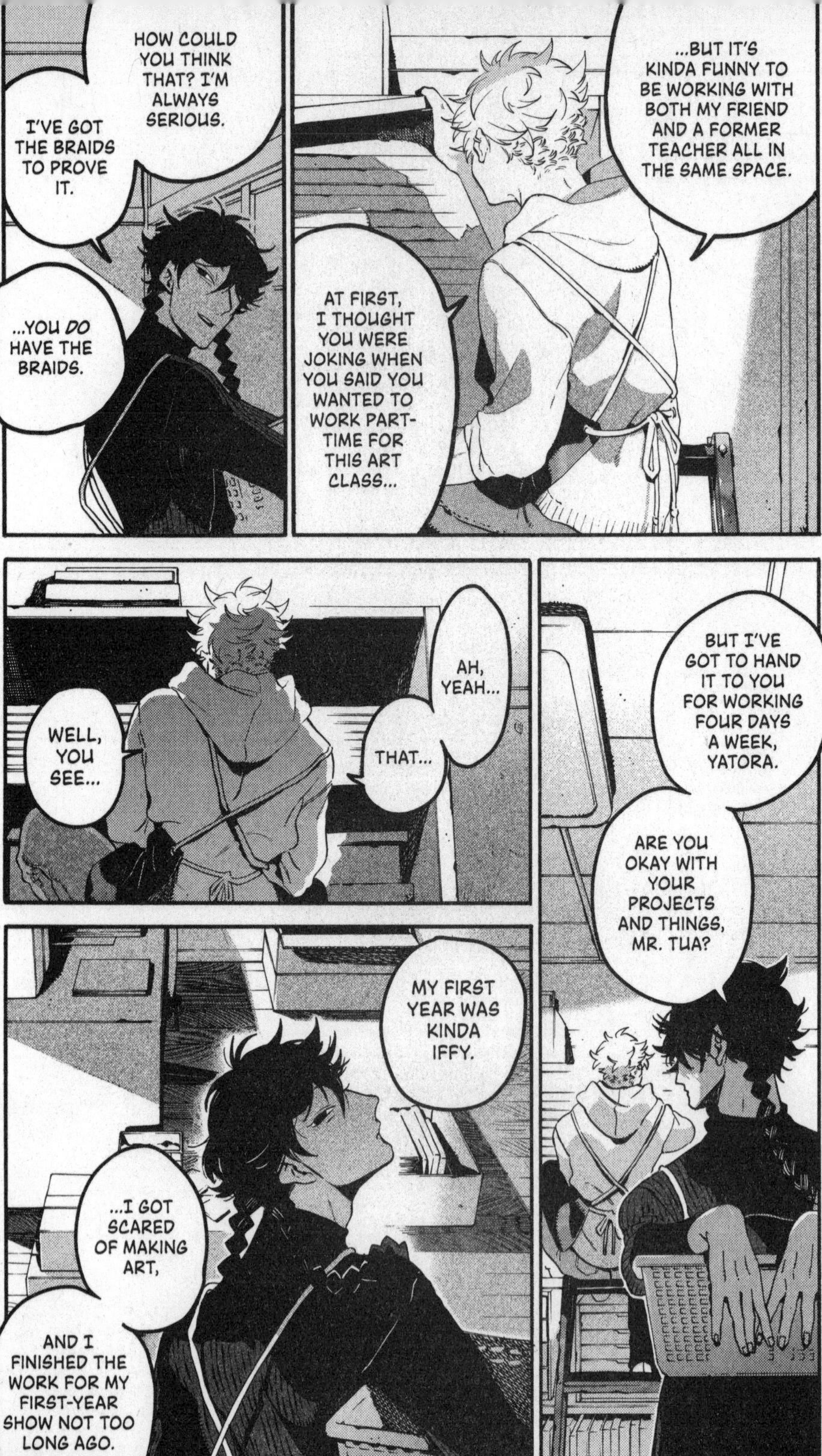
...BUT IT'S KINDA FUNNY TO BE WORKING WITH BOTH MY FRIEND AND A FORMER TEACHER ALL IN THE SAME SPACE.
AT FIRST, I THOUGHT YOU WERE JOKING WHEN YOU SAID YOU WANTED TO WORK PART-TIME FOR THIS ART CLASS...
HOW COULD YOU THINK THAT? I'M ALWAYS SERIOUS.
I'VE GOT THE BRAIDS TO PROVE IT.
...YOU *DO* HAVE THE BRAIDS.
BUT I'VE GOT TO HAND IT TO YOU FOR WORKING FOUR DAYS A WEEK, YATORA.
ARE YOU OKAY WITH YOUR PROJECTS AND THINGS, MR. TUA?
AH, YEAH...
THAT...
WELL, YOU SEE...
MY FIRST YEAR WAS KINDA IFFY.
...I GOT SCARED OF MAKING ART,
AND I FINISHED THE WORK FOR MY FIRST-YEAR SHOW NOT TOO LONG AGO.

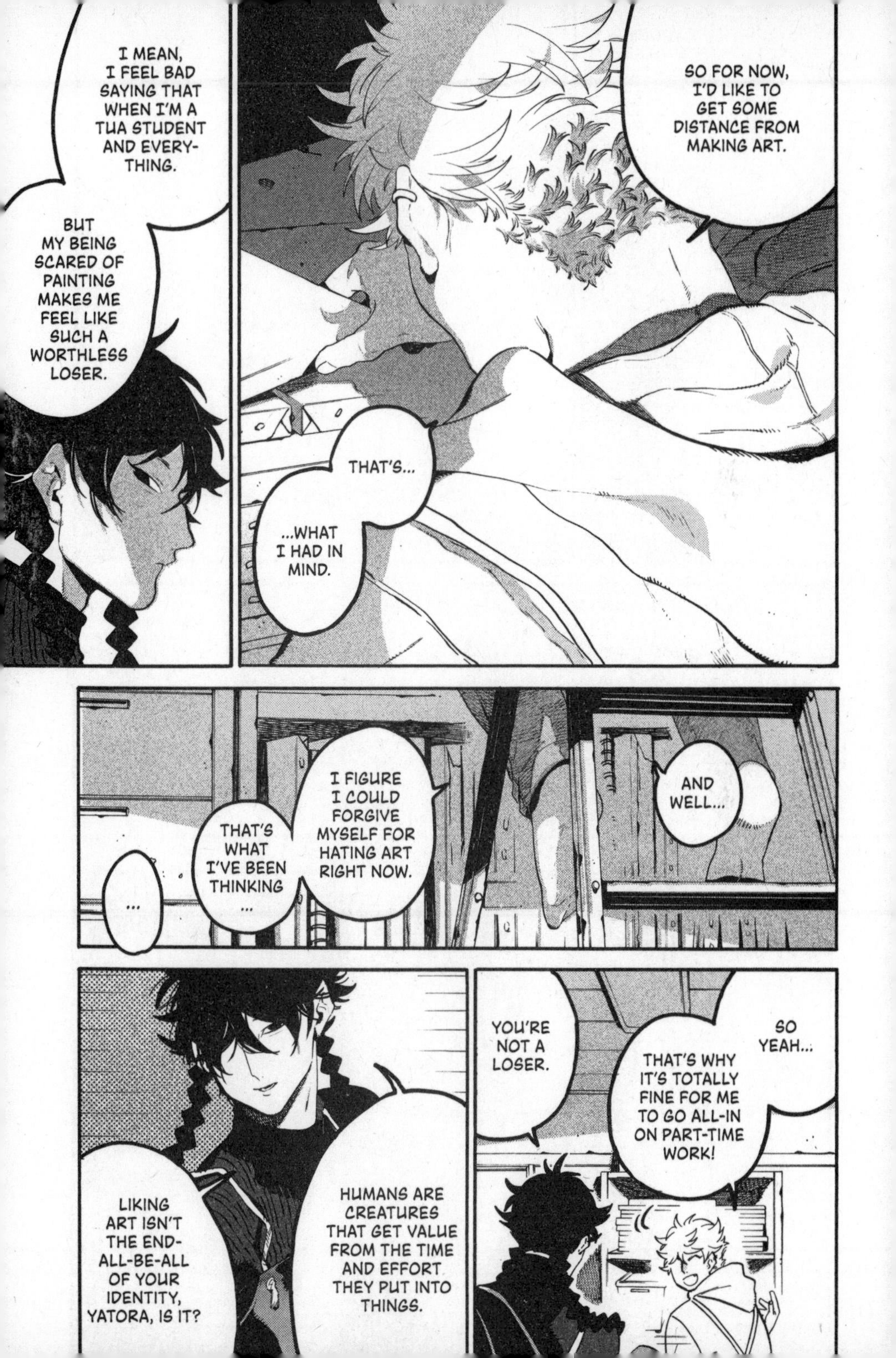
SO FOR NOW, I'D LIKE TO GET SOME DISTANCE FROM MAKING ART.
THAT'S...
...WHAT I HAD IN MIND.
I MEAN, I FEEL BAD SAYING THAT WHEN I'M A TUA STUDENT AND EVERY-THING.
BUT MY BEING SCARED OF PAINTING MAKES ME FEEL LIKE SUCH A WORTHLESS LOSER.
AND WELL...
I FIGURE I COULD FORGIVE MYSELF FOR HATING ART RIGHT NOW.
THAT'S WHAT I'VE BEEN THINKING...
...
SO YEAH...
THAT'S WHY IT'S TOTALLY FINE FOR ME TO GO ALL-IN ON PART-TIME WORK!
YOU'RE NOT A LOSER.
HUMANS ARE CREATURES THAT GET VALUE FROM THE TIME AND EFFORT THEY PUT INTO THINGS.
LIKING ART ISN'T THE END-ALL-BE-ALL OF YOUR IDENTITY, YATORA, IS IT?

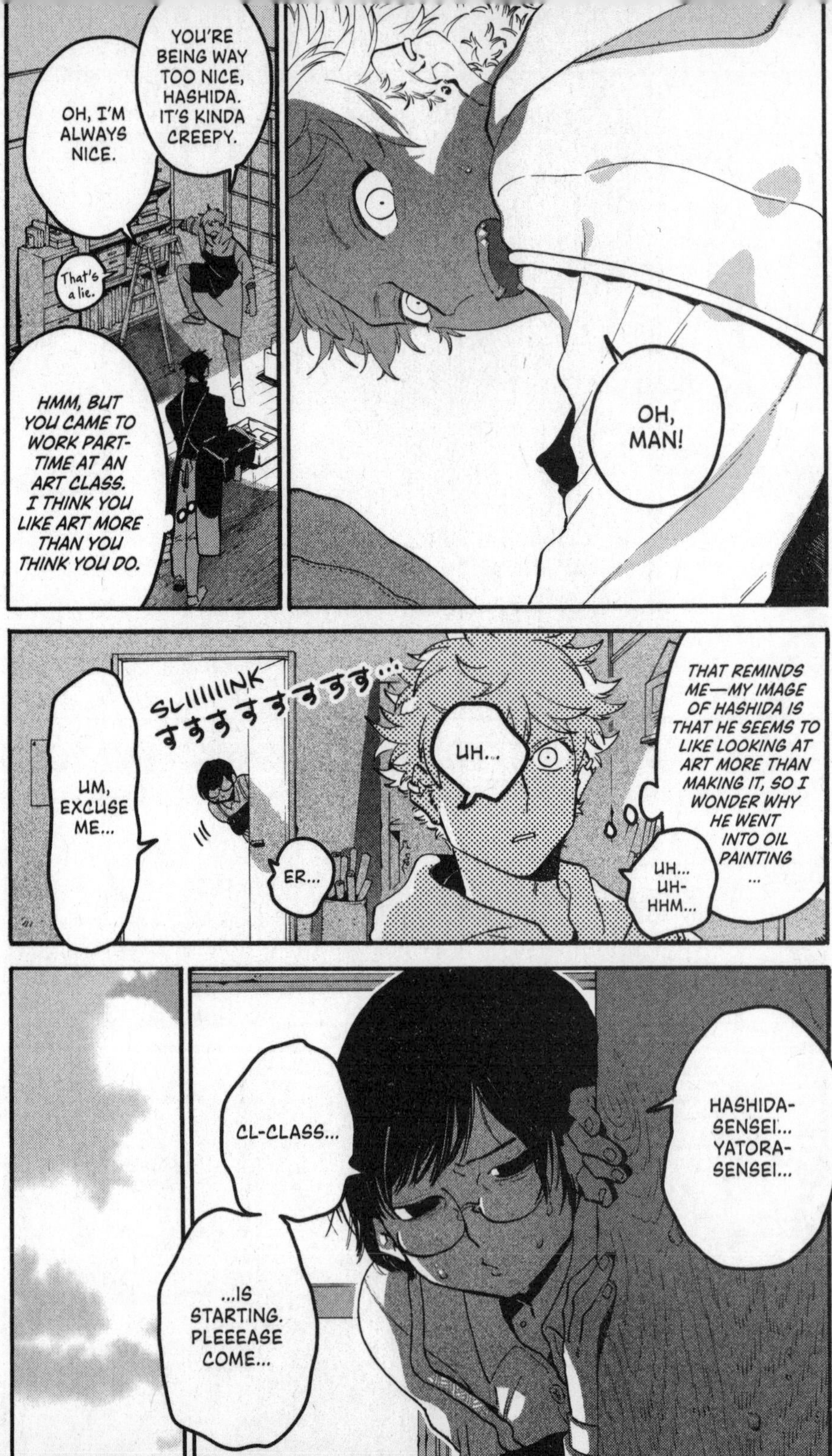
OH, MAN!
YOU'RE BEING WAY TOO NICE, HASHIDA. IT'S KINDA CREEPY.
OH, I'M ALWAYS NICE.
That's a lie.
HMM, BUT YOU CAME TO WORK PART-TIME AT AN ART CLASS. I THINK YOU LIKE ART MORE THAN YOU THINK YOU DO.
THAT REMINDS ME—MY IMAGE OF HASHIDA IS THAT HE SEEMS TO LIKE LOOKING AT ART MORE THAN MAKING IT, SO I WONDER WHY HE WENT INTO OIL PAINTING ...
UH... UH-HHM...
UH...
SLIIIIIINK すすすすすすすす...
UM, EXCUSE ME...
ER...
HASHIDA-SENSEI... YATORA-SENSEI...
CL-CLASS...
...IS STARTING. PLEEEASE COME...

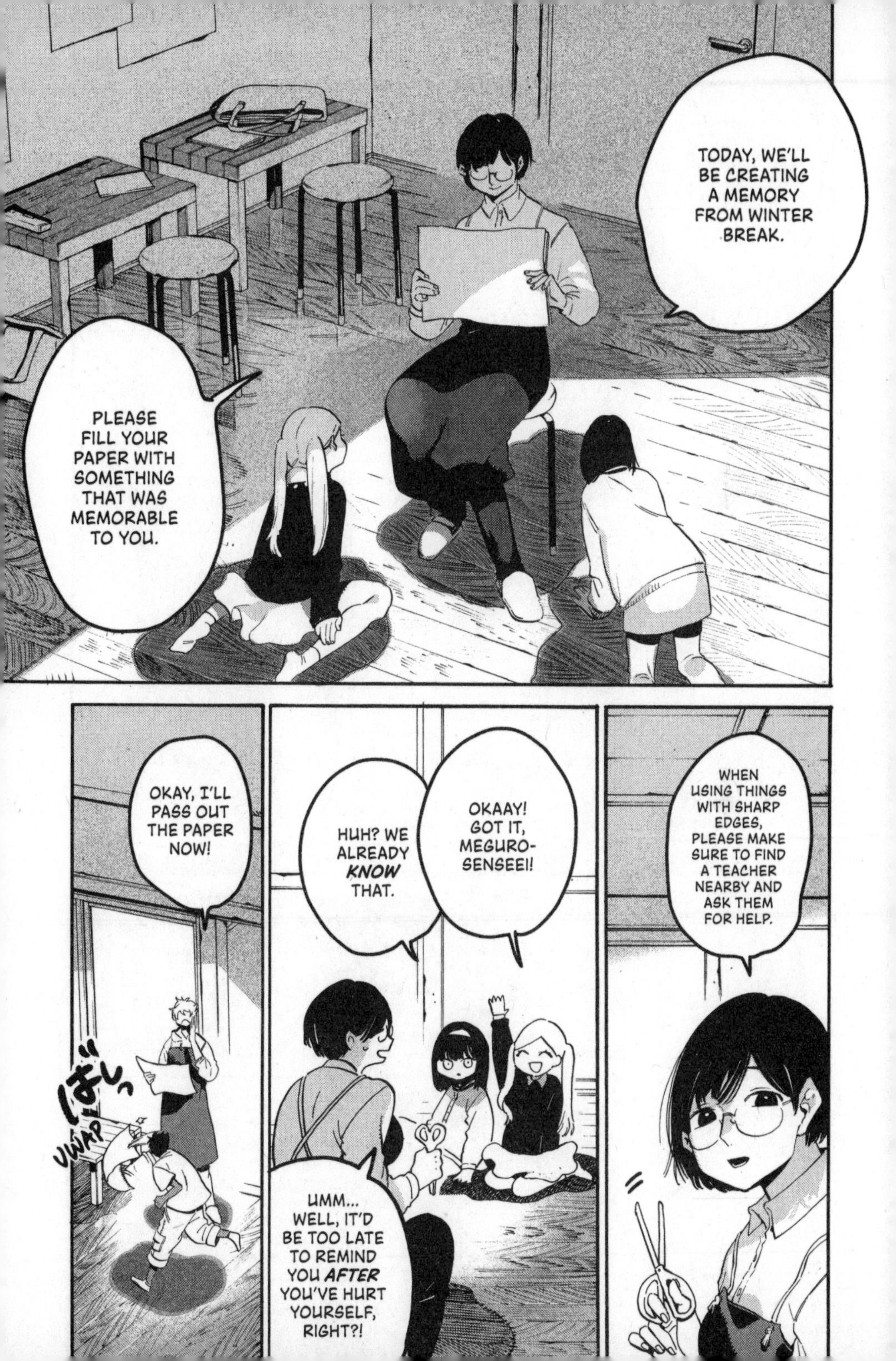
TODAY, WE'LL BE CREATING A MEMORY FROM WINTER BREAK.
PLEASE FILL YOUR PAPER WITH SOMETHING THAT WAS MEMORABLE TO YOU.
WHEN USING THINGS WITH SHARP EDGES, PLEASE MAKE SURE TO FIND A TEACHER NEARBY AND ASK THEM FOR HELP.
OKAAY! GOT IT, MEGURO-SENSEEI!
HUH? WE ALREADY *KNOW* THAT.
UMM... WELL, IT'D BE TOO LATE TO REMIND YOU *AFTER* YOU'VE HURT YOURSELF, RIGHT?!
OKAY, I'LL PASS OUT THE PAPER NOW!
ばしっ
UWAP

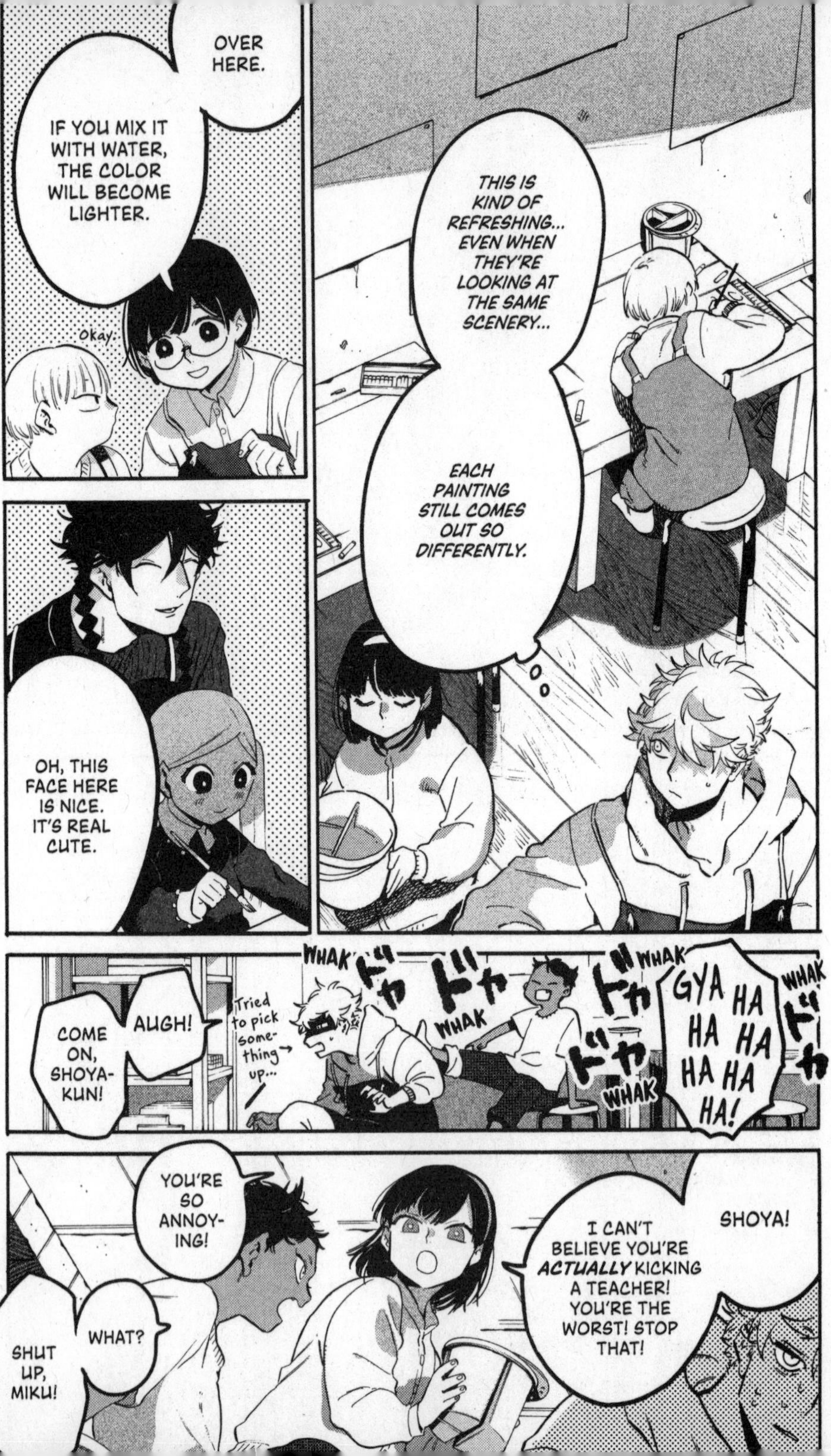
THIS IS KIND OF REFRESHING... EVEN WHEN THEY'RE LOOKING AT THE SAME SCENERY...
EACH PAINTING STILL COMES OUT SO DIFFERENTLY.
OVER HERE.
IF YOU MIX IT WITH WATER, THE COLOR WILL BECOME LIGHTER.
Okay.
OH, THIS FACE HERE IS NICE. IT'S REAL CUTE.
WHAK
WHAK
GYA HA HA HA HA HA HA HA!
WHAK
WHAK
WHAK
AUGH!
COME ON, SHOYA-KUN!
Tried to pick something up...
SHOYA!
I CAN'T BELIEVE YOU'RE ACTUALLY KICKING A TEACHER! YOU'RE THE WORST! STOP THAT!
YOU'RE SO ANNOYING!
WHAT?
SHUT UP, MIKU!

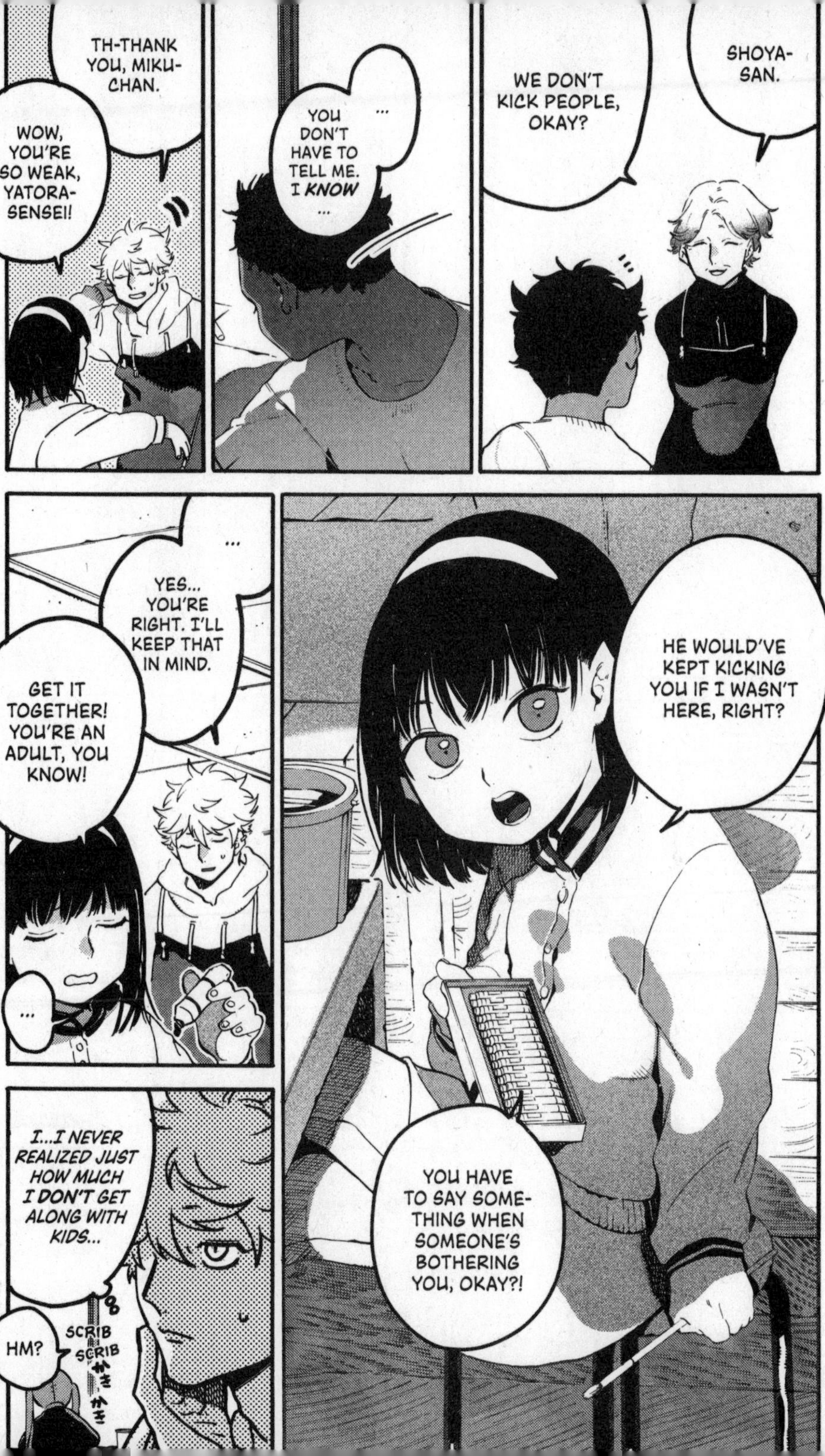
SHOYA-SAN.
WE DON'T KICK PEOPLE, OKAY?
...
YOU DON'T HAVE TO TELL ME. I *KNOW* ...
TH-THANK YOU, MIKU-CHAN.
WOW, YOU'RE SO WEAK, YATORA-SENSEI!
HE WOULD'VE KEPT KICKING YOU IF I WASN'T HERE, RIGHT?
YOU HAVE TO SAY SOME-THING WHEN SOMEONE'S BOTHERING YOU, OKAY?!
...
YES... YOU'RE RIGHT. I'LL KEEP THAT IN MIND.
GET IT TOGETHER! YOU'RE AN ADULT, YOU KNOW!
...
I...I NEVER REALIZED JUST HOW MUCH I DON'T GET ALONG WITH KIDS...
SCRIB SCRIB
かき かき
HM?

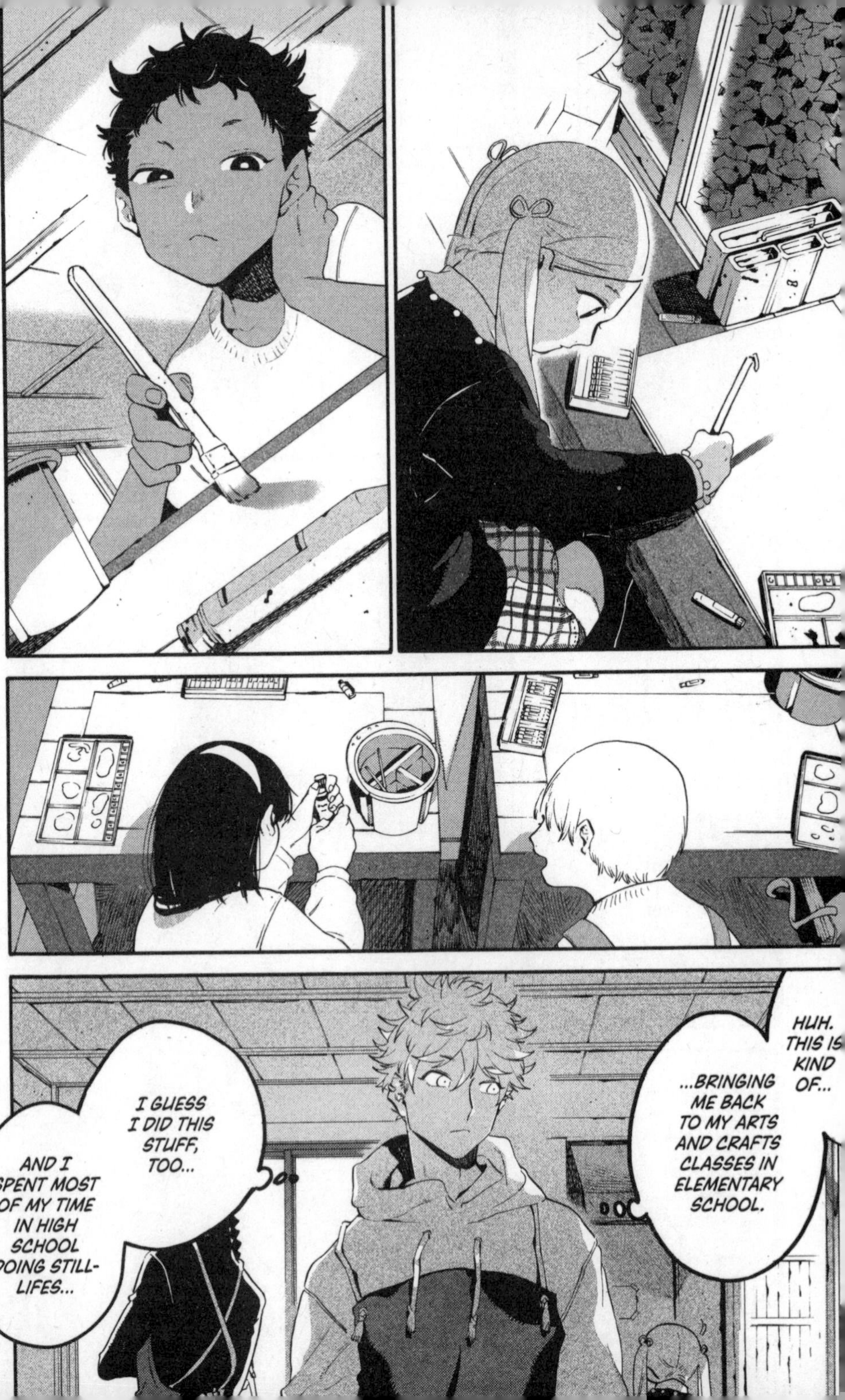
HUH. THIS IS KIND OF...
...BRINGING ME BACK TO MY ARTS AND CRAFTS CLASSES IN ELEMENTARY SCHOOL.
I GUESS I DID THIS STUFF, TOO...
AND I SPENT MOST OF MY TIME IN HIGH SCHOOL DOING STILL-LIFES...

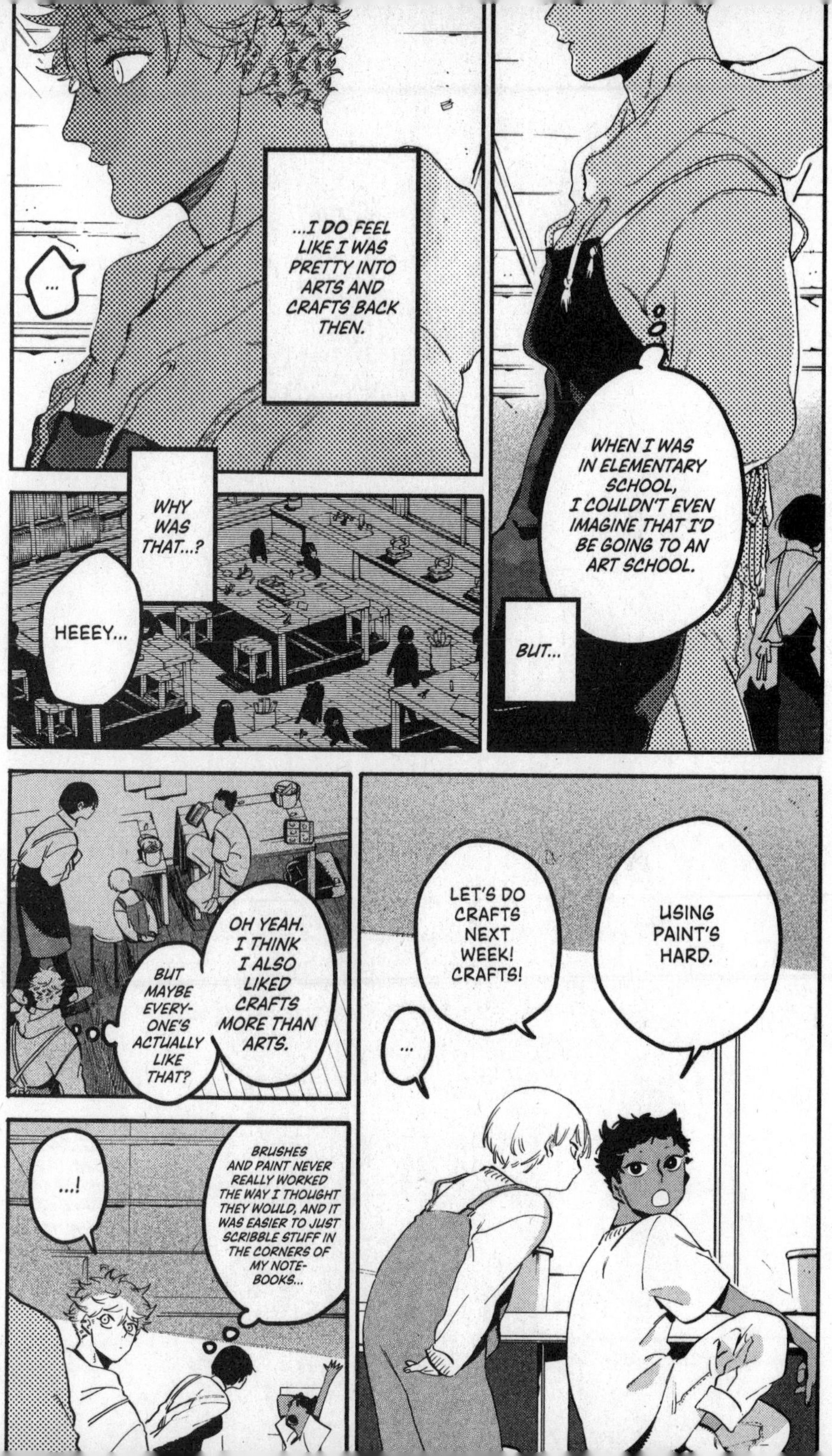
WHEN I WAS IN ELEMENTARY SCHOOL, I COULDN'T EVEN IMAGINE THAT I'D BE GOING TO AN ART SCHOOL.
BUT...
...I DO FEEL LIKE I WAS PRETTY INTO ARTS AND CRAFTS BACK THEN.
...
WHY WAS THAT...?
HEEEY...
USING PAINT'S HARD.
LET'S DO CRAFTS NEXT WEEK! CRAFTS!
...
OH YEAH. I THINK I ALSO LIKED CRAFTS MORE THAN ARTS.
BUT MAYBE EVERYONE'S ACTUALLY LIKE THAT?
...!
BRUSHES AND PAINT NEVER REALLY WORKED THE WAY I THOUGHT THEY WOULD, AND IT WAS EASIER TO JUST SCRIBBLE STUFF IN THE CORNERS OF MY NOTEBOOKS...

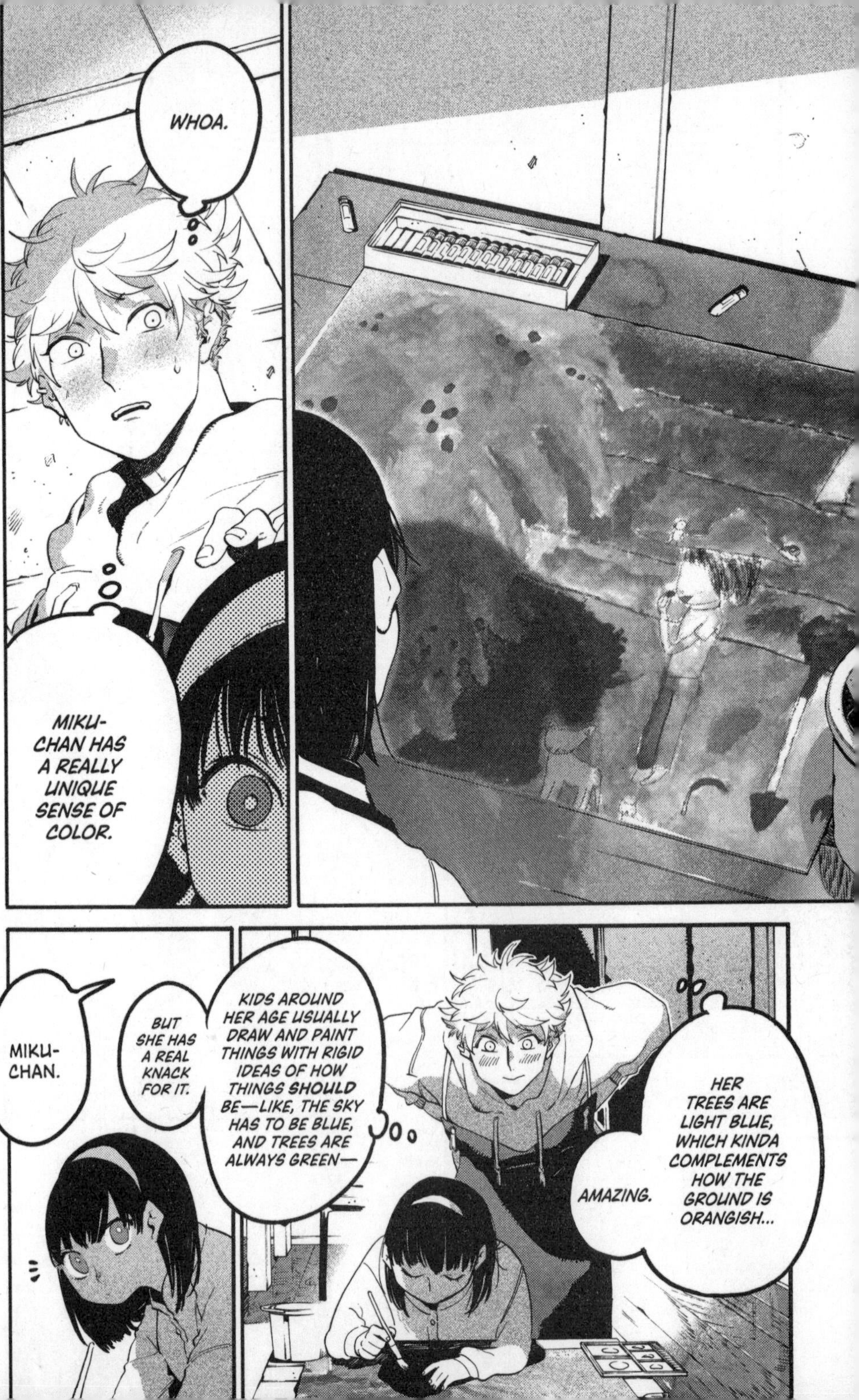
WHOA.
MIKU-CHAN HAS A REALLY UNIQUE SENSE OF COLOR.
HER TREES ARE LIGHT BLUE, WHICH KINDA COMPLEMENTS HOW THE GROUND IS ORANGISH...
AMAZING.
KIDS AROUND HER AGE USUALLY DRAW AND PAINT THINGS WITH RIGID IDEAS OF HOW THINGS **SHOULD** BE—LIKE, THE SKY HAS TO BE BLUE, AND TREES ARE ALWAYS GREEN—
BUT SHE HAS A REAL KNACK FOR IT.
MIKU-CHAN.

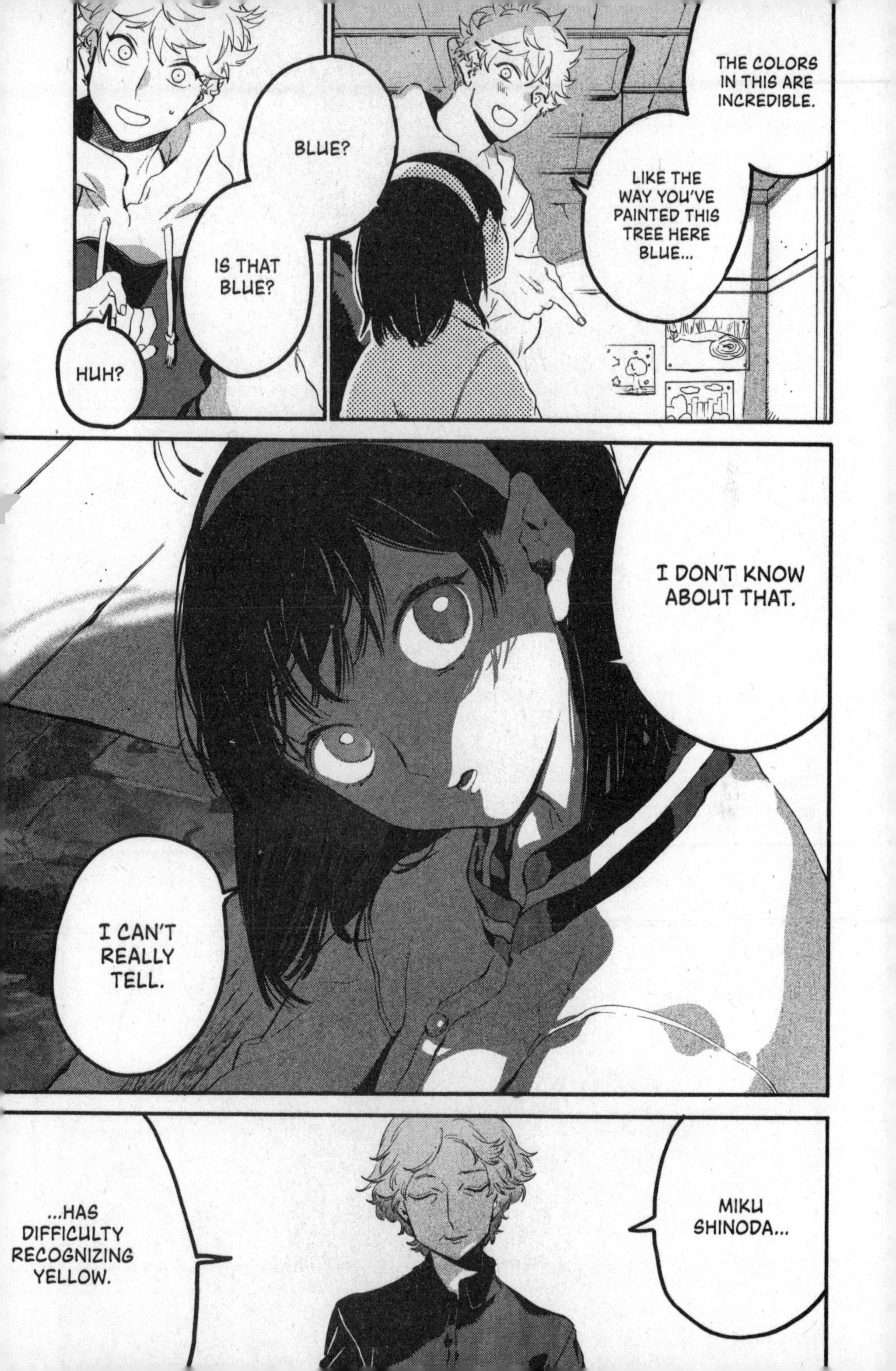
THE COLORS IN THIS ARE INCREDIBLE.
LIKE THE WAY YOU'VE PAINTED THIS TREE HERE BLUE...
BLUE?
IS THAT BLUE?
HUH?
I DON'T KNOW ABOUT THAT.
I CAN'T REALLY TELL.
MIKU SHINODA...
...HAS DIFFICULTY RECOGNIZING YELLOW.

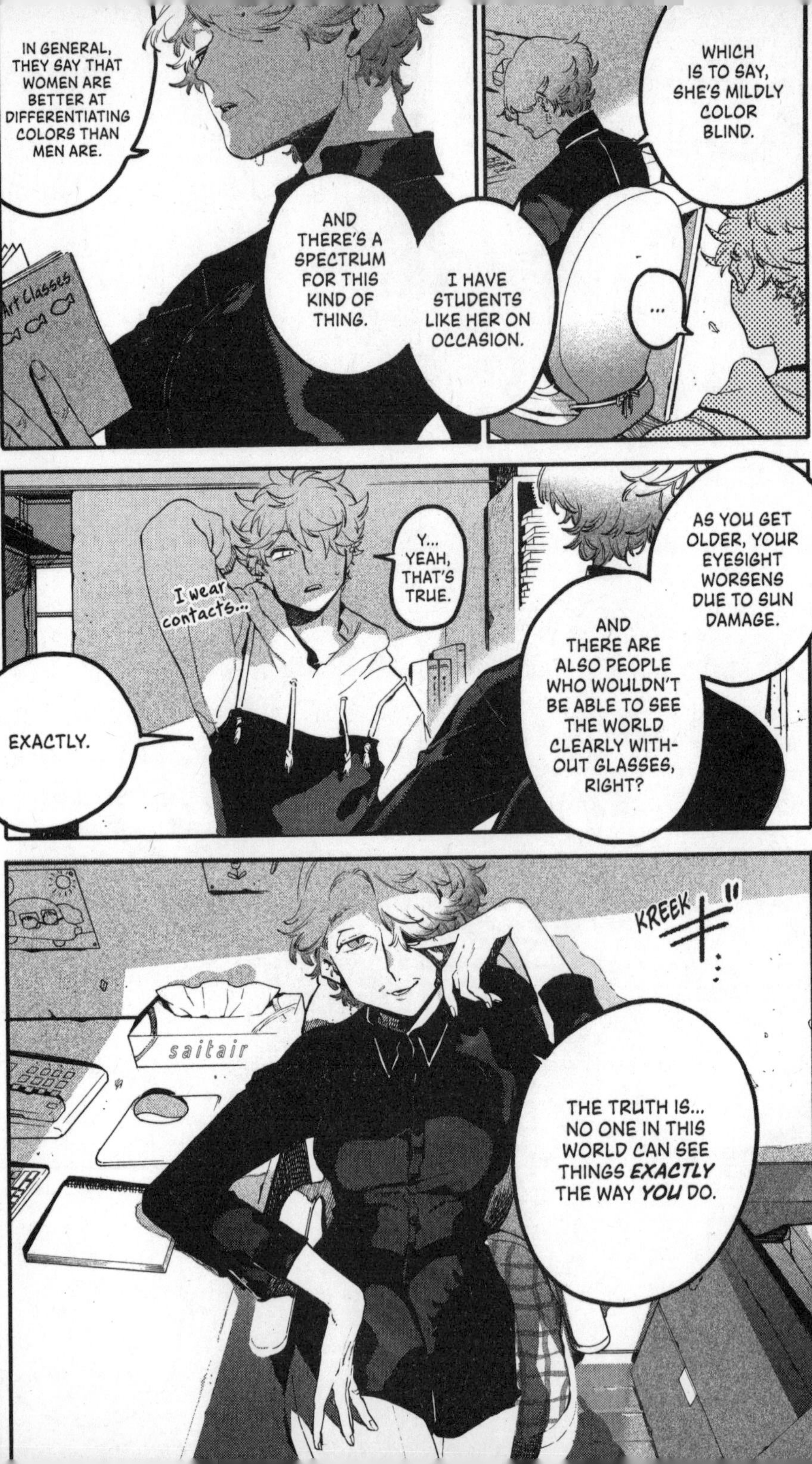

WHICH IS TO SAY, SHE'S MILDLY COLOR BLIND.
...
IN GENERAL, THEY SAY THAT WOMEN ARE BETTER AT DIFFERENTIATING COLORS THAN MEN ARE.
AND THERE'S A SPECTRUM FOR THIS KIND OF THING.
I HAVE STUDENTS LIKE HER ON OCCASION.
Art Classes
AS YOU GET OLDER, YOUR EYESIGHT WORSENS DUE TO SUN DAMAGE.
AND THERE ARE ALSO PEOPLE WHO WOULDN'T BE ABLE TO SEE THE WORLD CLEARLY WITH-OUT GLASSES, RIGHT?
Y... YEAH, THAT'S TRUE.
I wear contacts...
EXACTLY.
KREEK
THE TRUTH IS... NO ONE IN THIS WORLD CAN SEE THINGS *EXACTLY* THE WAY *YOU* DO.
saitair

THERE IS A CERTAIN THEORY THAT SUGGESTS THIS COMES FROM A CHROMOSOMAL DIFFERENCE BETWEEN MEN AND WOMEN. THIS ALSO VARIES AT THE INDIVIDUAL LEVEL, AND THERE ARE SEVERAL THEORIES ON THE TOPIC.

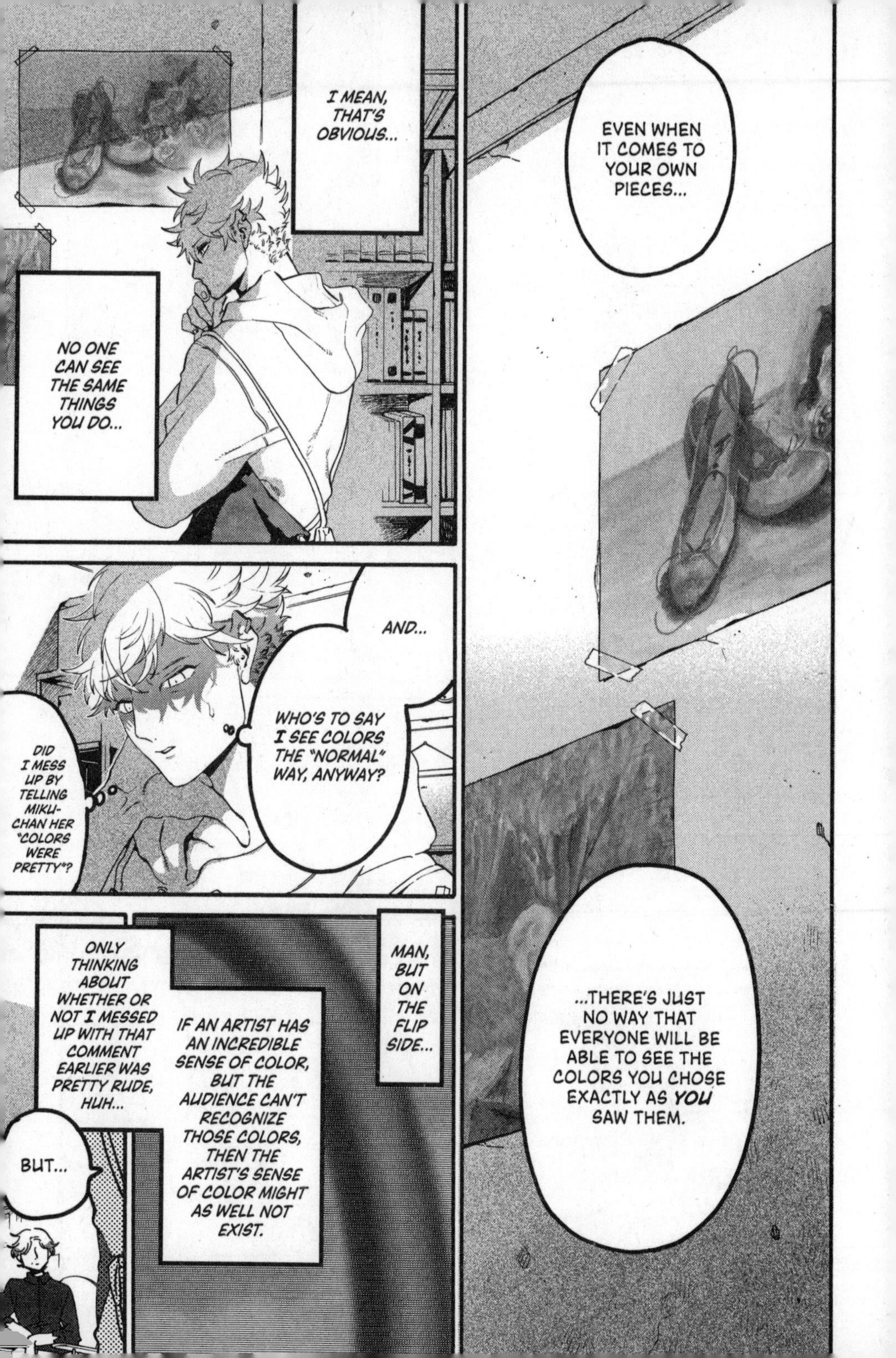
EVEN WHEN IT COMES TO YOUR OWN PIECES...
...THERE'S JUST NO WAY THAT EVERYONE WILL BE ABLE TO SEE THE COLORS YOU CHOSE EXACTLY AS *YOU* SAW THEM.
I MEAN, THAT'S OBVIOUS...
NO ONE CAN SEE THE SAME THINGS YOU DO...
AND...
WHO'S TO SAY I SEE COLORS THE "NORMAL" WAY, ANYWAY?
DID I MESS UP BY TELLING MIKU-CHAN HER "COLORS WERE PRETTY"?
MAN, BUT ON THE FLIP SIDE...
IF AN ARTIST HAS AN INCREDIBLE SENSE OF COLOR, BUT THE AUDIENCE CAN'T RECOGNIZE THOSE COLORS, THEN THE ARTIST'S SENSE OF COLOR MIGHT AS WELL NOT EXIST.
ONLY THINKING ABOUT WHETHER OR NOT I MESSED UP WITH THAT COMMENT EARLIER WAS PRETTY RUDE, HUH...
BUT...

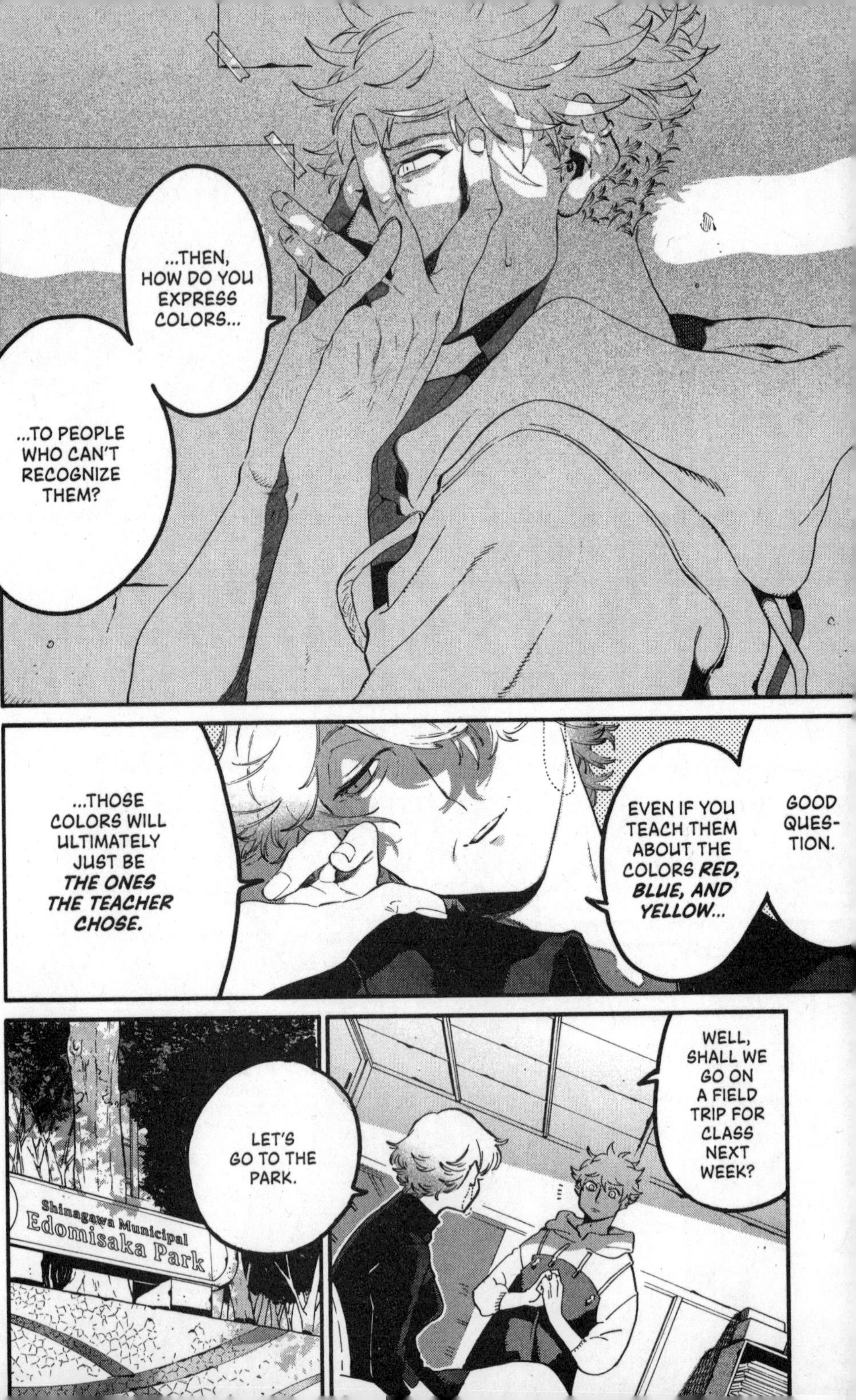
...THEN, HOW DO YOU EXPRESS COLORS...
...TO PEOPLE WHO CAN'T RECOGNIZE THEM?
GOOD QUESTION.
EVEN IF YOU TEACH THEM ABOUT THE COLORS *RED, BLUE, AND YELLOW*...
...THOSE COLORS WILL ULTIMATELY JUST BE *THE ONES THE TEACHER CHOSE.*
WELL, SHALL WE GO ON A FIELD TRIP FOR CLASS NEXT WEEK?
LET'S GO TO THE PARK.
Shinagawa Municipal
Edomisaka Park

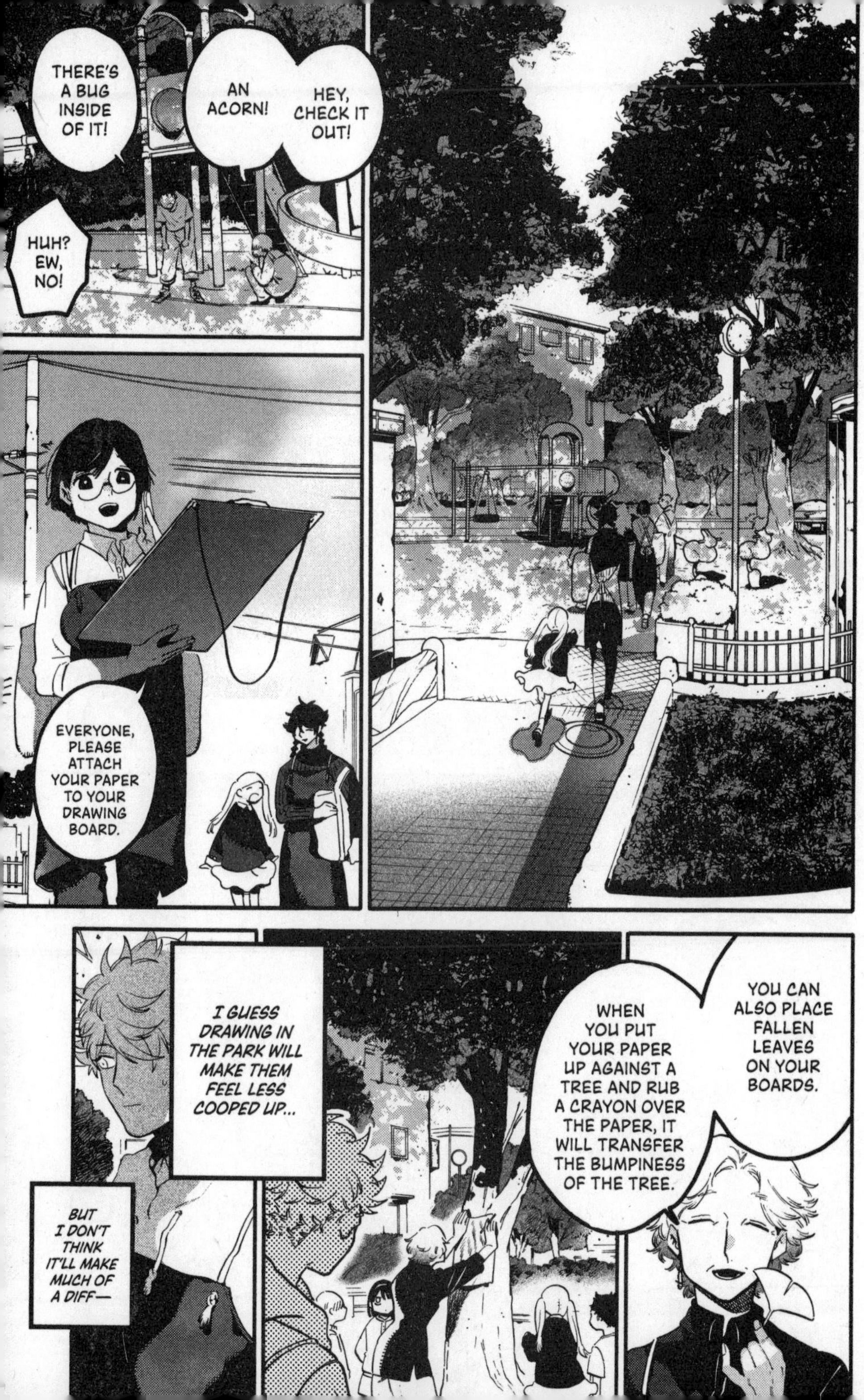
HEY, CHECK IT OUT!
AN ACORN!
THERE'S A BUG INSIDE OF IT!
HUH? EW, NO!
EVERYONE, PLEASE ATTACH YOUR PAPER TO YOUR DRAWING BOARD.
YOU CAN ALSO PLACE FALLEN LEAVES ON YOUR BOARDS.
WHEN YOU PUT YOUR PAPER UP AGAINST A TREE AND RUB A CRAYON OVER THE PAPER, IT WILL TRANSFER THE BUMPINESS OF THE TREE.
I GUESS DRAWING IN THE PARK WILL MAKE THEM FEEL LESS COOPED UP...
BUT I DON'T THINK IT'LL MAKE MUCH OF A DIFF—

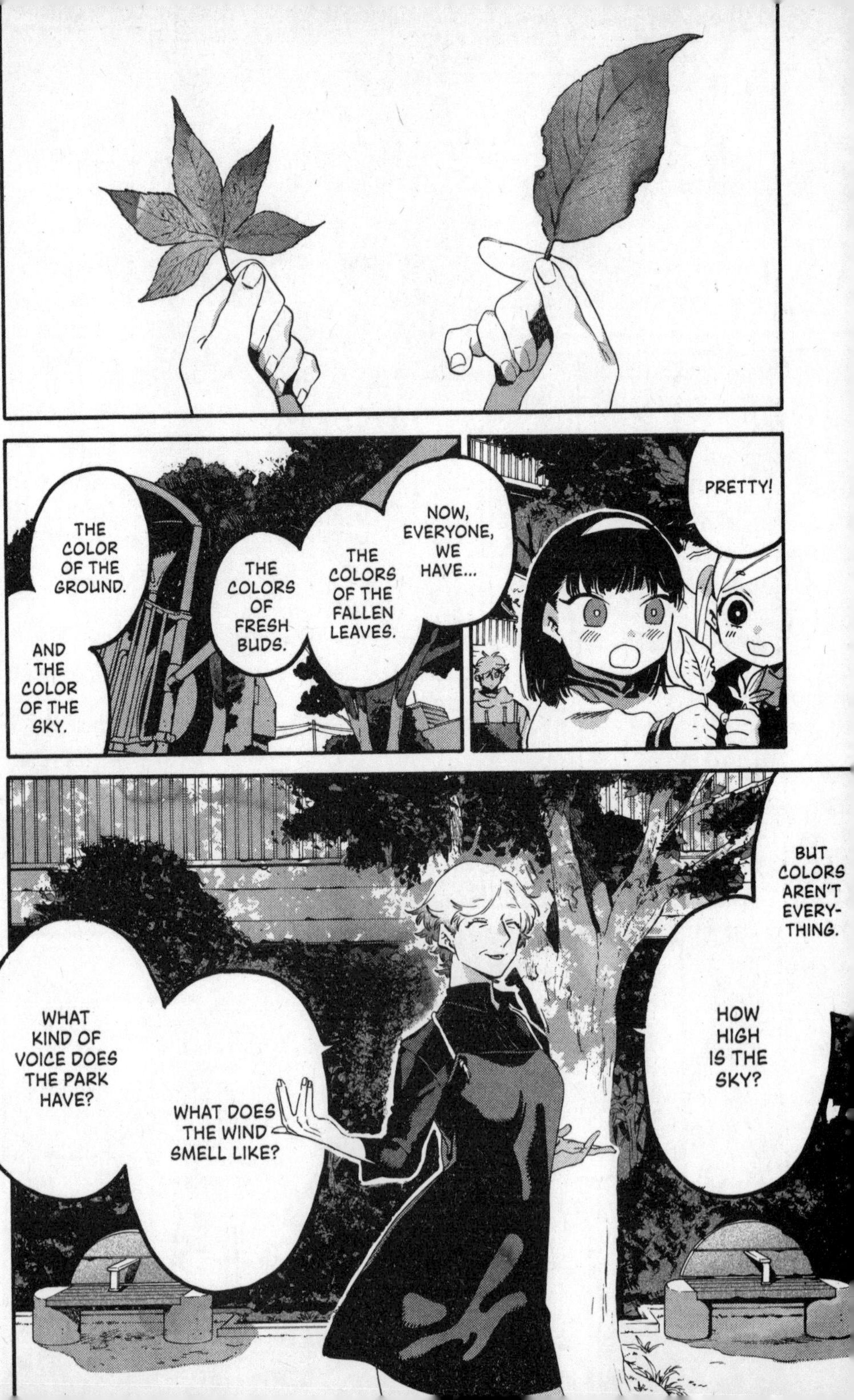
PRETTY!
NOW, EVERYONE, WE HAVE...
THE COLORS OF THE FALLEN LEAVES.
THE COLORS OF FRESH BUDS.
THE COLOR OF THE GROUND.
AND THE COLOR OF THE SKY.
BUT COLORS AREN'T EVERY-THING.
HOW HIGH IS THE SKY?
WHAT DOES THE WIND SMELL LIKE?
WHAT KIND OF VOICE DOES THE PARK HAVE?

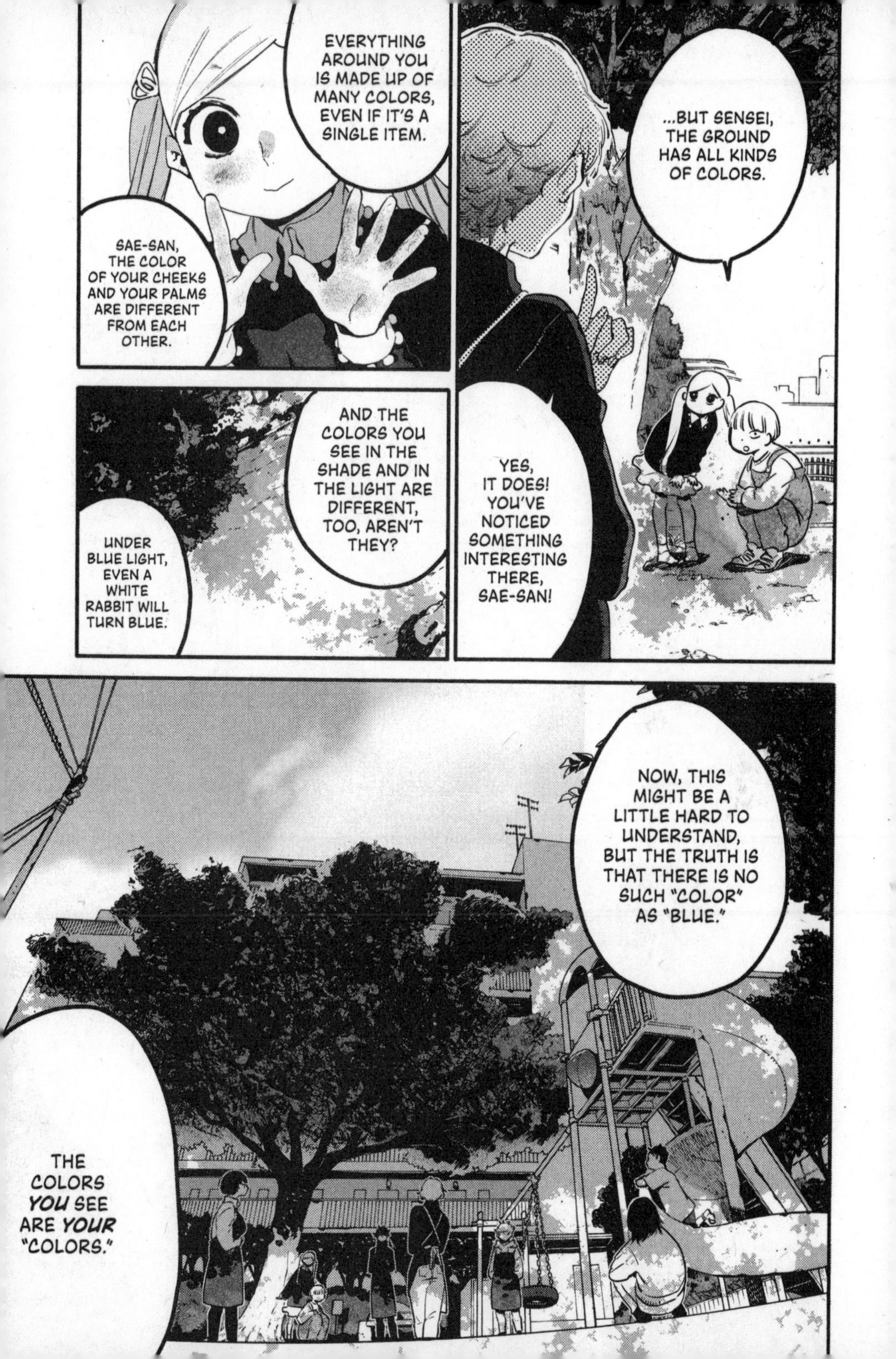
...BUT SENSEI, THE GROUND HAS ALL KINDS OF COLORS.
YES, IT DOES! YOU'VE NOTICED SOMETHING INTERESTING THERE, SAE-SAN!
EVERYTHING AROUND YOU IS MADE UP OF MANY COLORS, EVEN IF IT'S A SINGLE ITEM.
SAE-SAN, THE COLOR OF YOUR CHEEKS AND YOUR PALMS ARE DIFFERENT FROM EACH OTHER.
AND THE COLORS YOU SEE IN THE SHADE AND IN THE LIGHT ARE DIFFERENT, TOO, AREN'T THEY?
UNDER BLUE LIGHT, EVEN A WHITE RABBIT WILL TURN BLUE.
NOW, THIS MIGHT BE A LITTLE HARD TO UNDERSTAND, BUT THE TRUTH IS THAT THERE IS NO SUCH "COLOR" AS "BLUE."
THE COLORS *YOU* SEE ARE *YOUR* "COLORS."

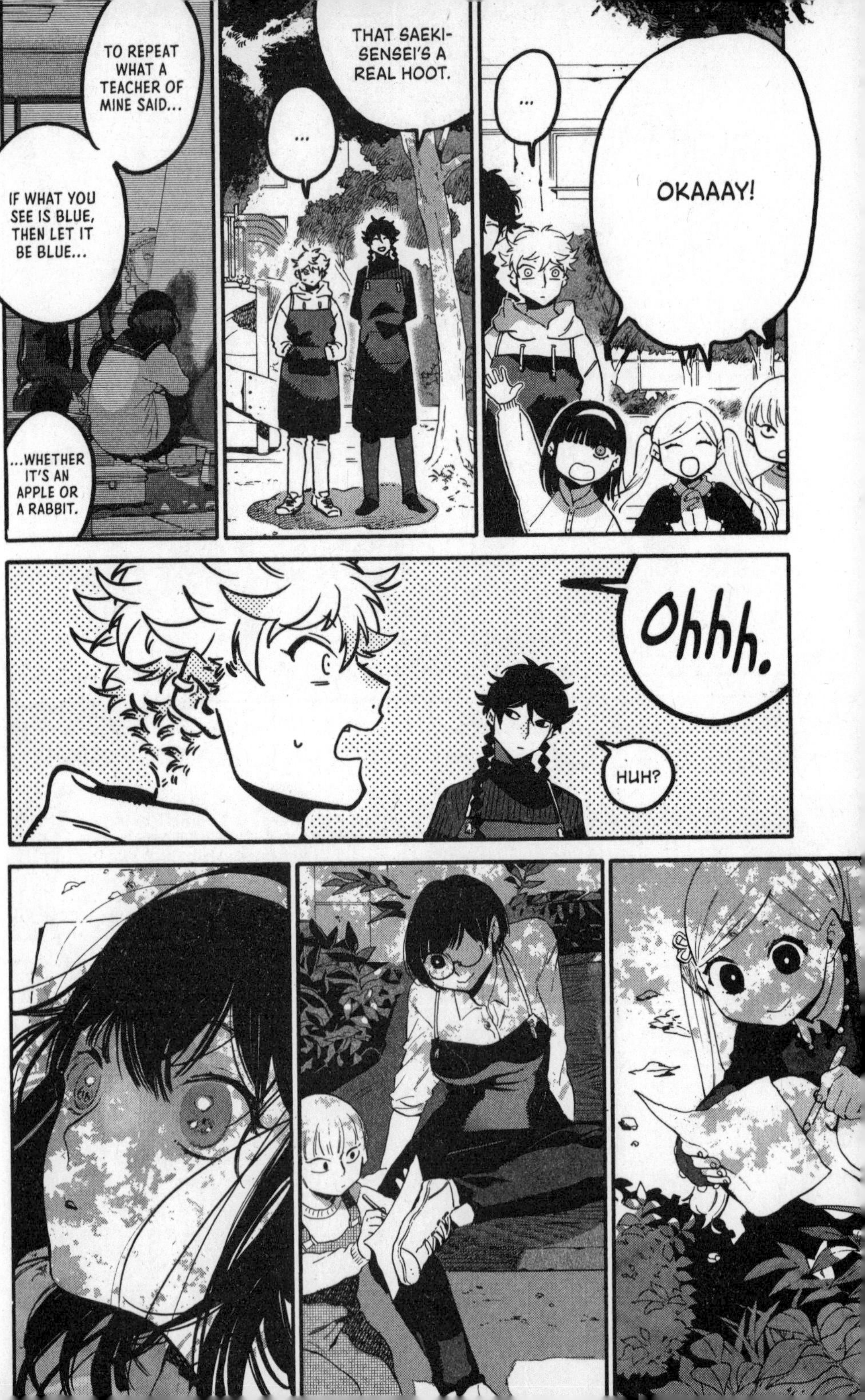

OKAAAY!
...
THAT SAEKI-SENSEI'S A REAL HOOT.
...
TO REPEAT WHAT A TEACHER OF MINE SAID...
IF WHAT YOU SEE IS BLUE, THEN LET IT BE BLUE...
...WHETHER IT'S AN APPLE OR A RABBIT.
Ohhh.
HUH?

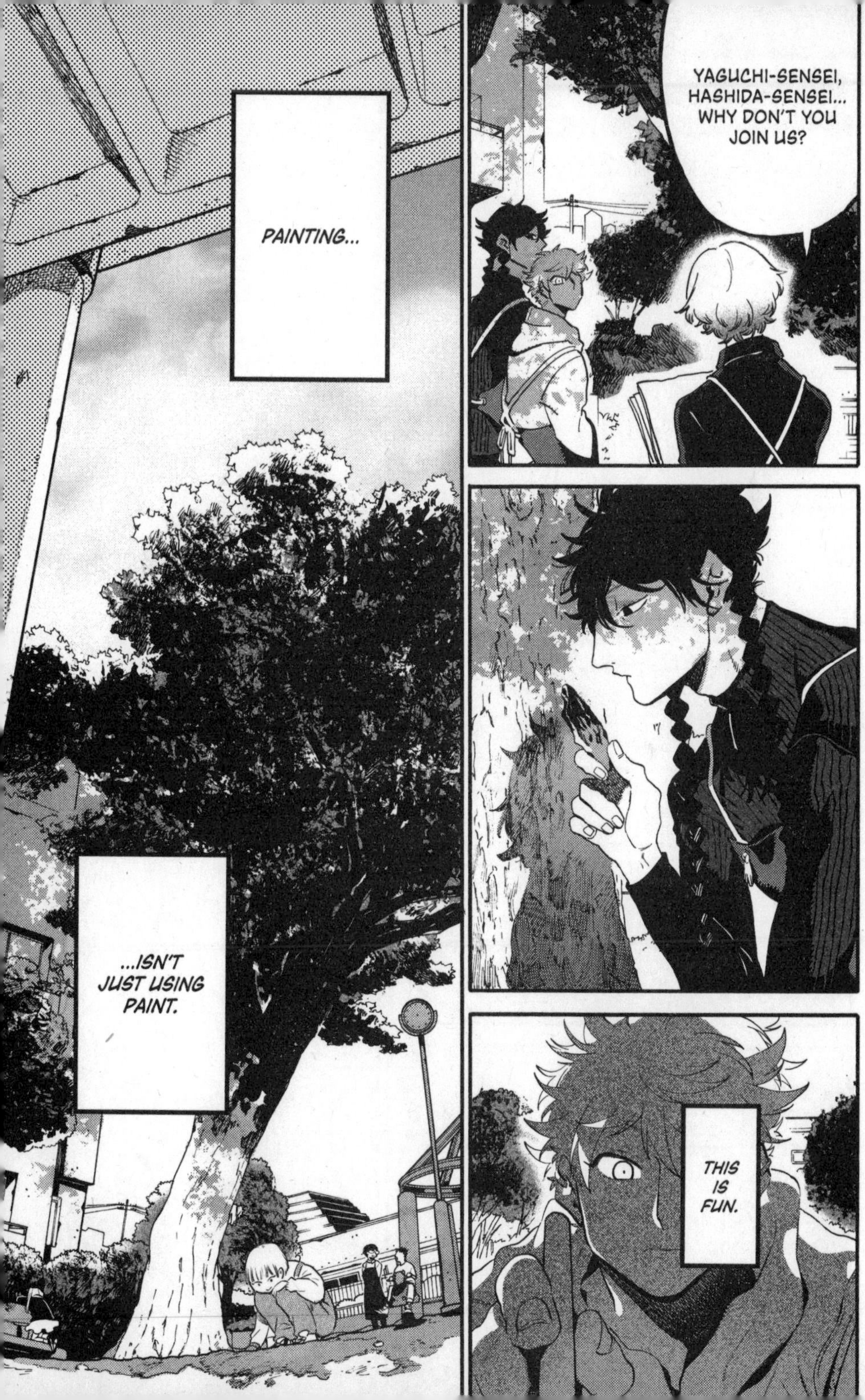
YAGUCHI-SENSEI, HASHIDA-SENSEI... WHY DON'T YOU JOIN US?
THIS IS FUN.
PAINTING...
...ISN'T JUST USING PAINT.

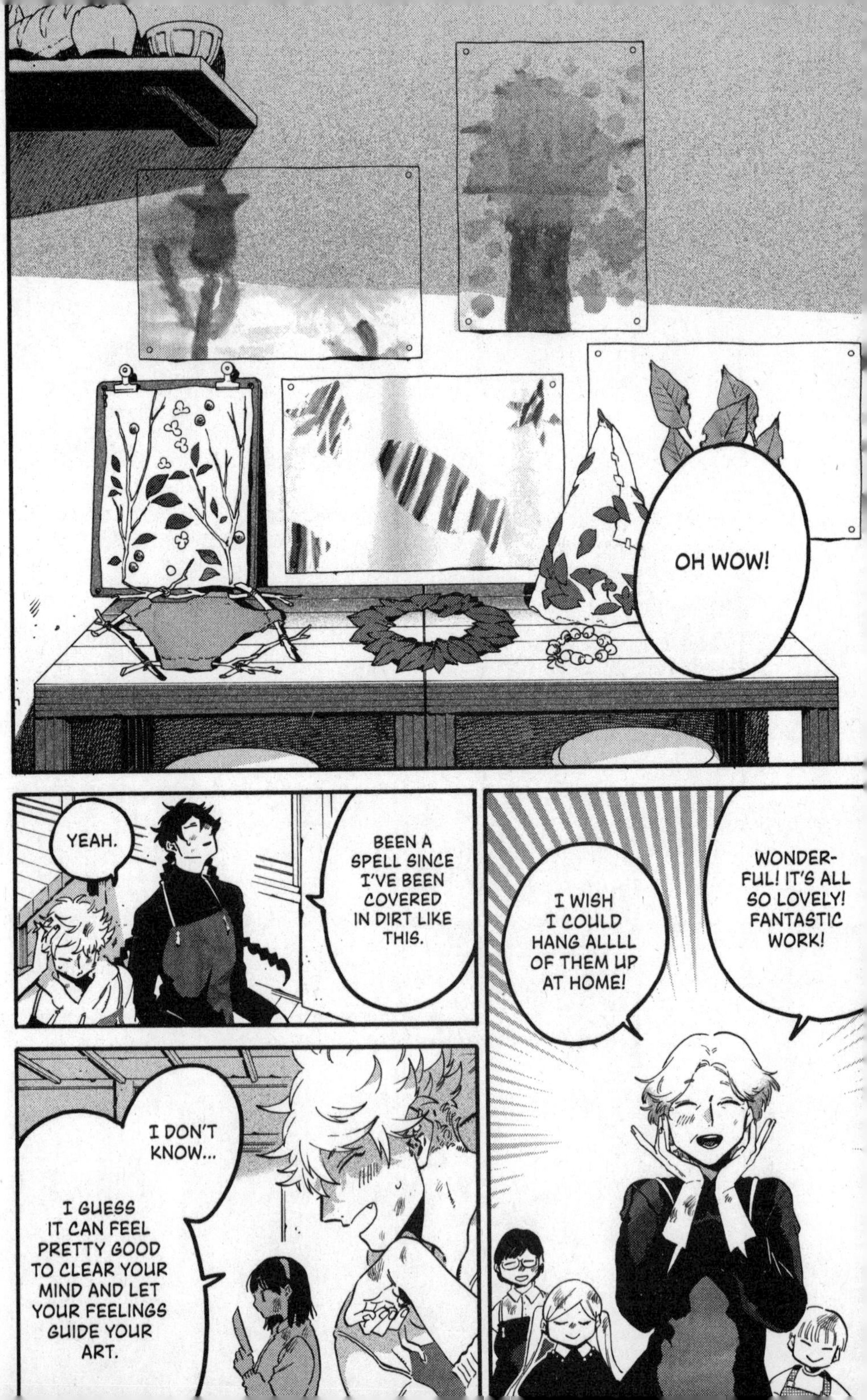
OH WOW!
WONDER-FUL! IT'S ALL SO LOVELY! FANTASTIC WORK!
I WISH I COULD HANG ALLLL OF THEM UP AT HOME!
BEEN A SPELL SINCE I'VE BEEN COVERED IN DIRT LIKE THIS.
YEAH.
I DON'T KNOW...
I GUESS IT CAN FEEL PRETTY GOOD TO CLEAR YOUR MIND AND LET YOUR FEELINGS GUIDE YOUR ART.

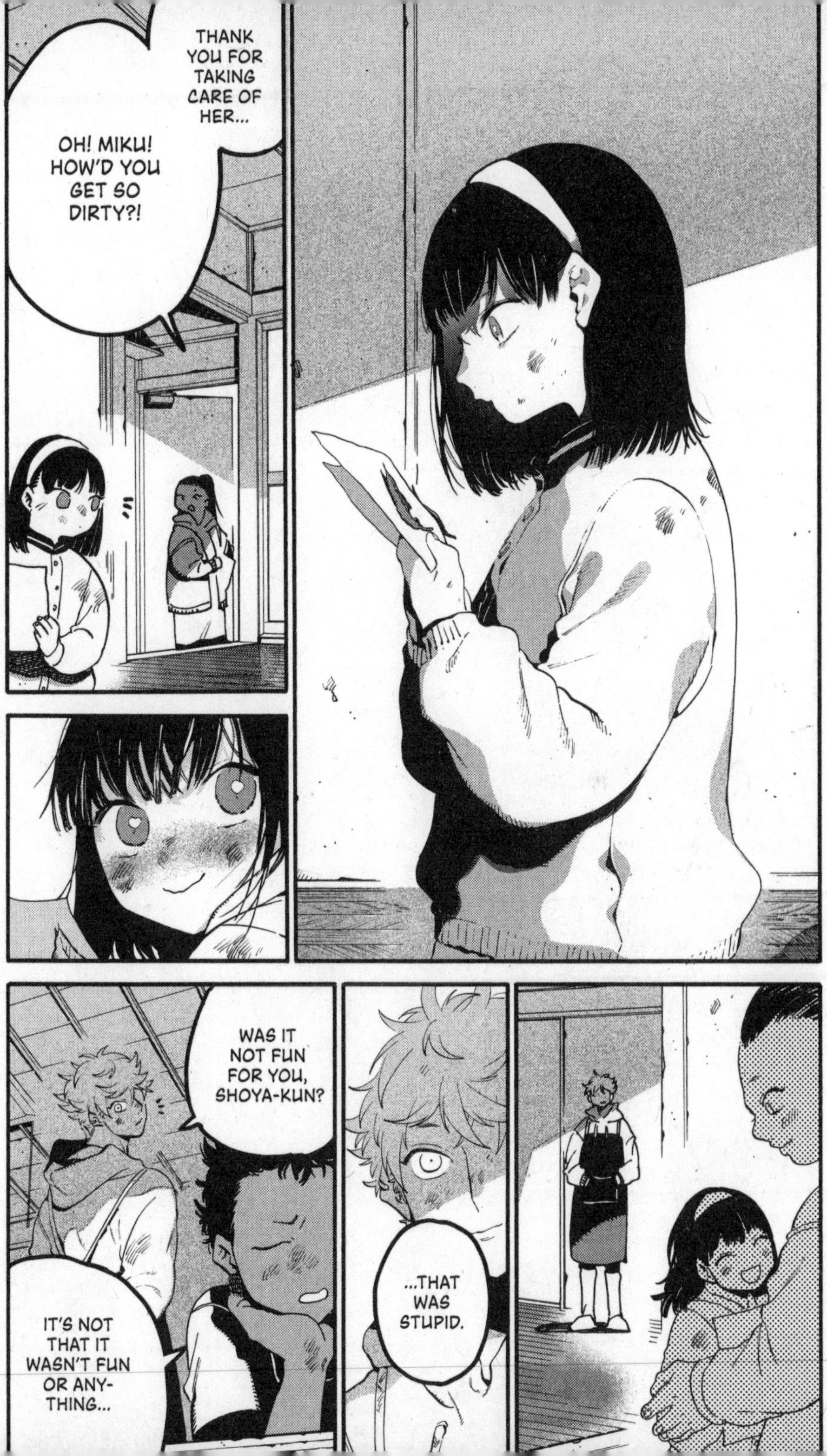
THANK YOU FOR TAKING CARE OF HER...
OH! MIKU! HOW'D YOU GET SO DIRTY?!
...THAT WAS STUPID.
WAS IT NOT FUN FOR YOU, SHOYA-KUN?
IT'S NOT THAT IT WASN'T FUN OR ANYTHING...

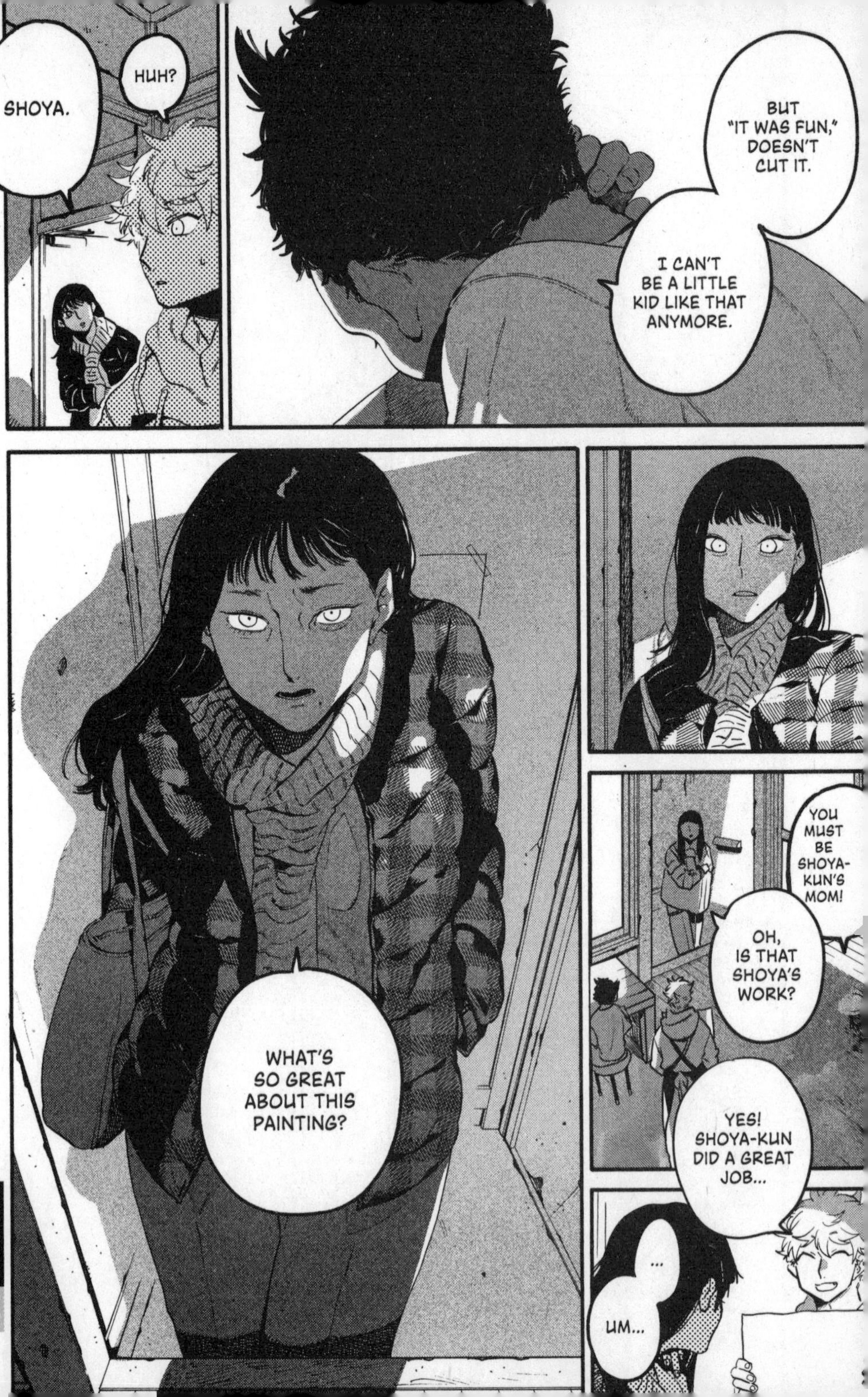
BUT "IT WAS FUN," DOESN'T CUT IT.
I CAN'T BE A LITTLE KID LIKE THAT ANYMORE.
HUH?
SHOYA.
YOU MUST BE SHOYA-KUN'S MOM!
OH, IS THAT SHOYA'S WORK?
YES! SHOYA-KUN DID A GREAT JOB...
...
UM...
WHAT'S SO GREAT ABOUT THIS PAINTING?
STROKE 44 END

HASHIDA'S UNPOPULAR WITH PARENTS

THOSE BRAIDS...
SO TALL...
WHAT A FAKE SMILE...

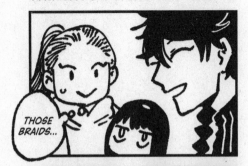

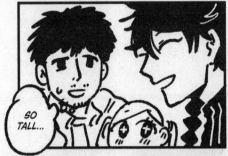

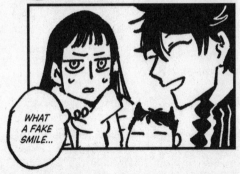

BLUE PERIOD

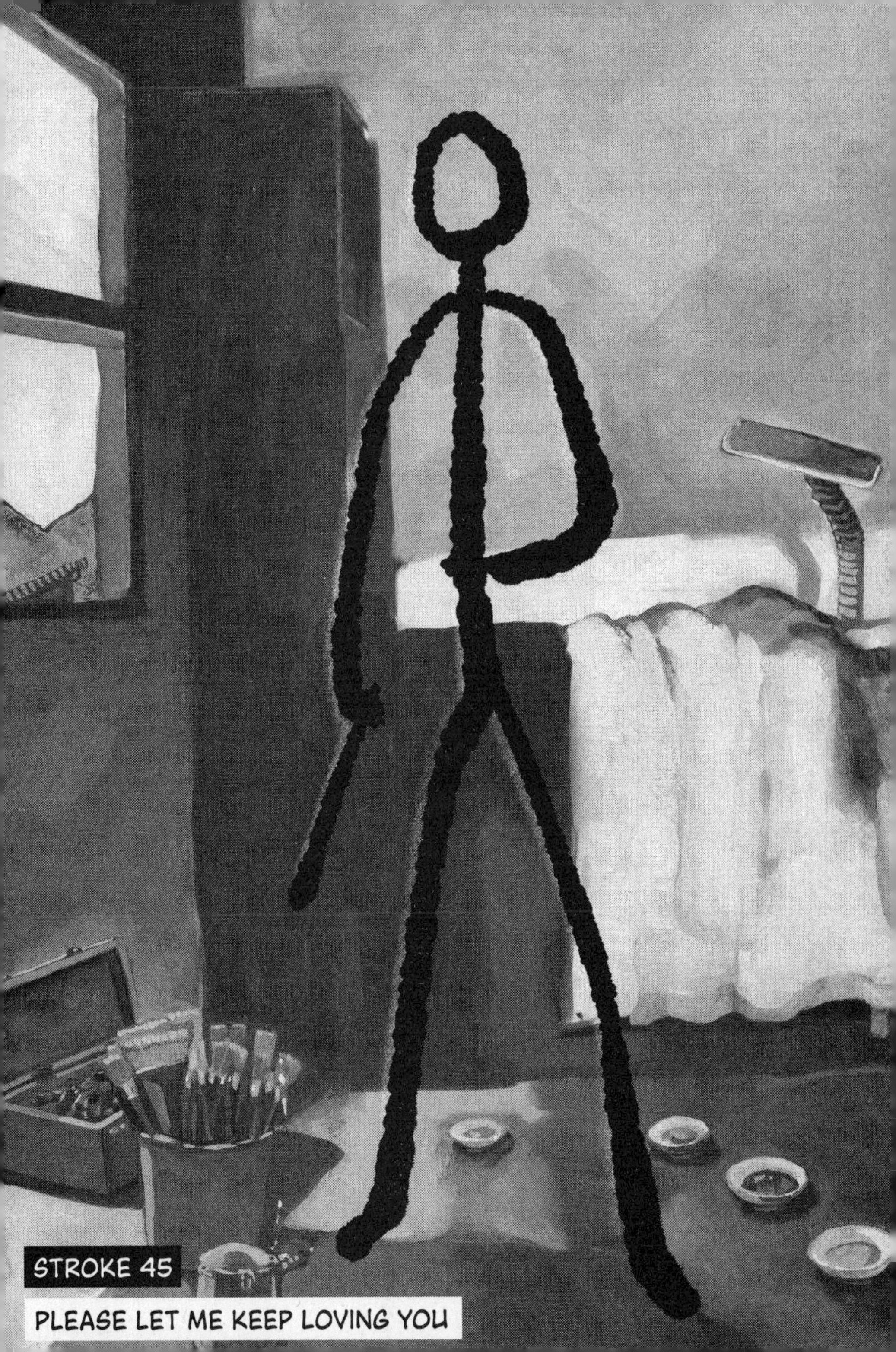
STROKE 45
PLEASE LET ME KEEP LOVING YOU

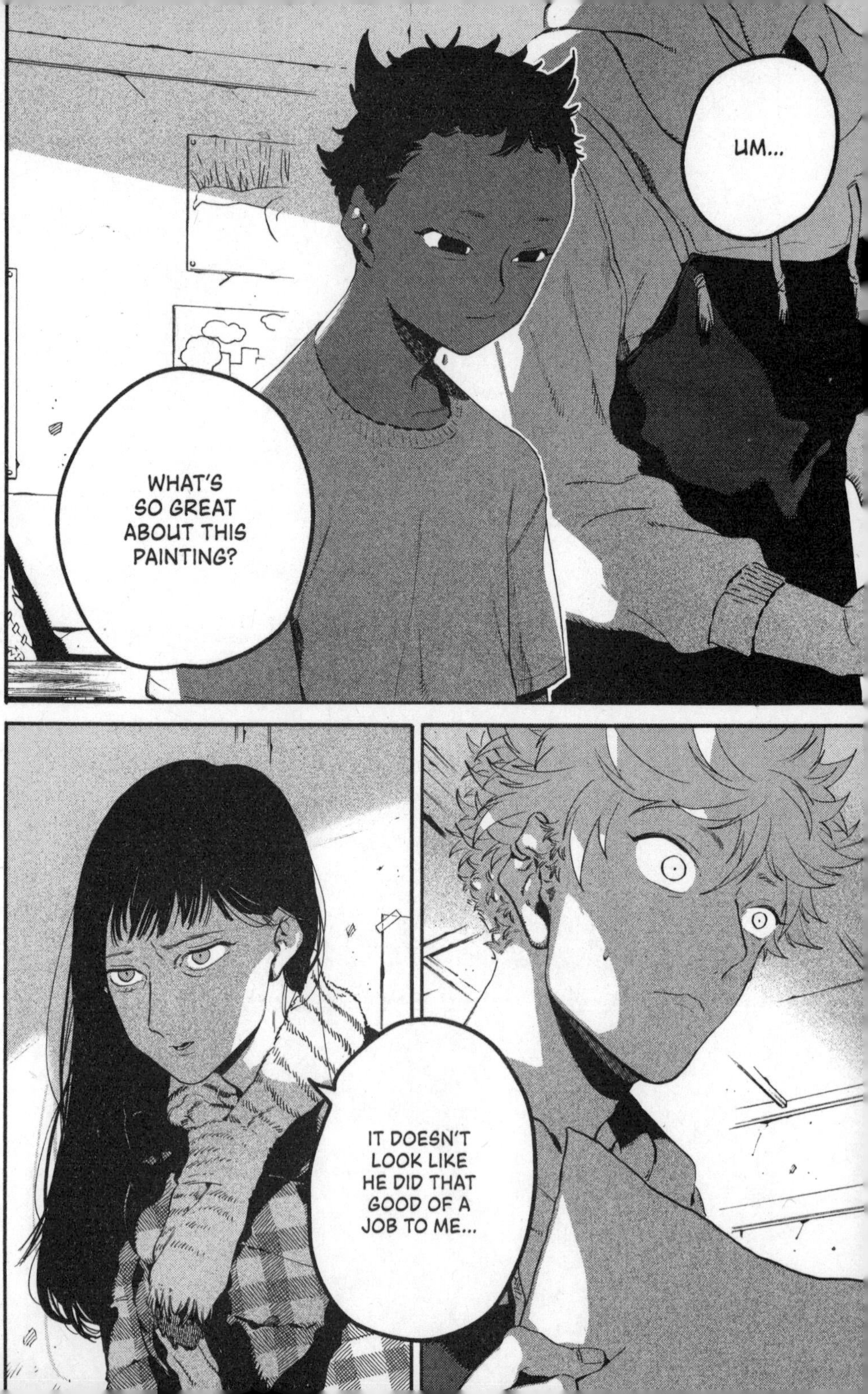
UM...
WHAT'S SO GREAT ABOUT THIS PAINTING?
IT DOESN'T LOOK LIKE HE DID THAT GOOD OF A JOB TO ME...

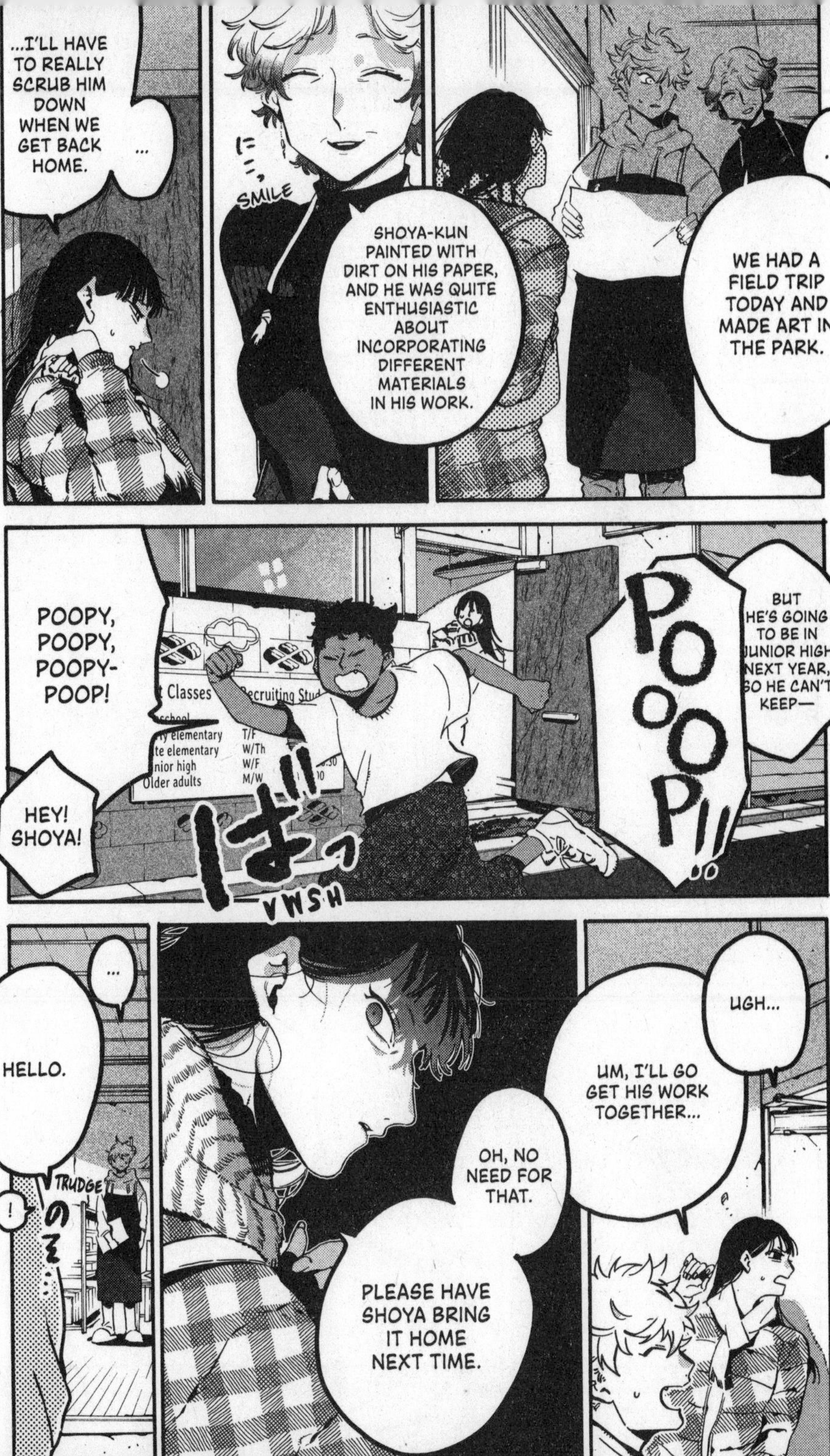
...
WE HAD A FIELD TRIP TODAY AND MADE ART IN THE PARK.
にっこ
SMILE
SHOYA-KUN PAINTED WITH DIRT ON HIS PAPER, AND HE WAS QUITE ENTHUSIASTIC ABOUT INCORPORATING DIFFERENT MATERIALS IN HIS WORK.
...I'LL HAVE TO REALLY SCRUB HIM DOWN WHEN WE GET BACK HOME.
...
BUT HE'S GOING TO BE IN JUNIOR HIGH NEXT YEAR, SO HE CAN'T KEEP—
POOOP!!
POOPY, POOPY, POOPY-POOP!
Classes
T/F
W/Th
W/F
Older adults
M/W
HEY! SHOYA!
ばっ
VWSH
UGH...
UM, I'LL GO GET HIS WORK TOGETHER...
OH, NO NEED FOR THAT.
PLEASE HAVE SHOYA BRING IT HOME NEXT TIME.
...
HELLO.
TRUDGE
のそ
!

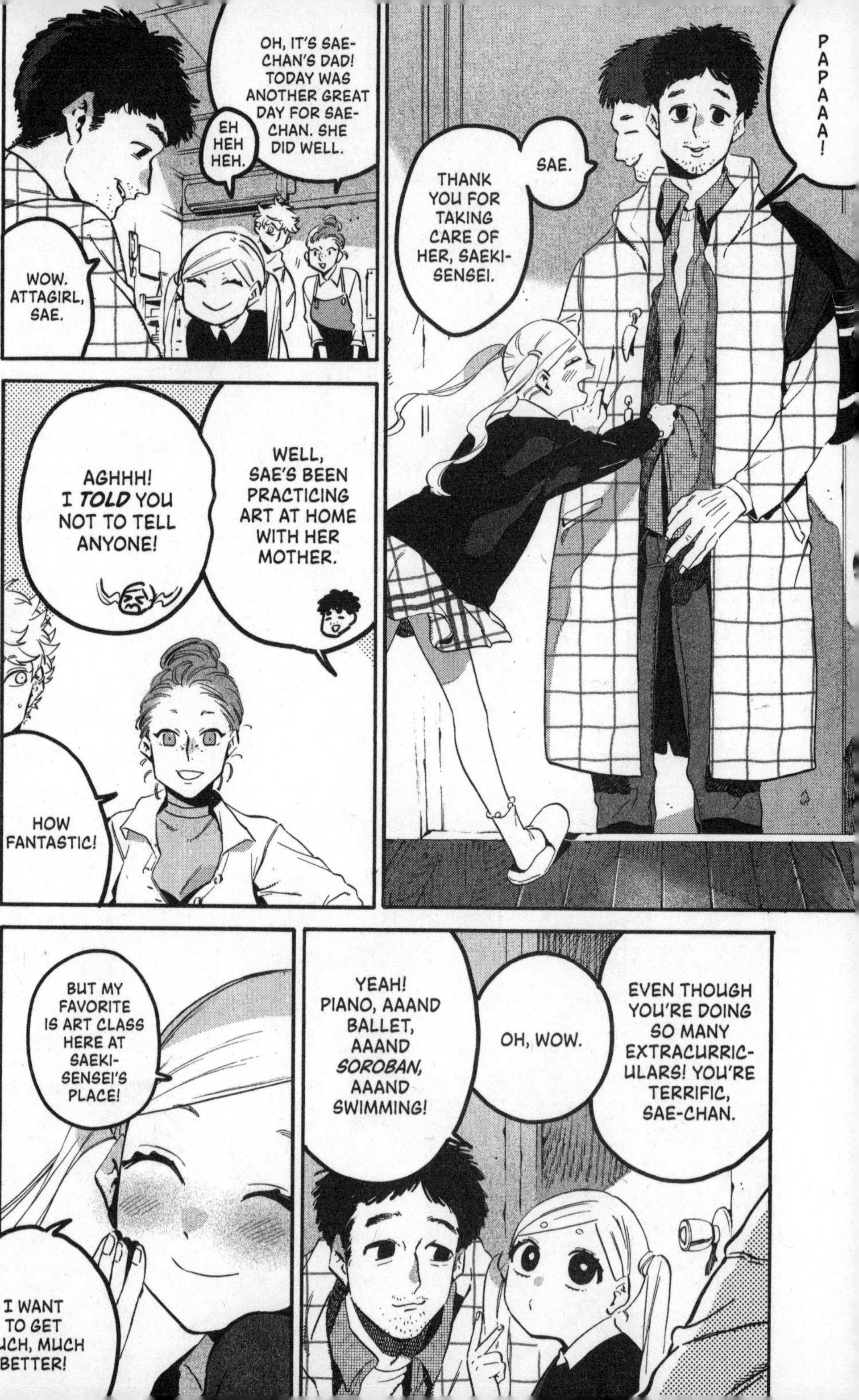
PAPAAA!
SAE.
THANK YOU FOR TAKING CARE OF HER, SAEKI-SENSEI.
OH, IT'S SAE-CHAN'S DAD! TODAY WAS ANOTHER GREAT DAY FOR SAE-CHAN. SHE DID WELL.
EH HEH HEH.
WOW. ATTAGIRL, SAE.
WELL, SAE'S BEEN PRACTICING ART AT HOME WITH HER MOTHER.
AGHHH! I *TOLD* YOU NOT TO TELL ANYONE!
HOW FANTASTIC!
EVEN THOUGH YOU'RE DOING SO MANY EXTRACURRICULARS! YOU'RE TERRIFIC, SAE-CHAN.
OH, WOW.
YEAH! PIANO, AAAND BALLET, AAAND *SOROBAN*, AAAND SWIMMING!
BUT MY FAVORITE IS ART CLASS HERE AT SAEKI-SENSEI'S PLACE!
I WANT TO GET MUCH, MUCH BETTER!

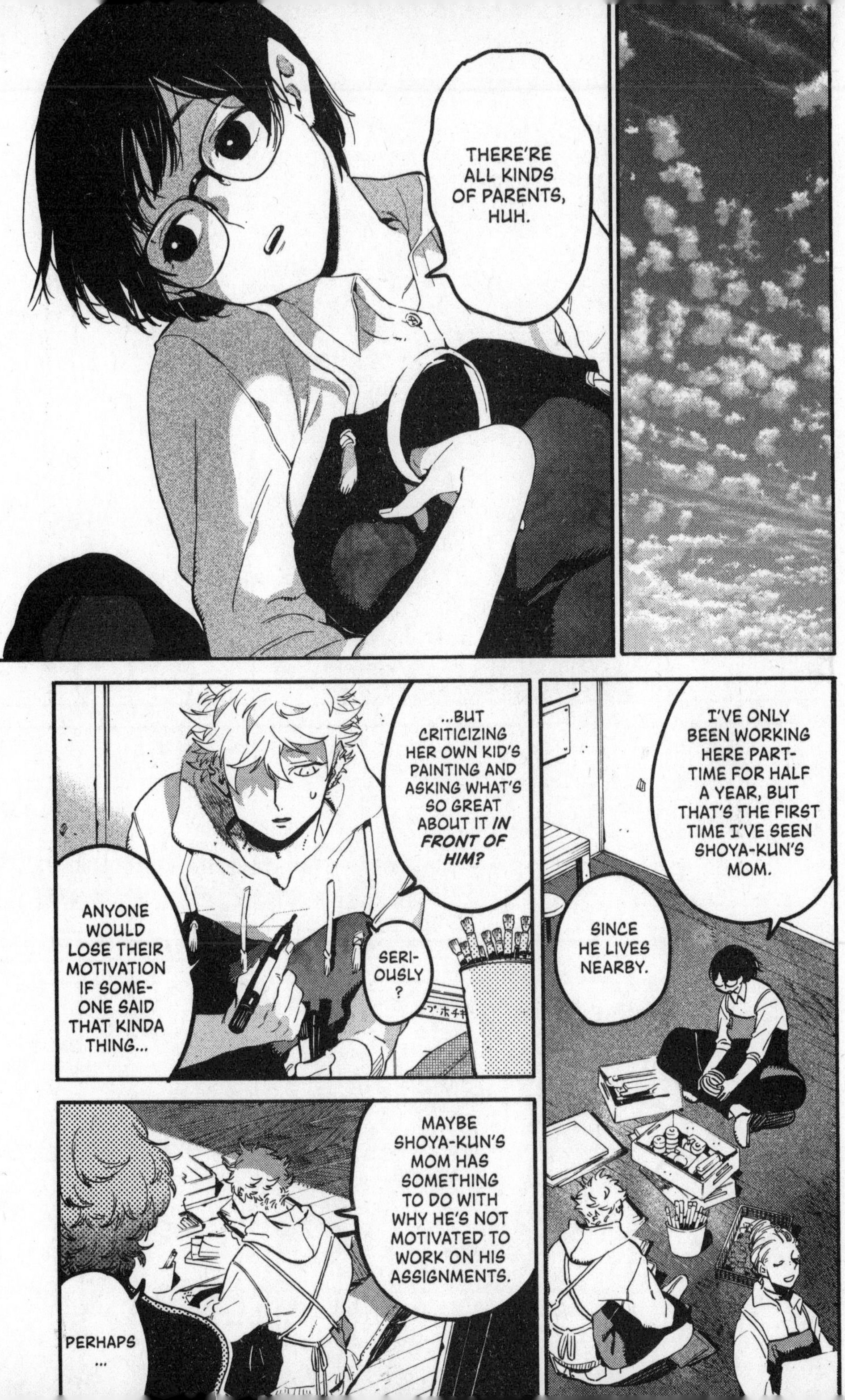
THERE'RE ALL KINDS OF PARENTS, HUH.
I'VE ONLY BEEN WORKING HERE PART-TIME FOR HALF A YEAR, BUT THAT'S THE FIRST TIME I'VE SEEN SHOYA-KUN'S MOM.
SINCE HE LIVES NEARBY.
...BUT CRITICIZING HER OWN KID'S PAINTING AND ASKING WHAT'S SO GREAT ABOUT IT *IN FRONT OF HIM?*
SERI-OUSLY?
ANYONE WOULD LOSE THEIR MOTIVATION IF SOME-ONE SAID THAT KINDA THING...
MAYBE SHOYA-KUN'S MOM HAS SOMETHING TO DO WITH WHY HE'S NOT MOTIVATED TO WORK ON HIS ASSIGNMENTS.
PERHAPS...

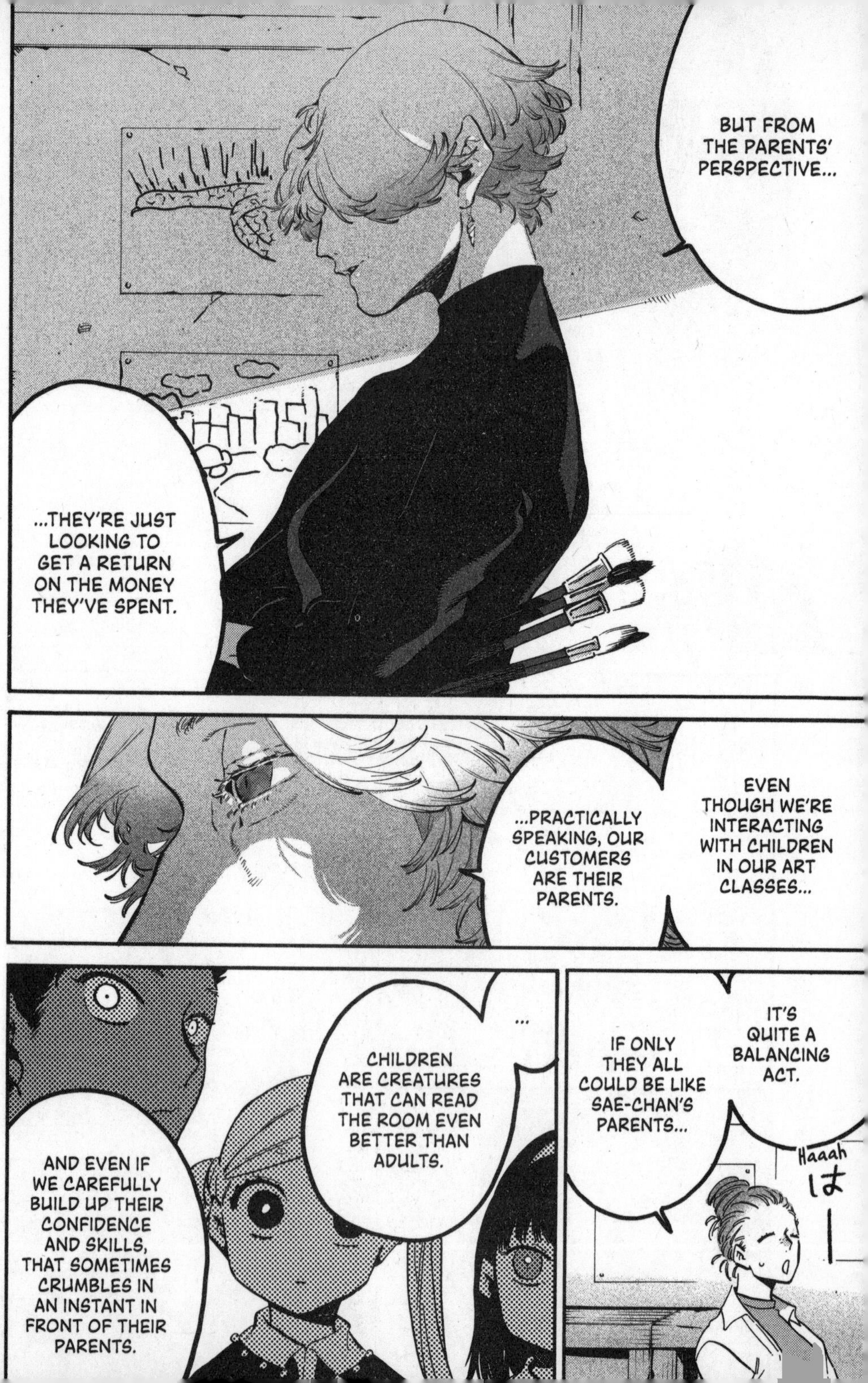
BUT FROM THE PARENTS' PERSPECTIVE...
...THEY'RE JUST LOOKING TO GET A RETURN ON THE MONEY THEY'VE SPENT.
EVEN THOUGH WE'RE INTERACTING WITH CHILDREN IN OUR ART CLASSES...
...PRACTICALLY SPEAKING, OUR CUSTOMERS ARE THEIR PARENTS.
IT'S QUITE A BALANCING ACT.
IF ONLY THEY ALL COULD BE LIKE SAE-CHAN'S PARENTS...
Haaah
はー
...
CHILDREN ARE CREATURES THAT CAN READ THE ROOM EVEN BETTER THAN ADULTS.
AND EVEN IF WE CAREFULLY BUILD UP THEIR CONFIDENCE AND SKILLS, THAT SOMETIMES CRUMBLES IN AN INSTANT IN FRONT OF THEIR PARENTS.

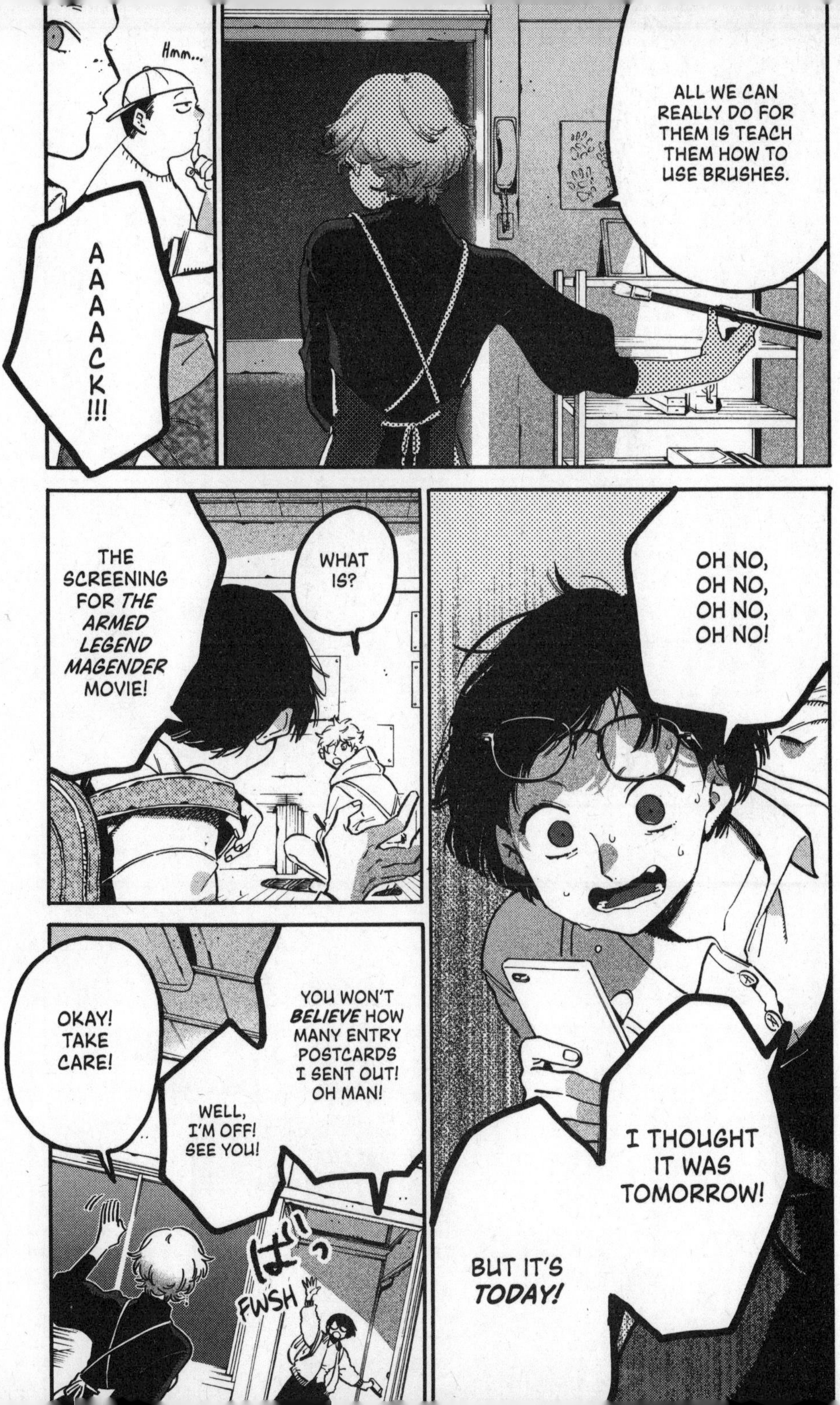

ALL WE CAN REALLY DO FOR THEM IS TEACH THEM HOW TO USE BRUSHES.
Hmm...
AAAACK!!!
OH NO, OH NO, OH NO, OH NO!
I THOUGHT IT WAS TOMORROW!
BUT IT'S *TODAY!*
WHAT IS?
THE SCREENING FOR *THE ARMED LEGEND MAGENDER* MOVIE!
YOU WON'T ***BELIEVE*** HOW MANY ENTRY POSTCARDS I SENT OUT! OH MAN!
WELL, I'M OFF! SEE YOU!
OKAY! TAKE CARE!
ばっ
FWSH

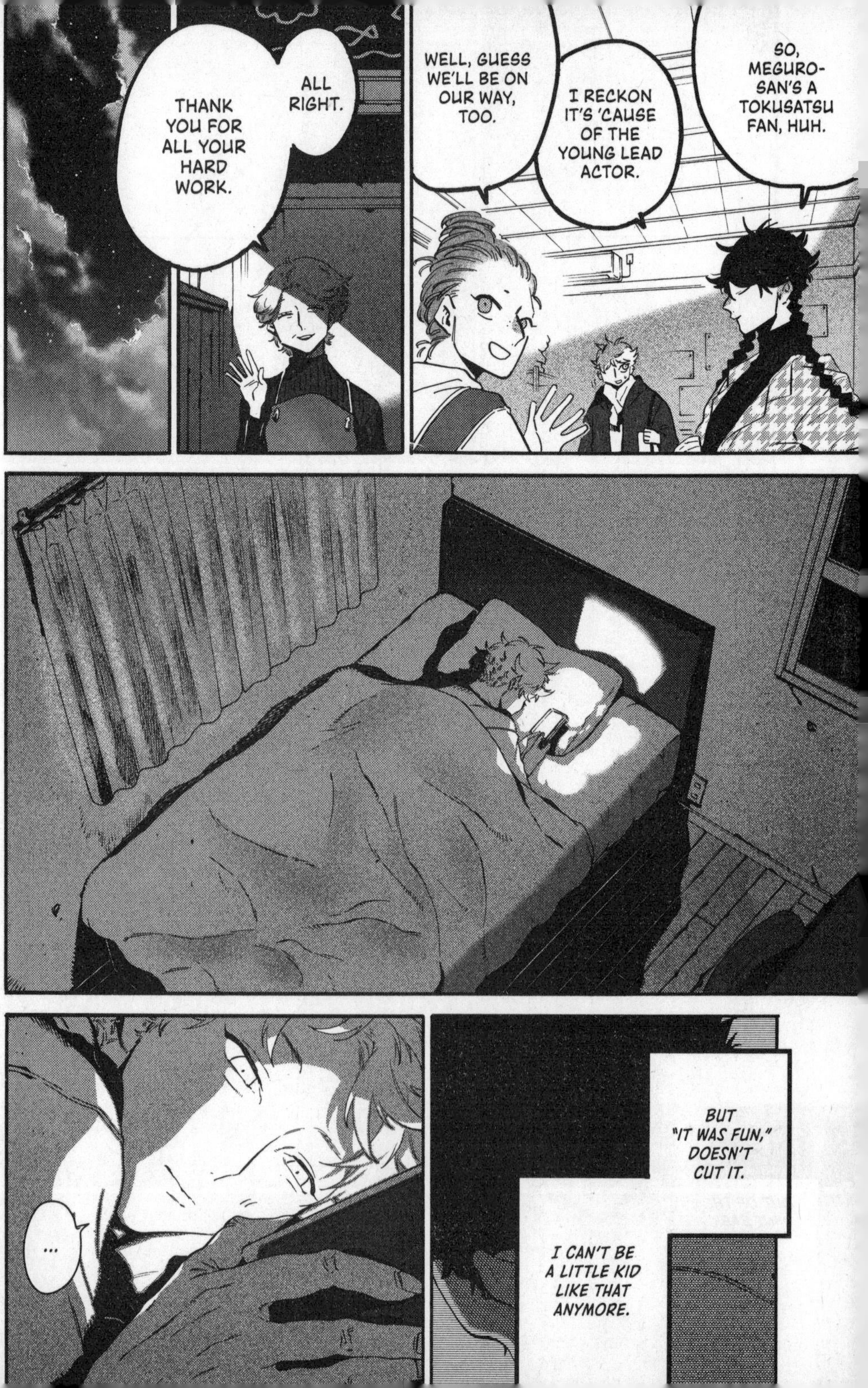
SO, MEGURO-SAN'S A TOKUSATSU FAN, HUH.
I RECKON IT'S 'CAUSE OF THE YOUNG LEAD ACTOR.
WELL, GUESS WE'LL BE ON OUR WAY, TOO.
ALL RIGHT.
THANK YOU FOR ALL YOUR HARD WORK.
BUT "IT WAS FUN," DOESN'T CUT IT.
I CAN'T BE A LITTLE KID LIKE THAT ANYMORE.
...

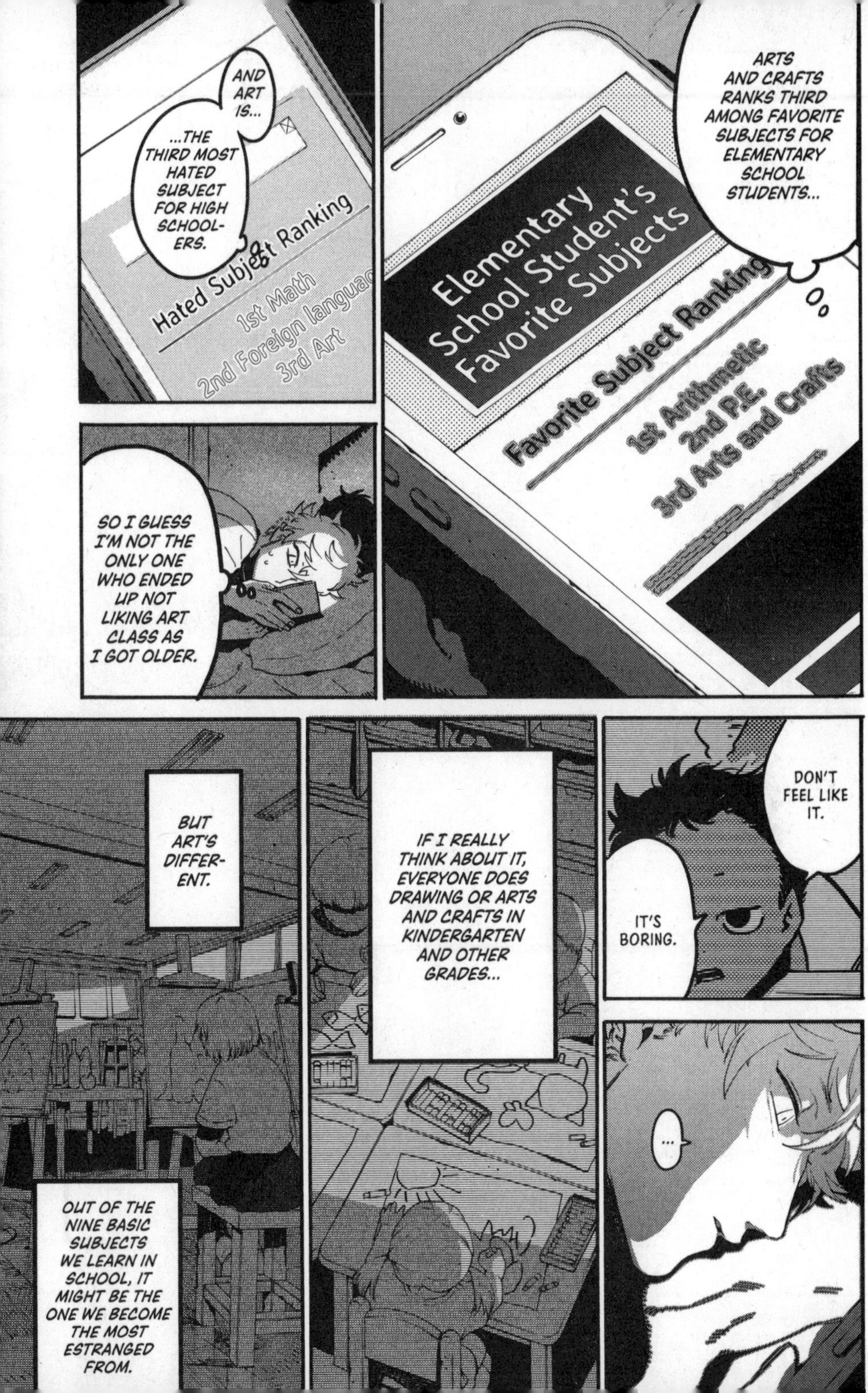
ARTS AND CRAFTS RANKS THIRD AMONG FAVORITE SUBJECTS FOR ELEMENTARY SCHOOL STUDENTS...
Elementary School Student's Favorite Subjects
Favorite Subject Ranking
1st Arithmetic
2nd P.E.
3rd Arts and Crafts
AND ART IS...
...THE THIRD MOST HATED SUBJECT FOR HIGH SCHOOL-ERS.
Hated Subject Ranking
1st Math
2nd Foreign languag
3rd Art
SO I GUESS I'M NOT THE ONLY ONE WHO ENDED UP NOT LIKING ART CLASS AS I GOT OLDER.
DON'T FEEL LIKE IT.
IT'S BORING.
...
IF I REALLY THINK ABOUT IT, EVERYONE DOES DRAWING OR ARTS AND CRAFTS IN KINDERGARTEN AND OTHER GRADES...
BUT ART'S DIFFER-ENT.
OUT OF THE NINE BASIC SUBJECTS WE LEARN IN SCHOOL, IT MIGHT BE THE ONE WE BECOME THE MOST ESTRANGED FROM.

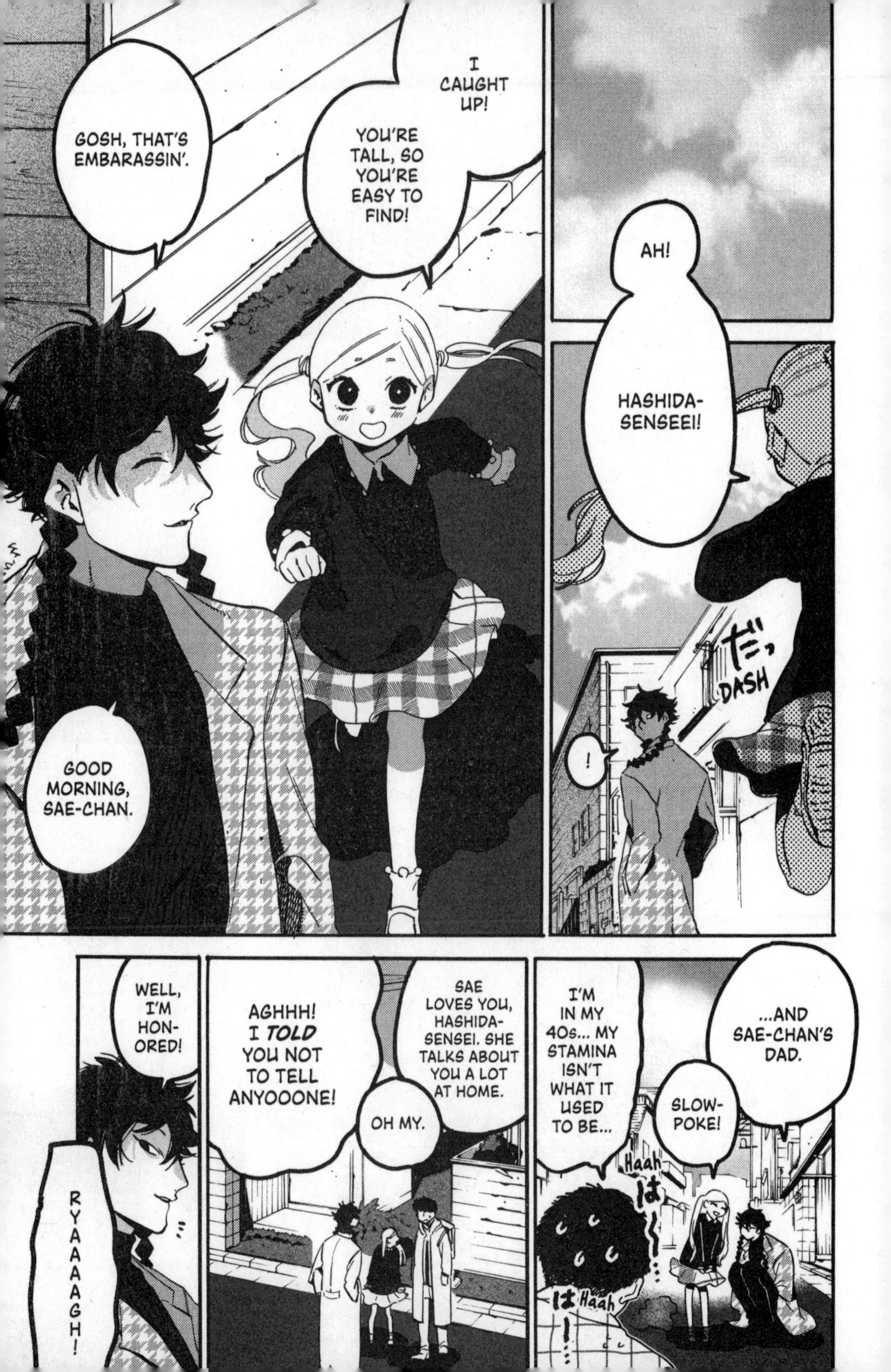
AH!
HASHIDA-SENSEEI!
だっ DASH
!
I CAUGHT UP!
YOU'RE TALL, SO YOU'RE EASY TO FIND!
GOSH, THAT'S EMBARASSIN'.
GOOD MORNING, SAE-CHAN.
...AND SAE-CHAN'S DAD.
I'M IN MY 40s... MY STAMINA ISN'T WHAT IT USED TO BE...
SLOW-POKE!
Haah
は~...
は Haah
~...
SAE LOVES YOU, HASHIDA-SENSEI. SHE TALKS ABOUT YOU A LOT AT HOME.
AGHHH! I *TOLD* YOU NOT TO TELL ANYOOONE!
OH MY.
WELL, I'M HON-ORED!
RYAAAAAGH!
...

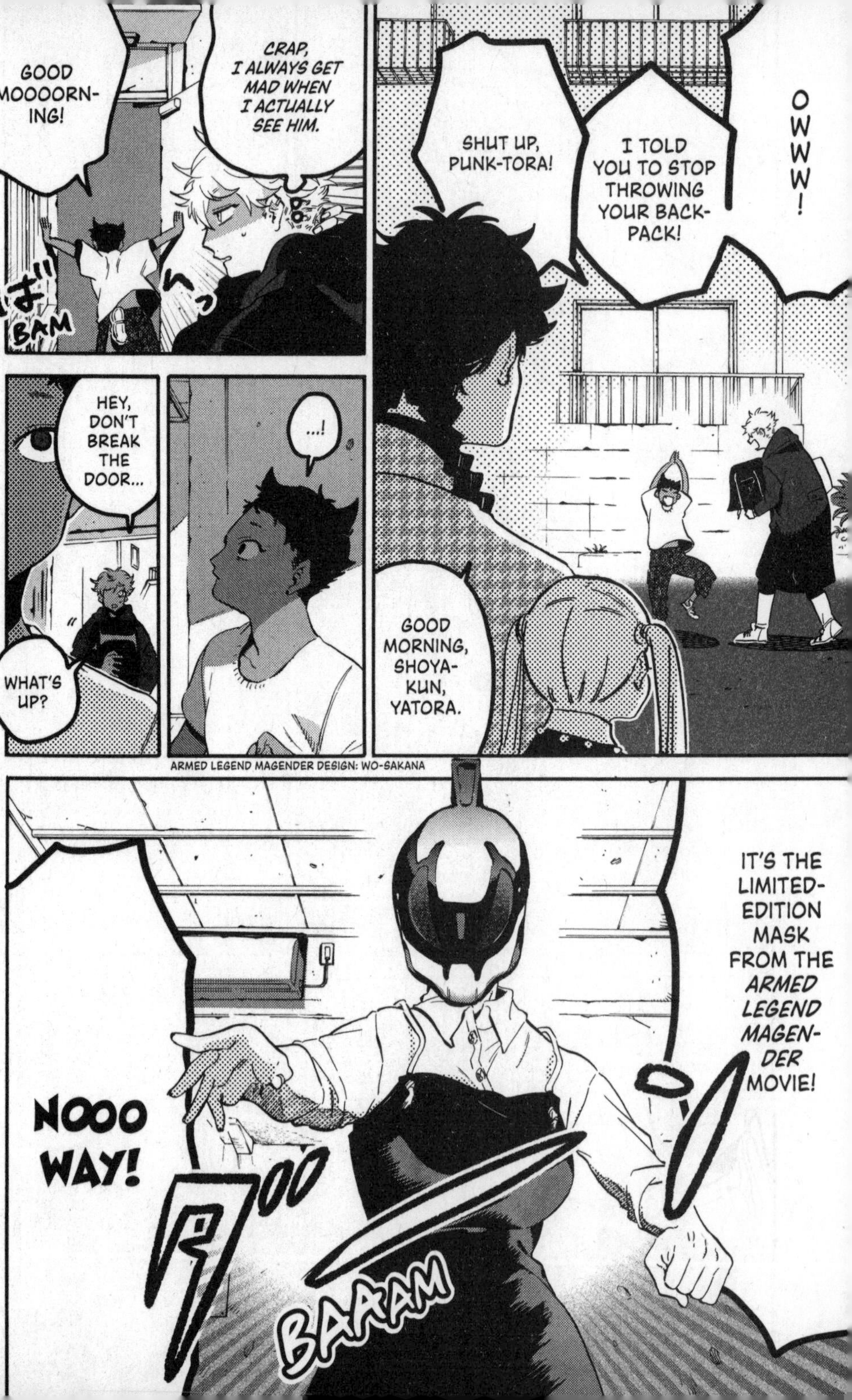
OWWW!
I TOLD YOU TO STOP THROWING YOUR BACK-PACK!
SHUT UP, PUNK-TORA!
GOOD MORNING, SHOYA-KUN, YATORA.
CRAP, I ALWAYS GET MAD WHEN I ACTUALLY SEE HIM.
GOOD MOOOORN-ING!
BAM
...!
HEY, DON'T BREAK THE DOOR...
WHAT'S UP?
ARMED LEGEND MAGENDER DESIGN: WO-SAKANA
IT'S THE LIMITED-EDITION MASK FROM THE *ARMED LEGEND MAGENDER* MOVIE!
NOOO WAY!
BAAAM

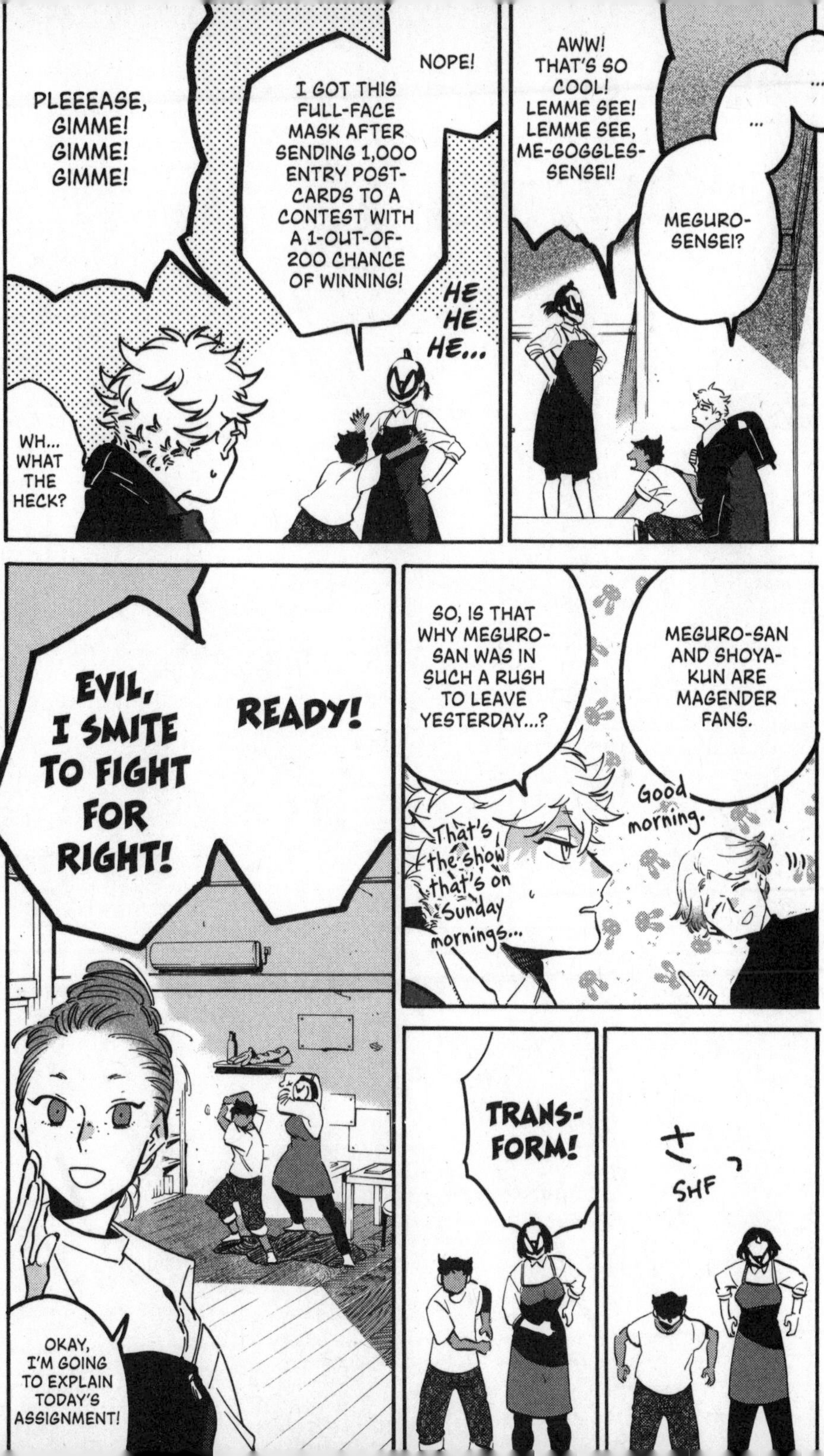
...
...
AWW! THAT'S SO COOL! LEMME SEE! LEMME SEE, ME-GOGGLES-SENSEI!
MEGURO-SENSEI?
NOPE!
I GOT THIS FULL-FACE MASK AFTER SENDING 1,000 ENTRY POST-CARDS TO A CONTEST WITH A 1-OUT-OF-200 CHANCE OF WINNING!
PLEEEASE, GIMME! GIMME! GIMME!
HE HE HE...
WH... WHAT THE HECK?
MEGURO-SAN AND SHOYA-KUN ARE MAGENDER FANS.
SO, IS THAT WHY MEGURO-SAN WAS IN SUCH A RUSH TO LEAVE YESTERDAY...?
Good morning.
That's the show that's on Sunday mornings...
さっ
SHF
TRANS-FORM!
READY!
EVIL, I SMITE TO FIGHT FOR RIGHT!
OKAY, I'M GOING TO EXPLAIN TODAY'S ASSIGNMENT!

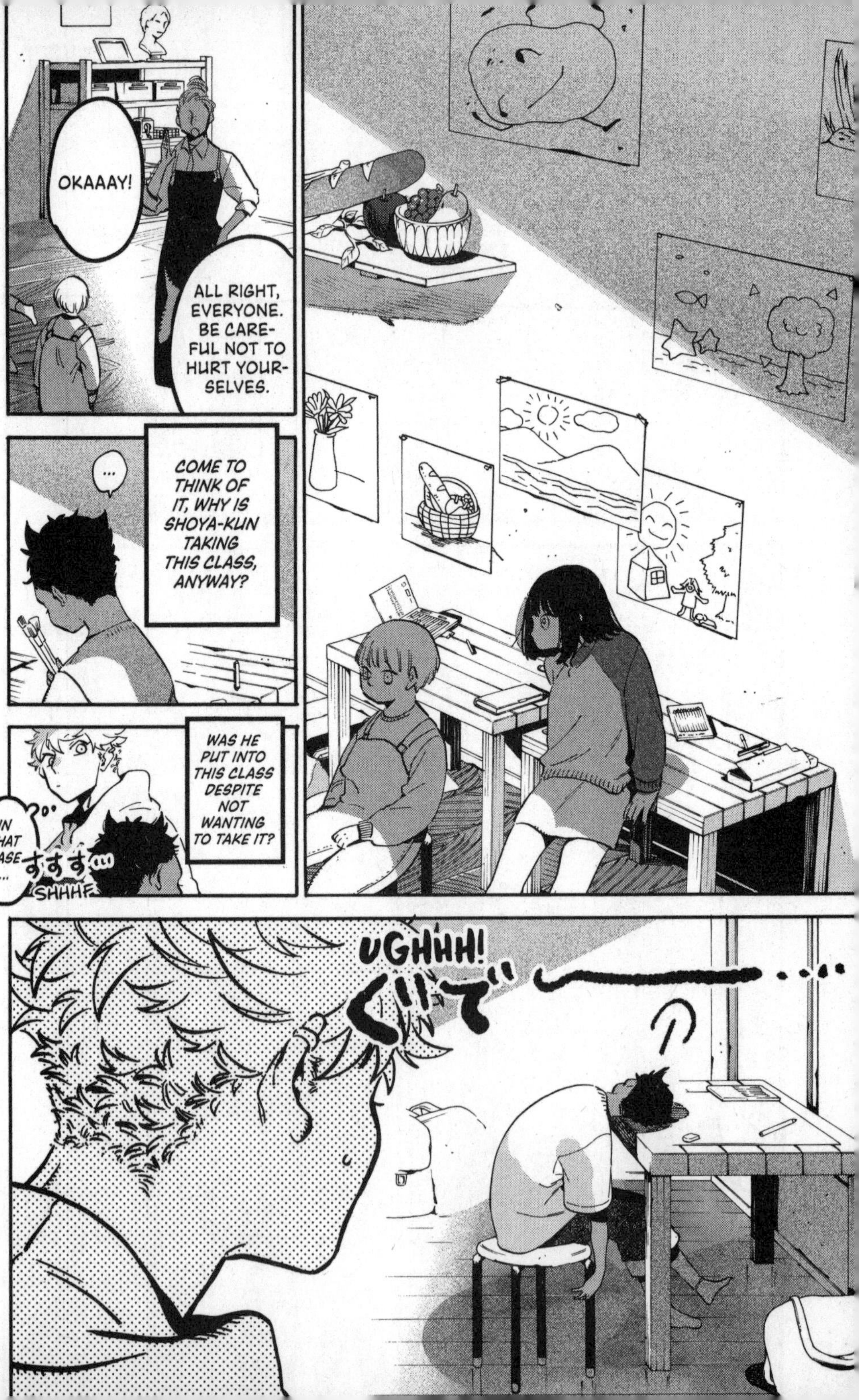
ALL RIGHT, EVERYONE. BE CARE-FUL NOT TO HURT YOUR-SELVES.
OKAAAY!
COME TO THINK OF IT, WHY IS SHOYA-KUN TAKING THIS CLASS, ANYWAY?
...
WAS HE PUT INTO THIS CLASS DESPITE NOT WANTING TO TAKE IT?
IN THAT CASE...
すすす
SHHHF
UGHHH!
ぐでー...
?

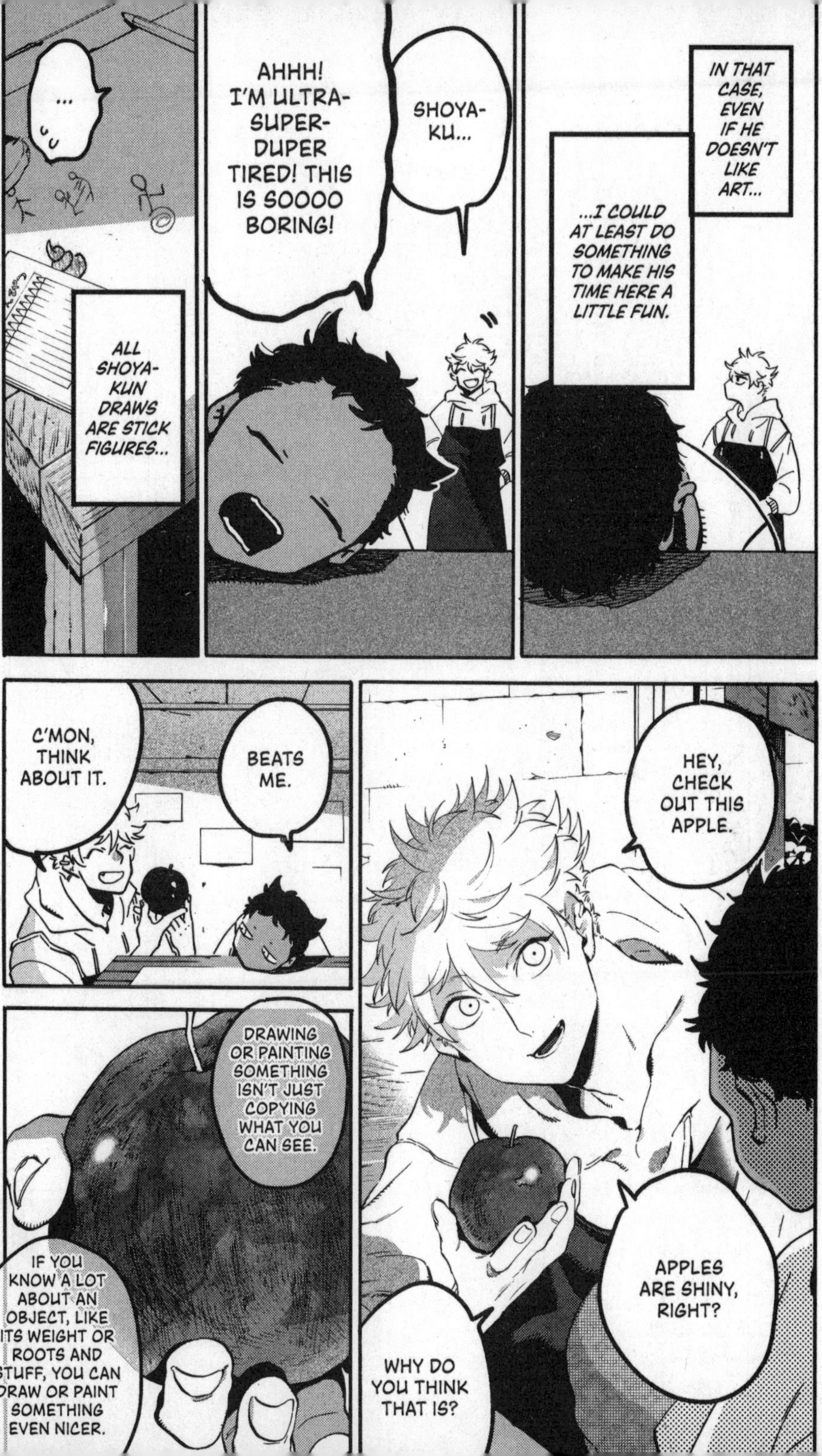
IN THAT CASE, EVEN IF HE DOESN'T LIKE ART...
...I COULD AT LEAST DO SOMETHING TO MAKE HIS TIME HERE A LITTLE FUN.
SHOYA-KU...
AHHH! I'M ULTRA-SUPER-DUPER TIRED! THIS IS SOOOO BORING!
...
ALL SHOYA-KUN DRAWS ARE STICK FIGURES...
HEY, CHECK OUT THIS APPLE.
APPLES ARE SHINY, RIGHT?
WHY DO YOU THINK THAT IS?
BEATS ME.
C'MON, THINK ABOUT IT.
DRAWING OR PAINTING SOMETHING ISN'T JUST COPYING WHAT YOU CAN SEE.
IF YOU KNOW A LOT ABOUT AN OBJECT, LIKE ITS WEIGHT OR ROOTS AND STUFF, YOU CAN DRAW OR PAINT SOMETHING EVEN NICER.

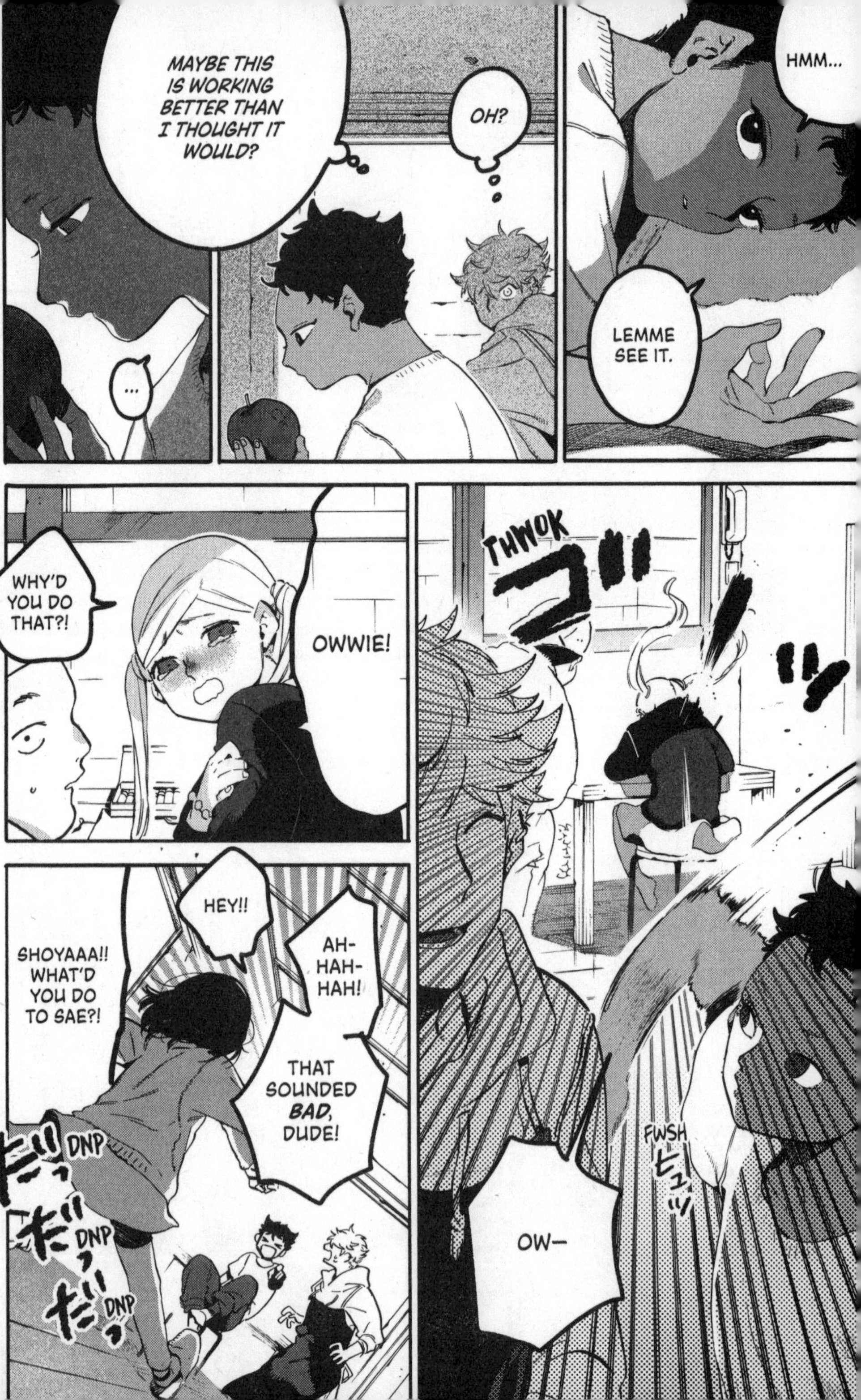
HMM...
LEMME SEE IT.
OH?
MAYBE THIS IS WORKING BETTER THAN I THOUGHT IT WOULD?
...
THWOK
FWSH
OW—
OWWIE!
WHY'D YOU DO THAT?!
HEY!!
AH-HAH-HAH!
THAT SOUNDED *BAD*, DUDE!
SHOYAAA!! WHAT'D YOU DO TO SAE?!
DNP
DNP
DNP

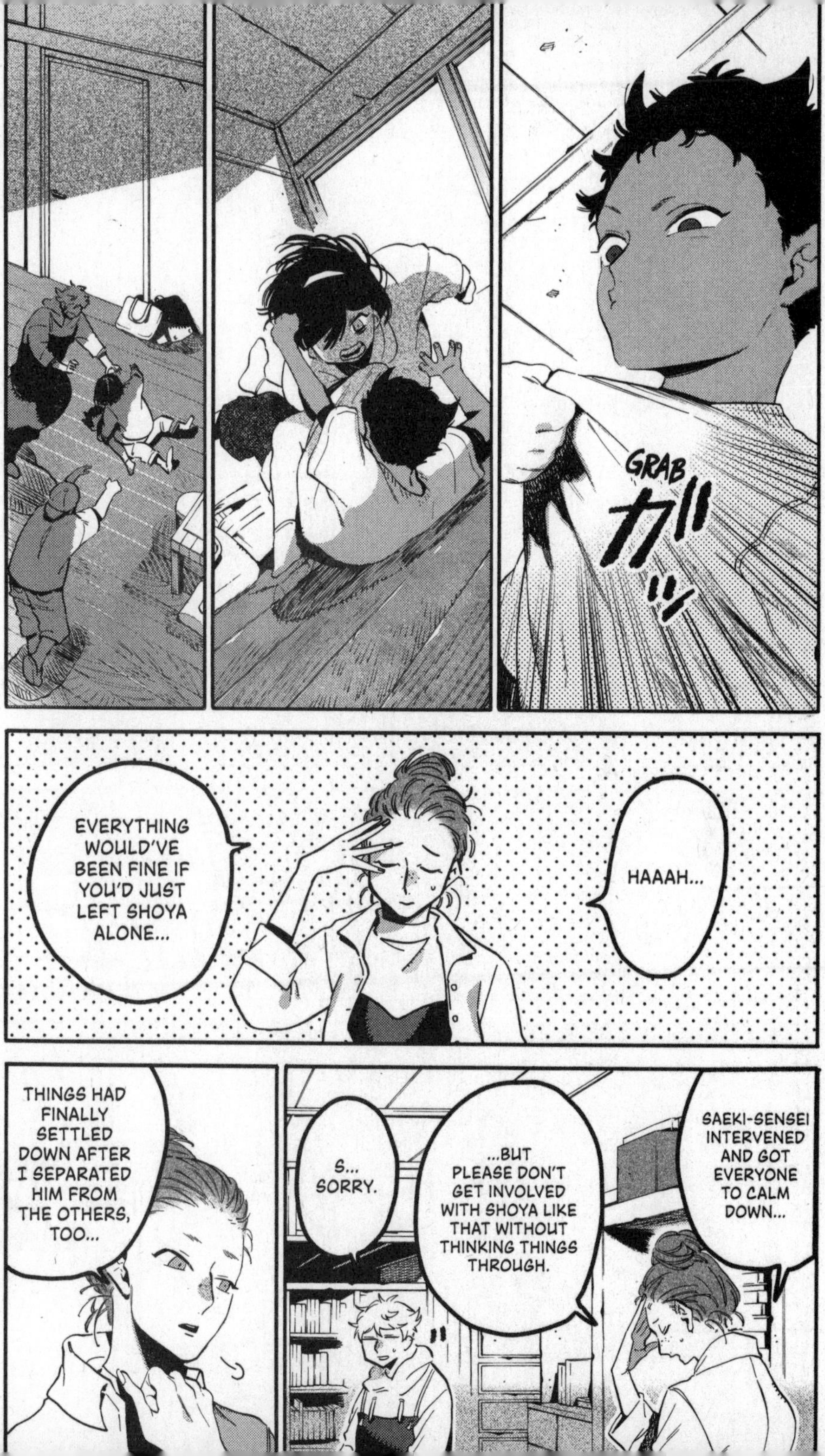
GRAB
ガッ
HAAAH...
EVERYTHING WOULD'VE BEEN FINE IF YOU'D JUST LEFT SHOYA ALONE...
SAEKI-SENSEI INTERVENED AND GOT EVERYONE TO CALM DOWN...
...BUT PLEASE DON'T GET INVOLVED WITH SHOYA LIKE THAT WITHOUT THINKING THINGS THROUGH.
S... SORRY.
THINGS HAD FINALLY SETTLED DOWN AFTER I SEPARATED HIM FROM THE OTHERS, TOO...

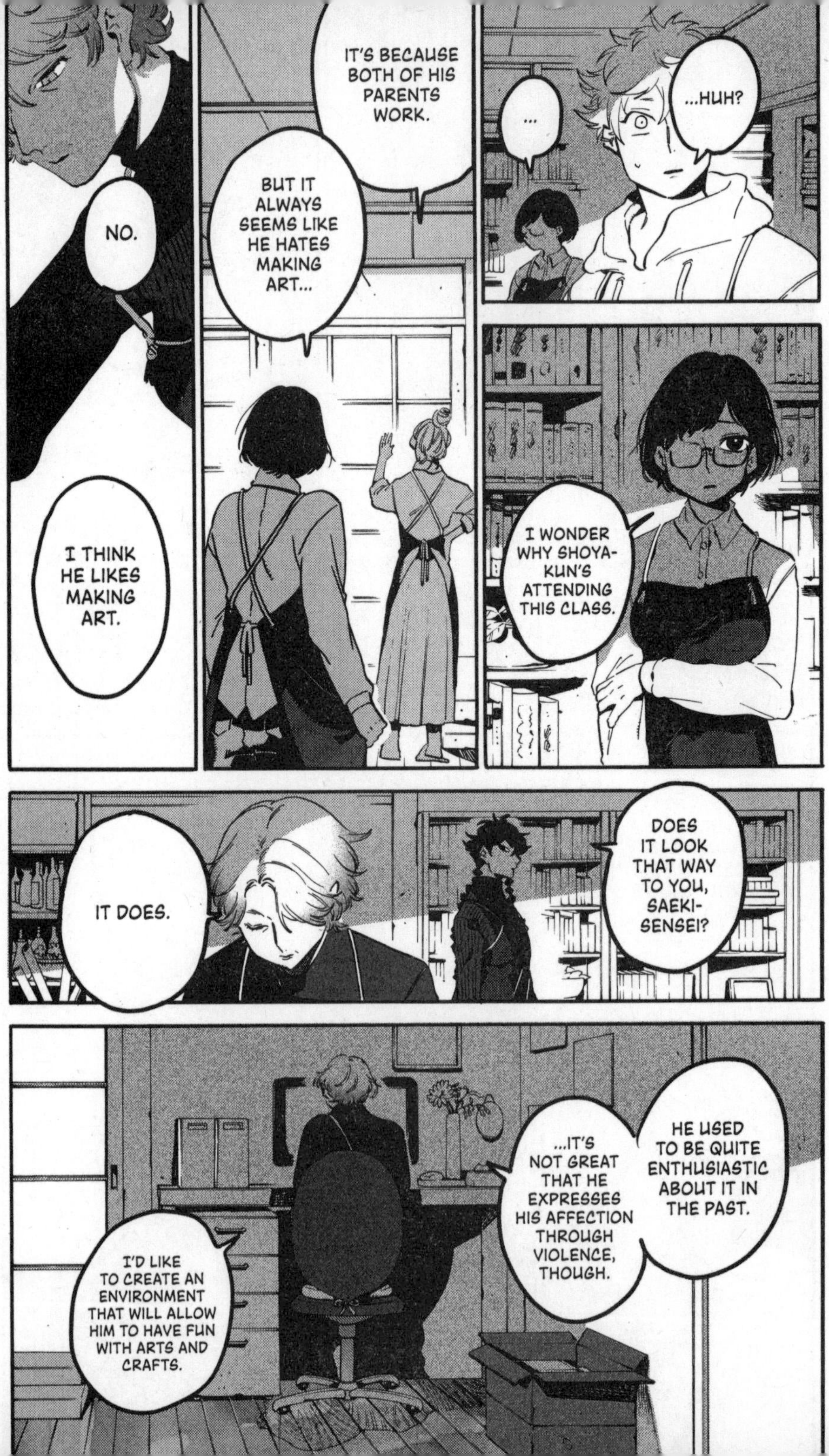

...HUH?
...
I WONDER WHY SHOYA-KUN'S ATTENDING THIS CLASS.
IT'S BECAUSE BOTH OF HIS PARENTS WORK.
BUT IT ALWAYS SEEMS LIKE HE HATES MAKING ART...
NO.
I THINK HE LIKES MAKING ART.
DOES IT LOOK THAT WAY TO YOU, SAEKI-SENSEI?
IT DOES.
HE USED TO BE QUITE ENTHUSIASTIC ABOUT IT IN THE PAST.
...IT'S NOT GREAT THAT HE EXPRESSES HIS AFFECTION THROUGH VIOLENCE, THOUGH.
I'D LIKE TO CREATE AN ENVIRONMENT THAT WILL ALLOW HIM TO HAVE FUN WITH ARTS AND CRAFTS.

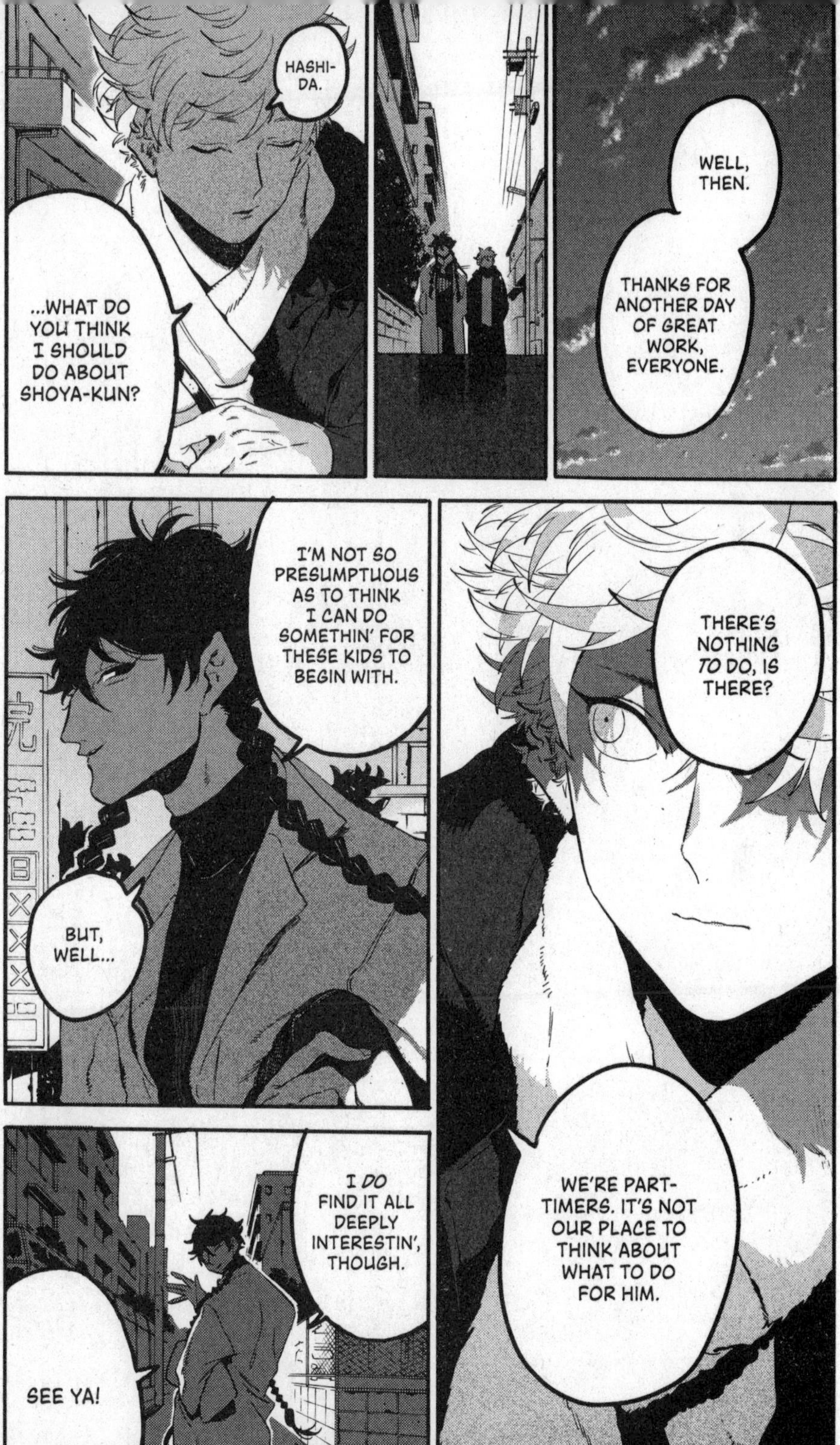
WELL, THEN.
THANKS FOR ANOTHER DAY OF GREAT WORK, EVERYONE.
HASHI-DA.
...WHAT DO YOU THINK I SHOULD DO ABOUT SHOYA-KUN?
THERE'S NOTHING *TO* DO, IS THERE?
WE'RE PART-TIMERS. IT'S NOT OUR PLACE TO THINK ABOUT WHAT TO DO FOR HIM.
I'M NOT SO PRESUMPTUOUS AS TO THINK I CAN DO SOMETHIN' FOR THESE KIDS TO BEGIN WITH.
BUT, WELL...
I *DO* FIND IT ALL DEEPLY INTERESTIN', THOUGH.
SEE YA!

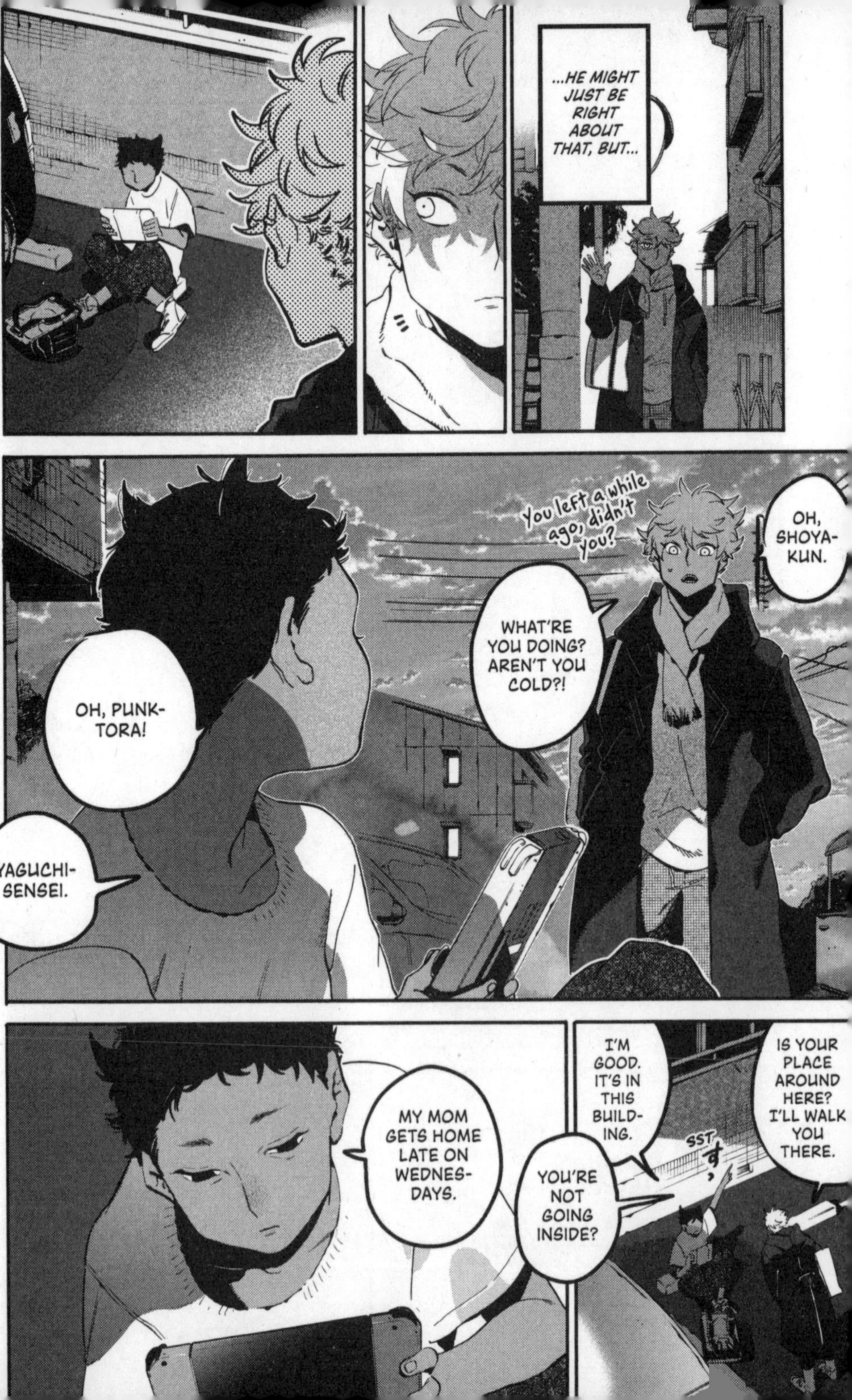
...HE MIGHT JUST BE RIGHT ABOUT THAT, BUT...
OH, SHOYA-KUN.
You left a while ago, didn't you?
WHAT'RE YOU DOING? AREN'T YOU COLD?!
OH, PUNK-TORA!
YAGUCHI-SENSEI.
IS YOUR PLACE AROUND HERE? I'LL WALK YOU THERE.
I'M GOOD. IT'S IN THIS BUILDING.
SST
YOU'RE NOT GOING INSIDE?
MY MOM GETS HOME LATE ON WEDNESDAYS.

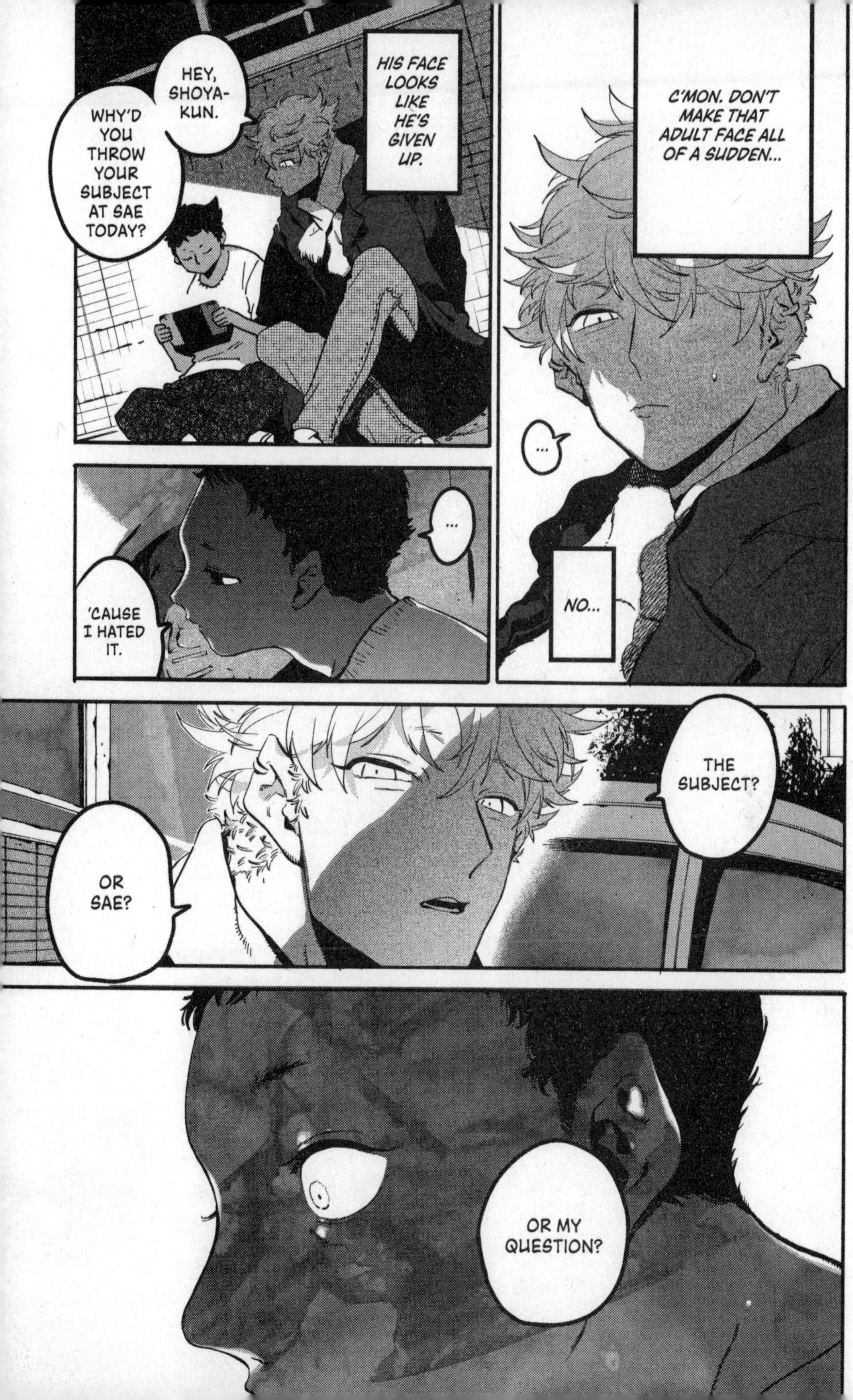
C'MON. DON'T MAKE THAT ADULT FACE ALL OF A SUDDEN...
...
NO...
HIS FACE LOOKS LIKE HE'S GIVEN UP.
HEY, SHOYA-KUN.
WHY'D YOU THROW YOUR SUBJECT AT SAE TODAY?
...
'CAUSE I HATED IT.
THE SUBJECT?
OR SAE?
OR MY QUESTION?

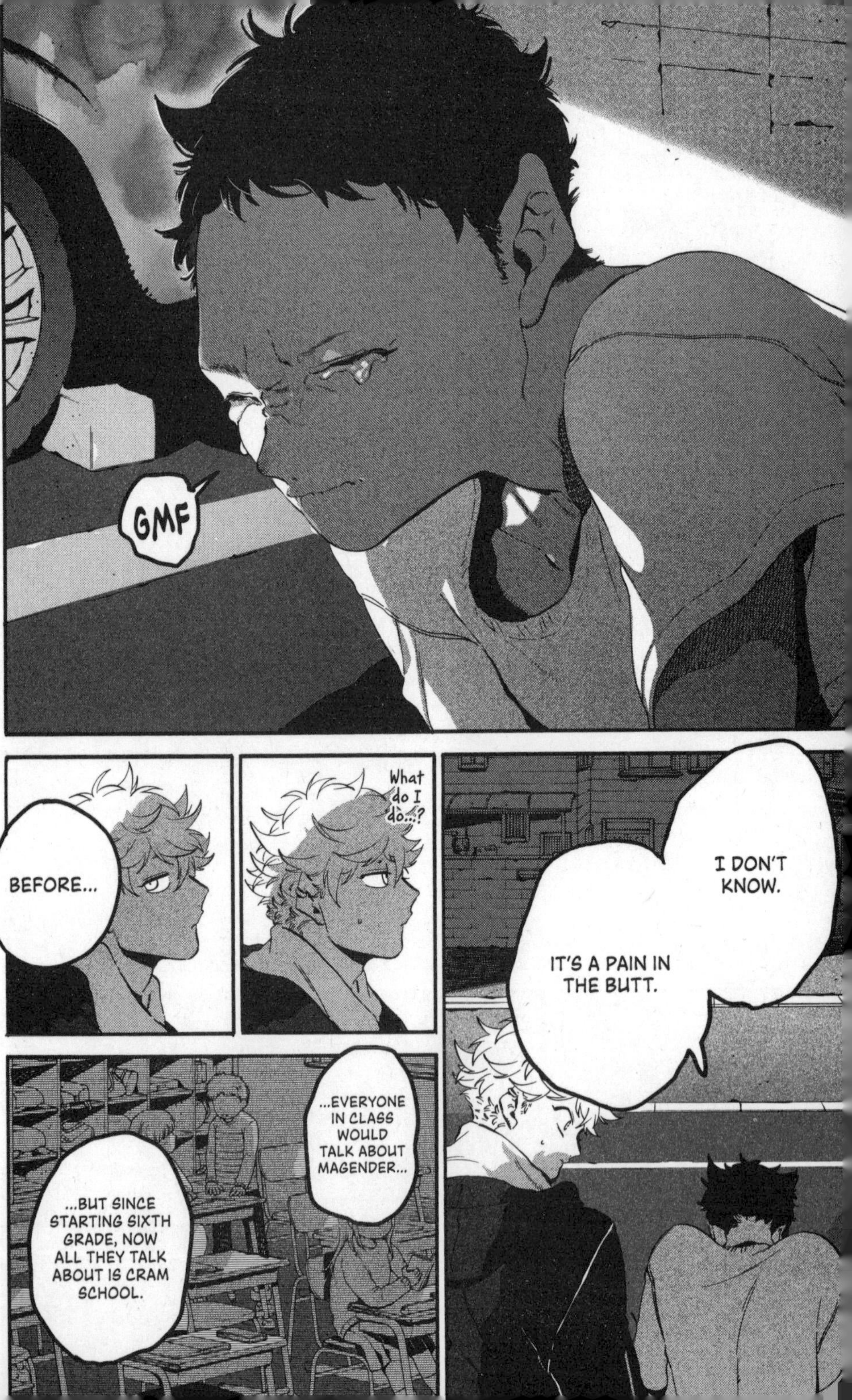
GMF
I DON'T KNOW.
IT'S A PAIN IN THE BUTT.
What do I do...?
BEFORE...
...EVERYONE IN CLASS WOULD TALK ABOUT MAGENDER...
...BUT SINCE STARTING SIXTH GRADE, NOW ALL THEY TALK ABOUT IS CRAM SCHOOL.

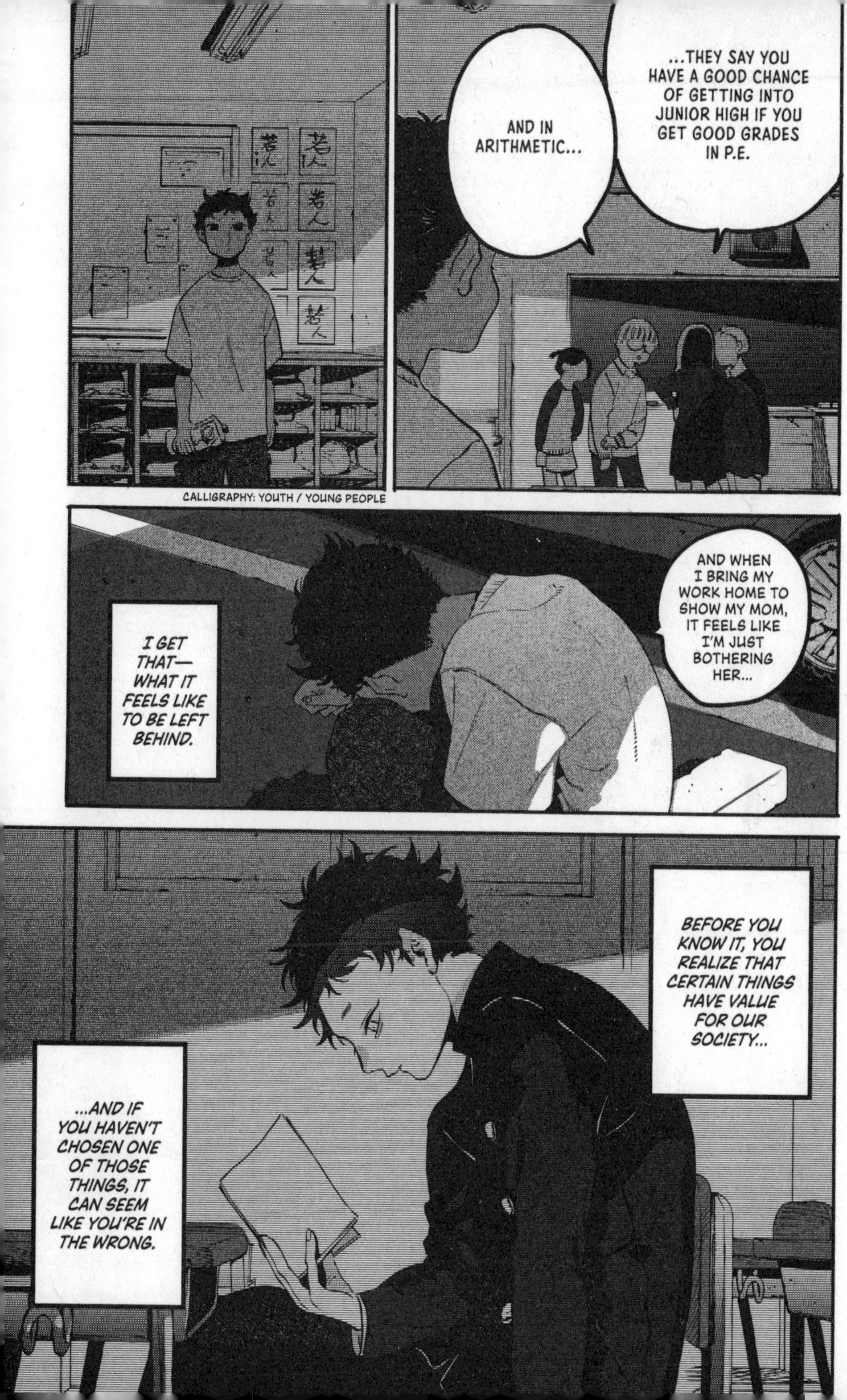
...THEY SAY YOU HAVE A GOOD CHANCE OF GETTING INTO JUNIOR HIGH IF YOU GET GOOD GRADES IN P.E.
AND IN ARITHMETIC...
AND WHEN I BRING MY WORK HOME TO SHOW MY MOM, IT FEELS LIKE I'M JUST BOTHERING HER...
I GET THAT—WHAT IT FEELS LIKE TO BE LEFT BEHIND.
BEFORE YOU KNOW IT, YOU REALIZE THAT CERTAIN THINGS HAVE VALUE FOR OUR SOCIETY...
...AND IF YOU HAVEN'T CHOSEN ONE OF THOSE THINGS, IT CAN SEEM LIKE YOU'RE IN THE WRONG.
CALLIGRAPHY: YOUTH / YOUNG PEOPLE

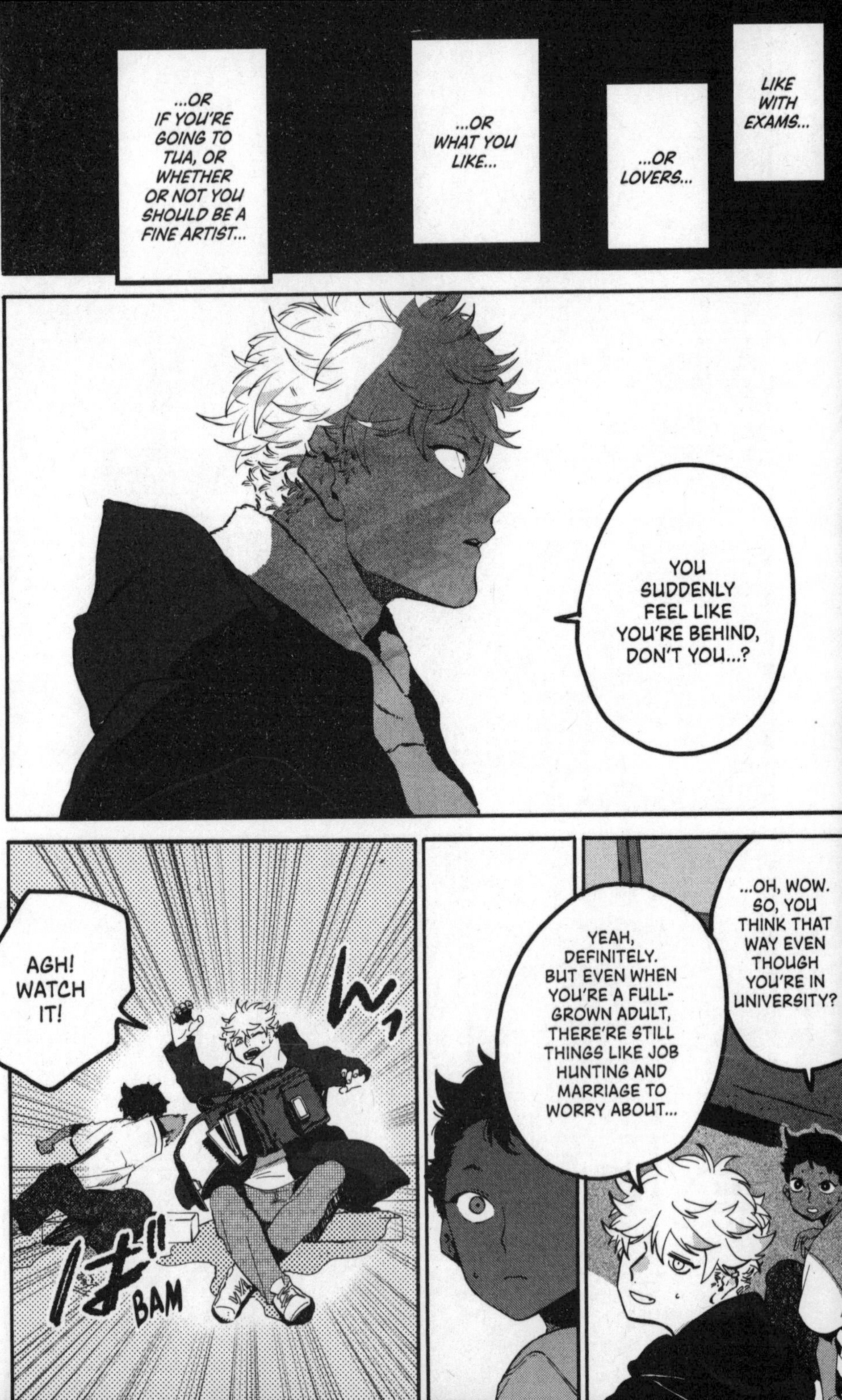
LIKE WITH EXAMS...
...OR LOVERS...
...OR WHAT YOU LIKE...
...OR IF YOU'RE GOING TO TUA, OR WHETHER OR NOT YOU SHOULD BE A FINE ARTIST...
YOU SUDDENLY FEEL LIKE YOU'RE BEHIND, DON'T YOU...?
...OH, WOW. SO, YOU THINK THAT WAY EVEN THOUGH YOU'RE IN UNIVERSITY?
YEAH, DEFINITELY. BUT EVEN WHEN YOU'RE A FULL-GROWN ADULT, THERE'RE STILL THINGS LIKE JOB HUNTING AND MARRIAGE TO WORRY ABOUT...
AGH! WATCH IT!
BAM

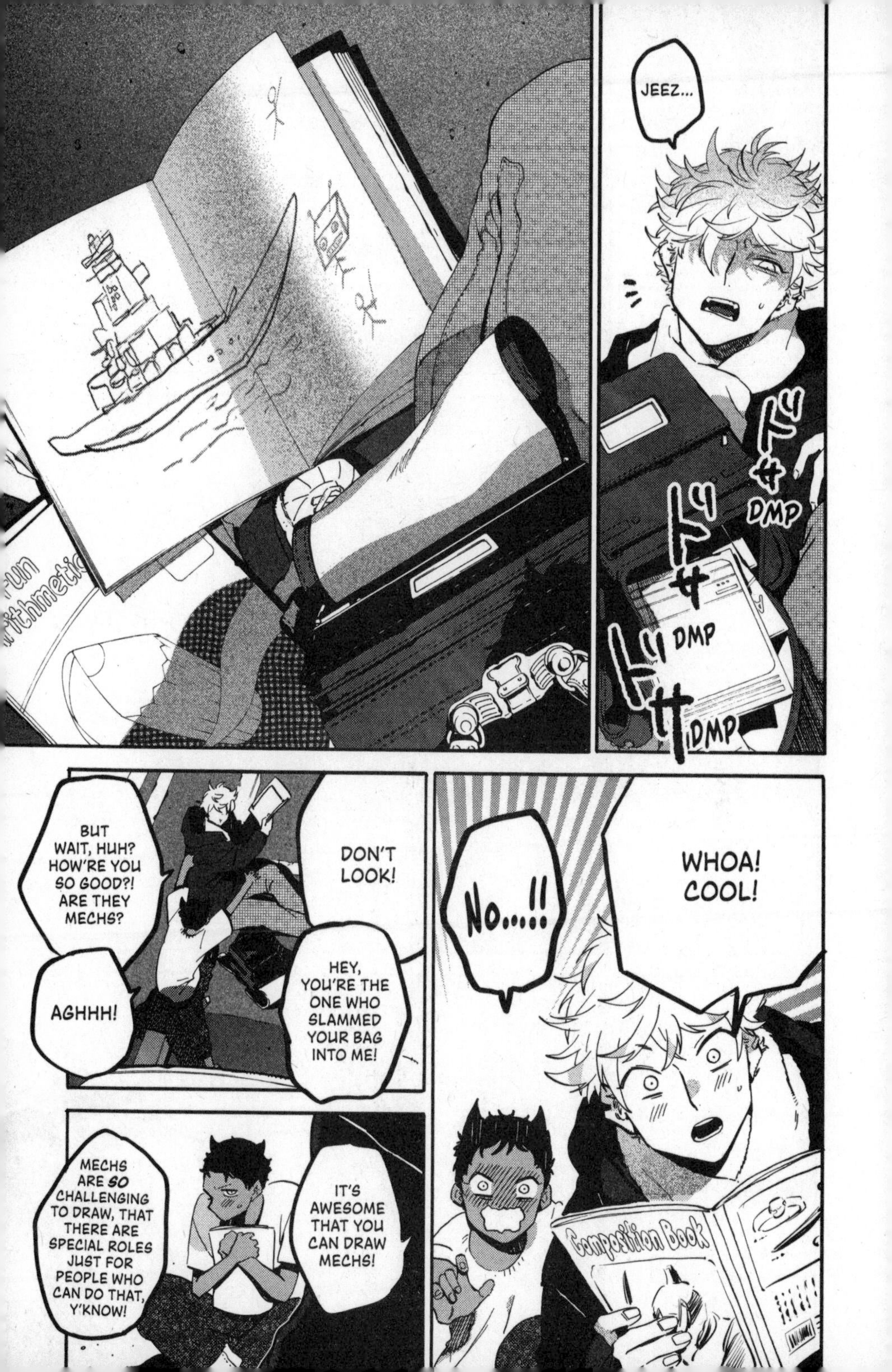
JEEZ...
ドサ
DMP
ドサ
DMP
ドサ
DMP
WHOA! COOL!
No...!!
Composition Book
DON'T LOOK!
BUT WAIT, HUH? HOW'RE YOU SO GOOD?! ARE THEY MECHS?
HEY, YOU'RE THE ONE WHO SLAMMED YOUR BAG INTO ME!
AGHHH!
IT'S AWESOME THAT YOU CAN DRAW MECHS!
MECHS ARE *SO* CHALLENGING TO DRAW, THAT THERE ARE SPECIAL ROLES JUST FOR PEOPLE WHO CAN DO THAT, Y'KNOW!

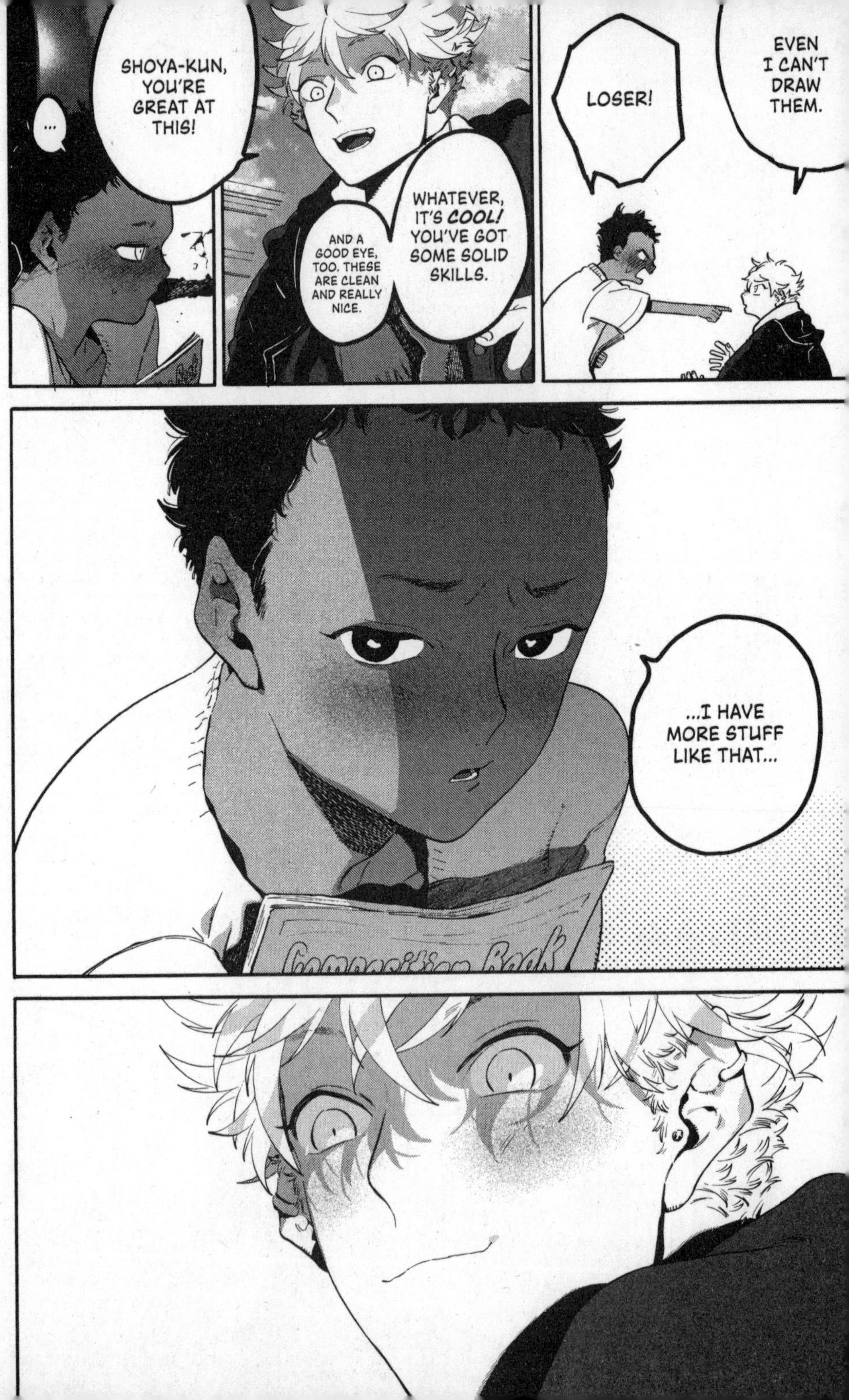
EVEN I CAN'T DRAW THEM.
LOSER!
WHATEVER, IT'S COOL! YOU'VE GOT SOME SOLID SKILLS.
AND A GOOD EYE, TOO. THESE ARE CLEAN AND REALLY NICE.
SHOYA-KUN, YOU'RE GREAT AT THIS!
...
...I HAVE MORE STUFF LIKE THAT...

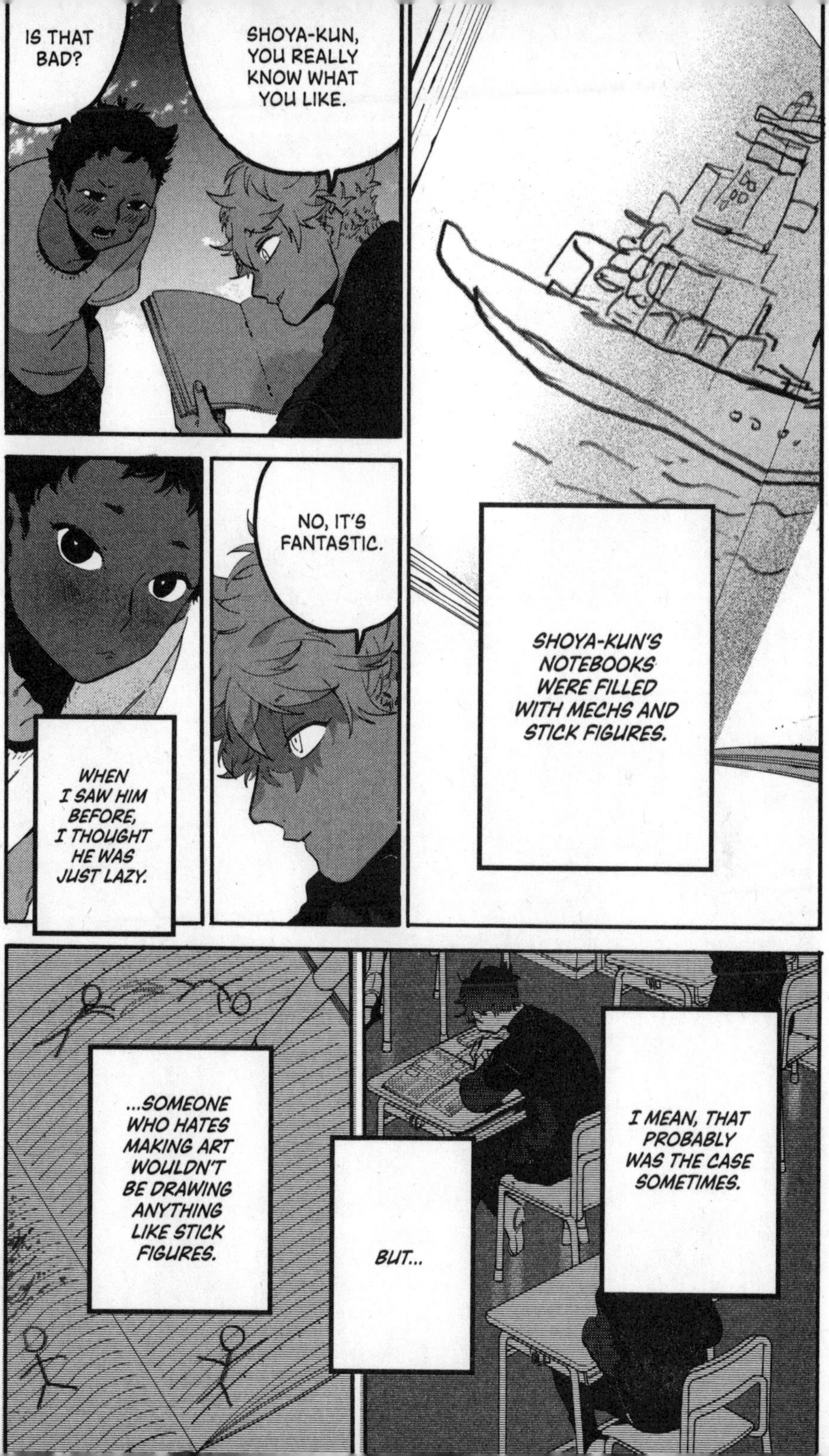
SHOYA-KUN'S NOTEBOOKS WERE FILLED WITH MECHS AND STICK FIGURES.
SHOYA-KUN, YOU REALLY KNOW WHAT YOU LIKE.
IS THAT BAD?
NO, IT'S FANTASTIC.
WHEN I SAW HIM BEFORE, I THOUGHT HE WAS JUST LAZY.
I MEAN, THAT PROBABLY WAS THE CASE SOMETIMES.
BUT...
...SOMEONE WHO HATES MAKING ART WOULDN'T BE DRAWING ANYTHING LIKE STICK FIGURES.

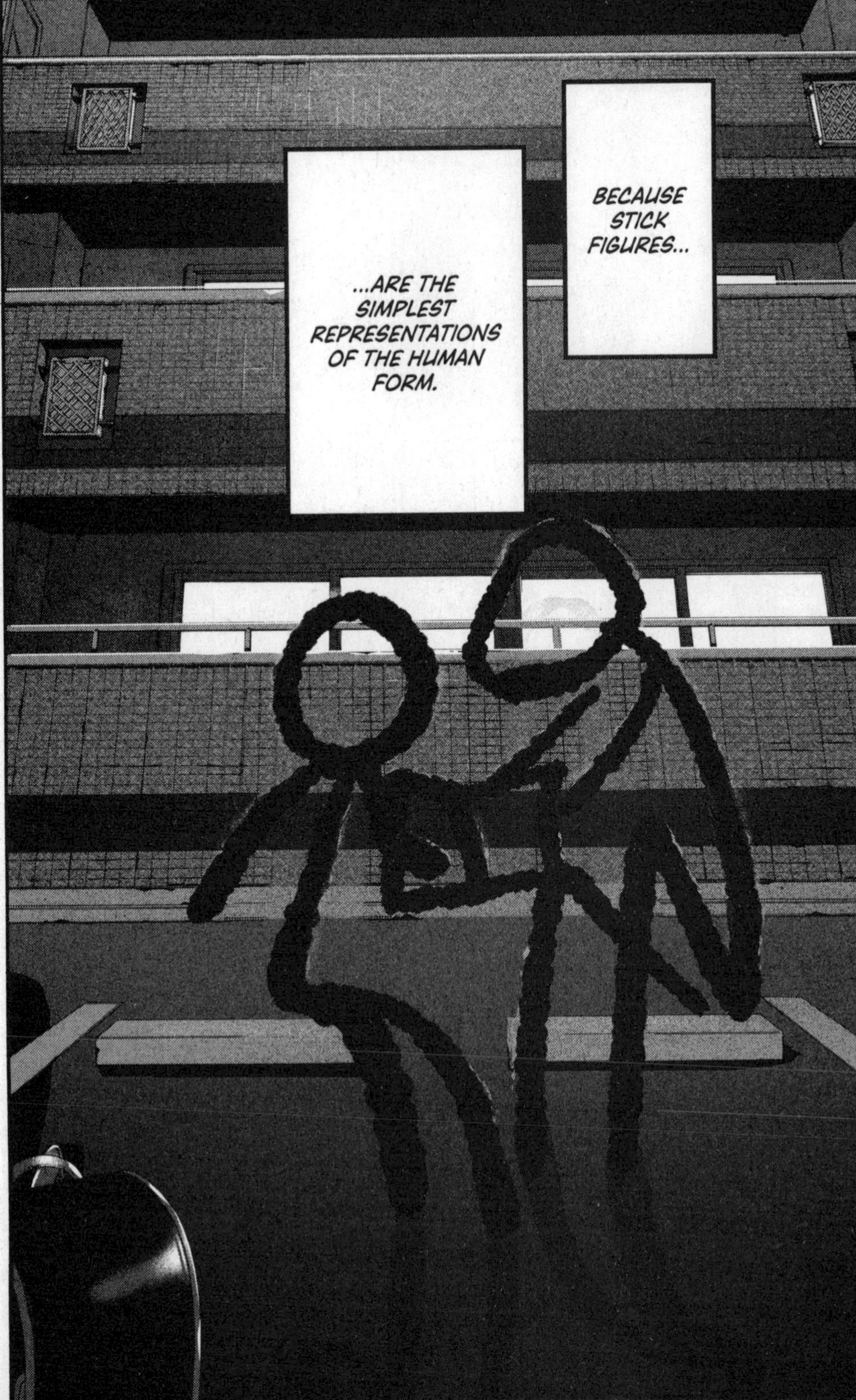
BECAUSE STICK FIGURES...
...ARE THE SIMPLEST REPRESENTATIONS OF THE HUMAN FORM.

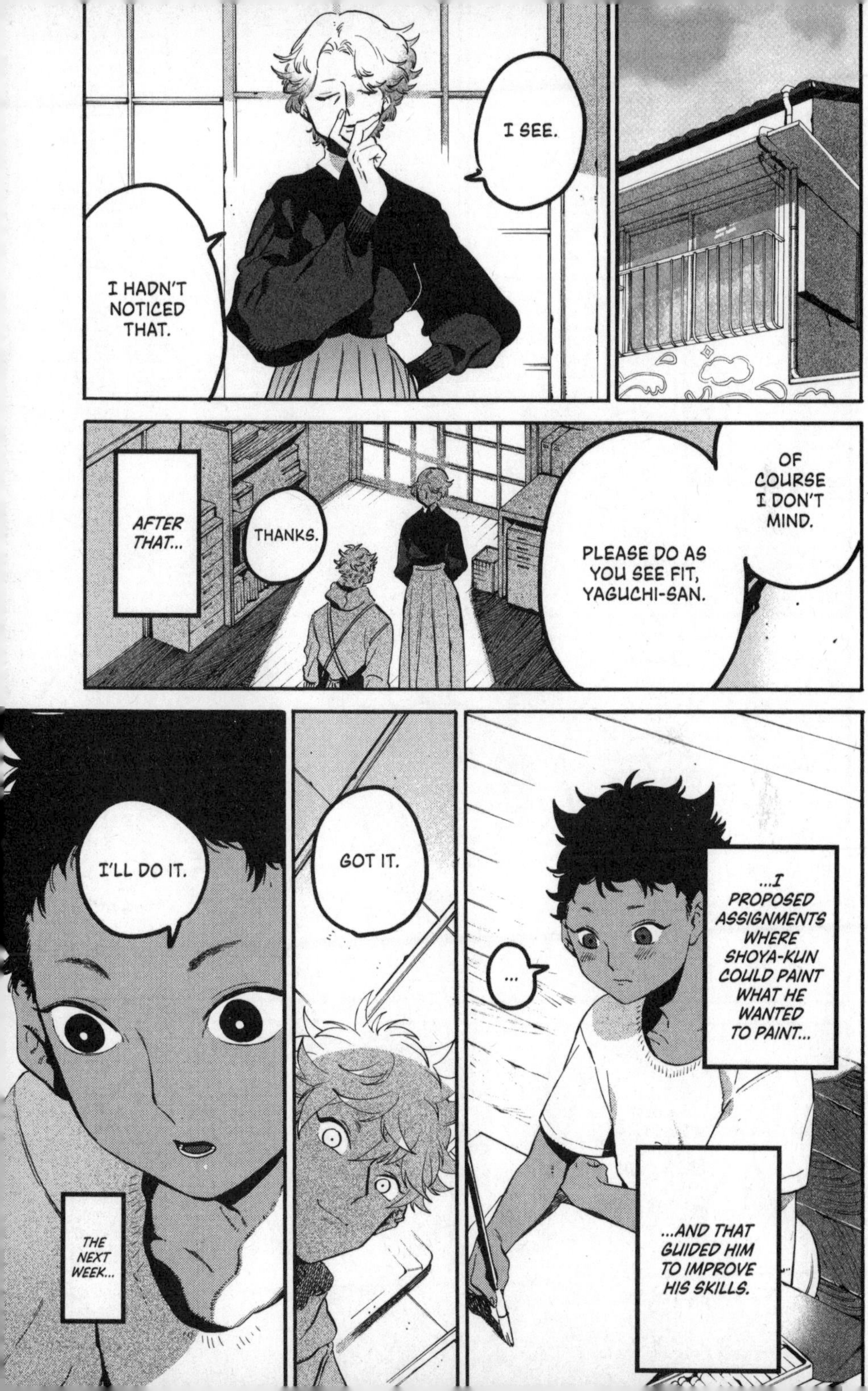
I SEE.
I HADN'T NOTICED THAT.
OF COURSE I DON'T MIND.
PLEASE DO AS YOU SEE FIT, YAGUCHI-SAN.
THANKS.
AFTER THAT...
...I PROPOSED ASSIGNMENTS WHERE SHOYA-KUN COULD PAINT WHAT HE WANTED TO PAINT...
...
...AND THAT GUIDED HIM TO IMPROVE HIS SKILLS.
GOT IT.
I'LL DO IT.
THE NEXT WEEK...

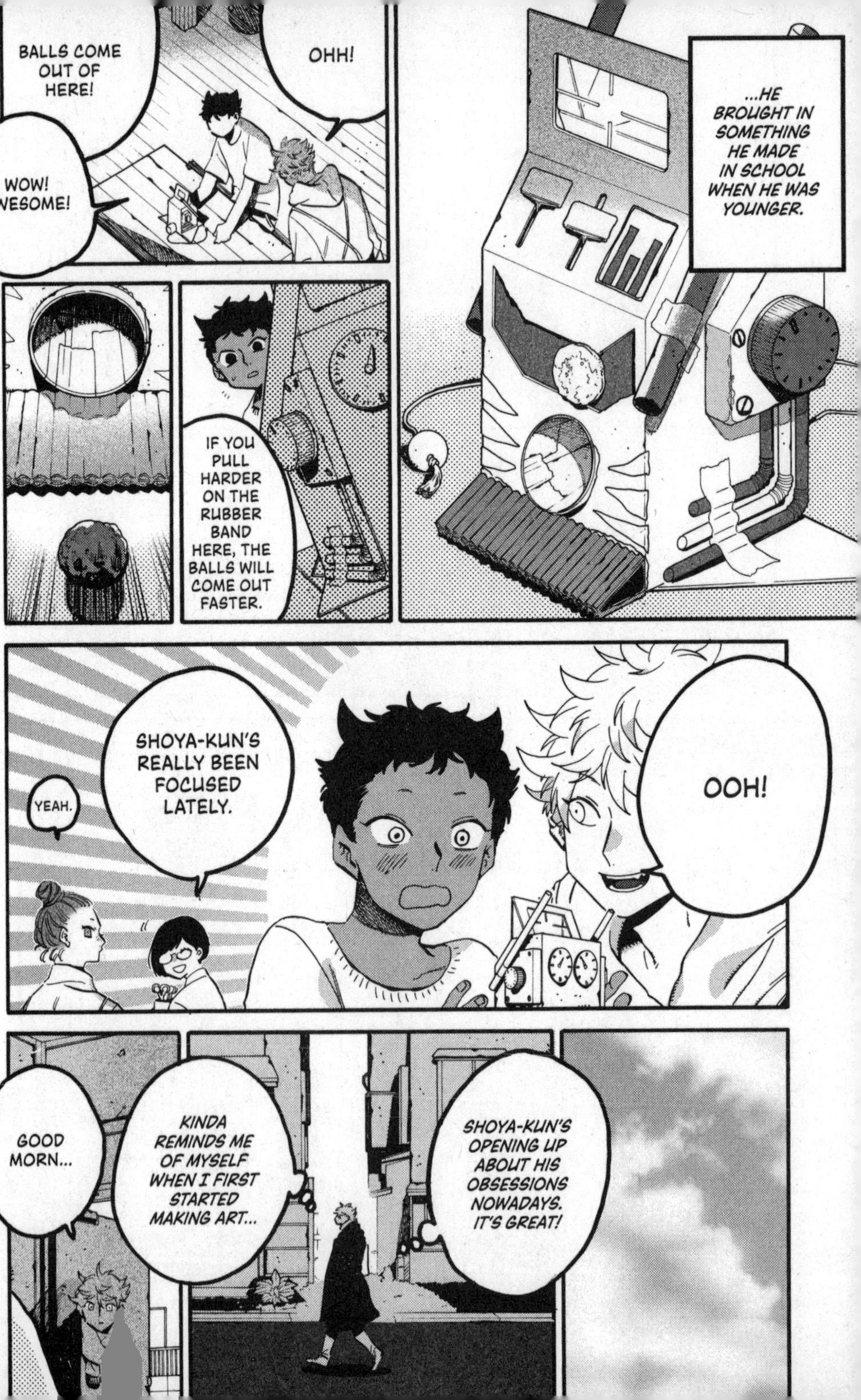
...HE BROUGHT IN SOMETHING HE MADE IN SCHOOL WHEN HE WAS YOUNGER.
OHH!
BALLS COME OUT OF HERE!
WOW! AWESOME!
IF YOU PULL HARDER ON THE RUBBER BAND HERE, THE BALLS WILL COME OUT FASTER.
OOH!
SHOYA-KUN'S REALLY BEEN FOCUSED LATELY.
YEAH.
SHOYA-KUN'S OPENING UP ABOUT HIS OBSESSIONS NOWADAYS. IT'S GREAT!
KINDA REMINDS ME OF MYSELF WHEN I FIRST STARTED MAKING ART...
GOOD MORN...

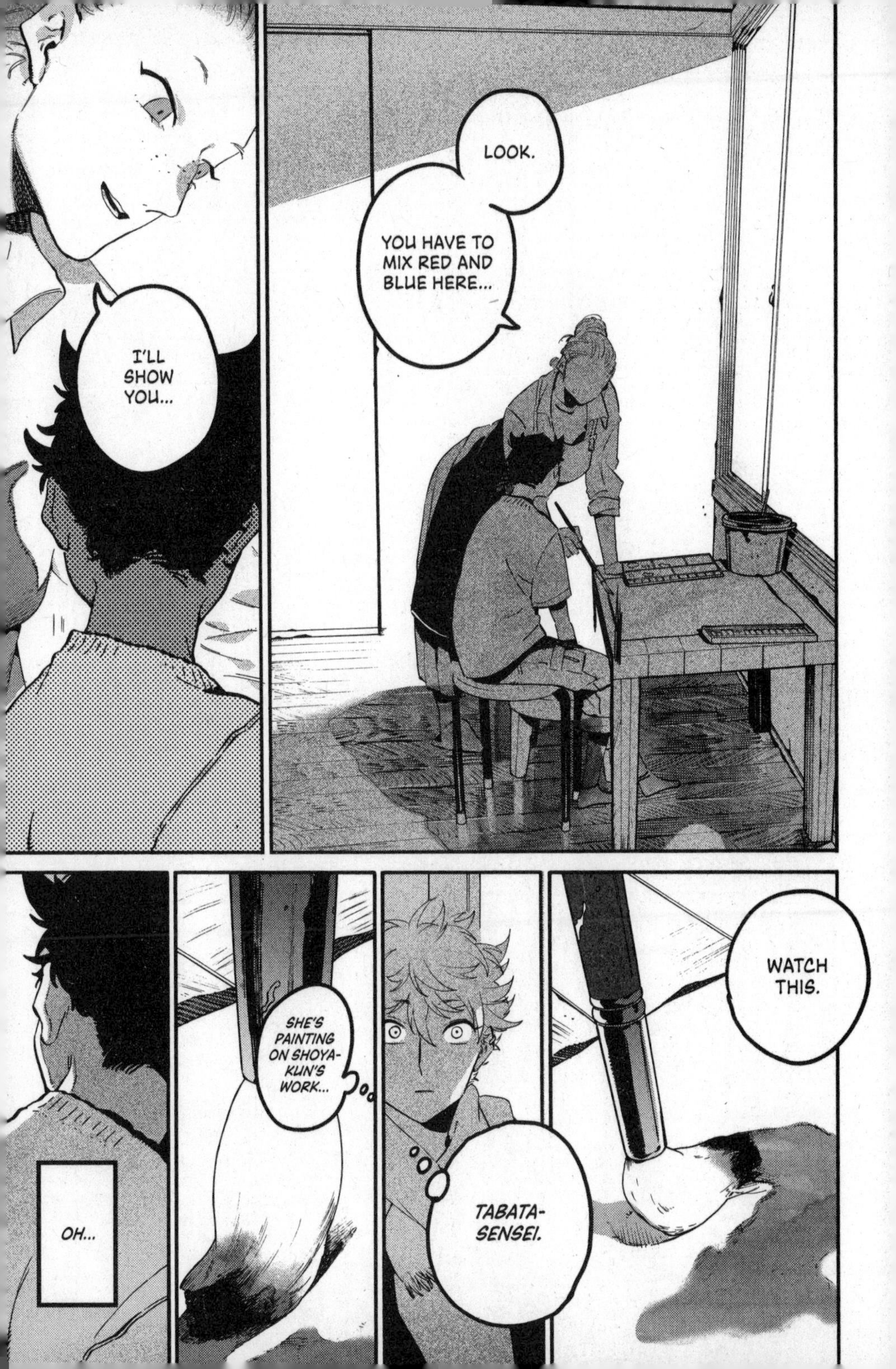
LOOK.
YOU HAVE TO MIX RED AND BLUE HERE...
I'LL SHOW YOU...
WATCH THIS.
TABATA-SENSEI.
SHE'S PAINTING ON SHOYA-KUN'S WORK...
OH...

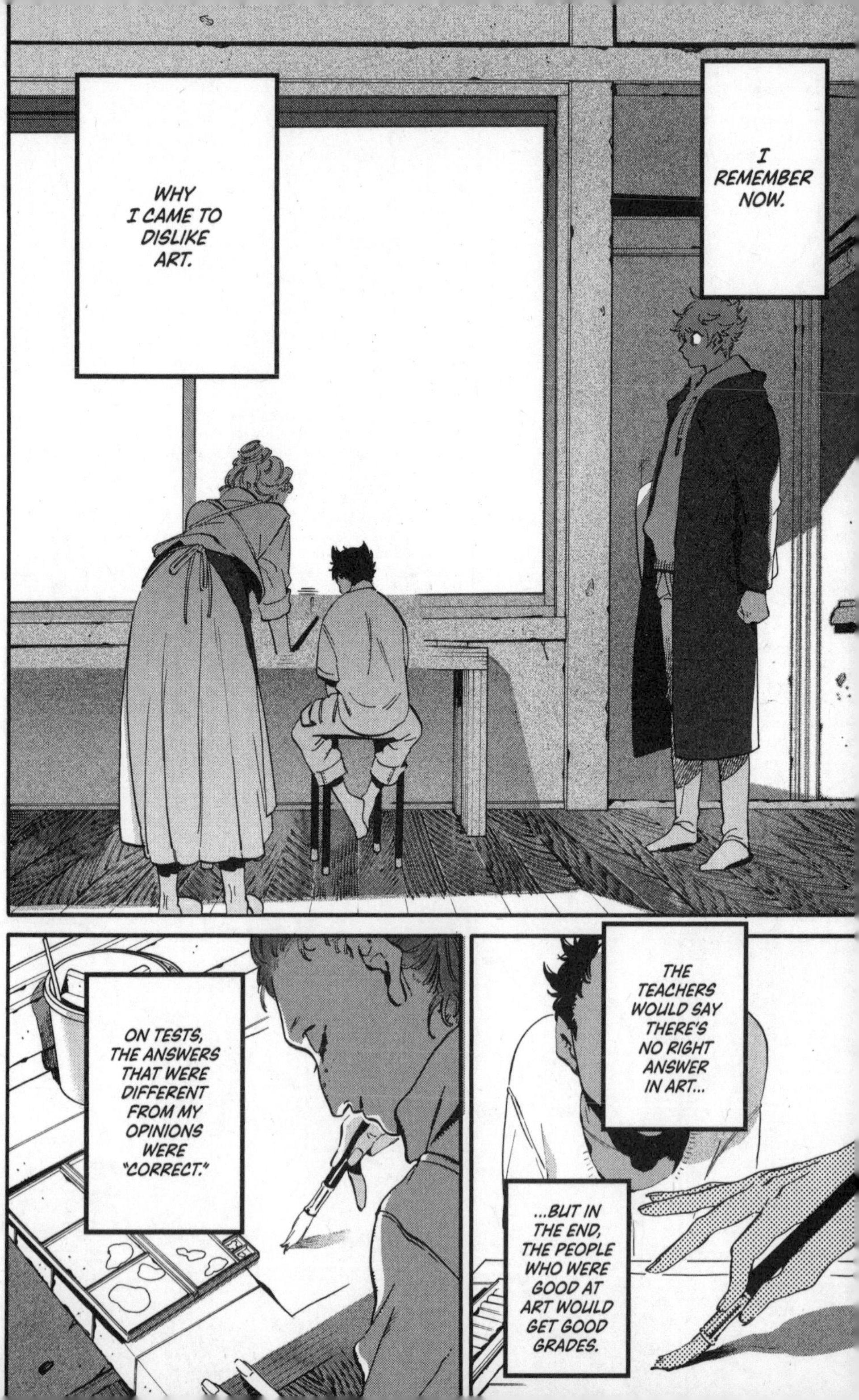
I REMEMBER NOW.
WHY I CAME TO DISLIKE ART.
THE TEACHERS WOULD SAY THERE'S NO RIGHT ANSWER IN ART...
...BUT IN THE END, THE PEOPLE WHO WERE GOOD AT ART WOULD GET GOOD GRADES.
ON TESTS, THE ANSWERS THAT WERE DIFFERENT FROM MY OPINIONS WERE "CORRECT."

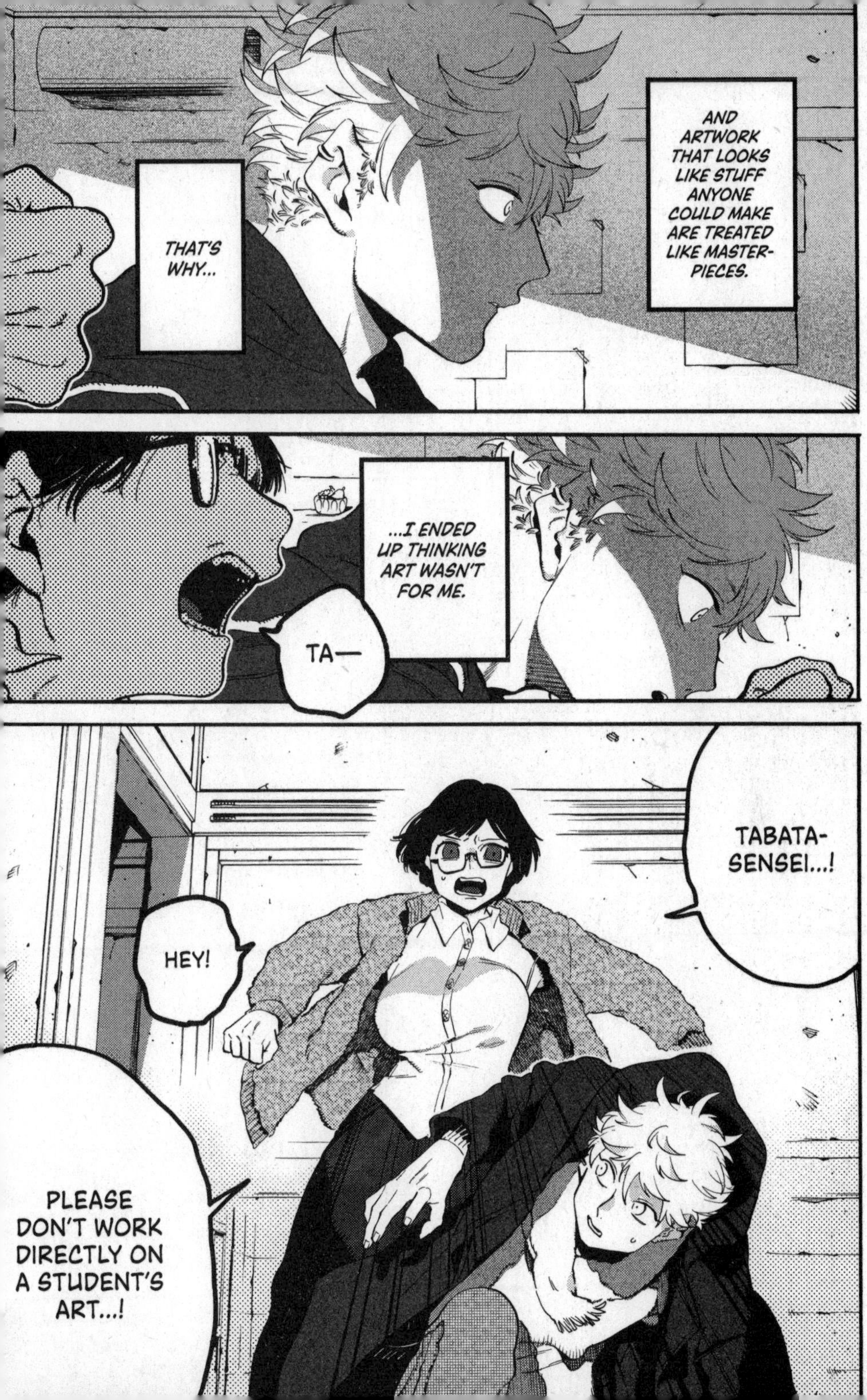
AND ARTWORK THAT LOOKS LIKE STUFF ANYONE COULD MAKE ARE TREATED LIKE MASTER-PIECES.
THAT'S WHY...
...I ENDED UP THINKING ART WASN'T FOR ME.
TA—
TABATA-SENSEI...!
HEY!
PLEASE DON'T WORK DIRECTLY ON A STUDENT'S ART...!

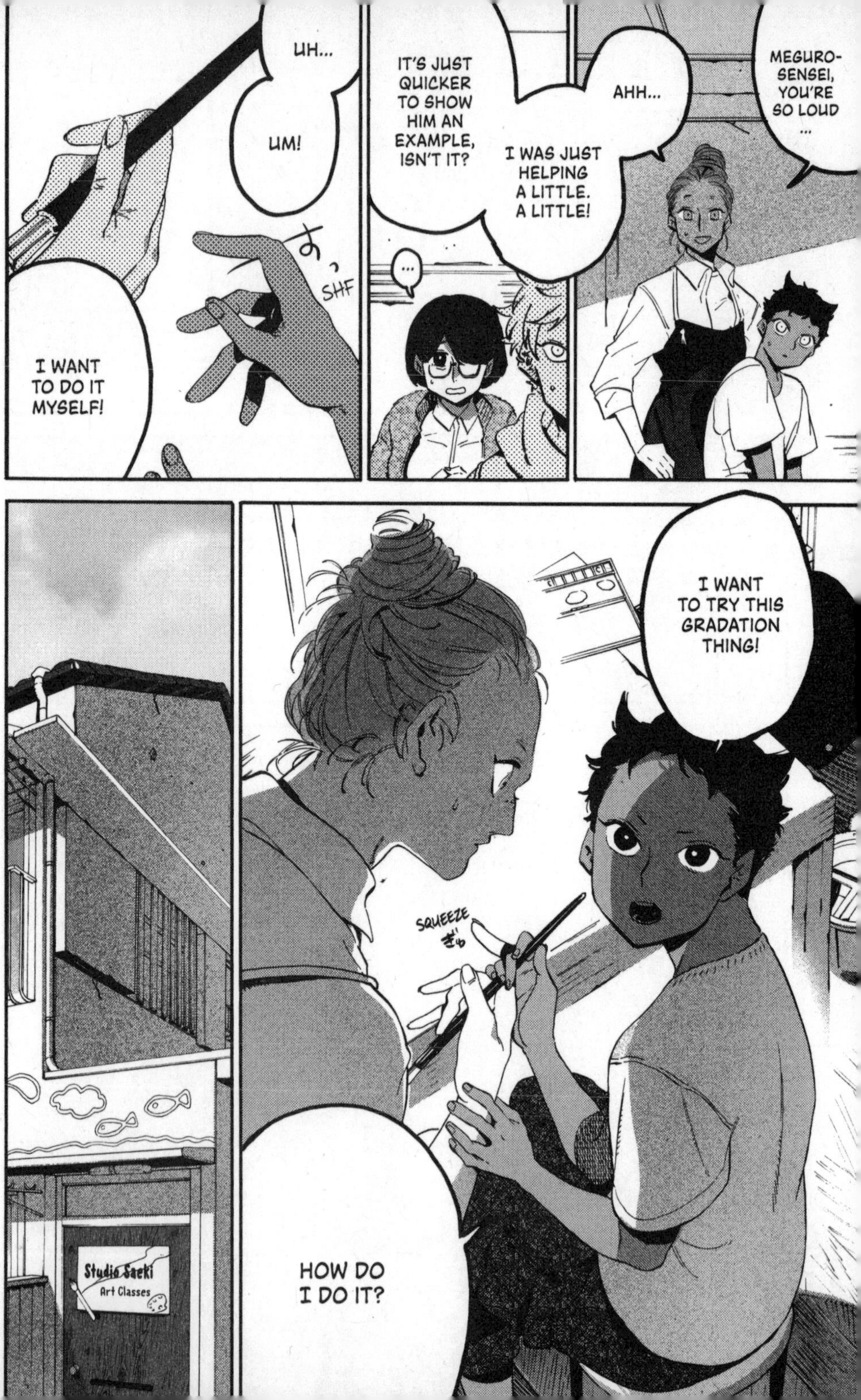
MEGURO-SENSEI, YOU'RE SO LOUD ...
AHH...
I WAS JUST HELPING A LITTLE. A LITTLE!
IT'S JUST QUICKER TO SHOW HIM AN EXAMPLE, ISN'T IT?
...
UH...
UM!
す SHF
I WANT TO DO IT MYSELF!
I WANT TO TRY THIS GRADATION THING!
SQUEEZE ぎゅ
HOW DO I DO IT?
Studio Saeki
Art Classes

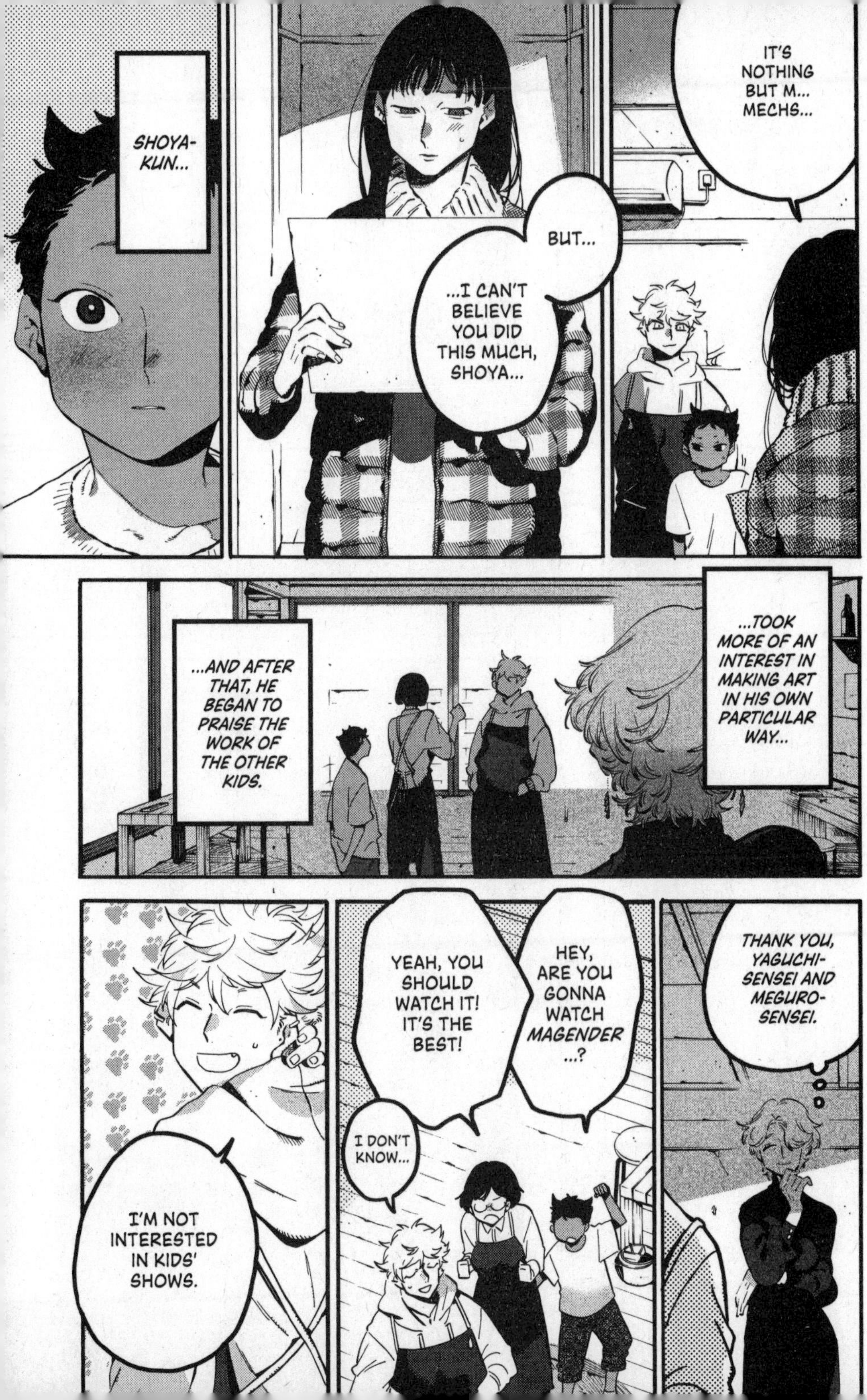
IT'S NOTHING BUT M... MECHS...
BUT...
...I CAN'T BELIEVE YOU DID THIS MUCH, SHOYA...
SHOYA-KUN...
...TOOK MORE OF AN INTEREST IN MAKING ART IN HIS OWN PARTICULAR WAY...
...AND AFTER THAT, HE BEGAN TO PRAISE THE WORK OF THE OTHER KIDS.
THANK YOU, YAGUCHI-SENSEI AND MEGURO-SENSEI.
HEY, ARE YOU GONNA WATCH MAGENDER ...?
YEAH, YOU SHOULD WATCH IT! IT'S THE BEST!
I DON'T KNOW...
I'M NOT INTERESTED IN KIDS' SHOWS.

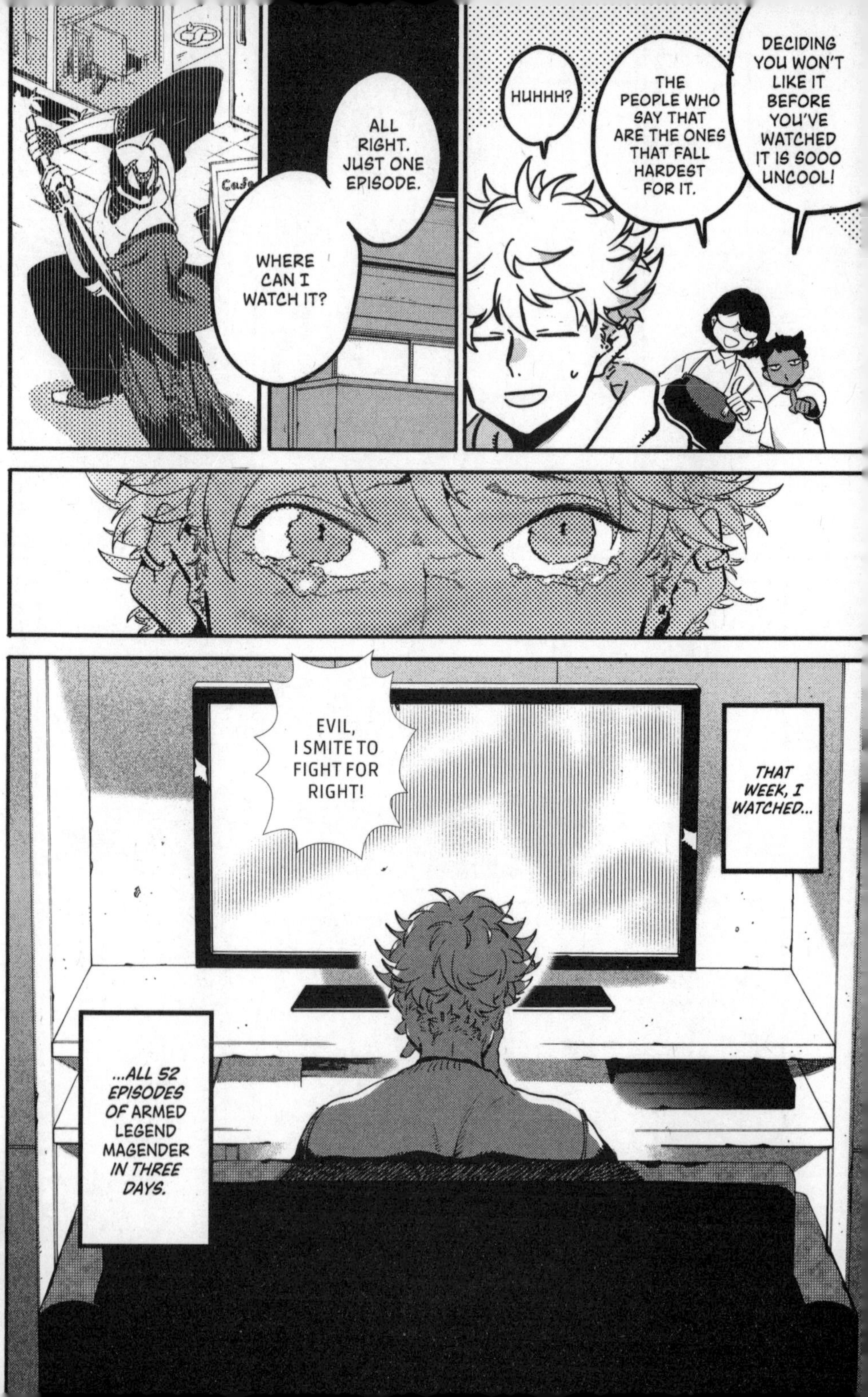
DECIDING YOU WON'T LIKE IT BEFORE YOU'VE WATCHED IT IS SOOO UNCOOL!
THE PEOPLE WHO SAY THAT ARE THE ONES THAT FALL HARDEST FOR IT.
HUHHH?
ALL RIGHT. JUST ONE EPISODE.
WHERE CAN I WATCH IT?
EVIL, I SMITE TO FIGHT FOR RIGHT!
THAT WEEK, I WATCHED...
...ALL 52 EPISODES OF ARMED LEGEND MAGENDER IN THREE DAYS.

STROKE 45 END

On spring break

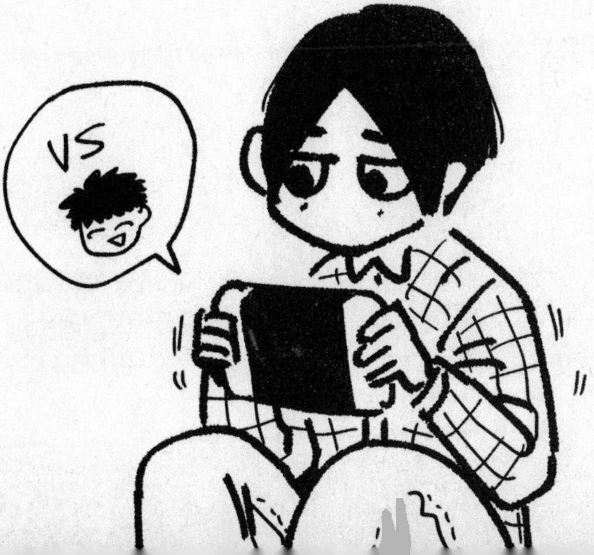
VS

BLUE PERIOD

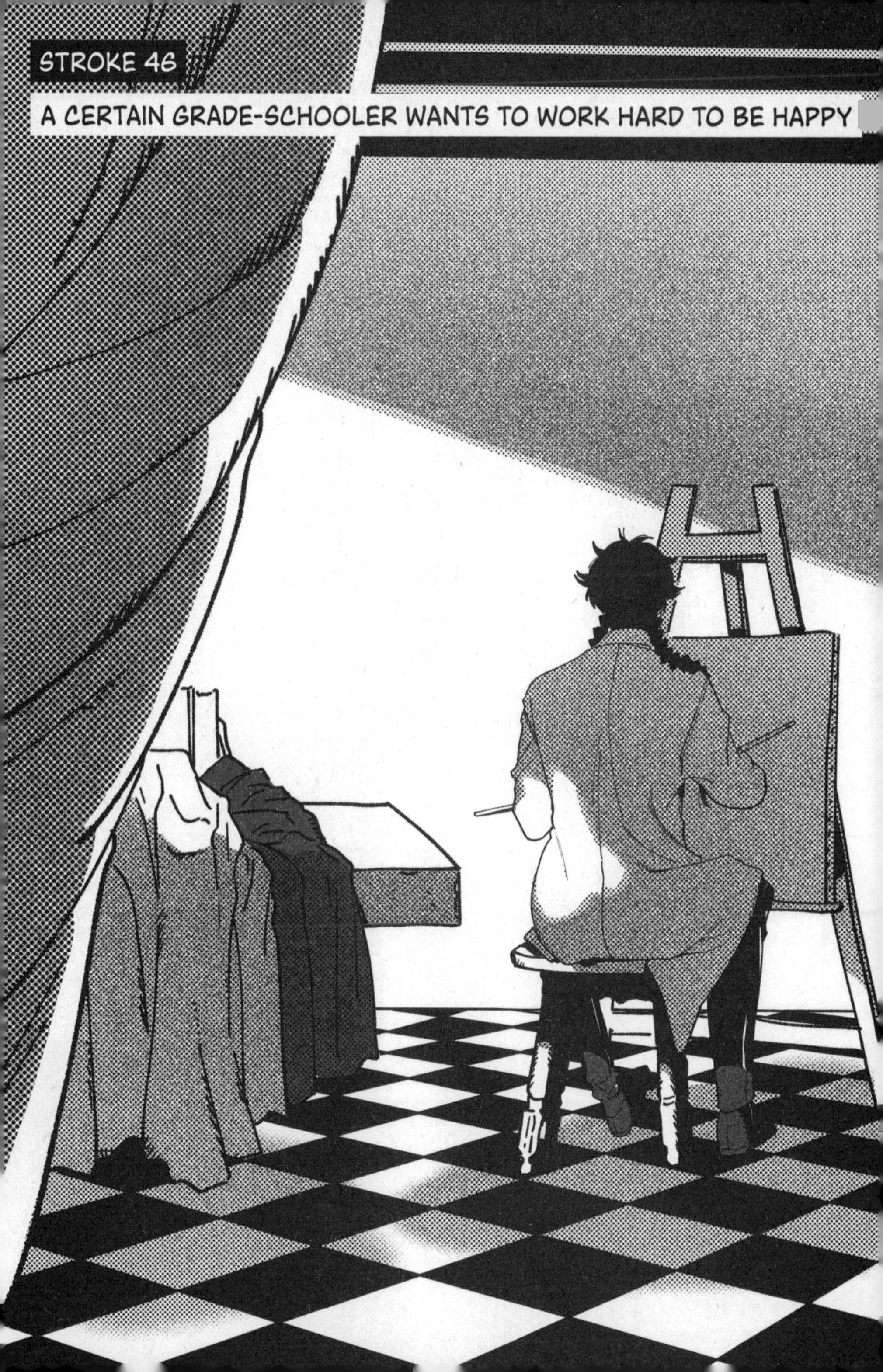
STROKE 46
A CERTAIN GRADE-SCHOOLER WANTS TO WORK HARD TO BE HAPPY

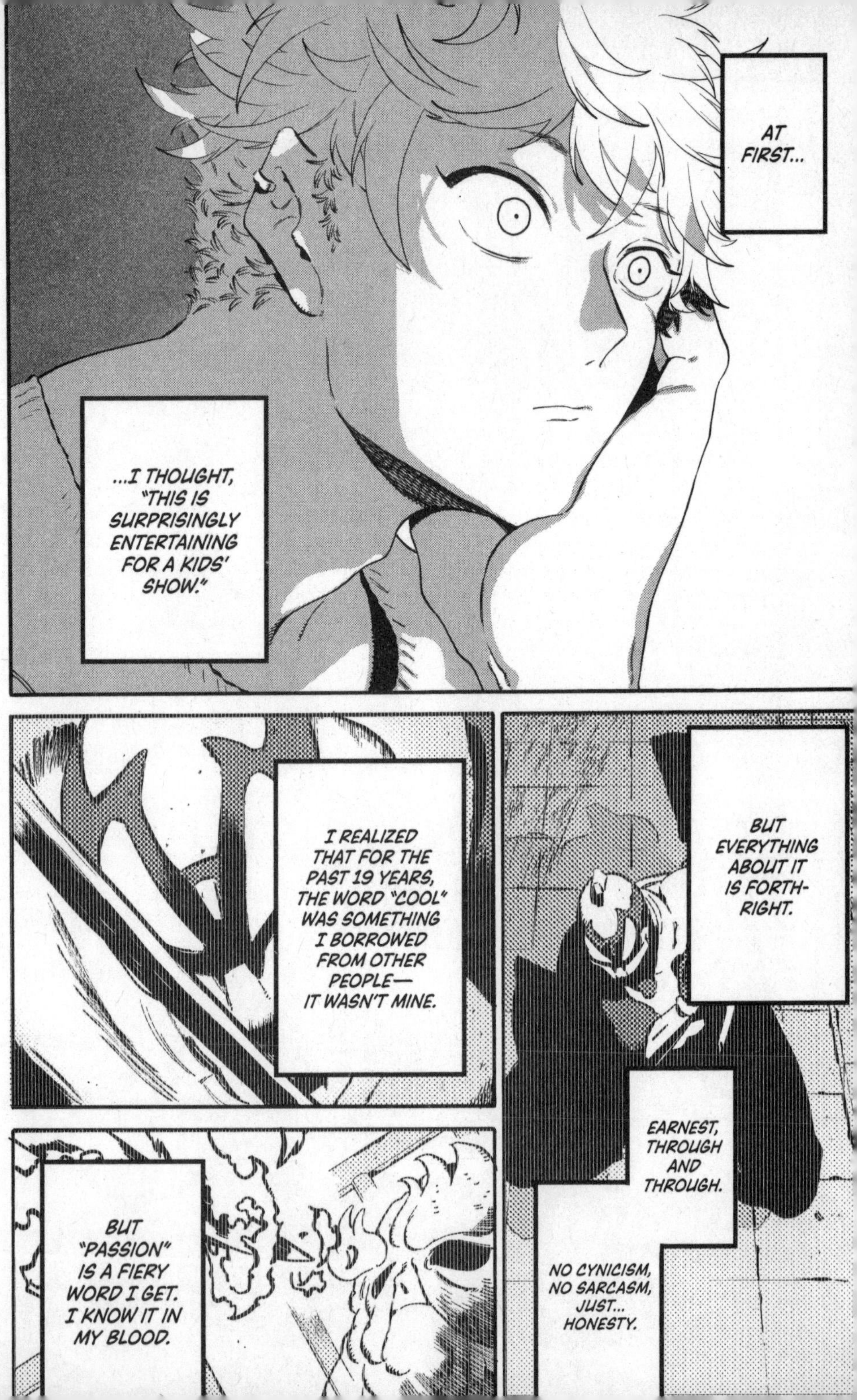
AT FIRST...
...I THOUGHT, "THIS IS SURPRISINGLY ENTERTAINING FOR A KIDS' SHOW."
BUT EVERYTHING ABOUT IT IS FORTH-RIGHT.
EARNEST, THROUGH AND THROUGH.
NO CYNICISM, NO SARCASM, JUST... HONESTY.
I REALIZED THAT FOR THE PAST 19 YEARS, THE WORD "COOL" WAS SOMETHING I BORROWED FROM OTHER PEOPLE— IT WASN'T MINE.
BUT "PASSION" IS A FIERY WORD I GET. I KNOW IT IN MY BLOOD.

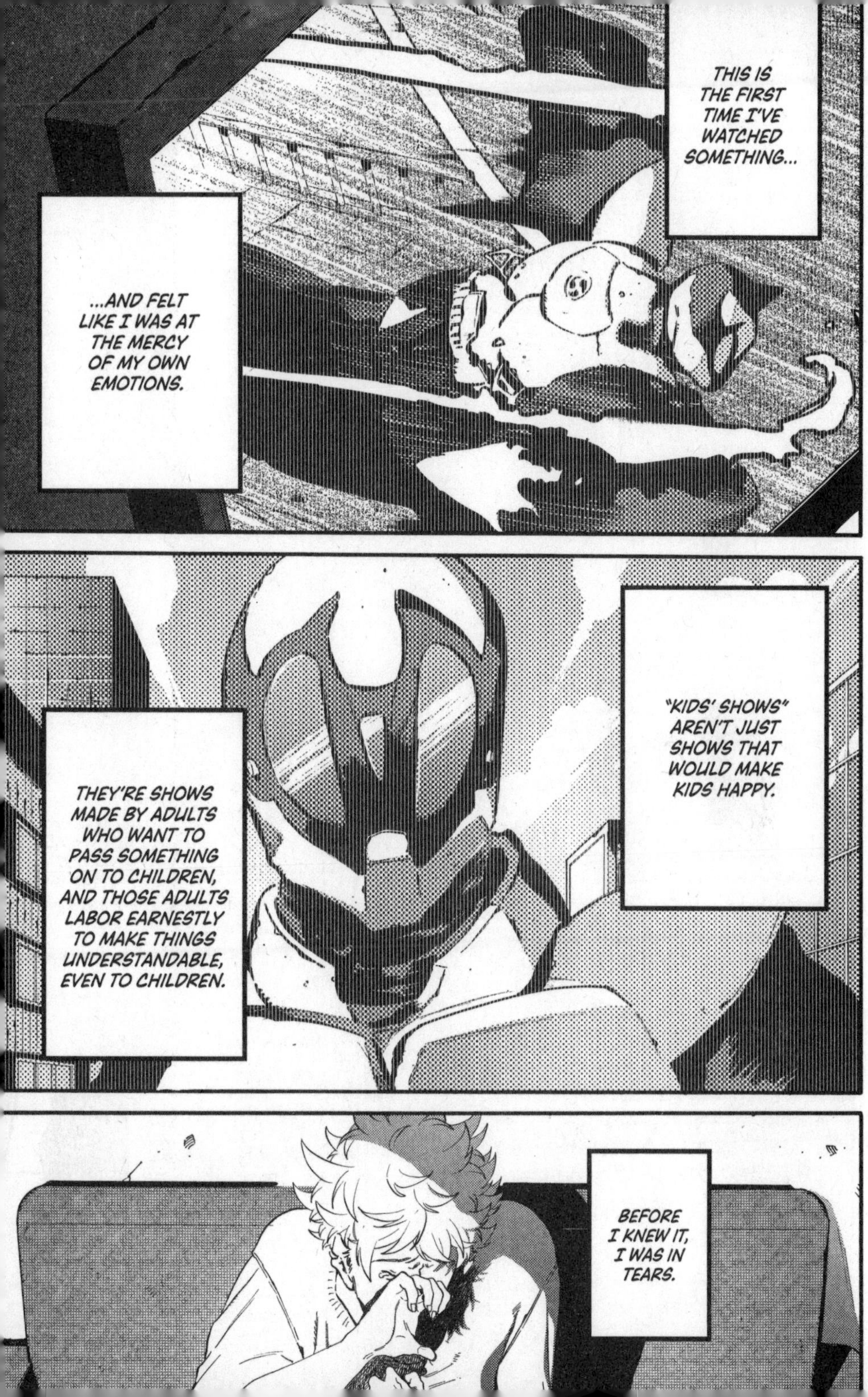
THIS IS THE FIRST TIME I'VE WATCHED SOMETHING...
...AND FELT LIKE I WAS AT THE MERCY OF MY OWN EMOTIONS.
"KIDS' SHOWS" AREN'T JUST SHOWS THAT WOULD MAKE KIDS HAPPY.
THEY'RE SHOWS MADE BY ADULTS WHO WANT TO PASS SOMETHING ON TO CHILDREN, AND THOSE ADULTS LABOR EARNESTLY TO MAKE THINGS UNDERSTANDABLE, EVEN TO CHILDREN.
BEFORE I KNEW IT, I WAS IN TEARS.

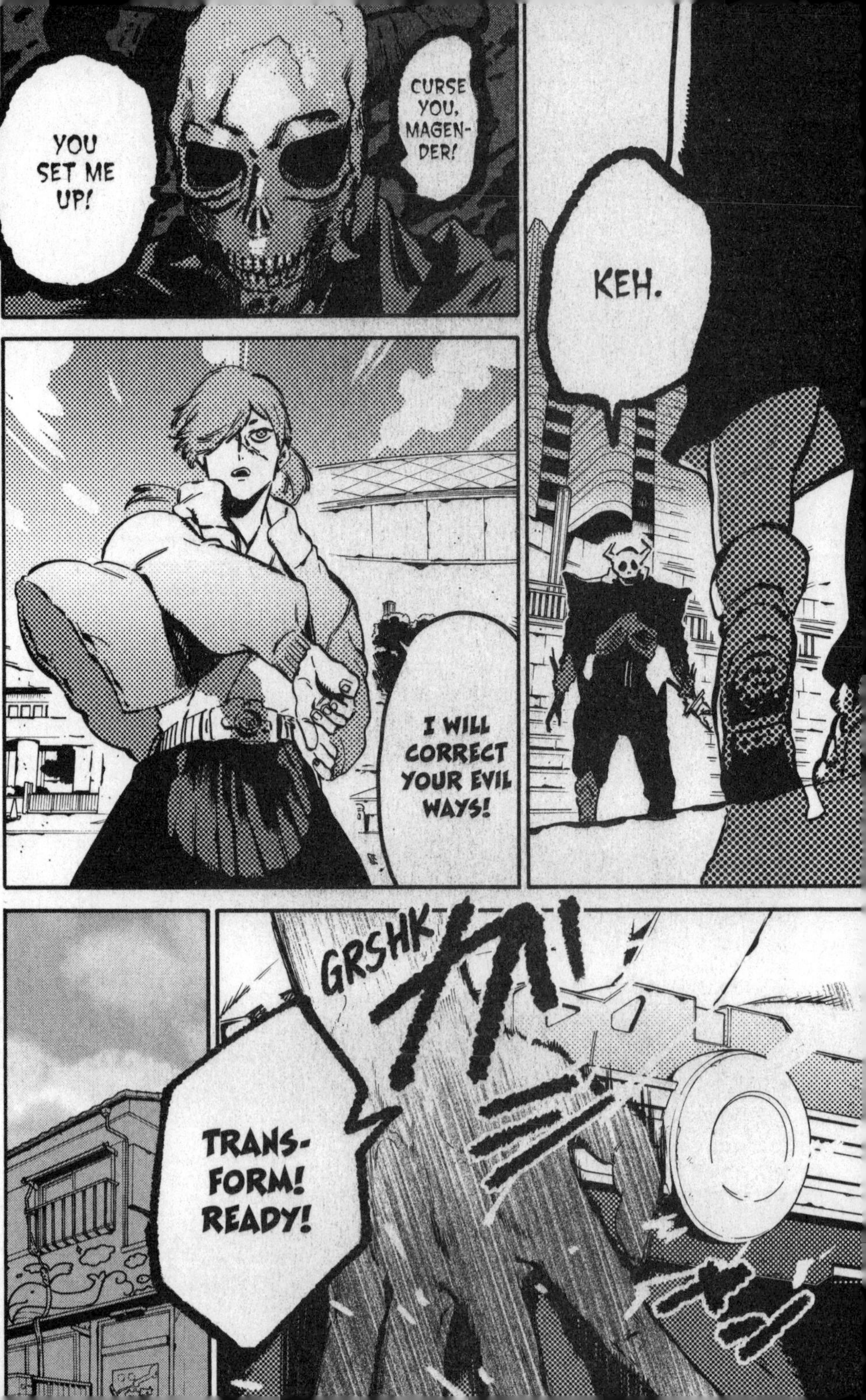
KEH.
CURSE YOU, MAGENDER!
YOU SET ME UP!
I WILL CORRECT YOUR EVIL WAYS!
GRSHK
TRANS-FORM! READY!

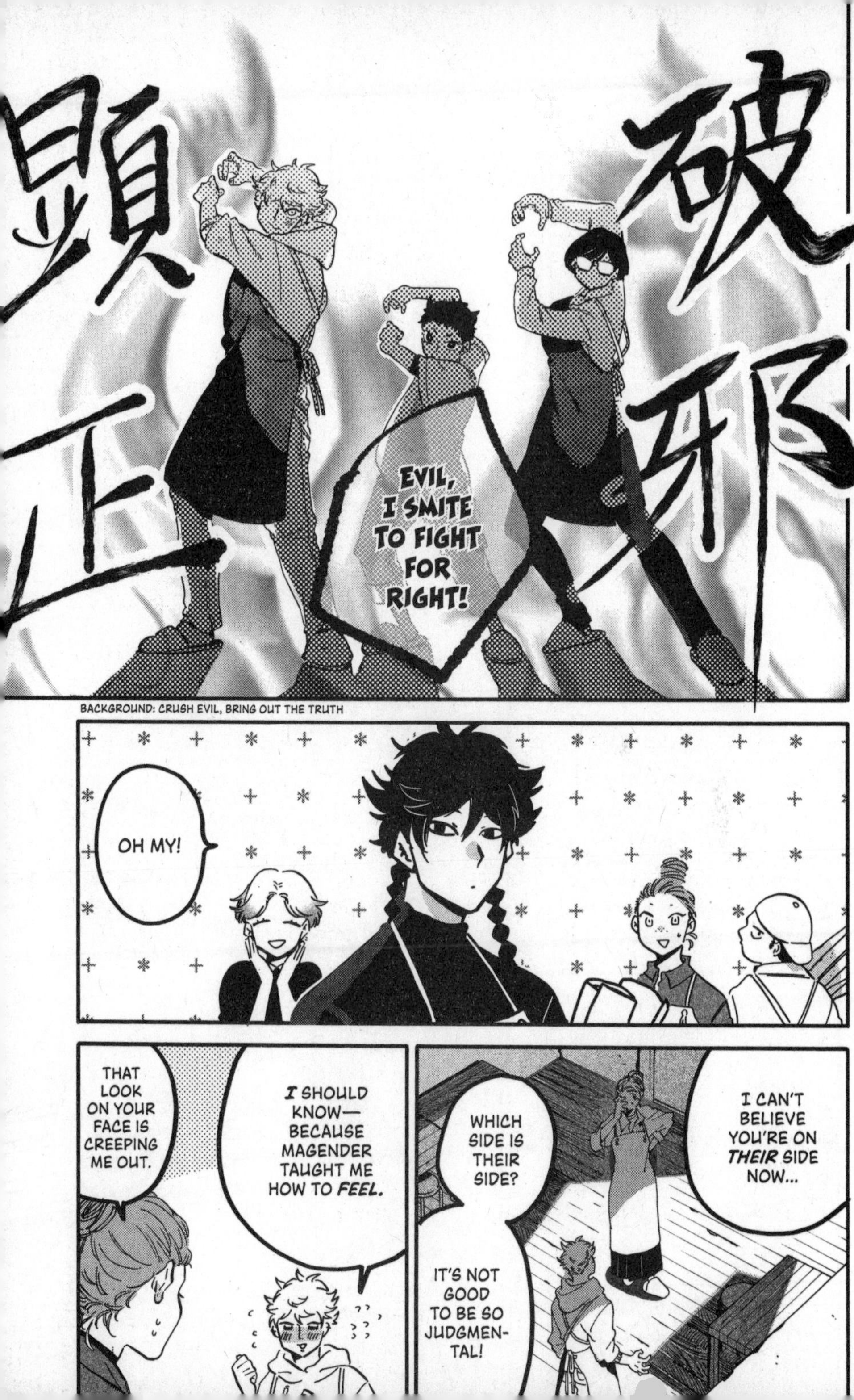
破邪
顕正
EVIL, I SMITE TO FIGHT FOR RIGHT!
BACKGROUND: CRUSH EVIL, BRING OUT THE TRUTH
OH MY!
I CAN'T BELIEVE YOU'RE ON *THEIR* SIDE NOW...
WHICH SIDE IS THEIR SIDE?
IT'S NOT GOOD TO BE SO JUDGMENTAL!
I SHOULD KNOW—BECAUSE MAGENDER TAUGHT ME HOW TO *FEEL.*
THAT LOOK ON YOUR FACE IS CREEPING ME OUT.

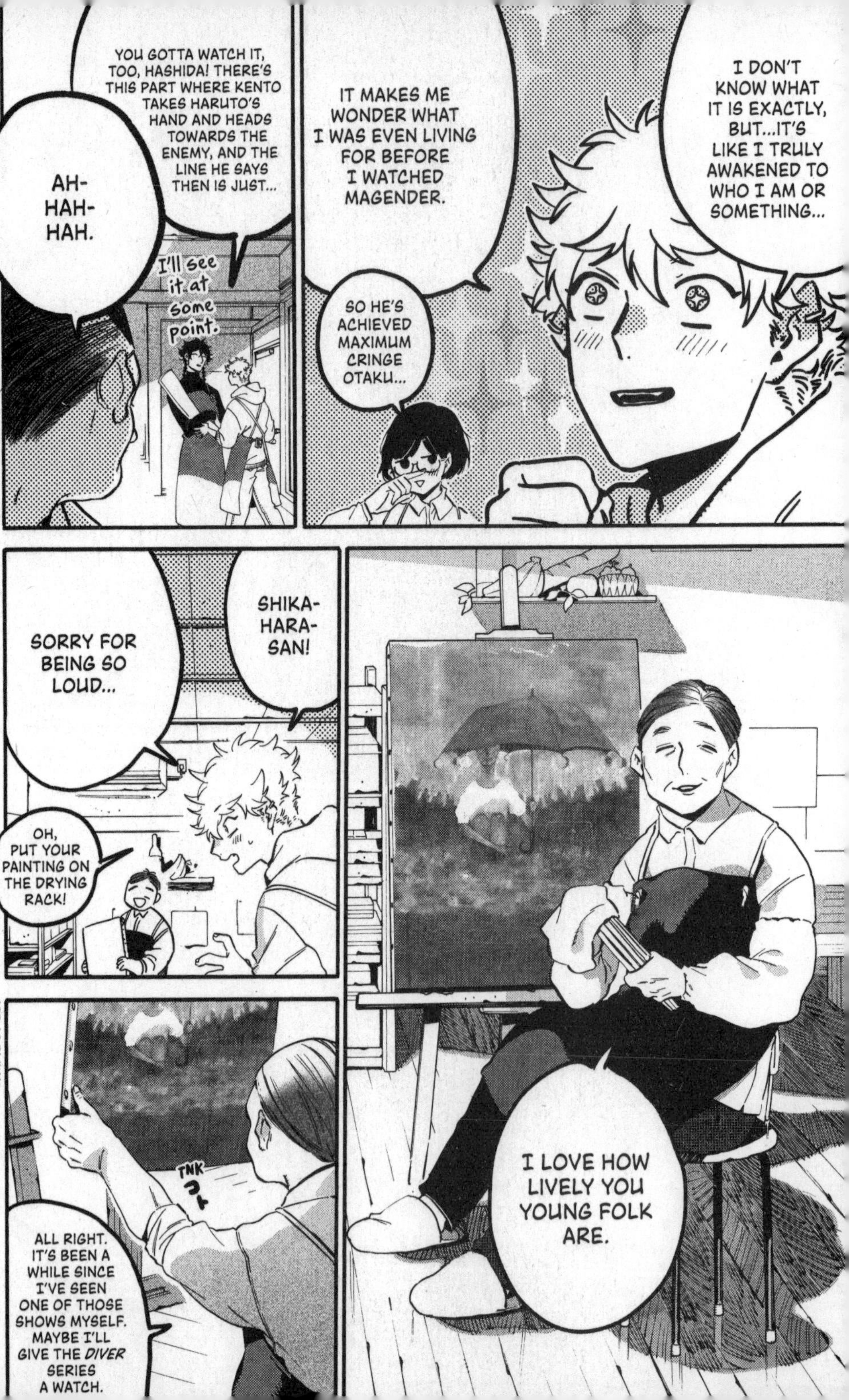
I DON'T KNOW WHAT IT IS EXACTLY, BUT...IT'S LIKE I TRULY AWAKENED TO WHO I AM OR SOMETHING...
IT MAKES ME WONDER WHAT I WAS EVEN LIVING FOR BEFORE I WATCHED MAGENDER.
SO HE'S ACHIEVED MAXIMUM CRINGE OTAKU...
YOU GOTTA WATCH IT, TOO, HASHIDA! THERE'S THIS PART WHERE KENTO TAKES HARUTO'S HAND AND HEADS TOWARDS THE ENEMY, AND THE LINE HE SAYS THEN IS JUST...
AH-HAH-HAH.
I'll see it at some point.
I LOVE HOW LIVELY YOU YOUNG FOLK ARE.
SHIKA-HARA-SAN!
SORRY FOR BEING SO LOUD...
OH, PUT YOUR PAINTING ON THE DRYING RACK!
TNK
コト
ALL RIGHT. IT'S BEEN A WHILE SINCE I'VE SEEN ONE OF THOSE SHOWS MYSELF. MAYBE I'LL GIVE THE *DIVER* SERIES A WATCH.

ART: AO TAJIMA

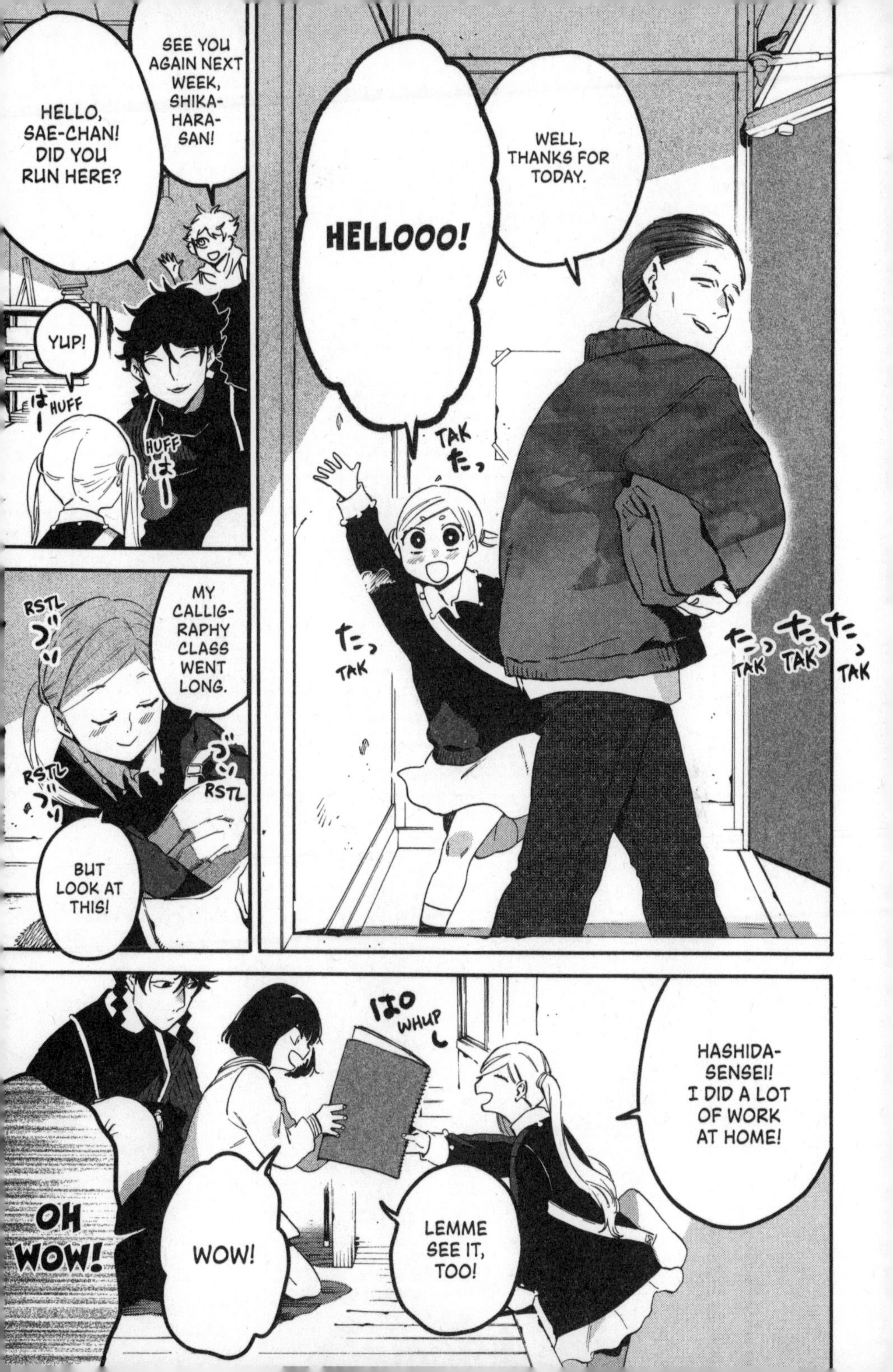
WELL, THANKS FOR TODAY.
HELLOOO!
TAK たっ
たっ TAK
たっ たっ たっ TAK TAK TAK
SEE YOU AGAIN NEXT WEEK, SHIKA-HARA-SAN!
HELLO, SAE-CHAN! DID YOU RUN HERE?
YUP!
HUFF
HUFF
MY CALLIG-RAPHY CLASS WENT LONG.
RSTL
RSTL
RSTL
BUT LOOK AT THIS!
HASHIDA-SENSEI! I DID A LOT OF WORK AT HOME!
WHUP
LEMME SEE IT, TOO!
WOW!
OH WOW!

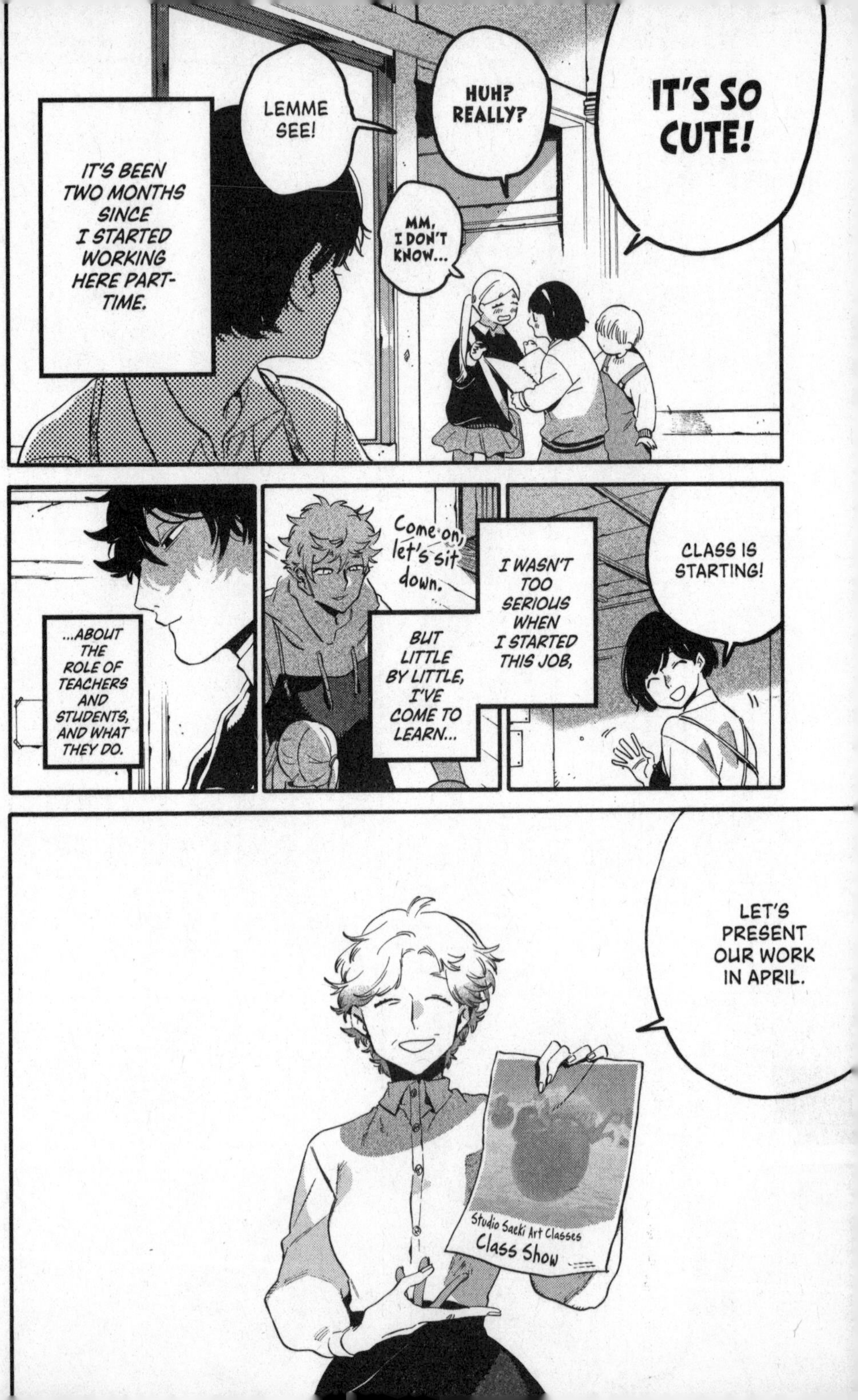
IT'S SO CUTE!
HUH? REALLY?
MM, I DON'T KNOW...
LEMME SEE!
IT'S BEEN TWO MONTHS SINCE I STARTED WORKING HERE PART-TIME.
CLASS IS STARTING!
I WASN'T TOO SERIOUS WHEN I STARTED THIS JOB,
Come on, let's sit down.
BUT LITTLE BY LITTLE, I'VE COME TO LEARN...
...ABOUT THE ROLE OF TEACHERS AND STUDENTS, AND WHAT THEY DO.
LET'S PRESENT OUR WORK IN APRIL.
Studio Saeki Art Classes
Class Show

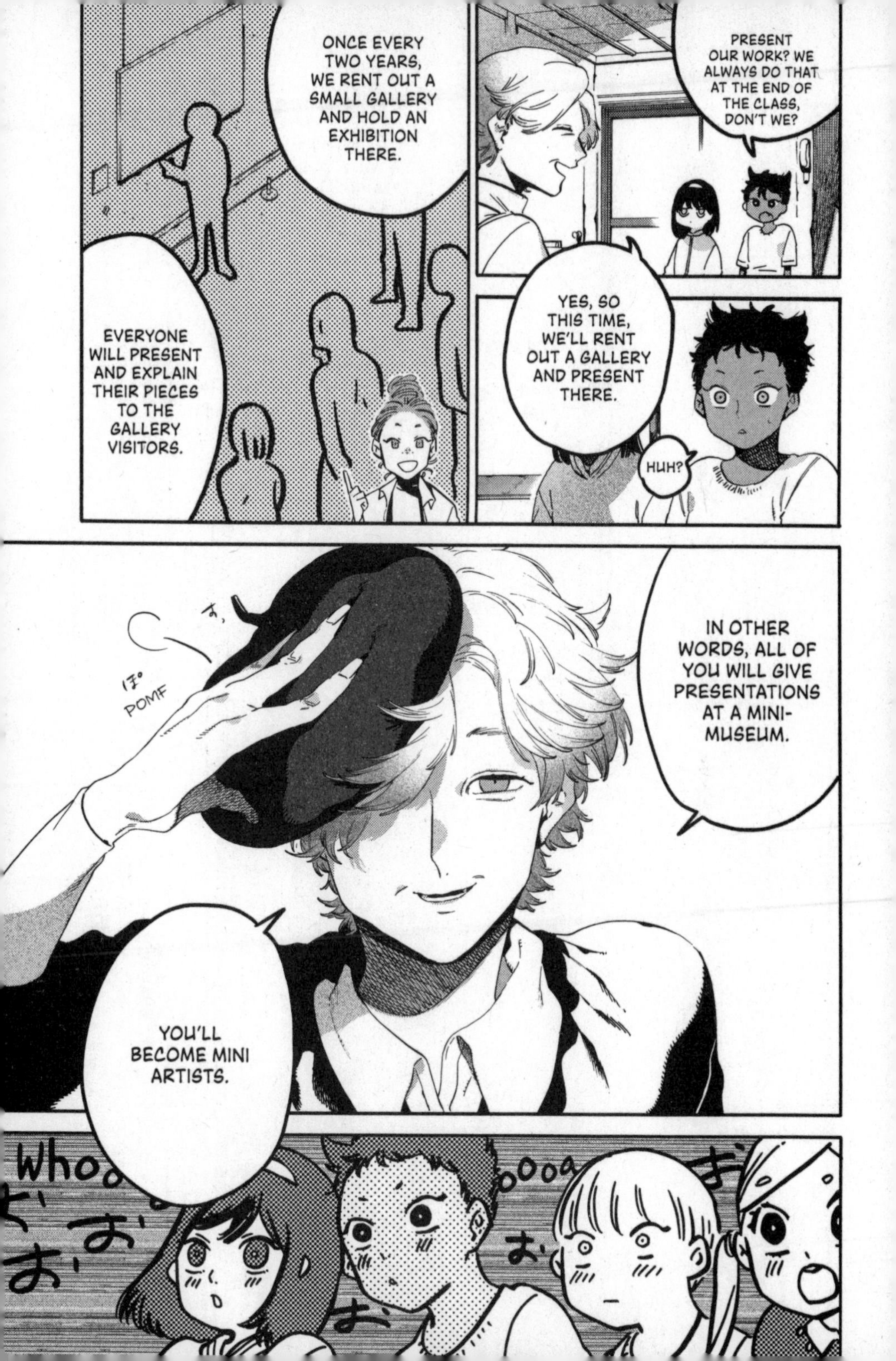
PRESENT OUR WORK? WE ALWAYS DO THAT AT THE END OF THE CLASS, DON'T WE?
YES, SO THIS TIME, WE'LL RENT OUT A GALLERY AND PRESENT THERE.
HUH?
ONCE EVERY TWO YEARS, WE RENT OUT A SMALL GALLERY AND HOLD AN EXHIBITION THERE.
EVERYONE WILL PRESENT AND EXPLAIN THEIR PIECES TO THE GALLERY VISITORS.
IN OTHER WORDS, ALL OF YOU WILL GIVE PRESENTATIONS AT A MINI-MUSEUM.
POMF
YOU'LL BECOME MINI ARTISTS.
Whoo

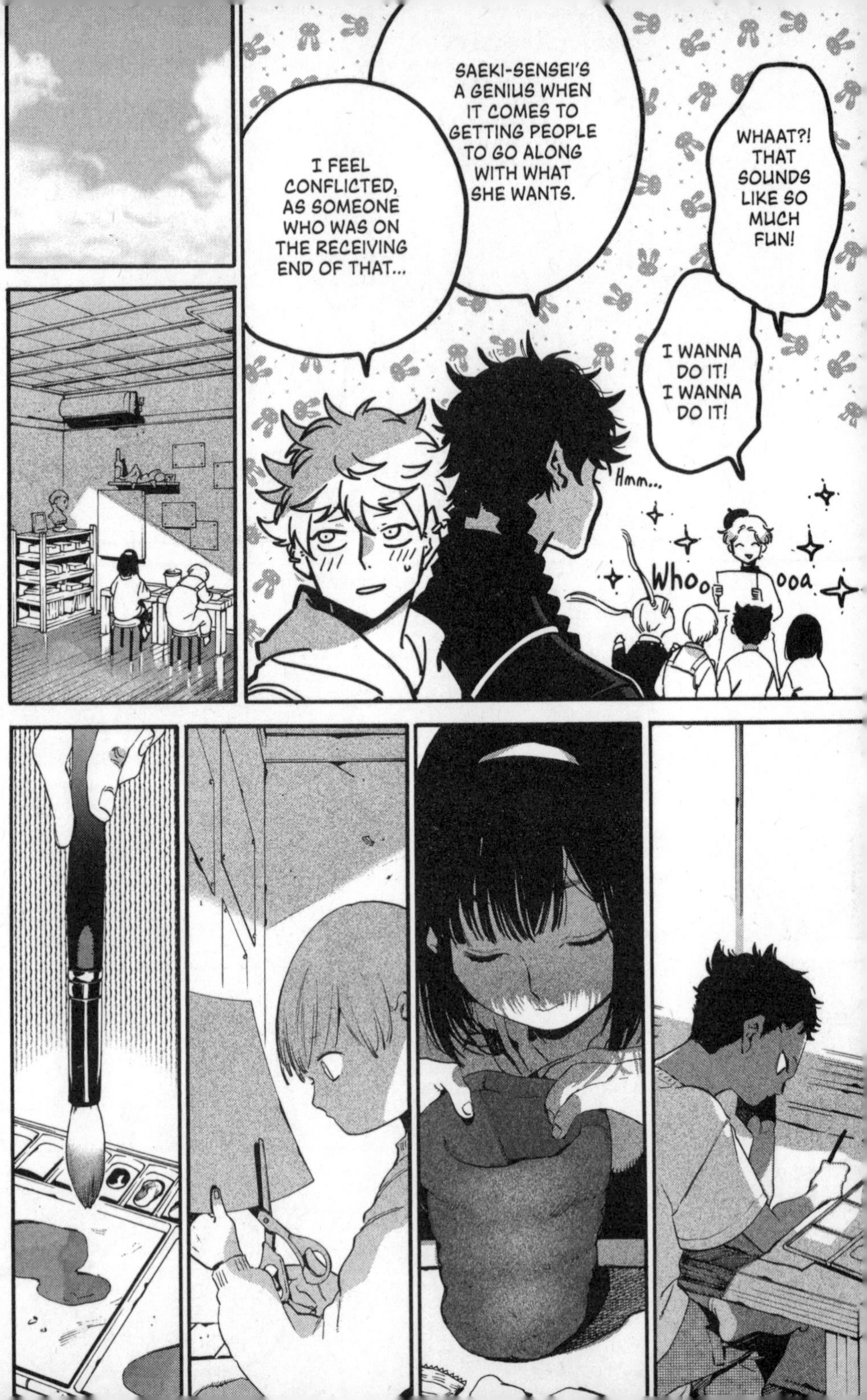
WHAAT?! THAT SOUNDS LIKE SO MUCH FUN!
I WANNA DO IT! I WANNA DO IT!
Whoooooa
Hmm...
SAEKI-SENSEI'S A GENIUS WHEN IT COMES TO GETTING PEOPLE TO GO ALONG WITH WHAT SHE WANTS.
I FEEL CONFLICTED, AS SOMEONE WHO WAS ON THE RECEIVING END OF THAT...

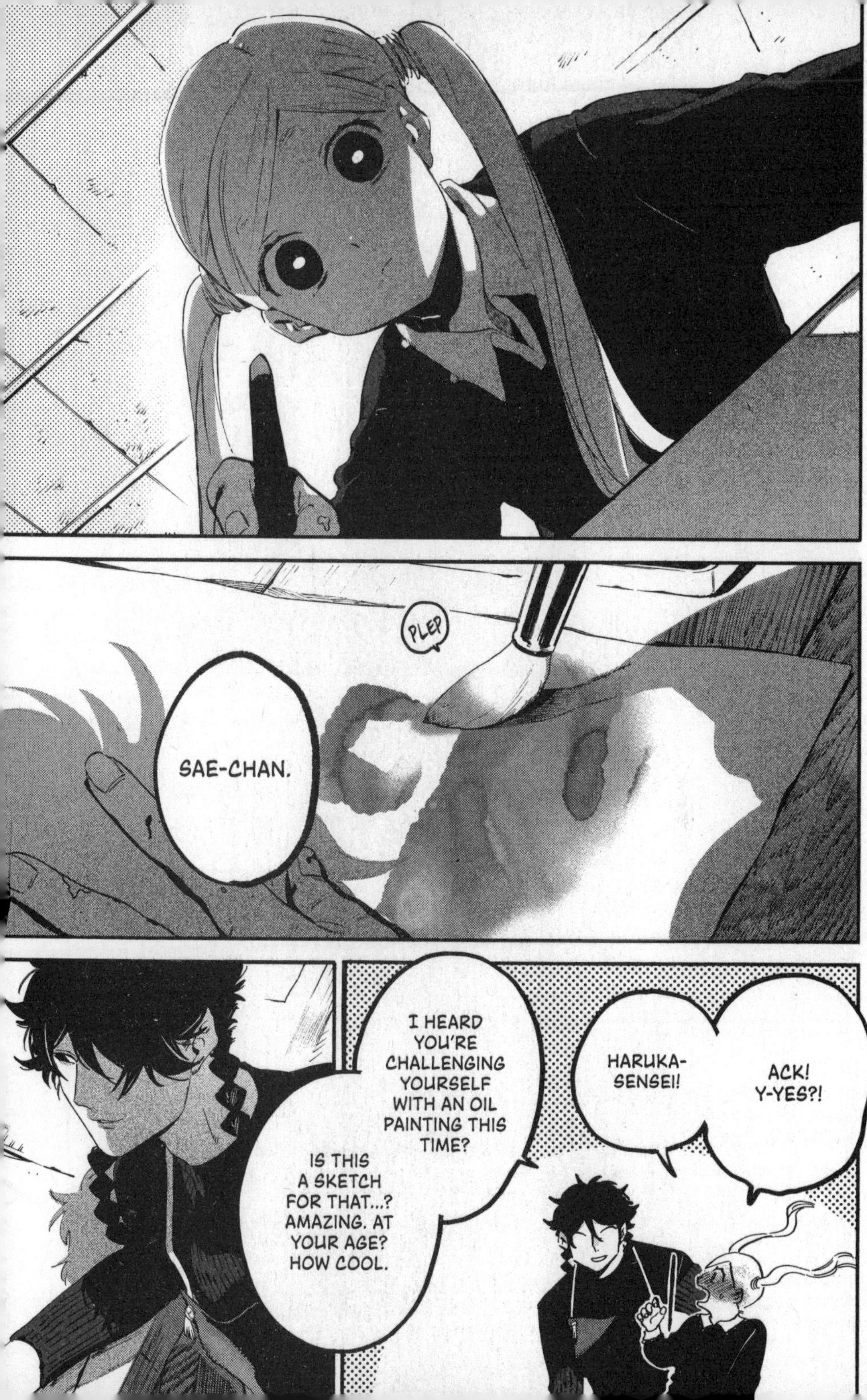
PLEP
SAE-CHAN.
ACK! Y-YES?!
HARUKA-SENSEI!
I HEARD YOU'RE CHALLENGING YOURSELF WITH AN OIL PAINTING THIS TIME?
IS THIS A SKETCH FOR THAT...? AMAZING. AT YOUR AGE? HOW COOL.

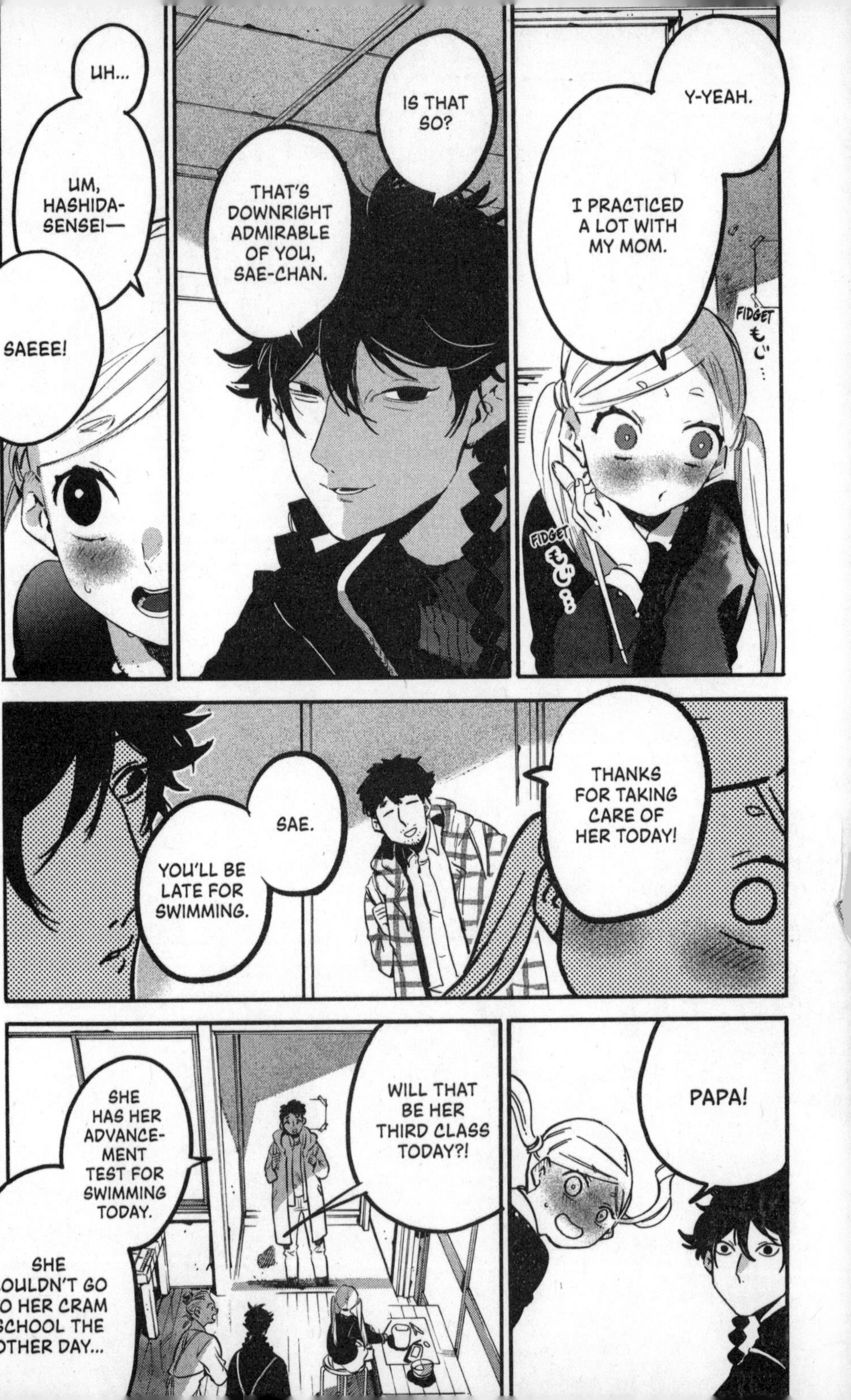
Y-YEAH.
I PRACTICED A LOT WITH MY MOM.
FIDGET もじ…
FIDGET もじ…
IS THAT SO?
THAT'S DOWNRIGHT ADMIRABLE OF YOU, SAE-CHAN.
UH...
UM, HASHIDA-SENSEI—
SAEEE!
THANKS FOR TAKING CARE OF HER TODAY!
SAE.
YOU'LL BE LATE FOR SWIMMING.
PAPA!
WILL THAT BE HER THIRD CLASS TODAY?!
SHE HAS HER ADVANCEMENT TEST FOR SWIMMING TODAY.
SHE COULDN'T GO TO HER CRAM SCHOOL THE OTHER DAY...

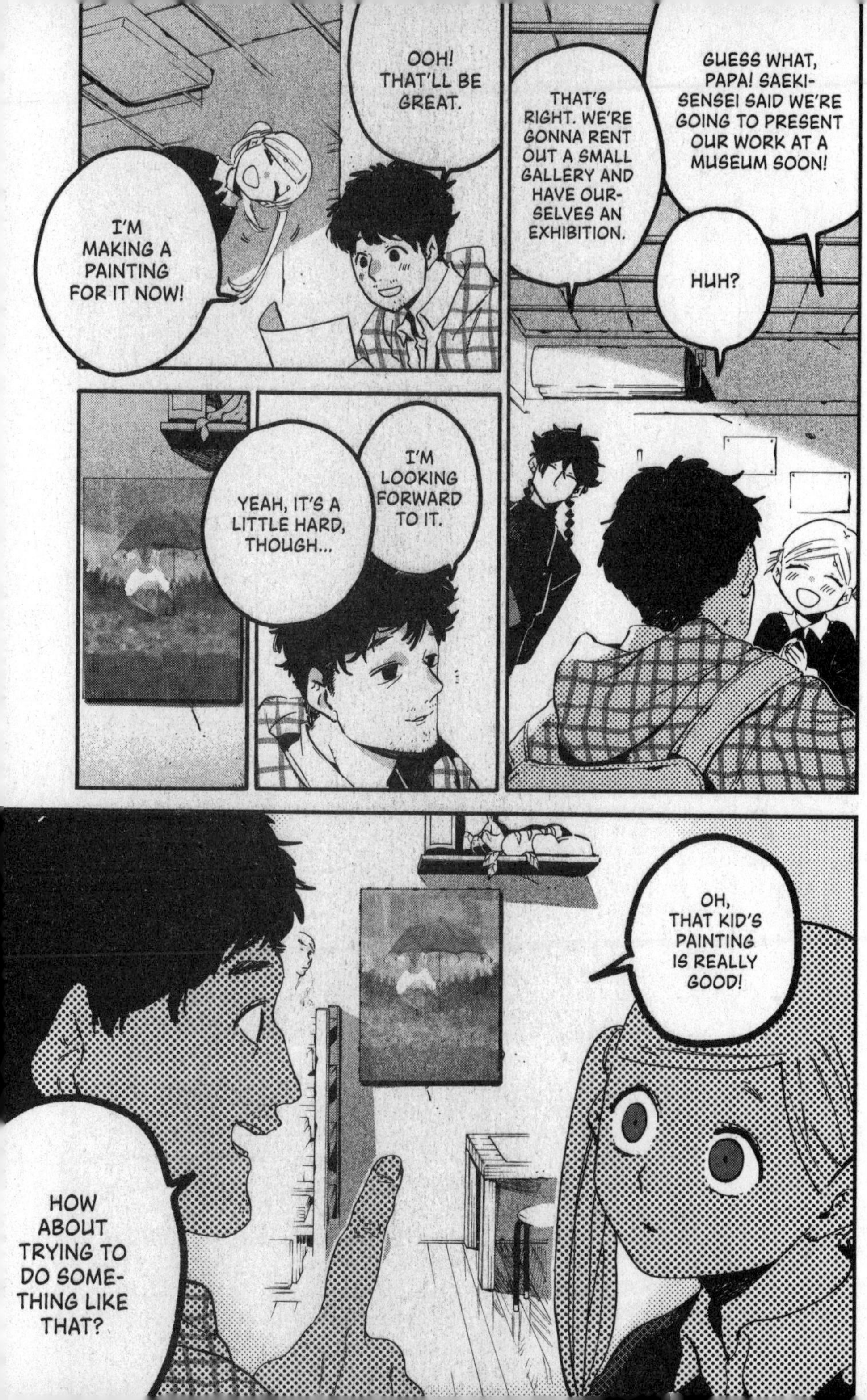
GUESS WHAT, PAPA! SAEKI-SENSEI SAID WE'RE GOING TO PRESENT OUR WORK AT A MUSEUM SOON!
THAT'S RIGHT. WE'RE GONNA RENT OUT A SMALL GALLERY AND HAVE OURSELVES AN EXHIBITION.
HUH?
OOH! THAT'LL BE GREAT.
I'M MAKING A PAINTING FOR IT NOW!
I'M LOOKING FORWARD TO IT.
YEAH, IT'S A LITTLE HARD, THOUGH...
OH, THAT KID'S PAINTING IS REALLY GOOD!
HOW ABOUT TRYING TO DO SOMETHING LIKE THAT?

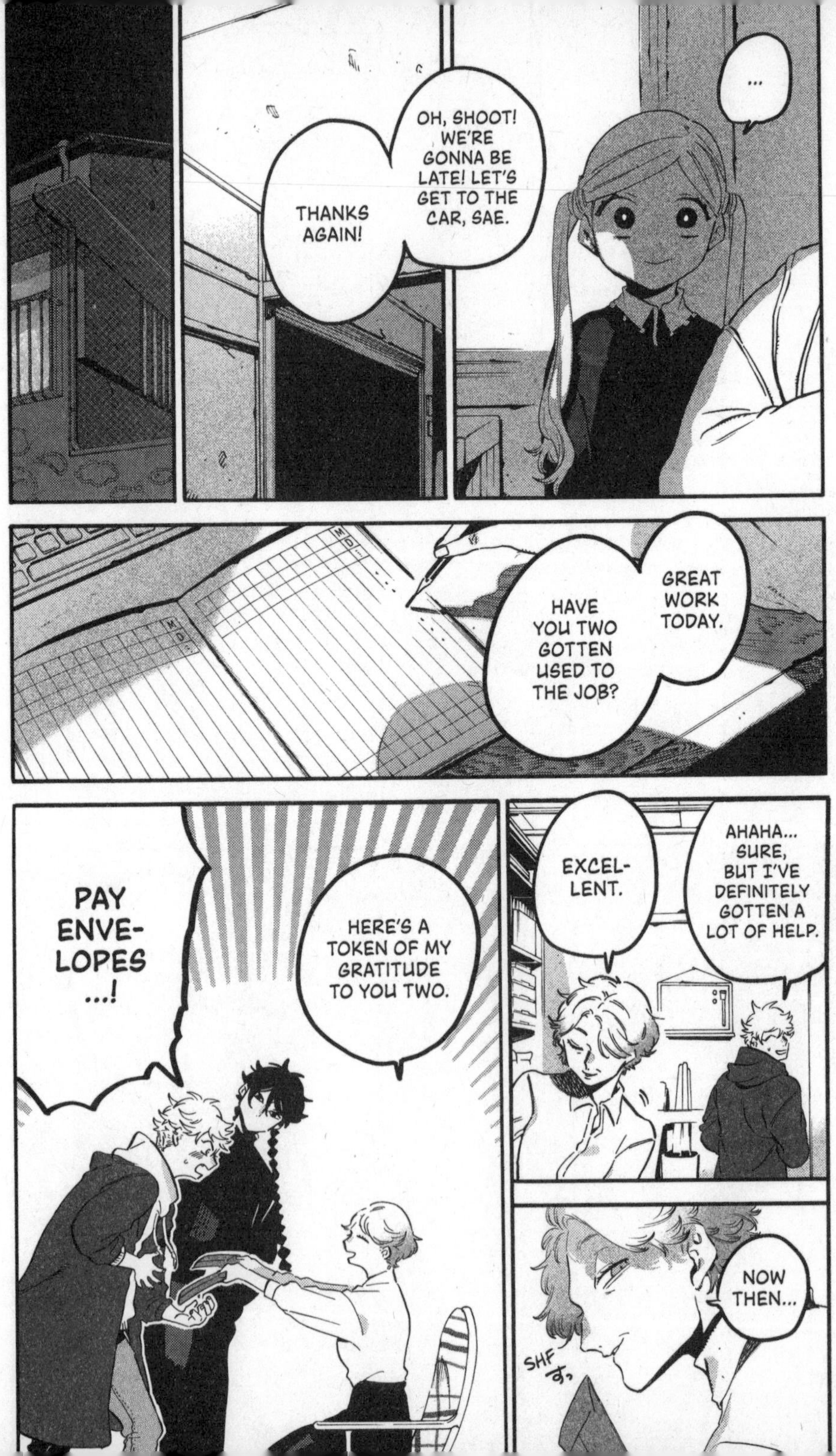
...
OH, SHOOT! WE'RE GONNA BE LATE! LET'S GET TO THE CAR, SAE.
THANKS AGAIN!
GREAT WORK TODAY.
HAVE YOU TWO GOTTEN USED TO THE JOB?
AHAHA... SURE, BUT I'VE DEFINITELY GOTTEN A LOT OF HELP.
EXCEL-LENT.
NOW THEN...
SHF
HERE'S A TOKEN OF MY GRATITUDE TO YOU TWO.
PAY ENVE-LOPES ...!

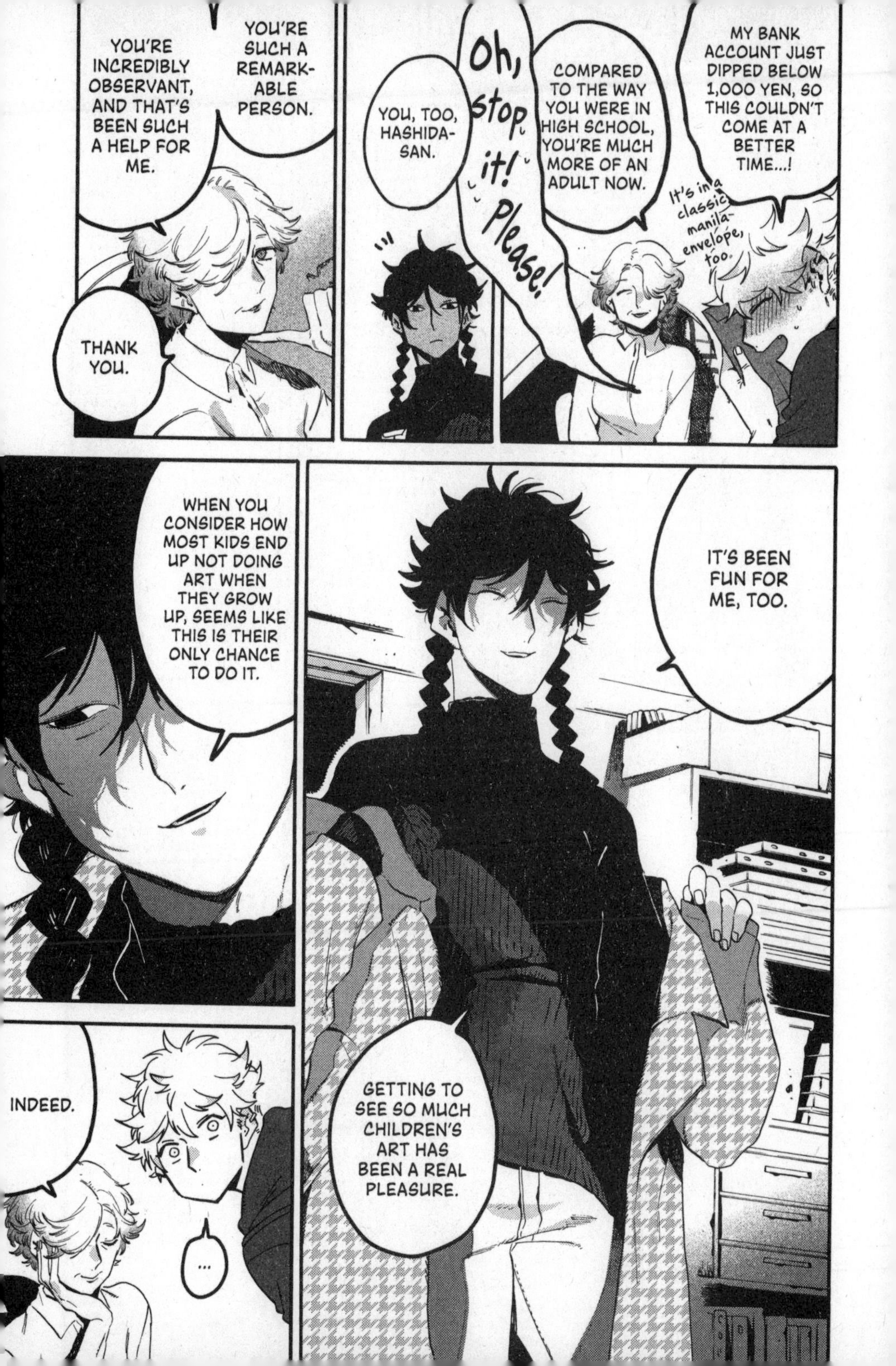
MY BANK ACCOUNT JUST DIPPED BELOW 1,000 YEN, SO THIS COULDN'T COME AT A BETTER TIME...!
It's in a classic manila envelope, too.
COMPARED TO THE WAY YOU WERE IN HIGH SCHOOL, YOU'RE MUCH MORE OF AN ADULT NOW.
Oh, stop it! Please!
YOU, TOO, HASHIDA-SAN.
YOU'RE SUCH A REMARKABLE PERSON.
YOU'RE INCREDIBLY OBSERVANT, AND THAT'S BEEN SUCH A HELP FOR ME.
THANK YOU.
IT'S BEEN FUN FOR ME, TOO.
GETTING TO SEE SO MUCH CHILDREN'S ART HAS BEEN A REAL PLEASURE.
WHEN YOU CONSIDER HOW MOST KIDS END UP NOT DOING ART WHEN THEY GROW UP, SEEMS LIKE THIS IS THEIR ONLY CHANCE TO DO IT.
INDEED.
...

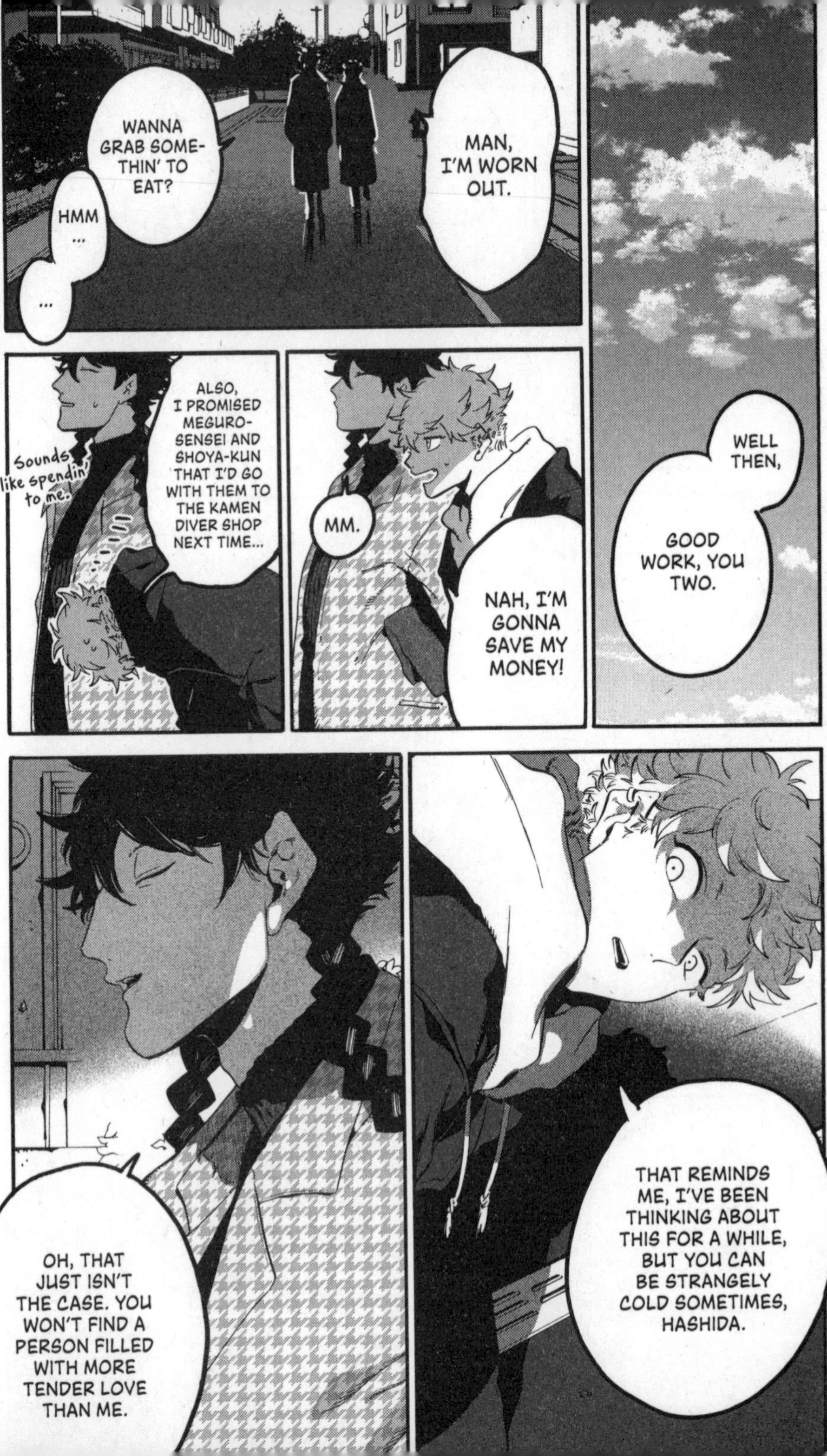
WELL THEN,
GOOD WORK, YOU TWO.
MAN, I'M WORN OUT.
WANNA GRAB SOME-THIN' TO EAT?
HMM ...
...
NAH, I'M GONNA SAVE MY MONEY!
MM.
ALSO, I PROMISED MEGURO-SENSEI AND SHOYA-KUN THAT I'D GO WITH THEM TO THE KAMEN DIVER SHOP NEXT TIME...
Sounds like spendin' to me.
THAT REMINDS ME, I'VE BEEN THINKING ABOUT THIS FOR A WHILE, BUT YOU CAN BE STRANGELY COLD SOMETIMES, HASHIDA.
OH, THAT JUST ISN'T THE CASE. YOU WON'T FIND A PERSON FILLED WITH MORE TENDER LOVE THAN ME.

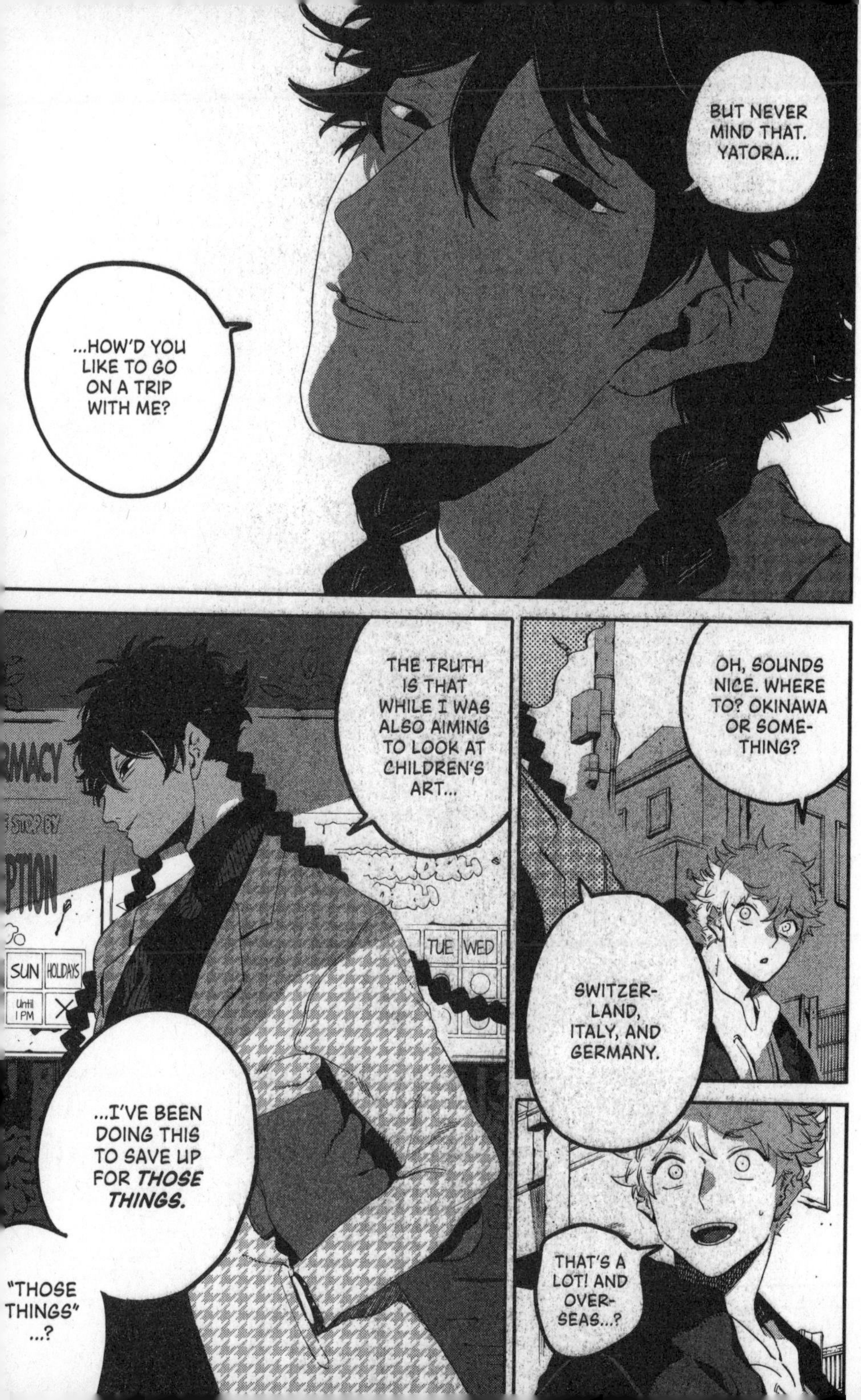
BUT NEVER MIND THAT. YATORA...
...HOW'D YOU LIKE TO GO ON A TRIP WITH ME?
OH, SOUNDS NICE. WHERE TO? OKINAWA OR SOME-THING?
SWITZER-LAND, ITALY, AND GERMANY.
THAT'S A LOT! AND OVER-SEAS...?
THE TRUTH IS THAT WHILE I WAS ALSO AIMING TO LOOK AT CHILDREN'S ART...
SUN
HOLIDAYS
Until 1 PM
TUE
WED
...I'VE BEEN DOING THIS TO SAVE UP FOR *THOSE THINGS.*
"THOSE THINGS" ...?

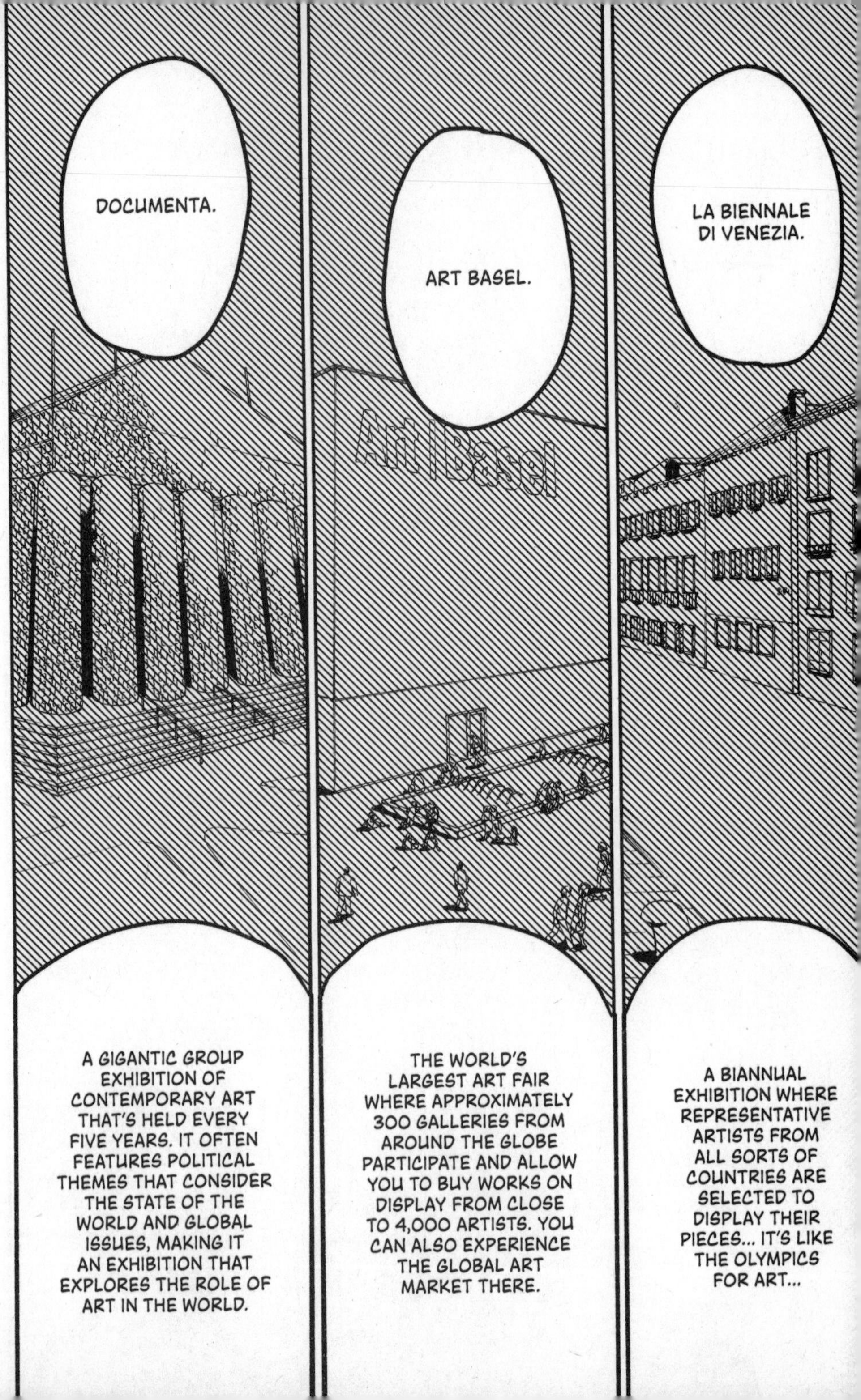
LA BIENNALE DI VENEZIA.
A BIANNUAL EXHIBITION WHERE REPRESENTATIVE ARTISTS FROM ALL SORTS OF COUNTRIES ARE SELECTED TO DISPLAY THEIR PIECES... IT'S LIKE THE OLYMPICS FOR ART...
ART BASEL.
Art Basel
THE WORLD'S LARGEST ART FAIR WHERE APPROXIMATELY 300 GALLERIES FROM AROUND THE GLOBE PARTICIPATE AND ALLOW YOU TO BUY WORKS ON DISPLAY FROM CLOSE TO 4,000 ARTISTS. YOU CAN ALSO EXPERIENCE THE GLOBAL ART MARKET THERE.
DOCUMENTA.
A GIGANTIC GROUP EXHIBITION OF CONTEMPORARY ART THAT'S HELD EVERY FIVE YEARS. IT OFTEN FEATURES POLITICAL THEMES THAT CONSIDER THE STATE OF THE WORLD AND GLOBAL ISSUES, MAKING IT AN EXHIBITION THAT EXPLORES THE ROLE OF ART IN THE WORLD.

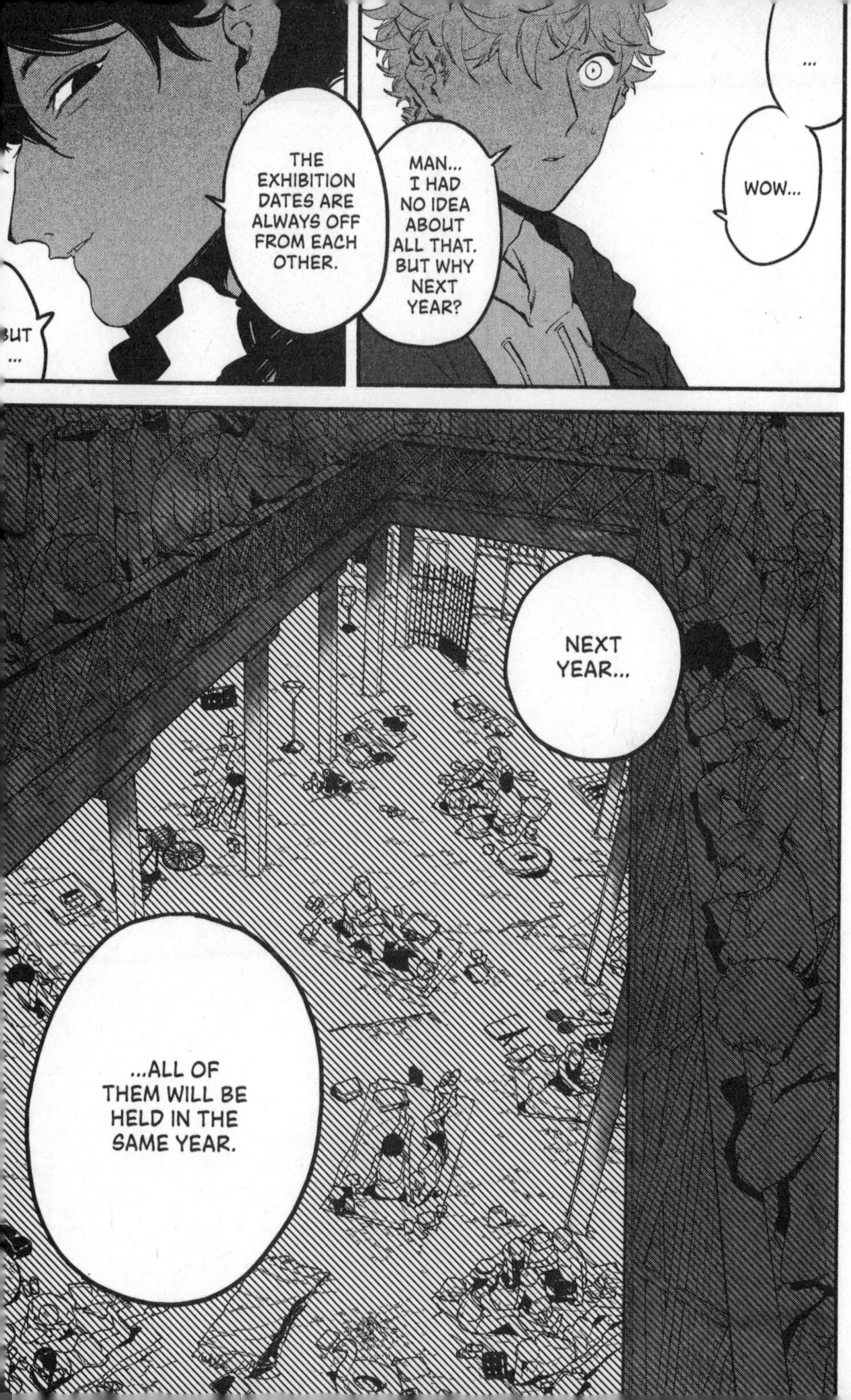
...
WOW...
MAN... I HAD NO IDEA ABOUT ALL THAT. BUT WHY NEXT YEAR?
THE EXHIBITION DATES ARE ALWAYS OFF FROM EACH OTHER.
BUT ...
NEXT YEAR...
...ALL OF THEM WILL BE HELD IN THE SAME YEAR.

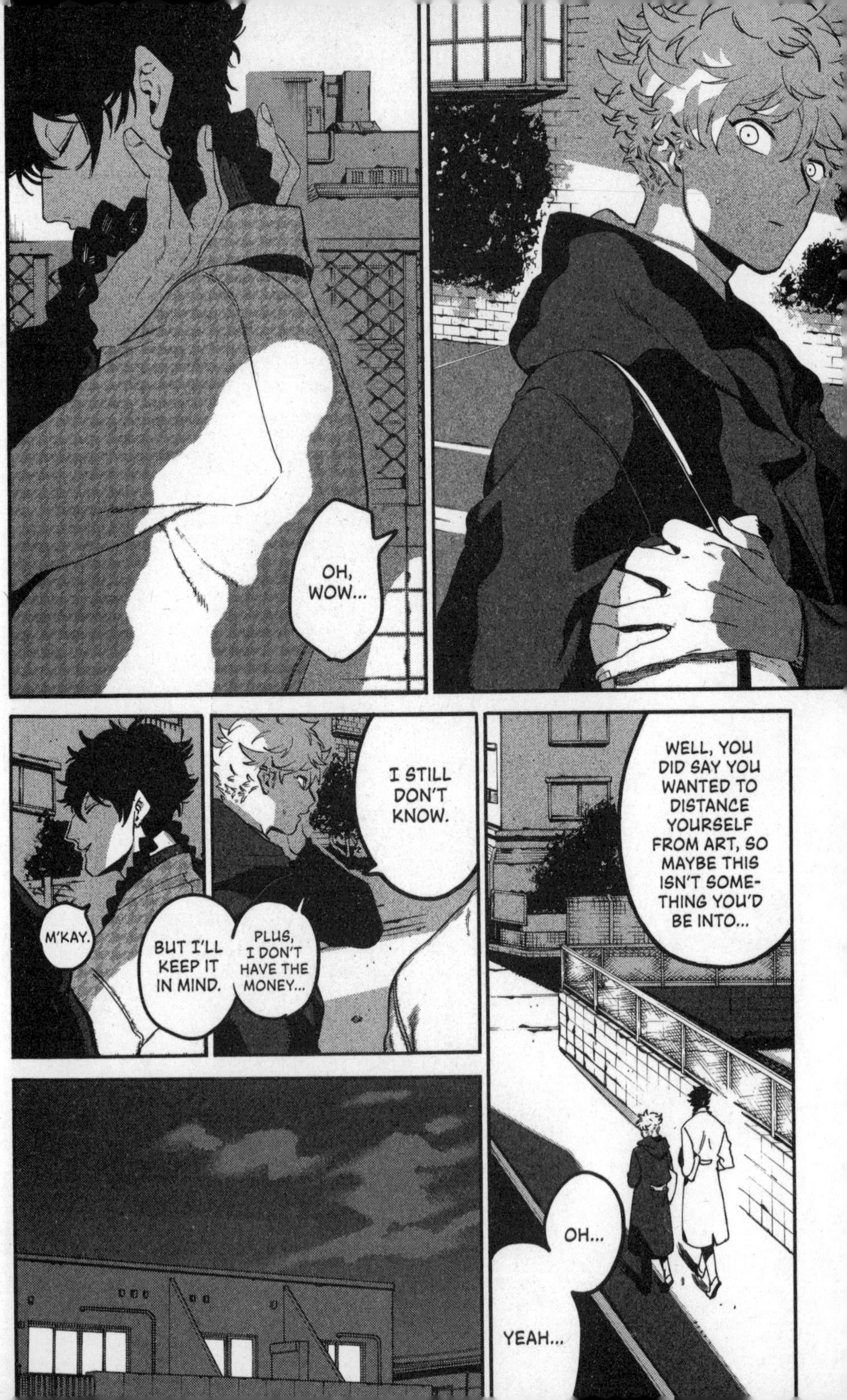
OH, WOW...
WELL, YOU DID SAY YOU WANTED TO DISTANCE YOURSELF FROM ART, SO MAYBE THIS ISN'T SOME-THING YOU'D BE INTO...
OH...
YEAH...
I STILL DON'T KNOW.
PLUS, I DON'T HAVE THE MONEY...
BUT I'LL KEEP IT IN MIND.
M'KAY.

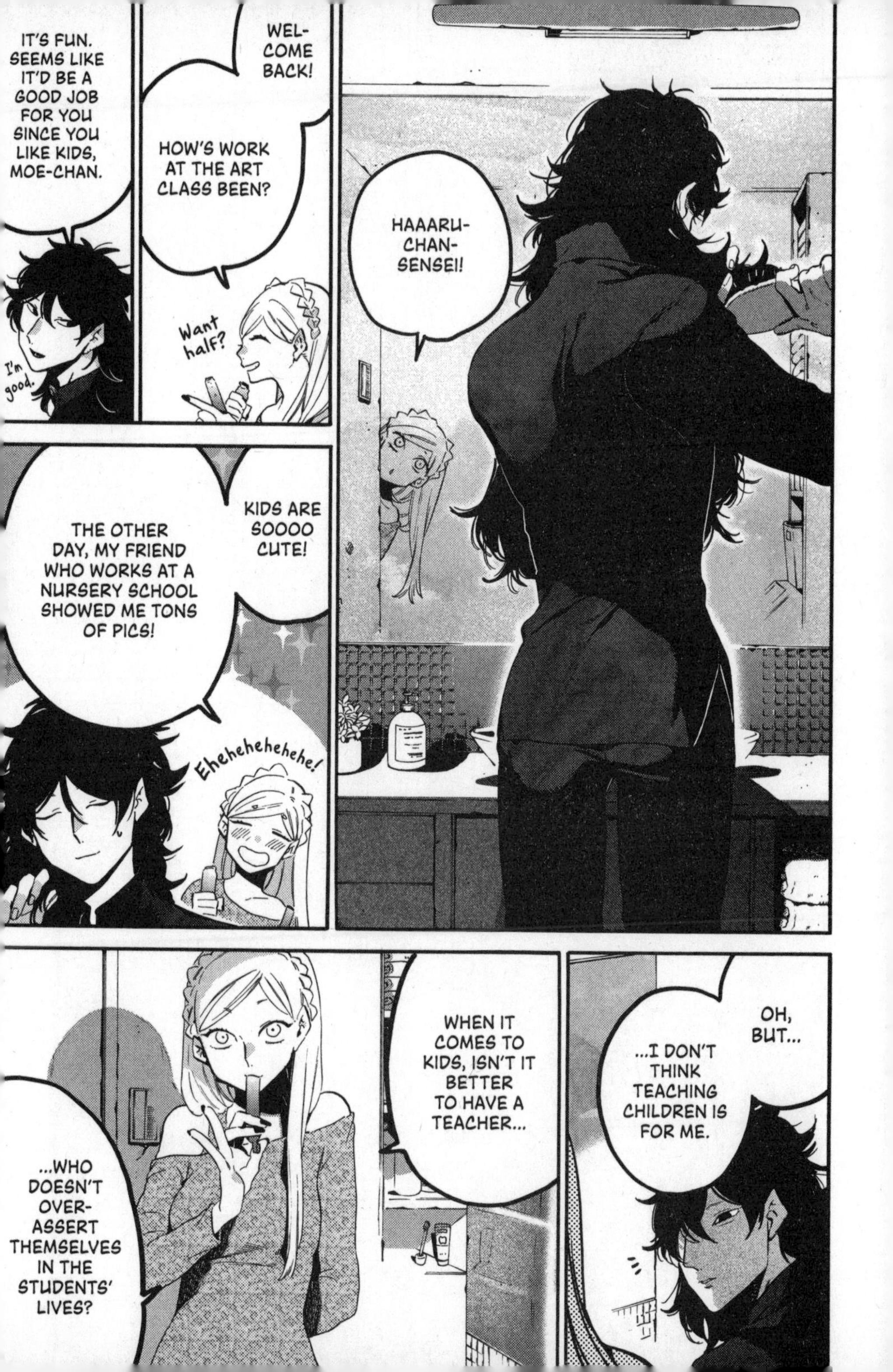
HAAARU-CHAN-SENSEI!
WEL-COME BACK!
HOW'S WORK AT THE ART CLASS BEEN?
Want half?
IT'S FUN. SEEMS LIKE IT'D BE A GOOD JOB FOR YOU SINCE YOU LIKE KIDS, MOE-CHAN.
I'm good.
KIDS ARE SOOOO CUTE!
THE OTHER DAY, MY FRIEND WHO WORKS AT A NURSERY SCHOOL SHOWED ME TONS OF PICS!
Ehehehehehehe!
OH, BUT...
...I DON'T THINK TEACHING CHILDREN IS FOR ME.
WHEN IT COMES TO KIDS, ISN'T IT BETTER TO HAVE A TEACHER...
...WHO DOESN'T OVER-ASSERT THEMSELVES IN THE STUDENTS' LIVES?

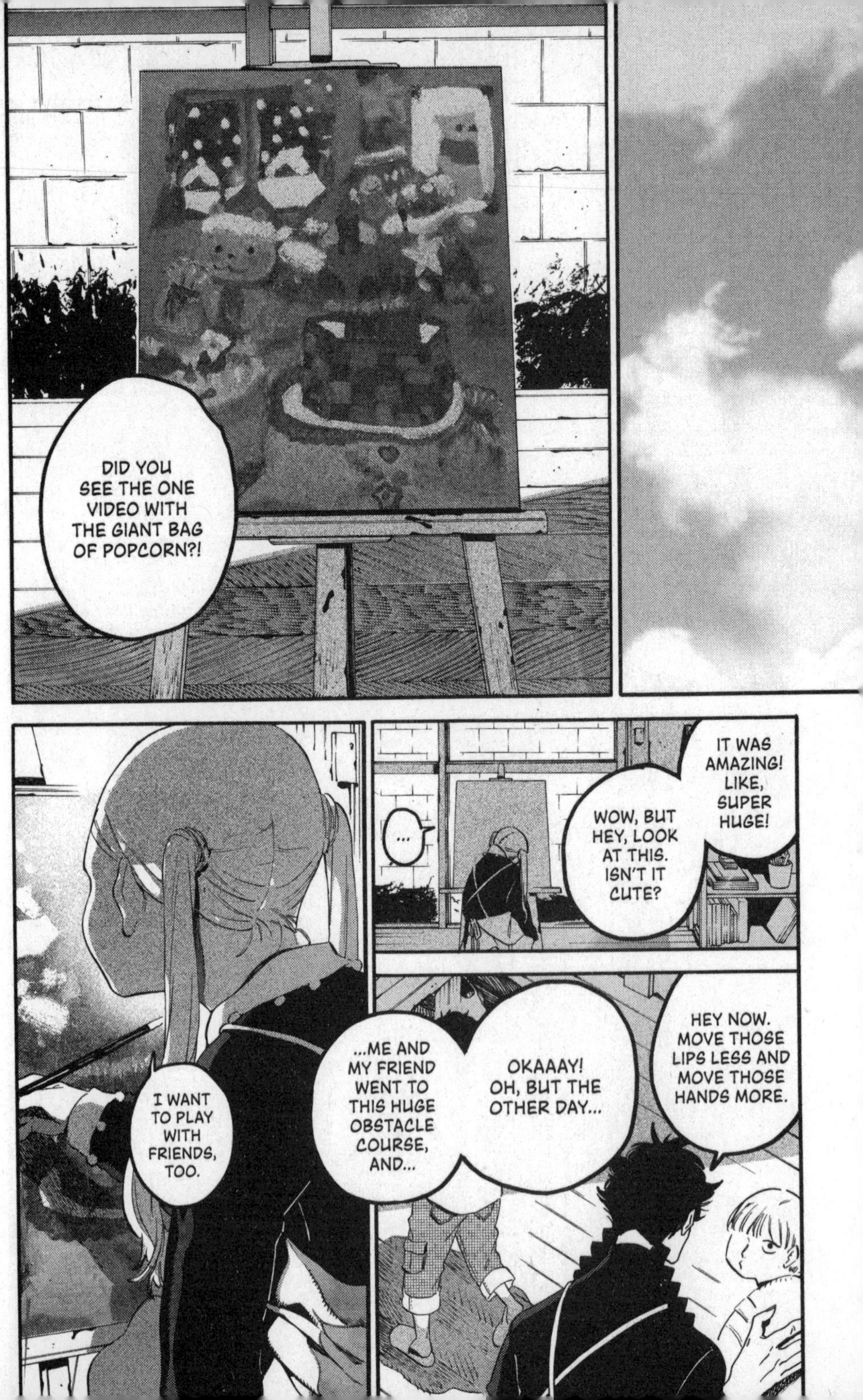
DID YOU SEE THE ONE VIDEO WITH THE GIANT BAG OF POPCORN?!
IT WAS AMAZING! LIKE, SUPER HUGE!
WOW, BUT HEY, LOOK AT THIS. ISN'T IT CUTE?
...
HEY NOW. MOVE THOSE LIPS LESS AND MOVE THOSE HANDS MORE.
OKAAAY! OH, BUT THE OTHER DAY...
...ME AND MY FRIEND WENT TO THIS HUGE OBSTACLE COURSE, AND...
I WANT TO PLAY WITH FRIENDS, TOO.

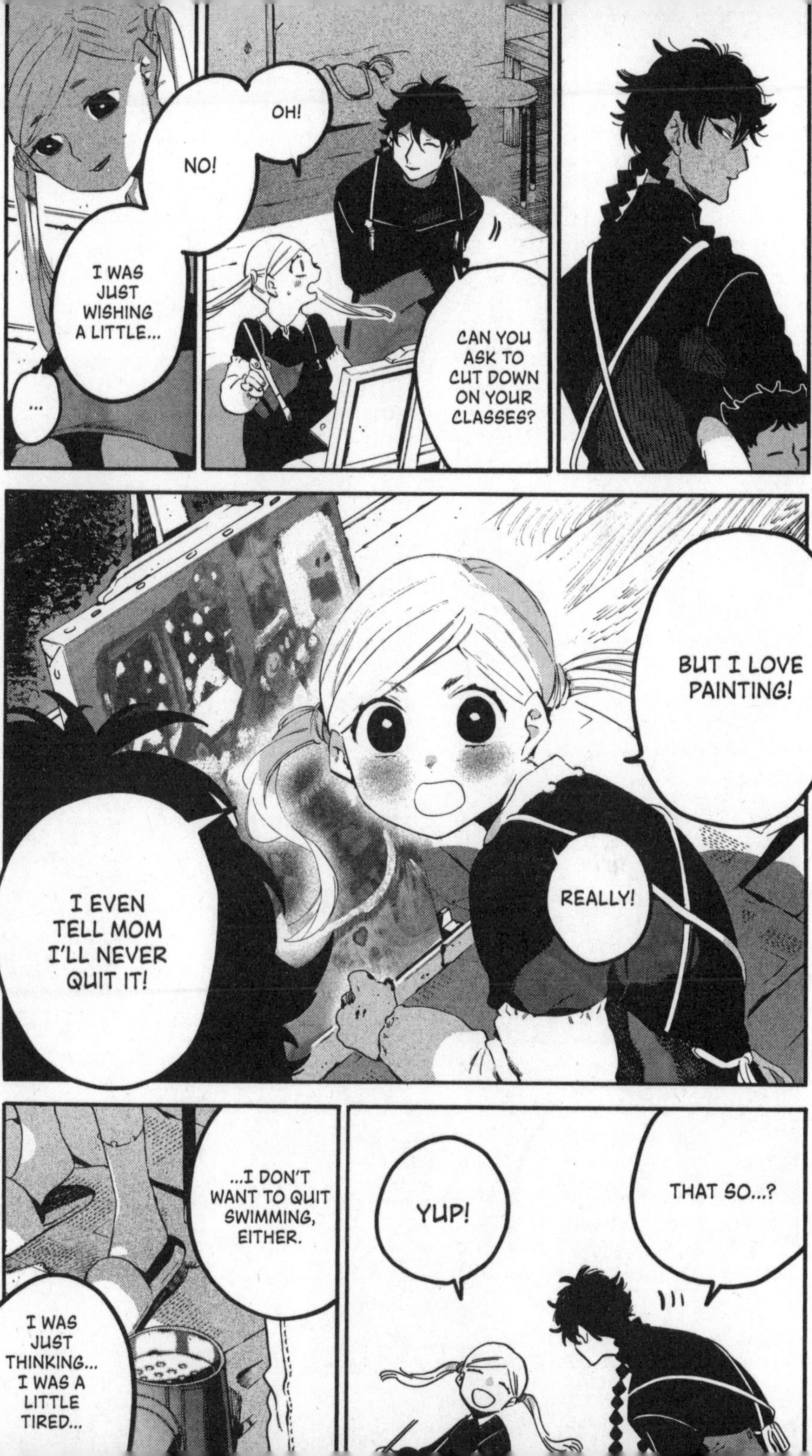
CAN YOU ASK TO CUT DOWN ON YOUR CLASSES?
OH!
NO!
I WAS JUST WISHING A LITTLE...
...
BUT I LOVE PAINTING!
REALLY!
I EVEN TELL MOM I'LL NEVER QUIT IT!
THAT SO...?
YUP!
...I DON'T WANT TO QUIT SWIMMING, EITHER.
I WAS JUST THINKING... I WAS A LITTLE TIRED...

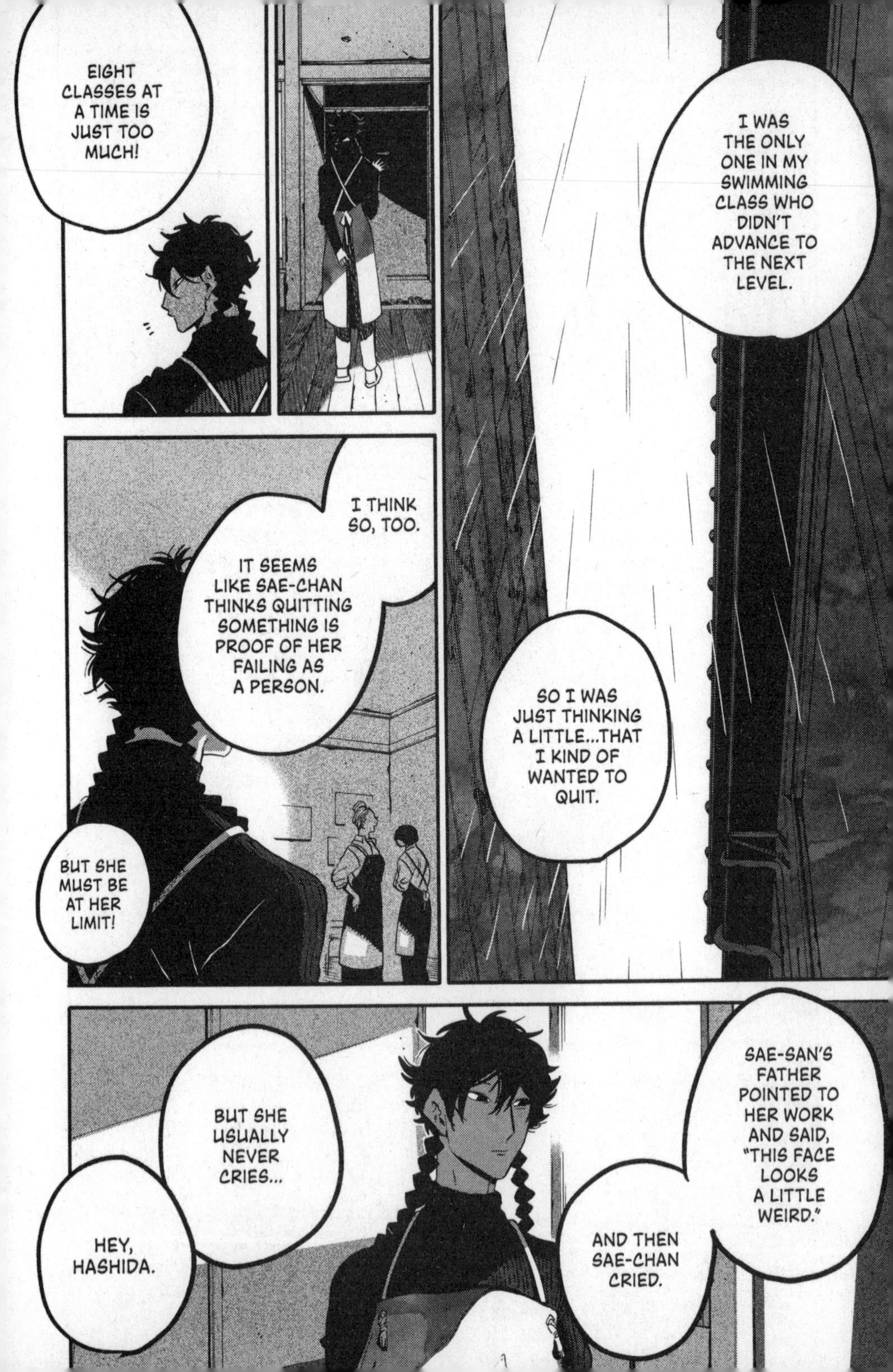
I WAS THE ONLY ONE IN MY SWIMMING CLASS WHO DIDN'T ADVANCE TO THE NEXT LEVEL.
SO I WAS JUST THINKING A LITTLE...THAT I KIND OF WANTED TO QUIT.
EIGHT CLASSES AT A TIME IS JUST TOO MUCH!
I THINK SO, TOO.
IT SEEMS LIKE SAE-CHAN THINKS QUITTING SOMETHING IS PROOF OF HER FAILING AS A PERSON.
BUT SHE MUST BE AT HER LIMIT!
SAE-SAN'S FATHER POINTED TO HER WORK AND SAID, "THIS FACE LOOKS A LITTLE WEIRD."
AND THEN SAE-CHAN CRIED.
BUT SHE USUALLY NEVER CRIES...
HEY, HASHIDA.

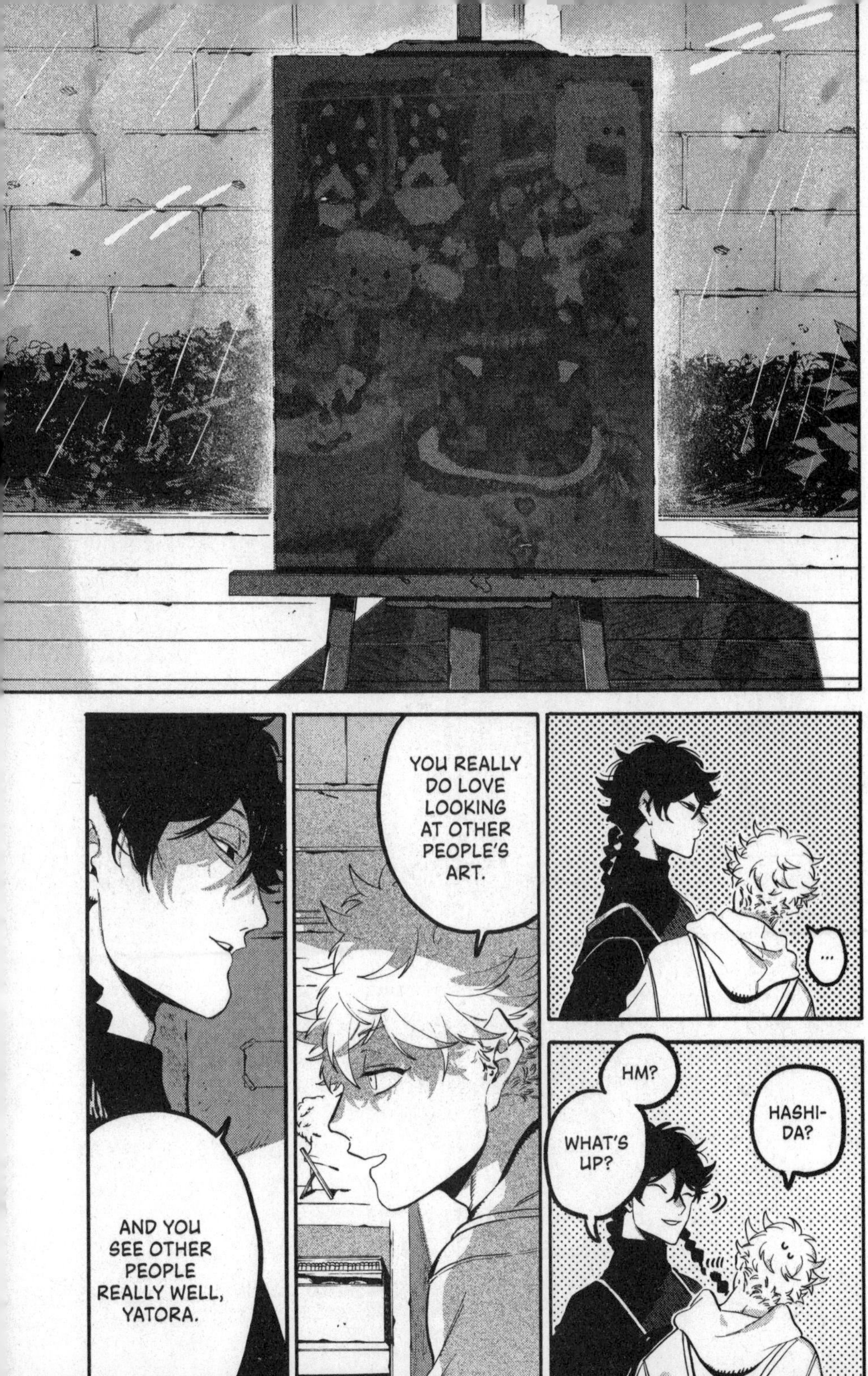
...
HASHI-DA?
HM?
WHAT'S UP?
YOU REALLY DO LOVE LOOKING AT OTHER PEOPLE'S ART.
AND YOU SEE OTHER PEOPLE REALLY WELL, YATORA.

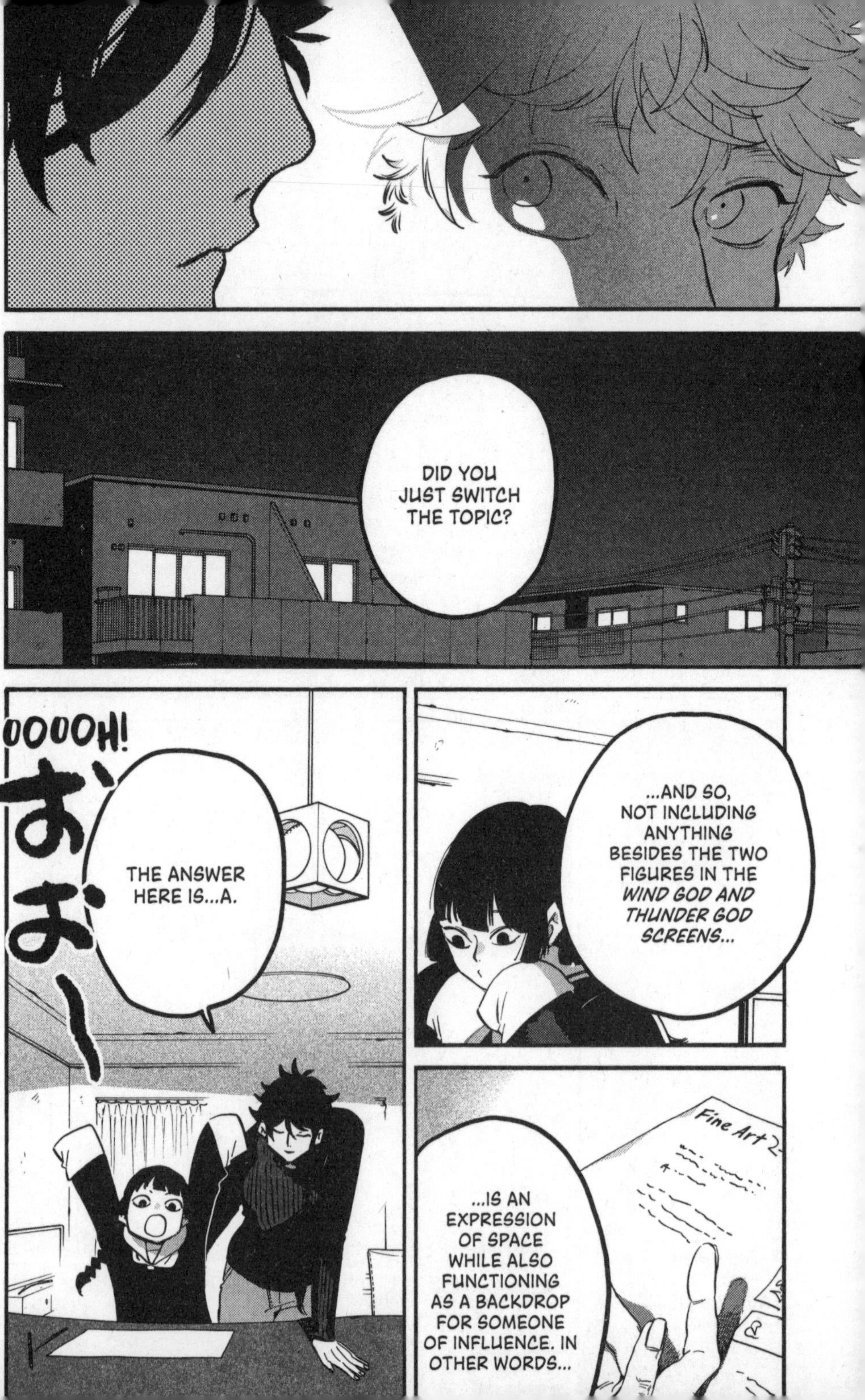
DID YOU JUST SWITCH THE TOPIC?
...AND SO, NOT INCLUDING ANYTHING BESIDES THE TWO FIGURES IN THE *WIND GOD AND THUNDER GOD SCREENS*...
Fine Art
...IS AN EXPRESSION OF SPACE WHILE ALSO FUNCTIONING AS A BACKDROP FOR SOMEONE OF INFLUENCE. IN OTHER WORDS...
THE ANSWER HERE IS...A.
OOOOH!
おお〜

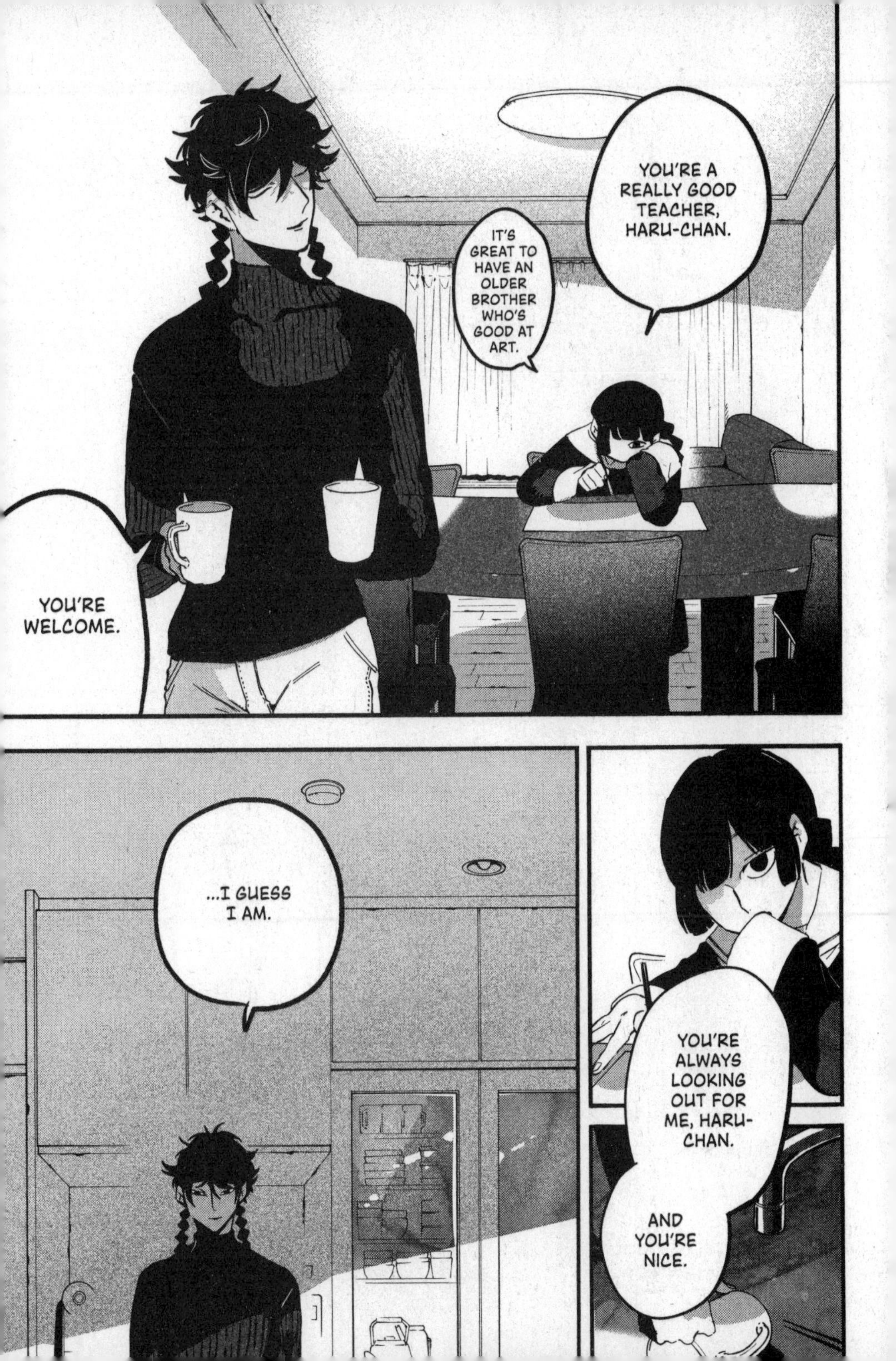
YOU'RE A REALLY GOOD TEACHER, HARU-CHAN.
IT'S GREAT TO HAVE AN OLDER BROTHER WHO'S GOOD AT ART.
YOU'RE WELCOME.
YOU'RE ALWAYS LOOKING OUT FOR ME, HARU-CHAN.
AND YOU'RE NICE.
...I GUESS I AM.

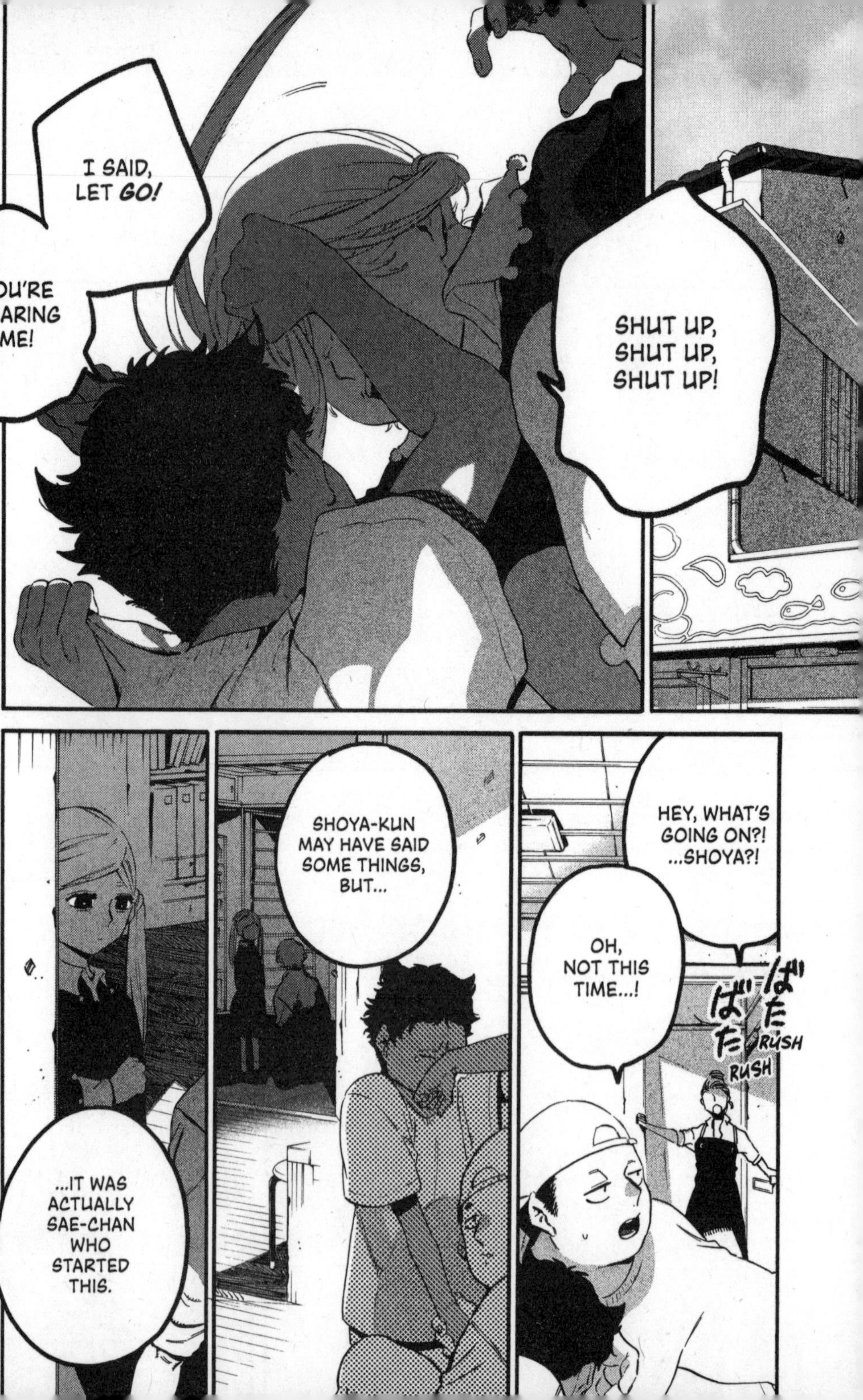
I SAID, LET GO!
YOU'RE SCARING ME!
SHUT UP, SHUT UP, SHUT UP!
HEY, WHAT'S GOING ON?! ...SHOYA?!
OH, NOT THIS TIME...!
ばたばた RUSH RUSH
SHOYA-KUN MAY HAVE SAID SOME THINGS, BUT...
...IT WAS ACTUALLY SAE-CHAN WHO STARTED THIS.

SOMETHING'S BEEN WRONG WITH SAE-CHAN LATELY...

COULD IT BE THAT SAE-CHAN'S PARENTS ARE ACTUALLY BAD PEOPLE?

NO.

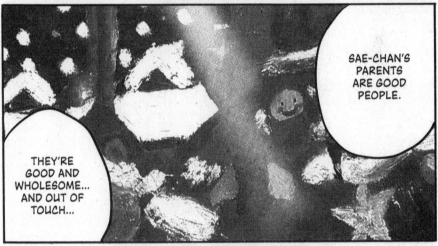

SAE-CHAN'S PARENTS ARE GOOD PEOPLE.

THEY'RE GOOD AND WHOLESOME... AND OUT OF TOUCH...

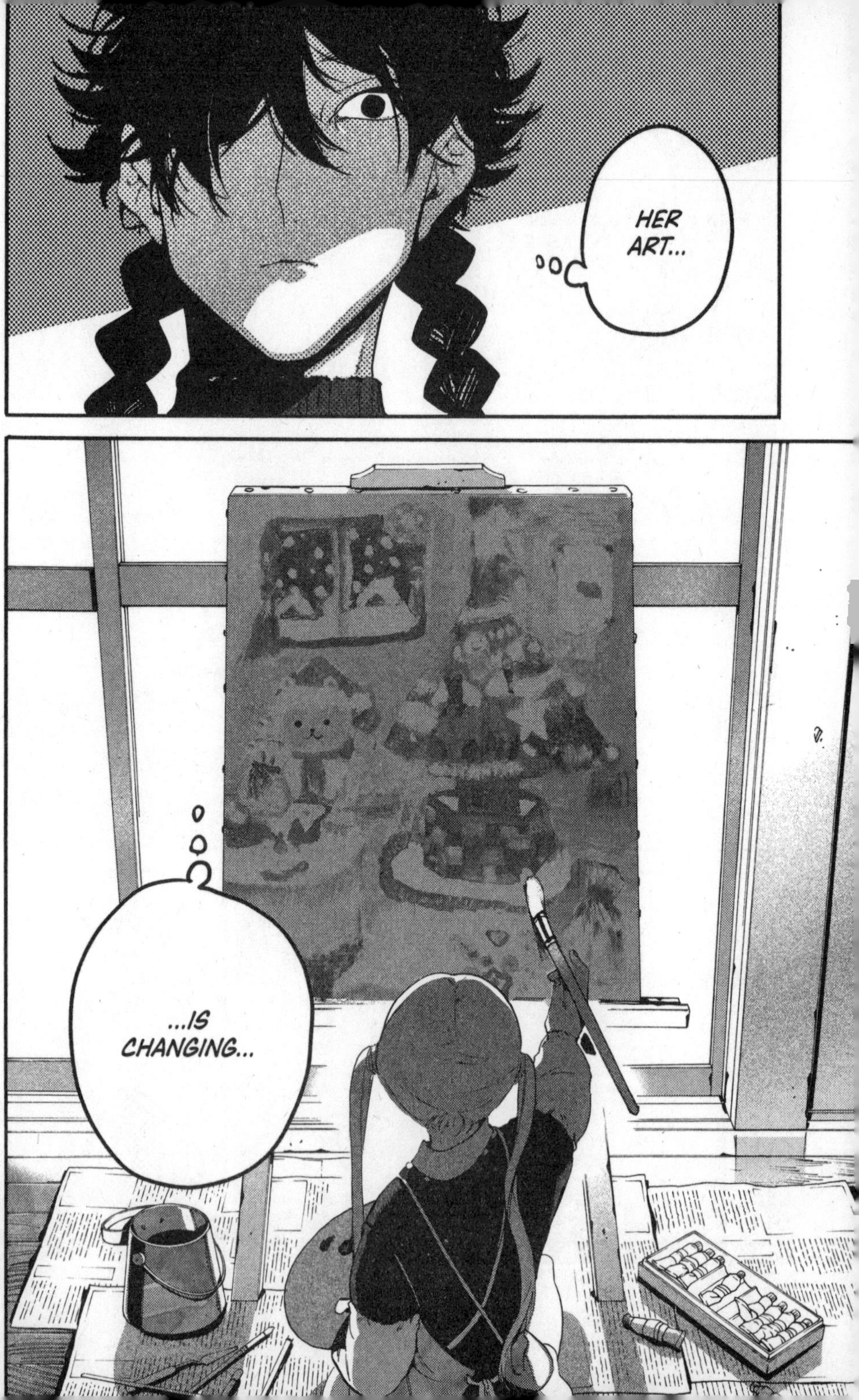
HER ART...
...IS CHANGING...

STROKE 46 END

Armed Legend

MAGENDER

One day, Kento, the second-born son in a family that runs a prestigious Kendo dojo, was visited by a mysterious man who came to lay waste to the dojo. This mysterious man fights to resurrect demons and has the ability to drain the life force out of those he defeats, turning them into lifeless beings. Just then, Kento found a mysterious sword in his shed—a sword that was once bequeathed to his ancestors by the imperial court. As he drew this sword that would give him the power to fight back against the demons, light filled the room... And from that moment on, Kento gained the ability to transform into "Magender"...

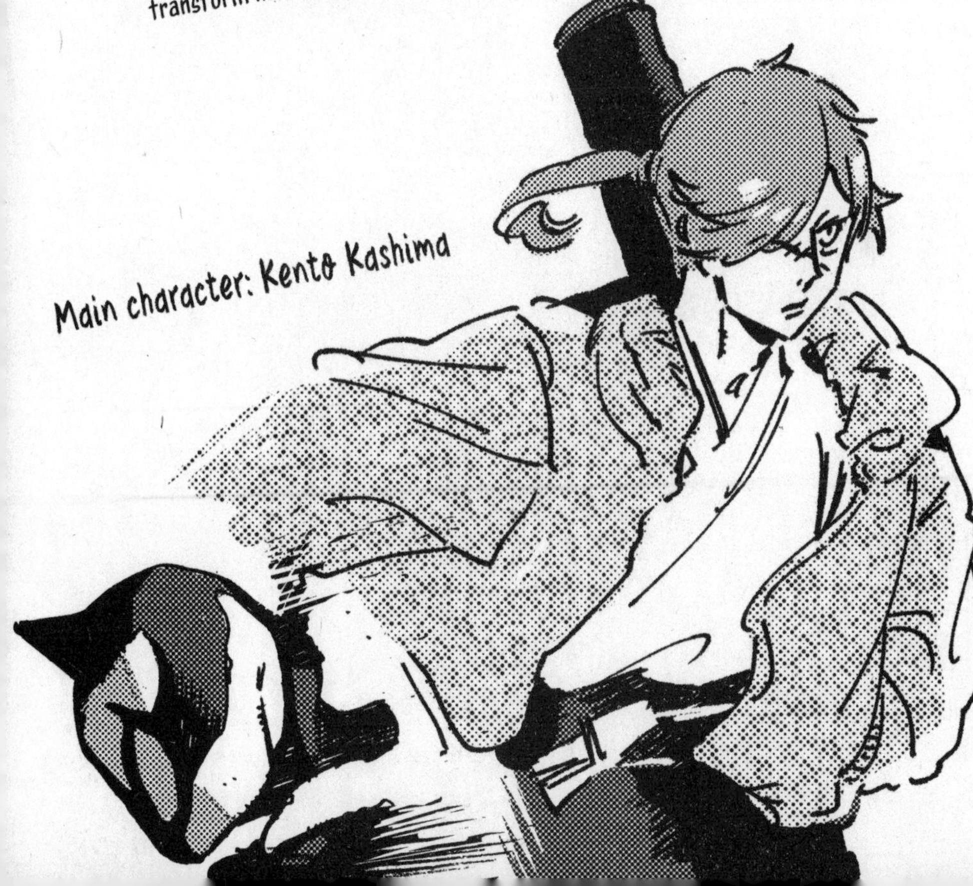

Main character: Kento Kashima

BLUE PERIOD

STROKE 47 SHAKY BRUSH TIP

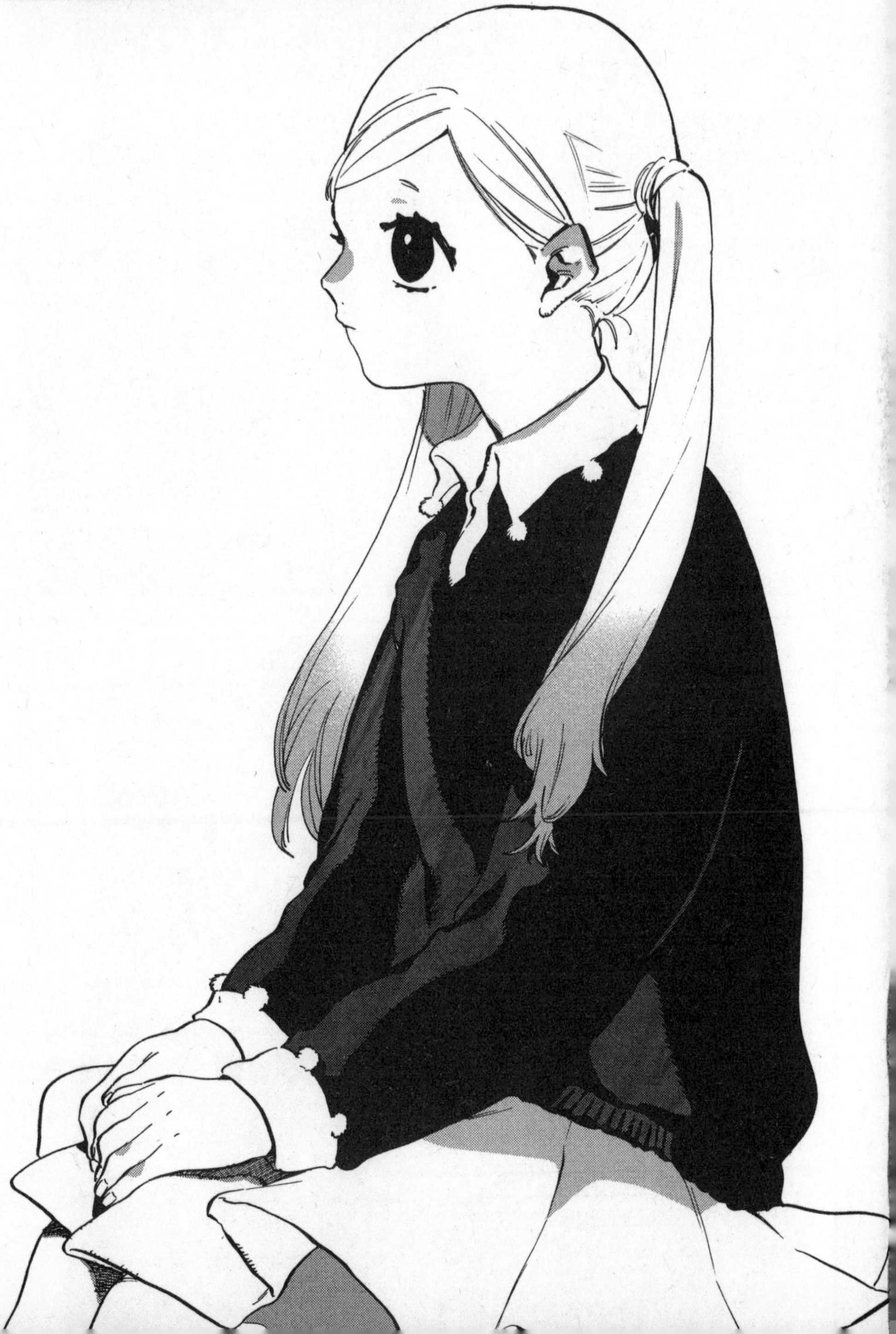

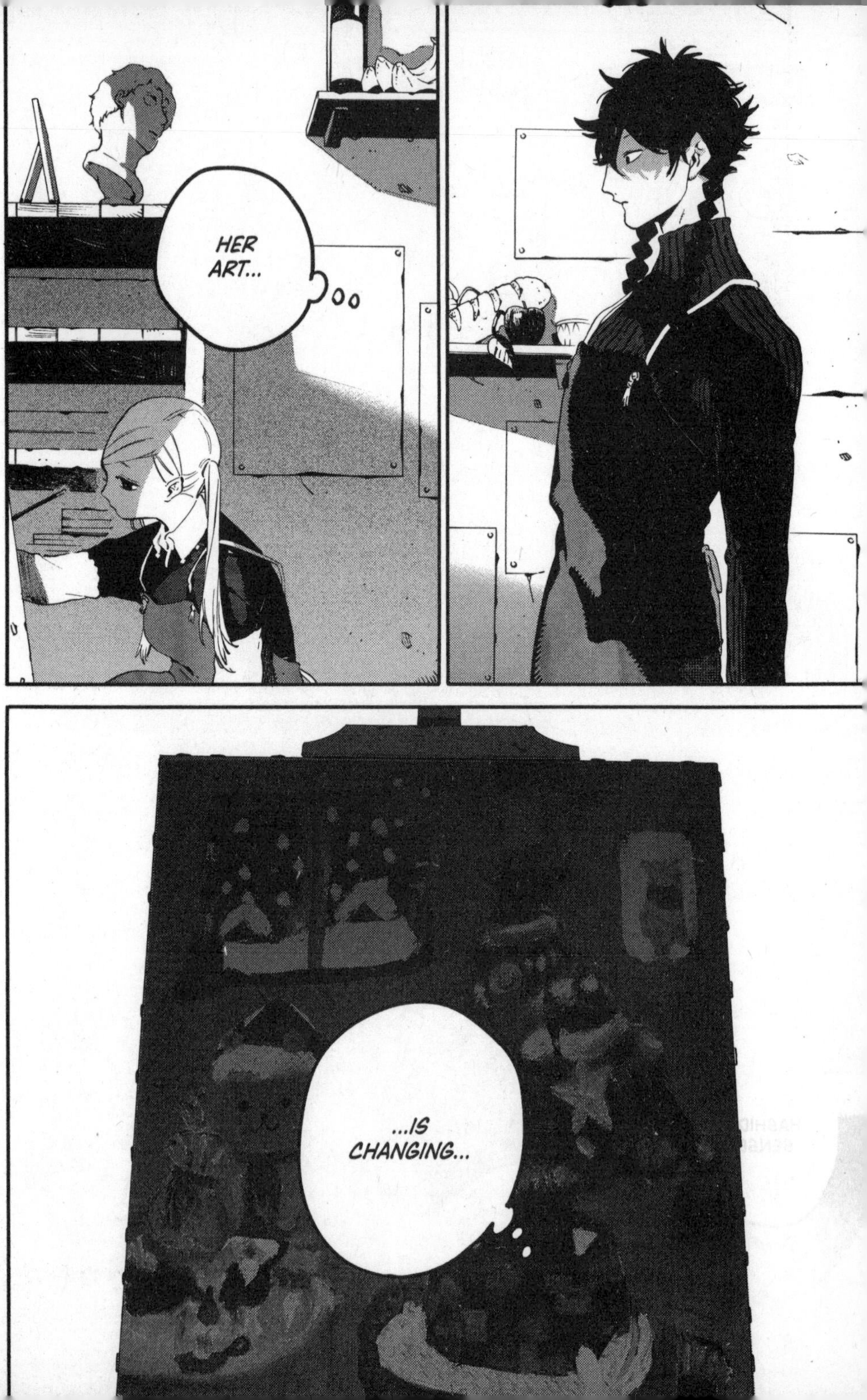
HER ART...
...IS CHANGING...

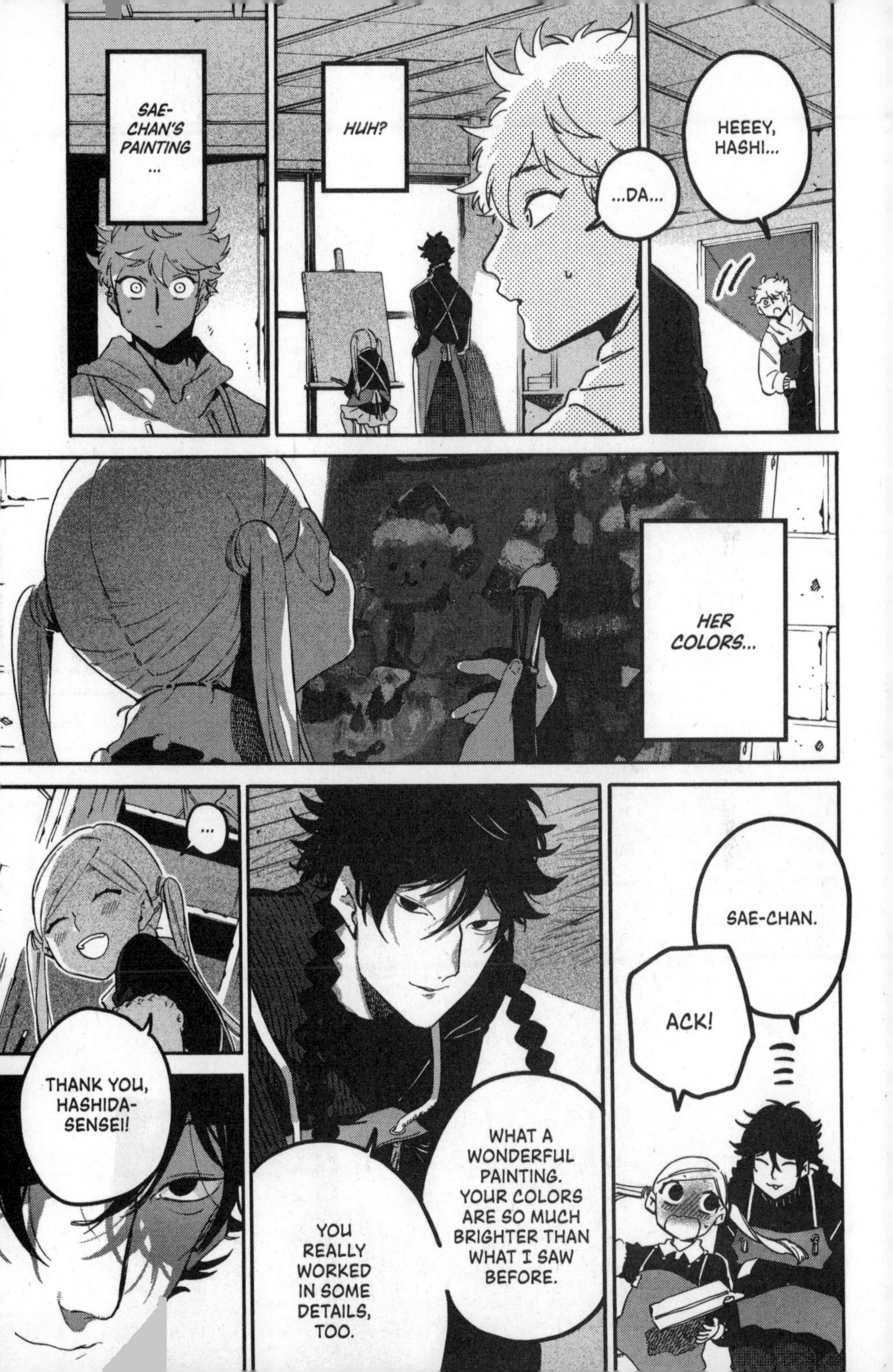
HEEEY, HASHI...
...DA...
HUH?
SAE-CHAN'S PAINTING ...
HER COLORS...
SAE-CHAN.
ACK!
WHAT A WONDERFUL PAINTING. YOUR COLORS ARE SO MUCH BRIGHTER THAN WHAT I SAW BEFORE.
YOU REALLY WORKED IN SOME DETAILS, TOO.
...
THANK YOU, HASHIDA-SENSEI!

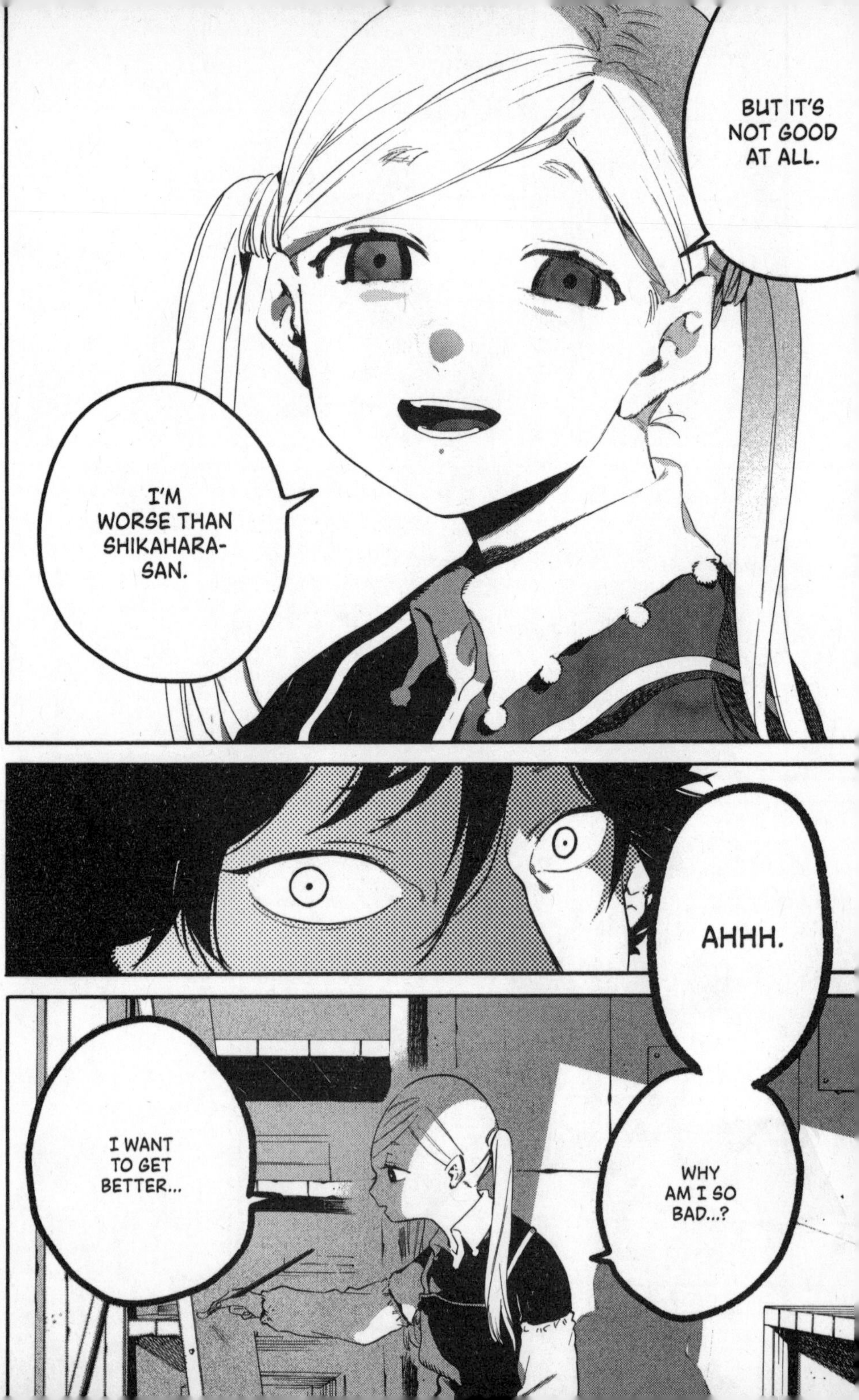
BUT IT'S NOT GOOD AT ALL.
I'M WORSE THAN SHIKAHARA-SAN.
AHHH.
WHY AM I SO BAD...?
I WANT TO GET BETTER...

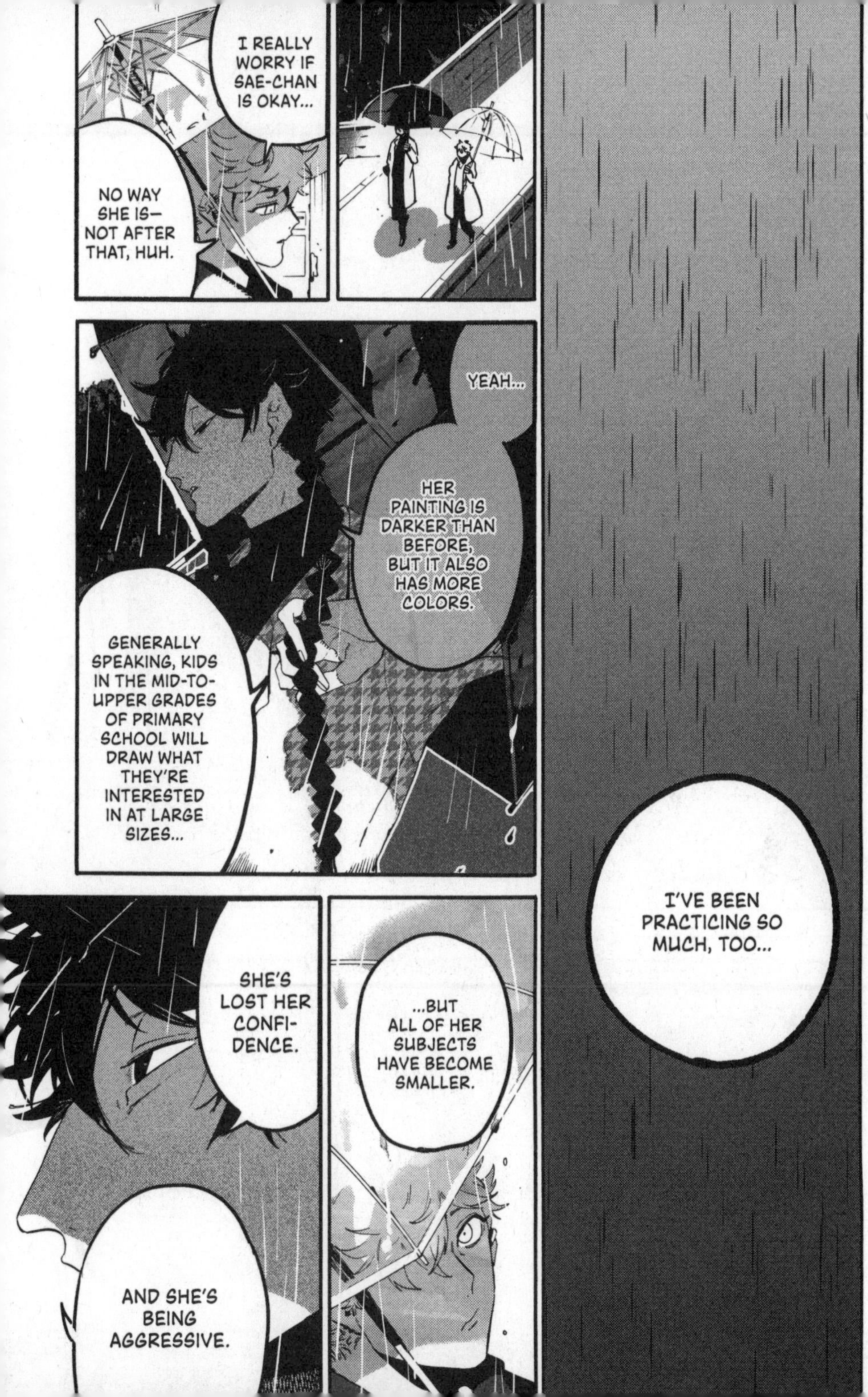
I'VE BEEN PRACTICING SO MUCH, TOO...
I REALLY WORRY IF SAE-CHAN IS OKAY...
NO WAY SHE IS— NOT AFTER THAT, HUH.
YEAH...
HER PAINTING IS DARKER THAN BEFORE, BUT IT ALSO HAS MORE COLORS.
GENERALLY SPEAKING, KIDS IN THE MID-TO-UPPER GRADES OF PRIMARY SCHOOL WILL DRAW WHAT THEY'RE INTERESTED IN AT LARGE SIZES...
...BUT ALL OF HER SUBJECTS HAVE BECOME SMALLER.
SHE'S LOST HER CONFI-DENCE.
AND SHE'S BEING AGGRESSIVE.

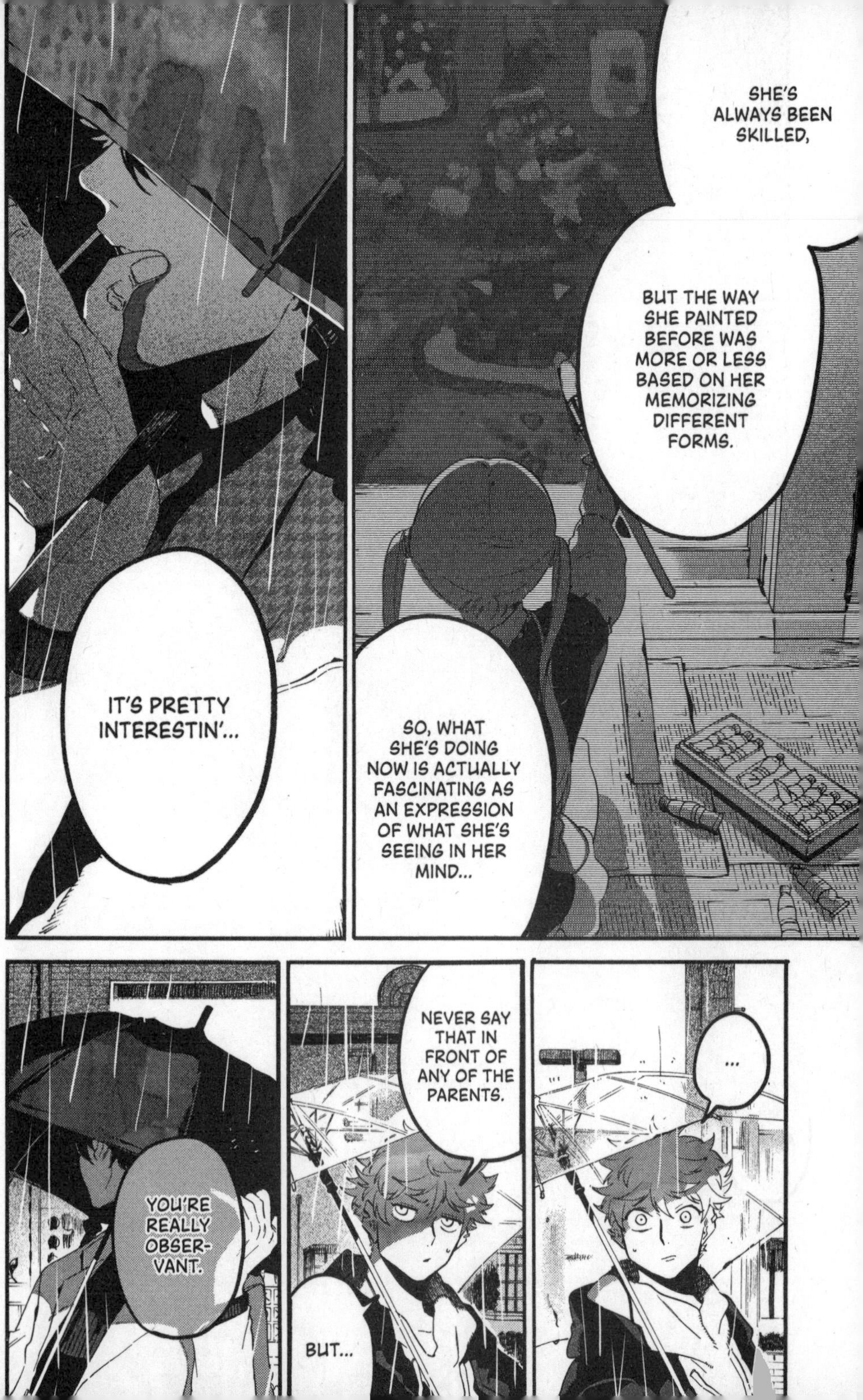
SHE'S ALWAYS BEEN SKILLED,
BUT THE WAY SHE PAINTED BEFORE WAS MORE OR LESS BASED ON HER MEMORIZING DIFFERENT FORMS.
SO, WHAT SHE'S DOING NOW IS ACTUALLY FASCINATING AS AN EXPRESSION OF WHAT SHE'S SEEING IN HER MIND...
IT'S PRETTY INTERESTIN'...
...
NEVER SAY THAT IN FRONT OF ANY OF THE PARENTS.
BUT...
YOU'RE REALLY OBSERVANT.

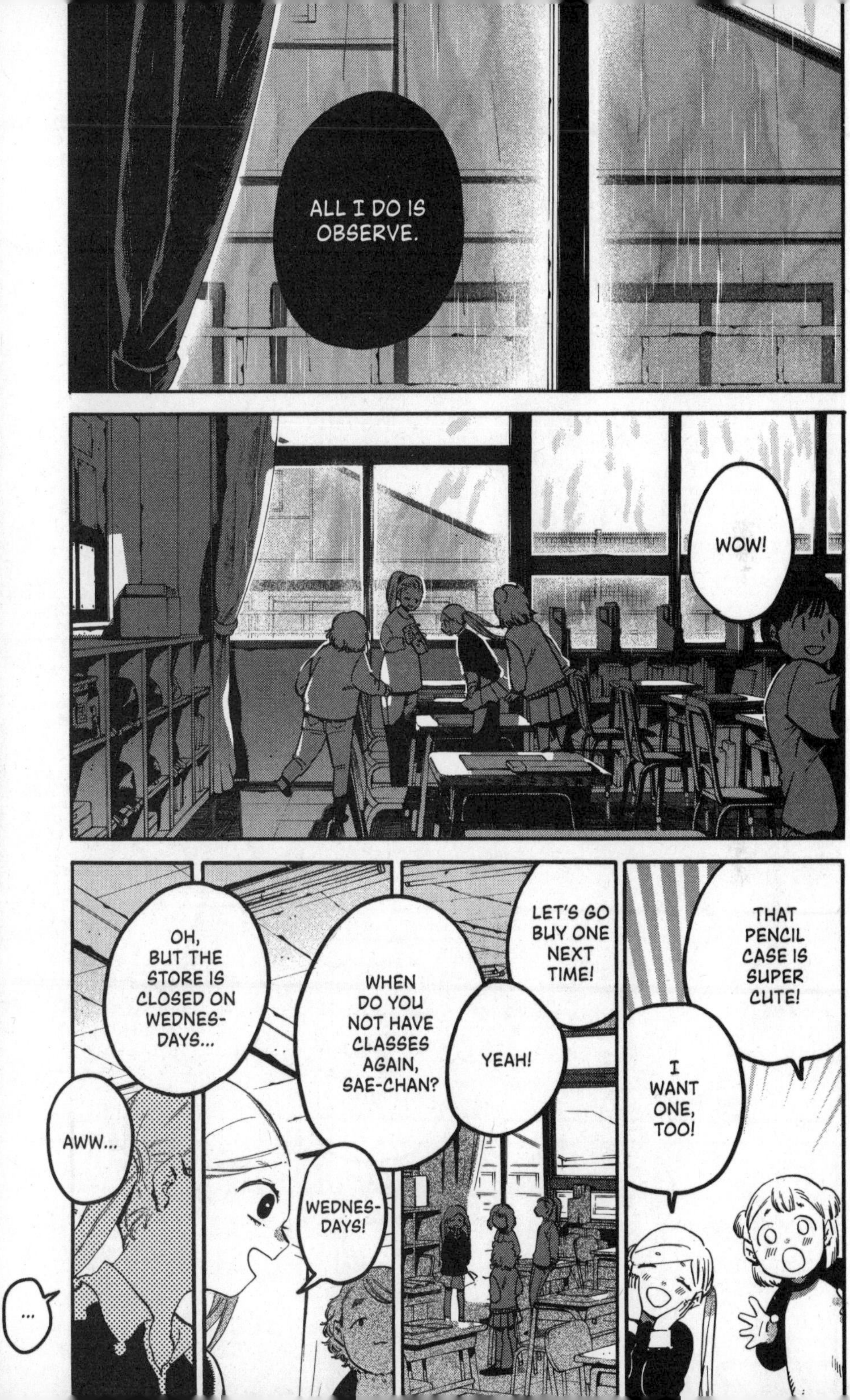
ALL I DO IS OBSERVE.
WOW!
THAT PENCIL CASE IS SUPER CUTE!
I WANT ONE, TOO!
LET'S GO BUY ONE NEXT TIME!
YEAH!
WHEN DO YOU NOT HAVE CLASSES AGAIN, SAE-CHAN?
WEDNES-DAYS!
OH, BUT THE STORE IS CLOSED ON WEDNES-DAYS...
AWW...
...

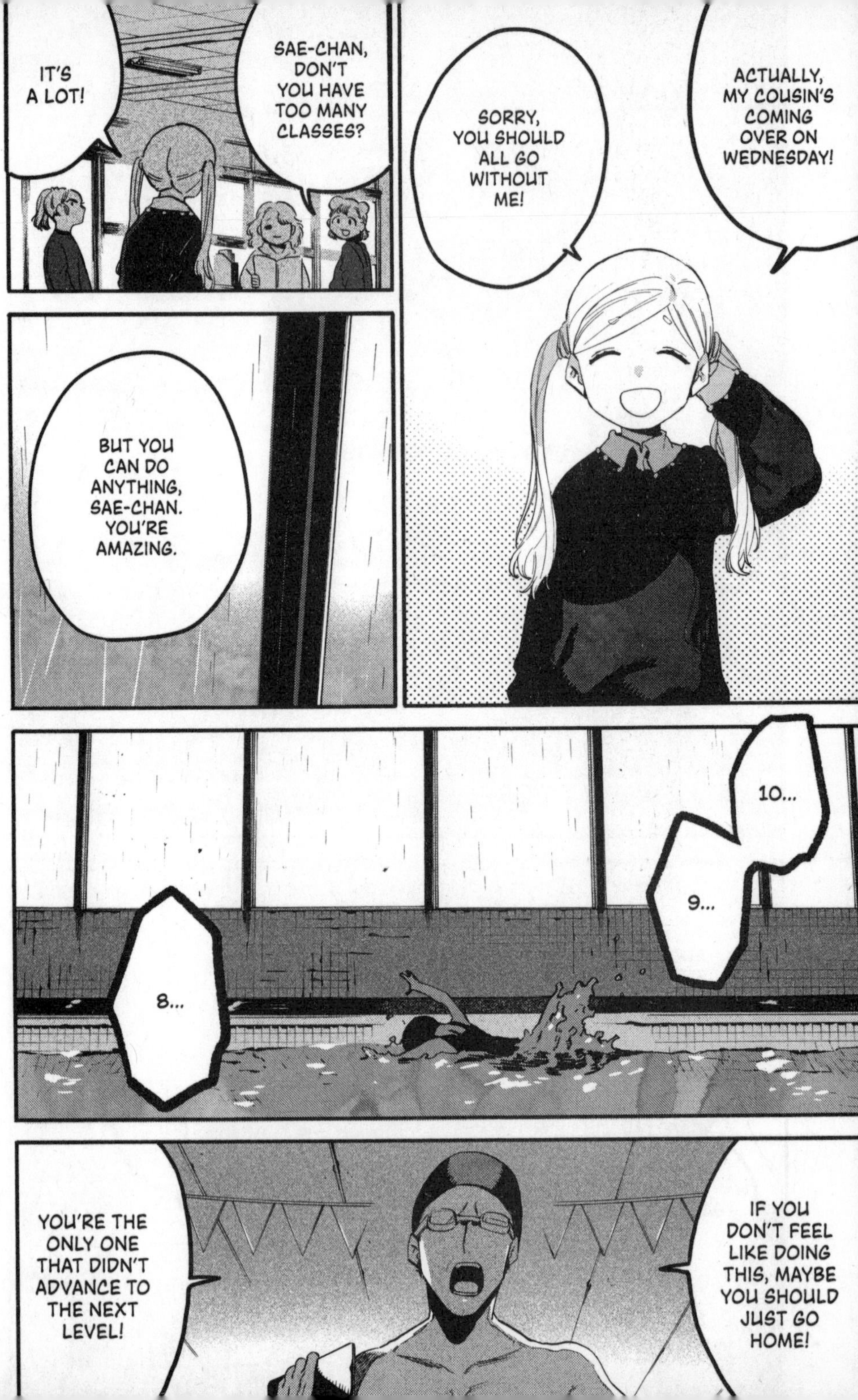
ACTUALLY, MY COUSIN'S COMING OVER ON WEDNESDAY!
SORRY, YOU SHOULD ALL GO WITHOUT ME!
SAE-CHAN, DON'T YOU HAVE TOO MANY CLASSES?
IT'S A LOT!
BUT YOU CAN DO ANYTHING, SAE-CHAN. YOU'RE AMAZING.
10...
9...
8...
IF YOU DON'T FEEL LIKE DOING THIS, MAYBE YOU SHOULD JUST GO HOME!
YOU'RE THE ONLY ONE THAT DIDN'T ADVANCE TO THE NEXT LEVEL!

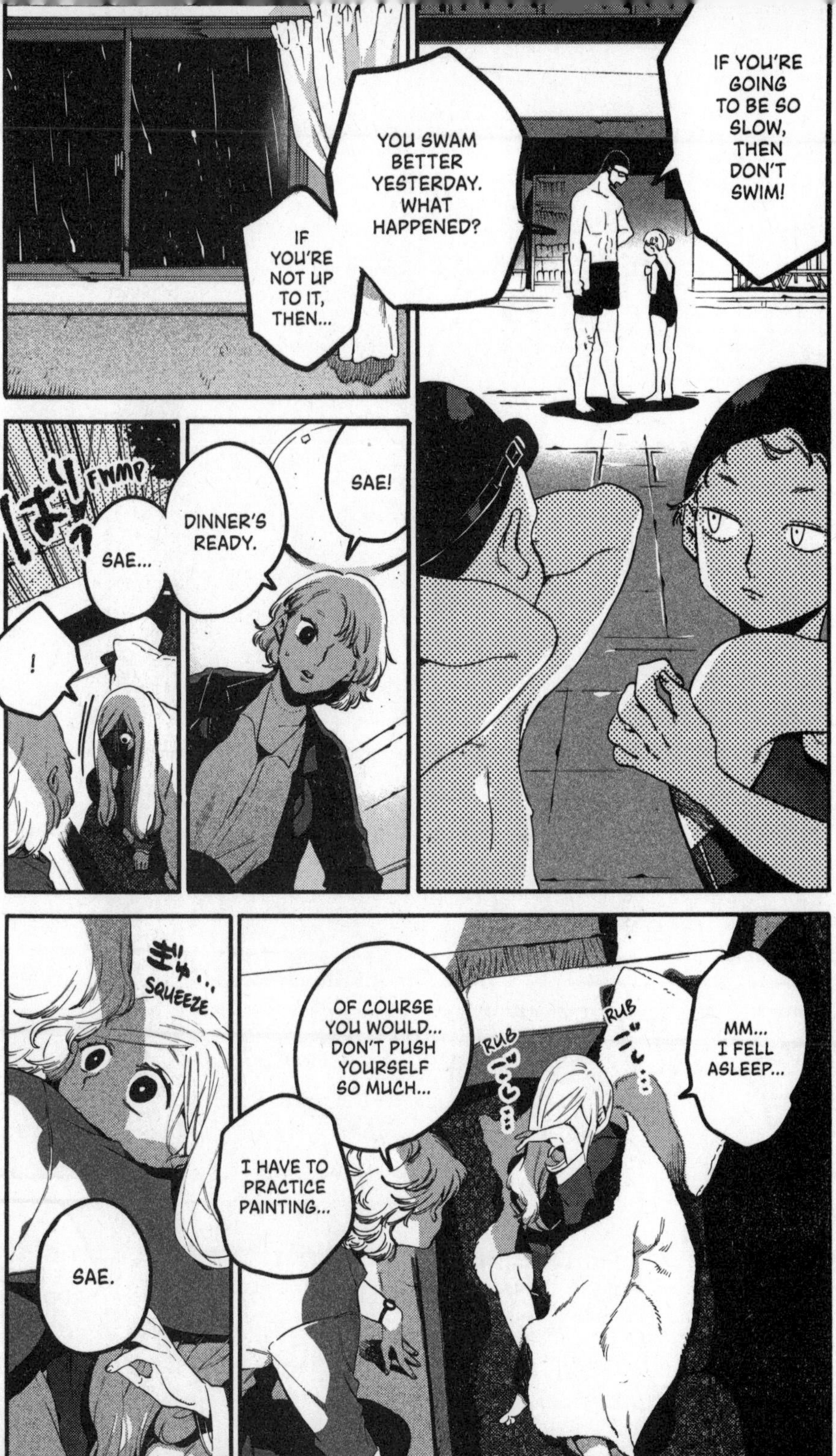
IF YOU'RE GOING TO BE SO SLOW, THEN DON'T SWIM!
YOU SWAM BETTER YESTERDAY. WHAT HAPPENED?
IF YOU'RE NOT UP TO IT, THEN...
SAE!
DINNER'S READY.
SAE...
FWMP
!
MM... I FELL ASLEEP...
RUB
RUB
OF COURSE YOU WOULD... DON'T PUSH YOURSELF SO MUCH...
I HAVE TO PRACTICE PAINTING...
SQUEEZE
SAE.

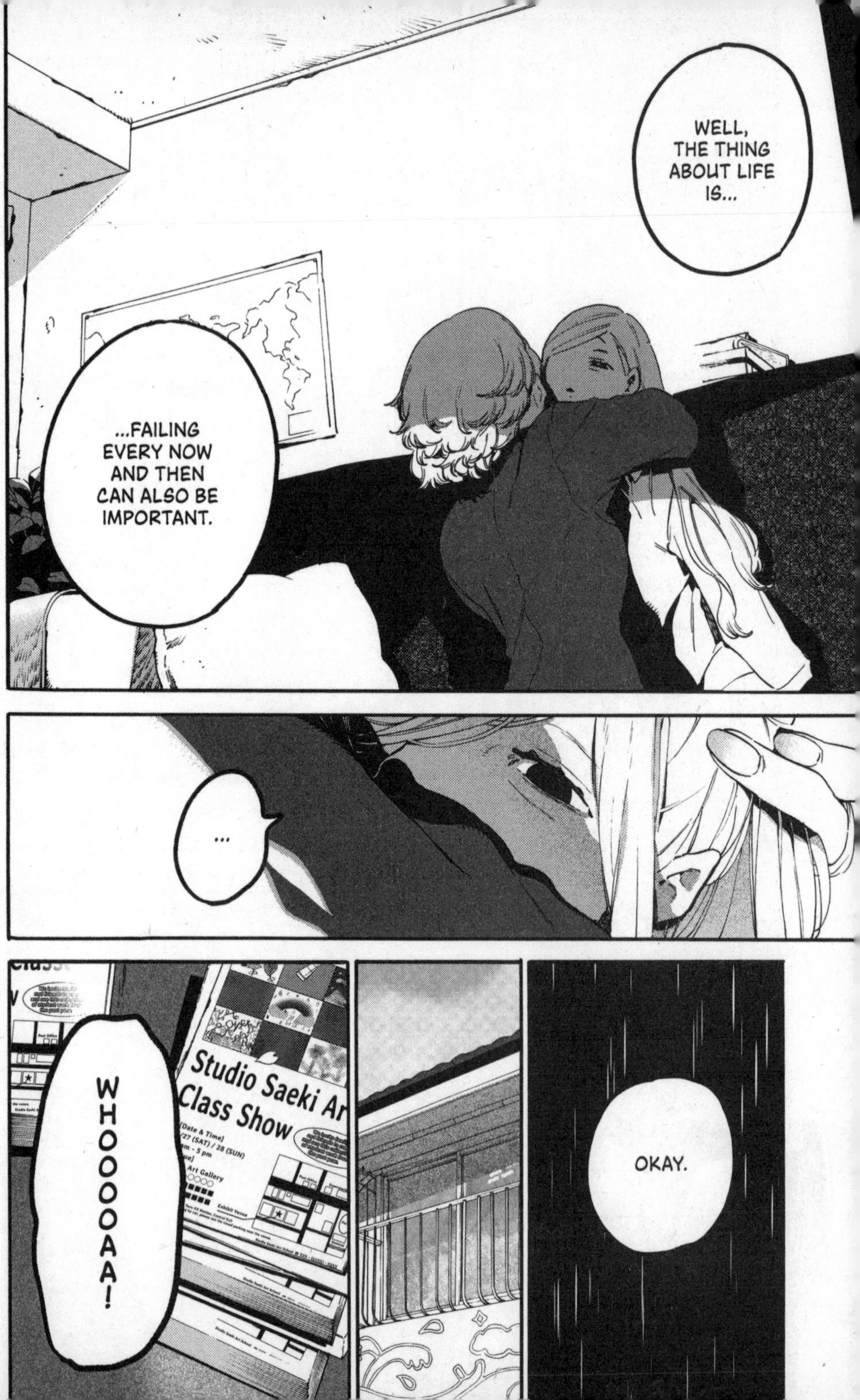
WELL, THE THING ABOUT LIFE IS...
...FAILING EVERY NOW AND THEN CAN ALSO BE IMPORTANT.
...
OKAY.
WHOOOOAA!
Studio Saeki Ar
Class Show

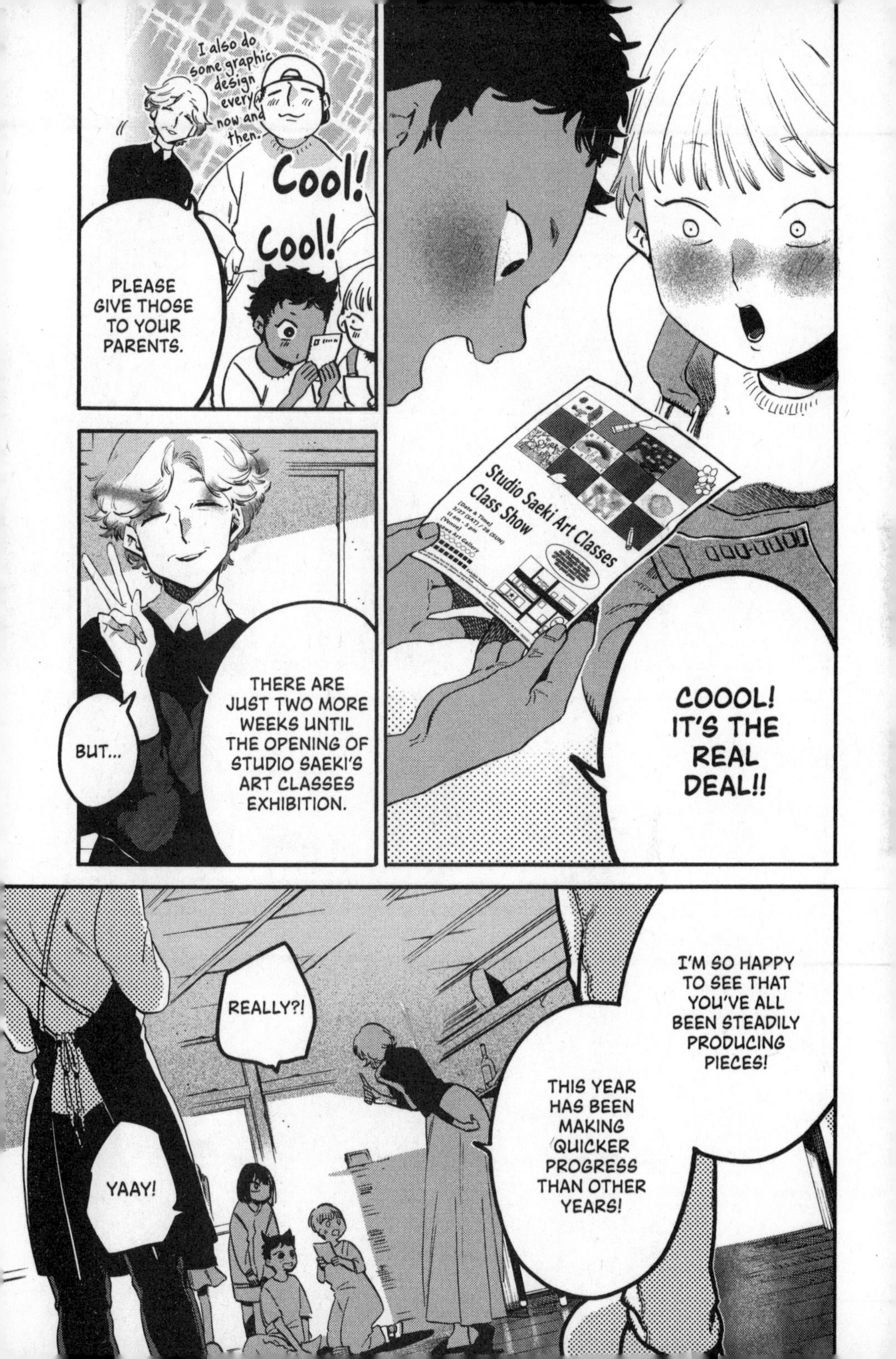
Studio Saeki Art Classes
Class Show
COOOL! IT'S THE REAL DEAL!!
I also do some graphic design every now and then.
Cool!
Cool!
PLEASE GIVE THOSE TO YOUR PARENTS.
THERE ARE JUST TWO MORE WEEKS UNTIL THE OPENING OF STUDIO SAEKI'S ART CLASSES EXHIBITION.
BUT...
I'M SO HAPPY TO SEE THAT YOU'VE ALL BEEN STEADILY PRODUCING PIECES!
THIS YEAR HAS BEEN MAKING QUICKER PROGRESS THAN OTHER YEARS!
REALLY?!
YAAY!

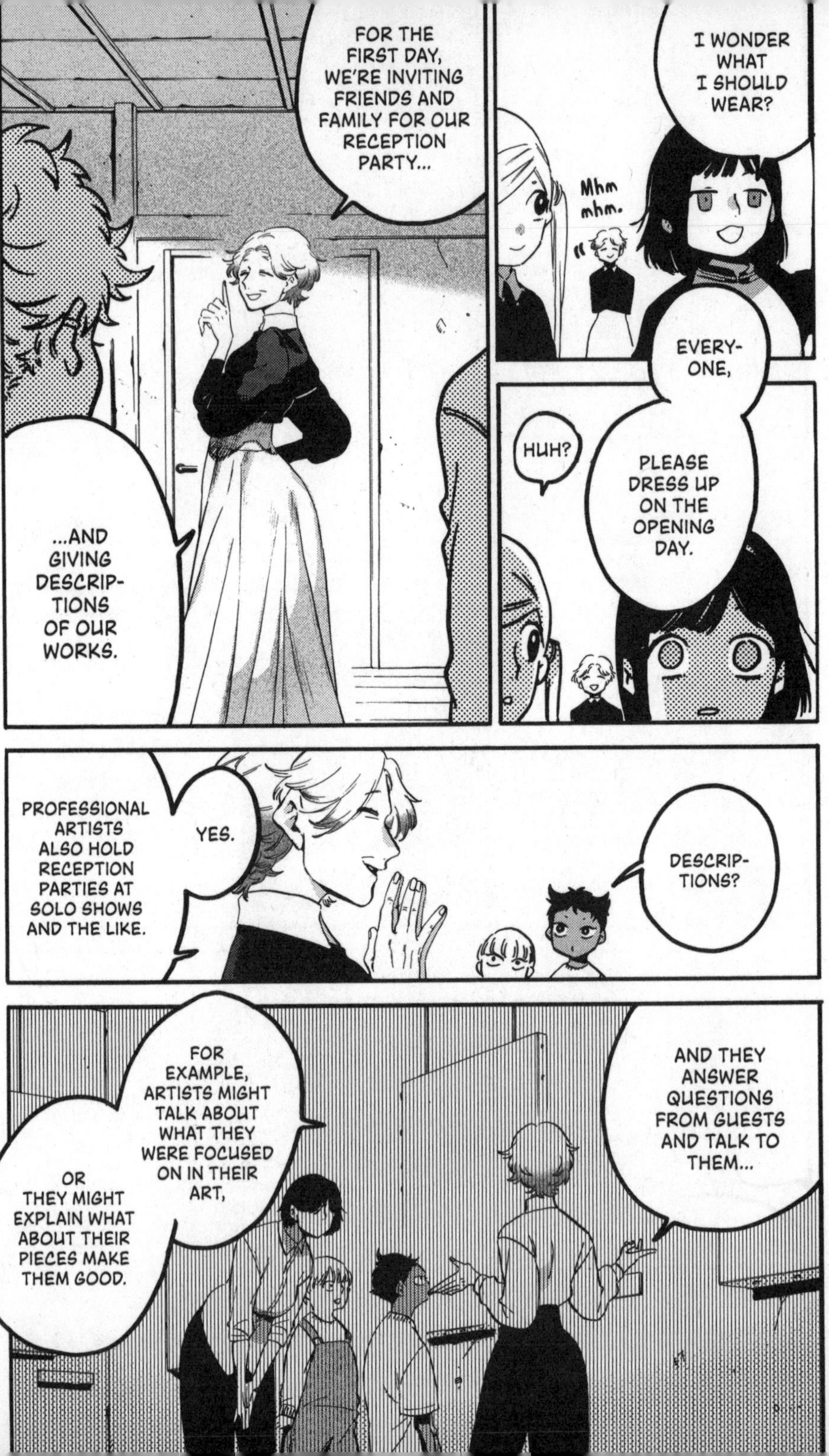
I WONDER WHAT I SHOULD WEAR?
Mhm mhm.
EVERY-ONE,
HUH?
PLEASE DRESS UP ON THE OPENING DAY.
FOR THE FIRST DAY, WE'RE INVITING FRIENDS AND FAMILY FOR OUR RECEPTION PARTY...
...AND GIVING DESCRIPTIONS OF OUR WORKS.
DESCRIP-TIONS?
YES.
PROFESSIONAL ARTISTS ALSO HOLD RECEPTION PARTIES AT SOLO SHOWS AND THE LIKE.
AND THEY ANSWER QUESTIONS FROM GUESTS AND TALK TO THEM...
FOR EXAMPLE, ARTISTS MIGHT TALK ABOUT WHAT THEY WERE FOCUSED ON IN THEIR ART,
OR THEY MIGHT EXPLAIN WHAT ABOUT THEIR PIECES MAKE THEM GOOD.

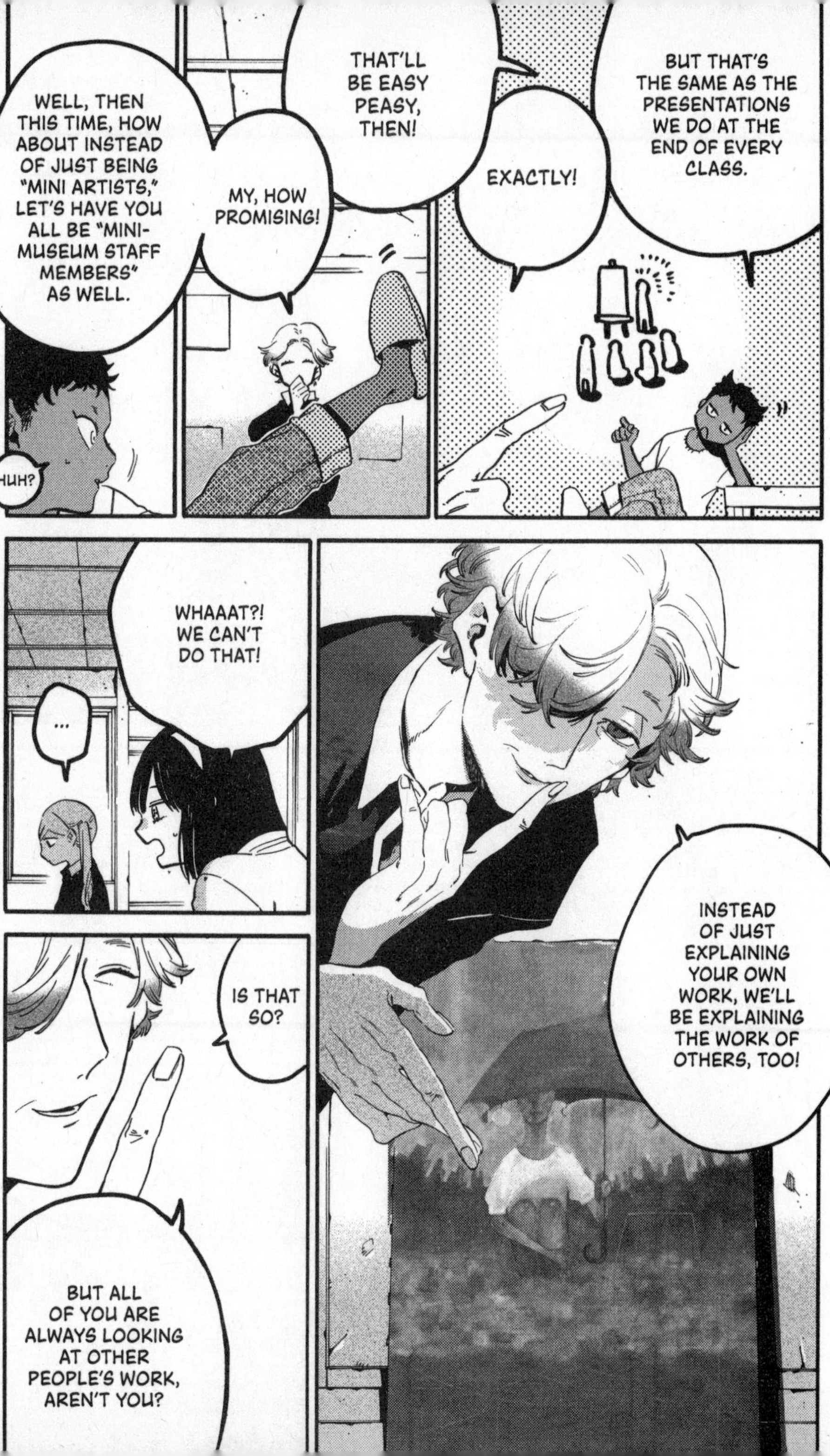
BUT THAT'S THE SAME AS THE PRESENTATIONS WE DO AT THE END OF EVERY CLASS.
THAT'LL BE EASY PEASY, THEN!
EXACTLY!
MY, HOW PROMISING!
WELL, THEN THIS TIME, HOW ABOUT INSTEAD OF JUST BEING "MINI ARTISTS," LET'S HAVE YOU ALL BE "MINI-MUSEUM STAFF MEMBERS" AS WELL.
HUH?
INSTEAD OF JUST EXPLAINING YOUR OWN WORK, WE'LL BE EXPLAINING THE WORK OF OTHERS, TOO!
WHAAAT?! WE CAN'T DO THAT!
...
IS THAT SO?
BUT ALL OF YOU ARE ALWAYS LOOKING AT OTHER PEOPLE'S WORK, AREN'T YOU?

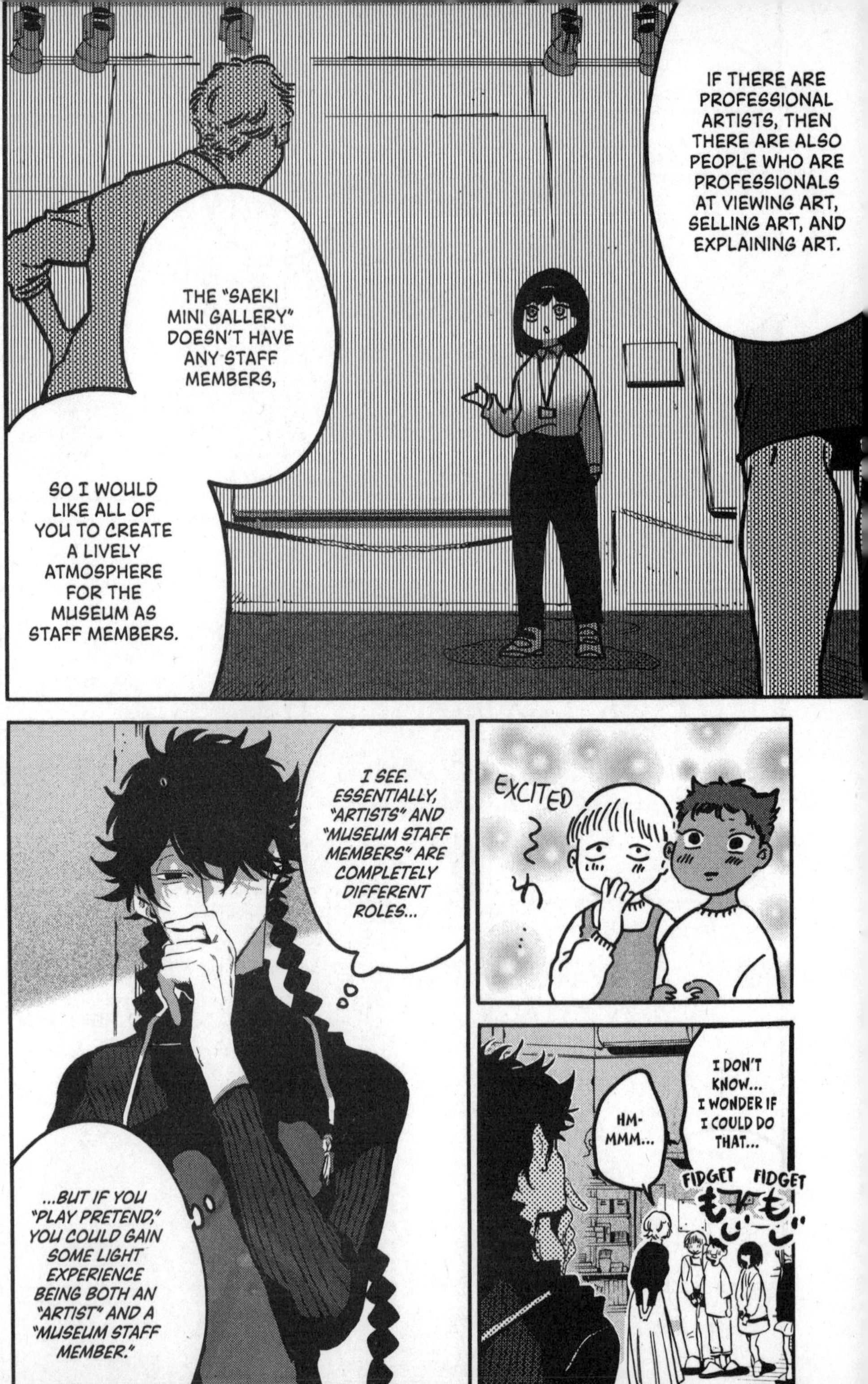
IF THERE ARE PROFESSIONAL ARTISTS, THEN THERE ARE ALSO PEOPLE WHO ARE PROFESSIONALS AT VIEWING ART, SELLING ART, AND EXPLAINING ART.
THE "SAEKI MINI GALLERY" DOESN'T HAVE ANY STAFF MEMBERS,
SO I WOULD LIKE ALL OF YOU TO CREATE A LIVELY ATMOSPHERE FOR THE MUSEUM AS STAFF MEMBERS.
EXCITED
I DON'T KNOW... I WONDER IF I COULD DO THAT...
HM-MMM...
FIDGET FIDGET
I SEE. ESSENTIALLY, "ARTISTS" AND "MUSEUM STAFF MEMBERS" ARE COMPLETELY DIFFERENT ROLES...
...BUT IF YOU "PLAY PRETEND," YOU COULD GAIN SOME LIGHT EXPERIENCE BEING BOTH AN "ARTIST" AND A "MUSEUM STAFF MEMBER."

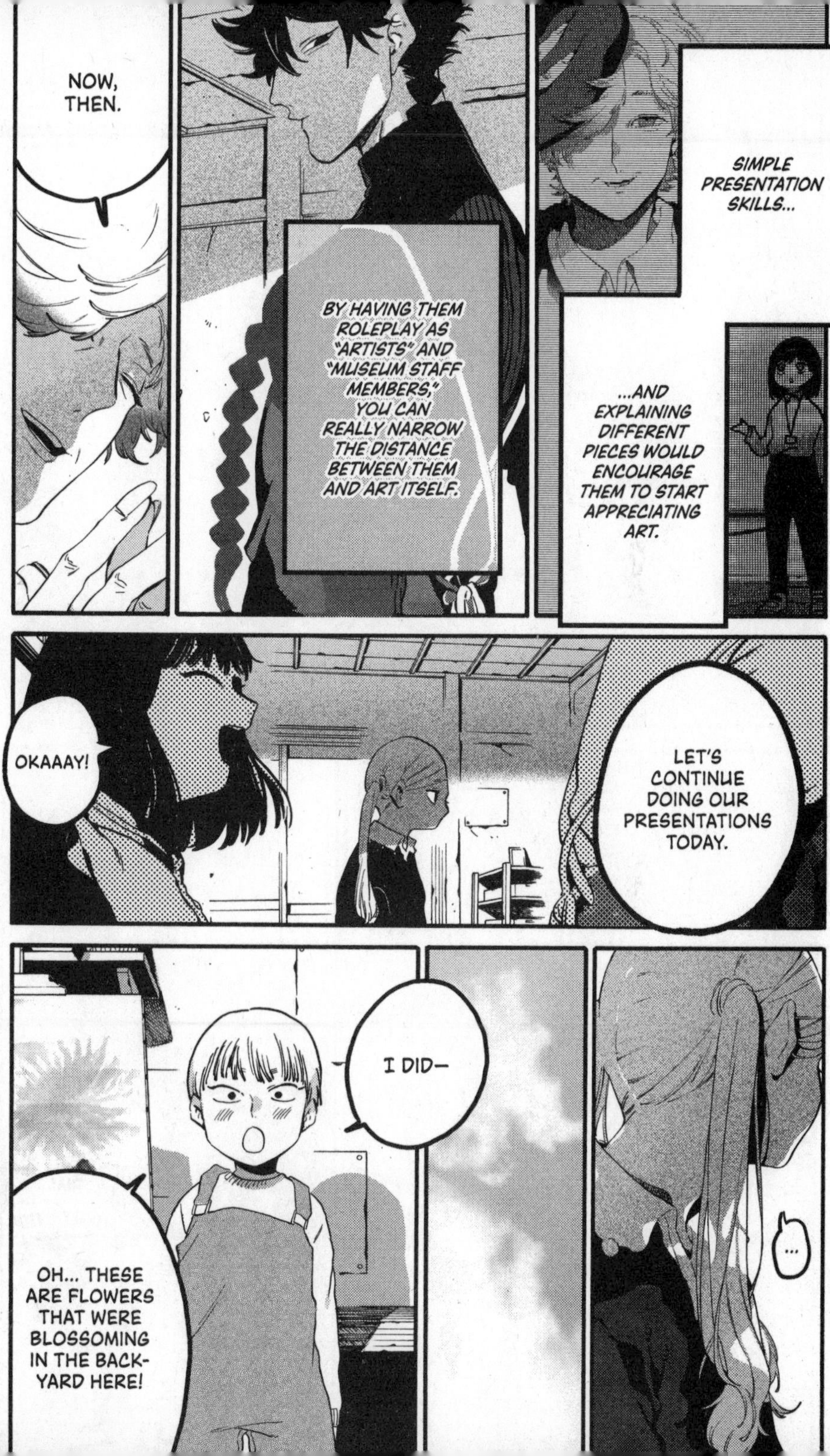
SIMPLE PRESENTATION SKILLS...
...AND EXPLAINING DIFFERENT PIECES WOULD ENCOURAGE THEM TO START APPRECIATING ART.
BY HAVING THEM ROLEPLAY AS "ARTISTS" AND "MUSEUM STAFF MEMBERS," YOU CAN REALLY NARROW THE DISTANCE BETWEEN THEM AND ART ITSELF.
NOW, THEN.
LET'S CONTINUE DOING OUR PRESENTATIONS TODAY.
OKAAAY!
...
I DID—
OH... THESE ARE FLOWERS THAT WERE BLOSSOMING IN THE BACK-YARD HERE!

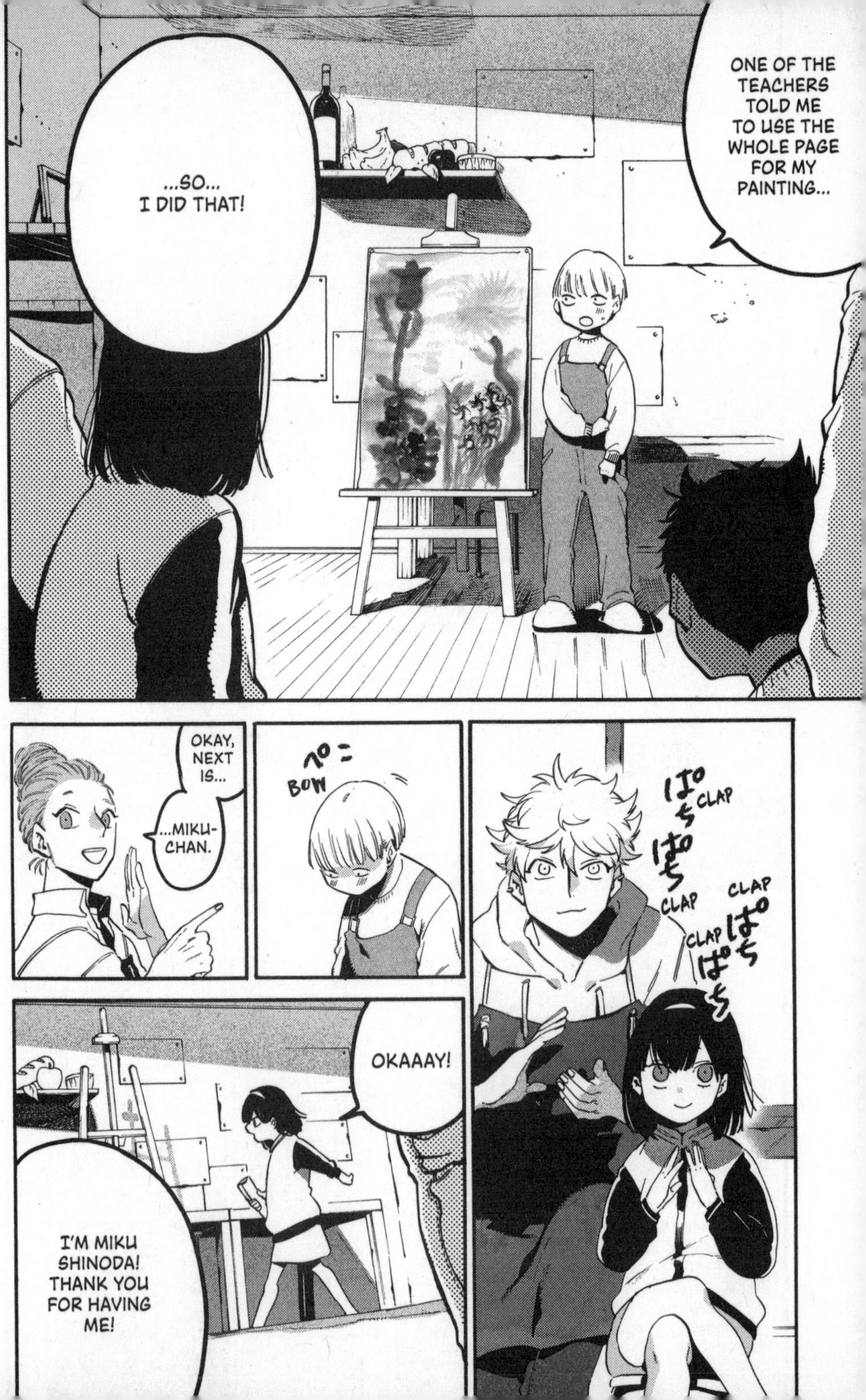
ONE OF THE TEACHERS TOLD ME TO USE THE WHOLE PAGE FOR MY PAINTING...
...SO... I DID THAT!
ぱち CLAP
ぱち CLAP
CLAP ぱち
CLAP ぱち
ぺこ BOW
OKAY, NEXT IS...
...MIKU-CHAN.
OKAAAY!
I'M MIKU SHINODA! THANK YOU FOR HAVING ME!

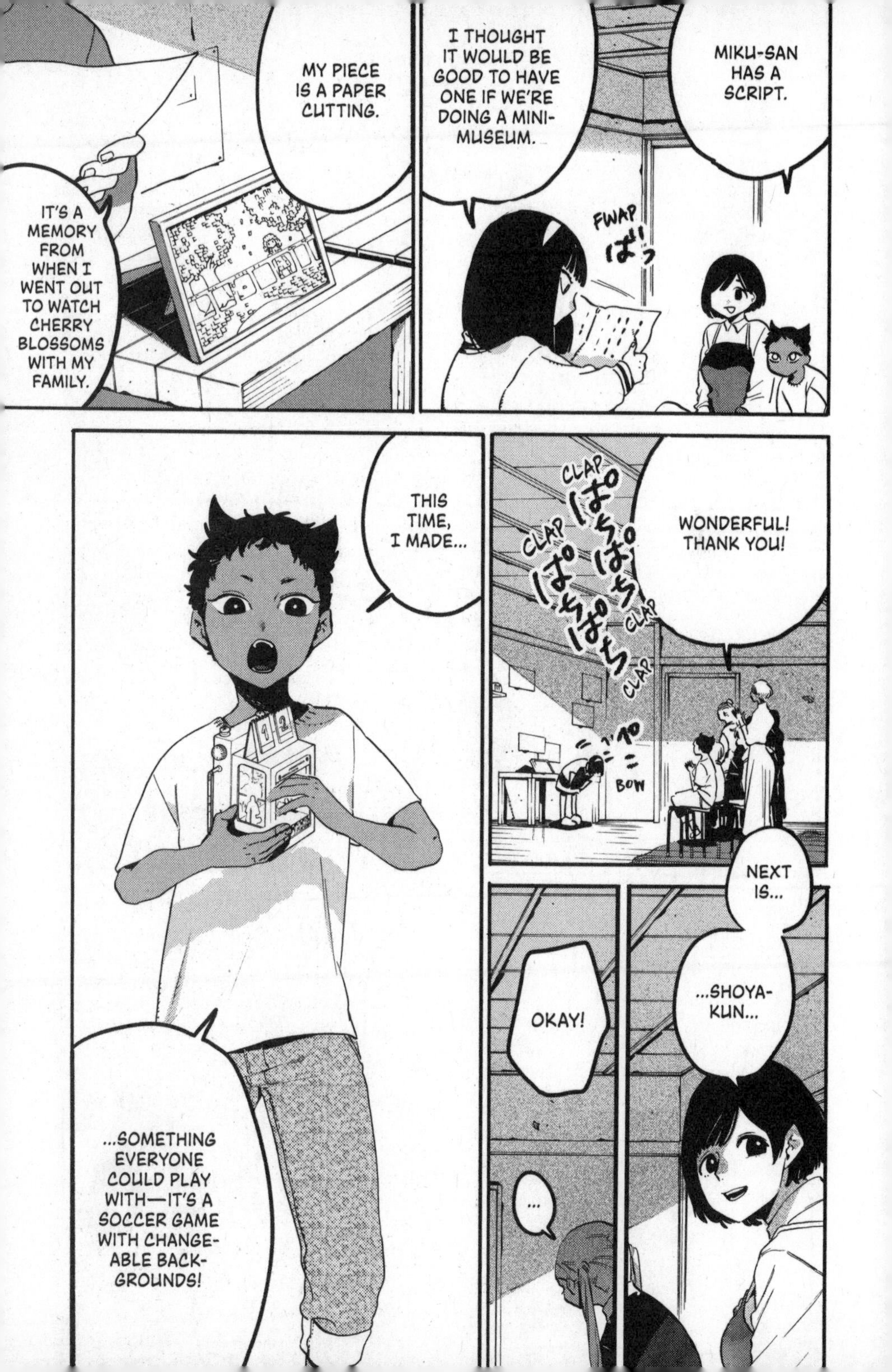

MIKU-SAN HAS A SCRIPT.
I THOUGHT IT WOULD BE GOOD TO HAVE ONE IF WE'RE DOING A MINI-MUSEUM.
FWAP
ばっ
MY PIECE IS A PAPER CUTTING.
IT'S A MEMORY FROM WHEN I WENT OUT TO WATCH CHERRY BLOSSOMS WITH MY FAMILY.
WONDERFUL! THANK YOU!
CLAP
ぱち
CLAP
ぱち
CLAP
ぱち
CLAP
ぱち
BOW
NEXT IS...
...SHOYA-KUN...
OKAY!
...
THIS TIME, I MADE...
...SOMETHING EVERYONE COULD PLAY WITH—IT'S A SOCCER GAME WITH CHANGE-ABLE BACK-GROUNDS!

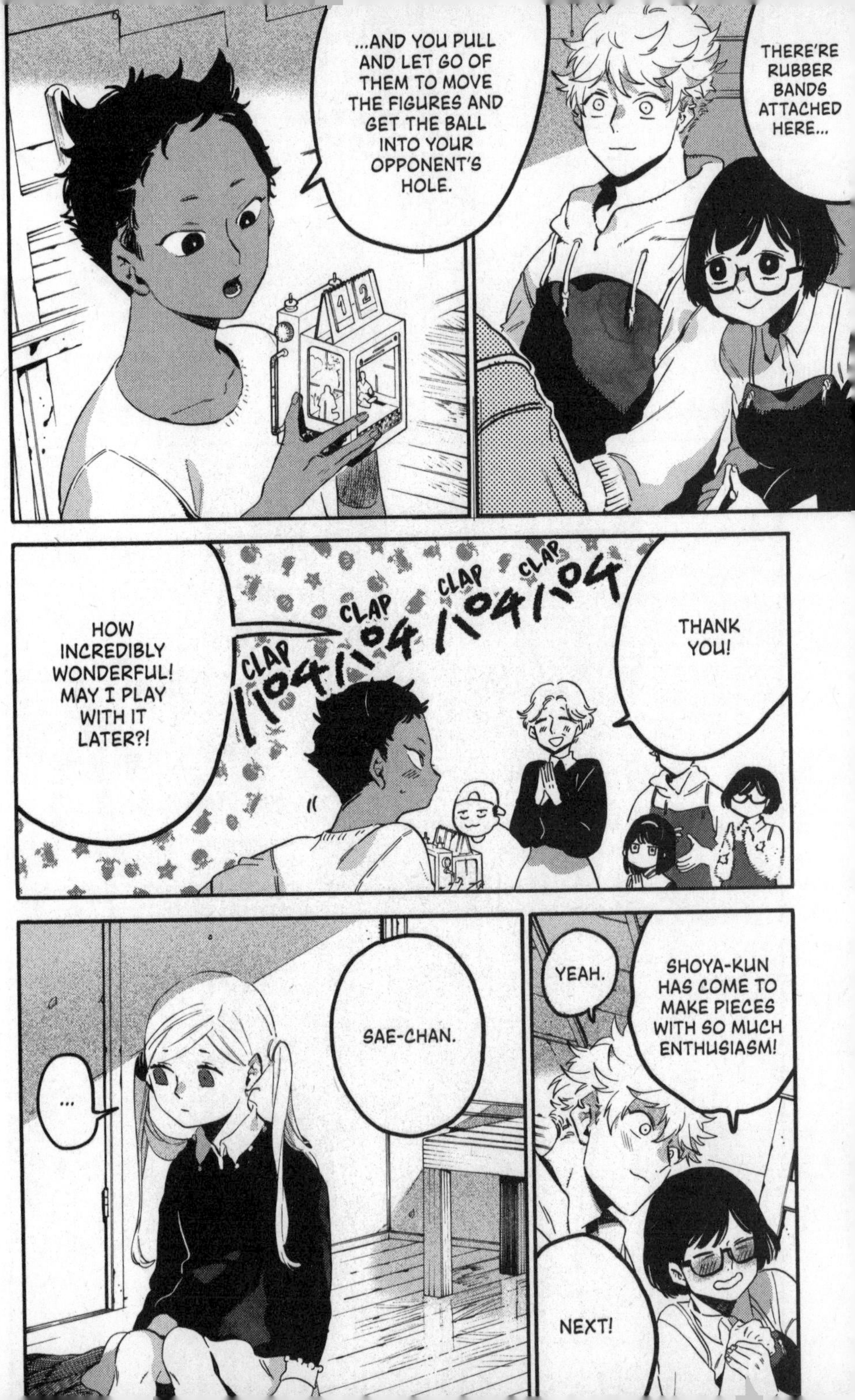
THERE'RE RUBBER BANDS ATTACHED HERE...
...AND YOU PULL AND LET GO OF THEM TO MOVE THE FIGURES AND GET THE BALL INTO YOUR OPPONENT'S HOLE.
THANK YOU!
CLAP
CLAP
CLAP
CLAP
HOW INCREDIBLY WONDERFUL! MAY I PLAY WITH IT LATER?!
SHOYA-KUN HAS COME TO MAKE PIECES WITH SO MUCH ENTHUSIASM!
YEAH.
NEXT!
SAE-CHAN.
...

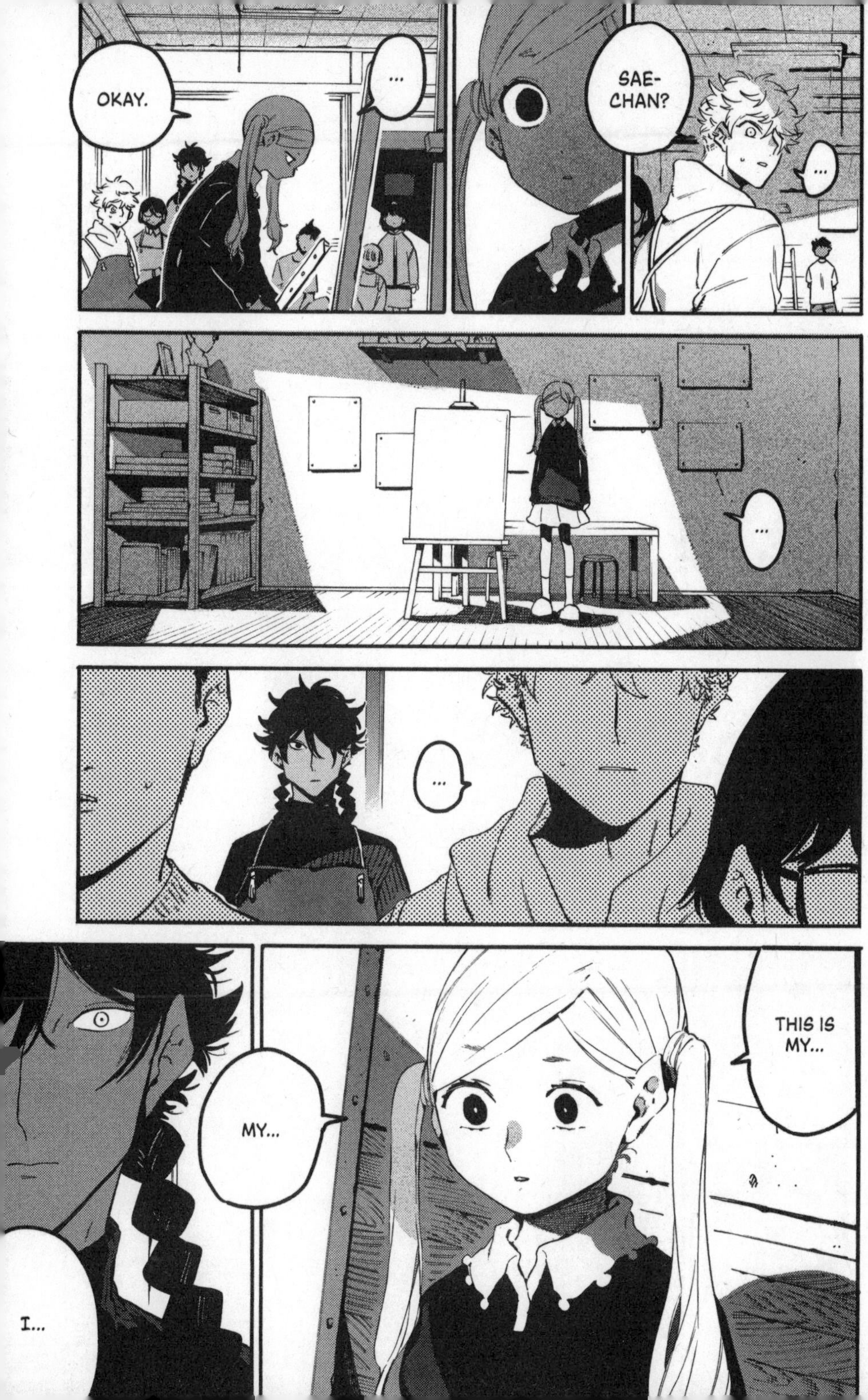
...
SAE-CHAN?
...
OKAY.
...
...
THIS IS MY...
MY...
I...

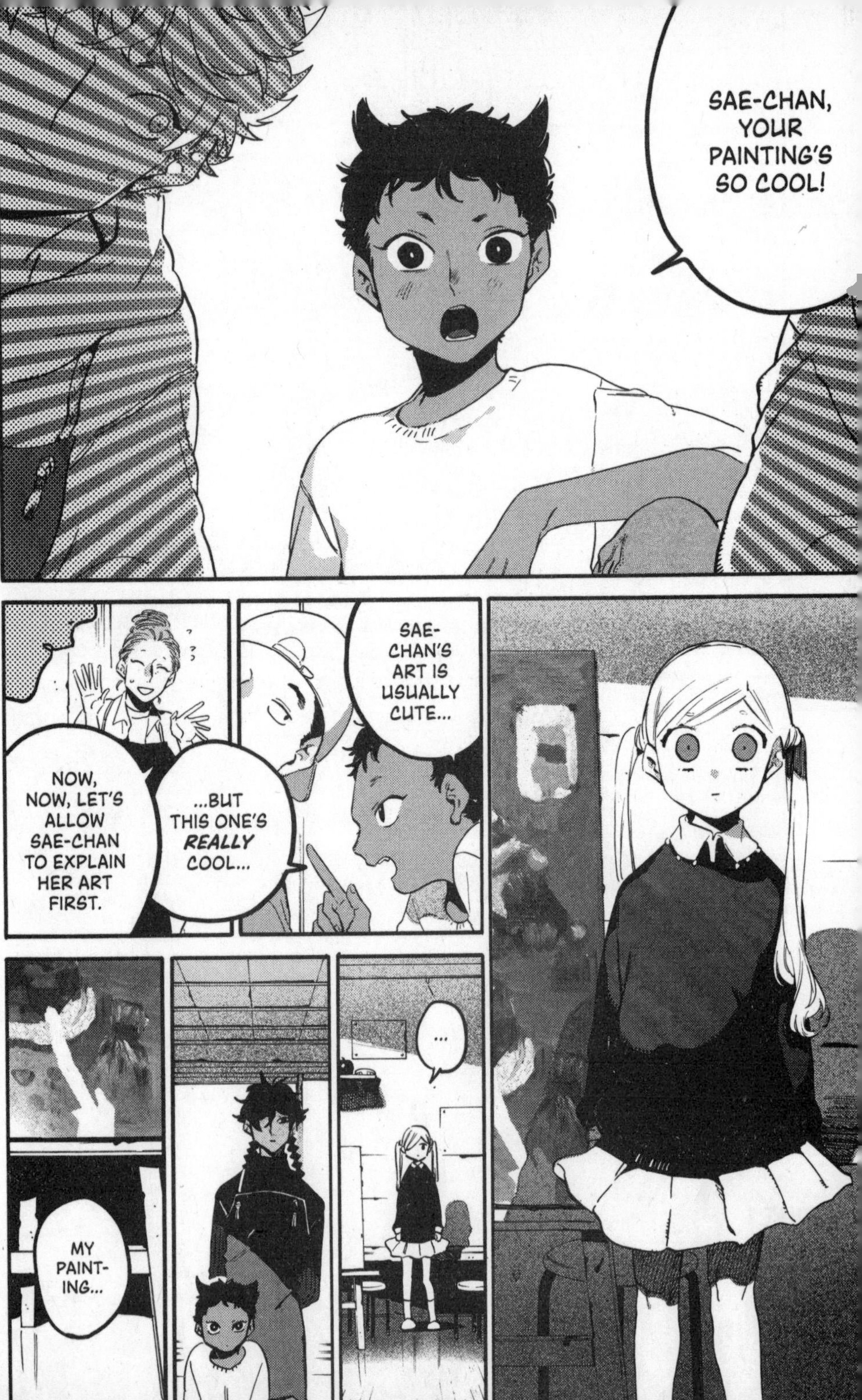
SAE-CHAN, YOUR PAINTING'S SO COOL!
SAE-CHAN'S ART IS USUALLY CUTE...
...BUT THIS ONE'S *REALLY* COOL...
NOW, NOW, LET'S ALLOW SAE-CHAN TO EXPLAIN HER ART FIRST.
...
MY PAINTING...

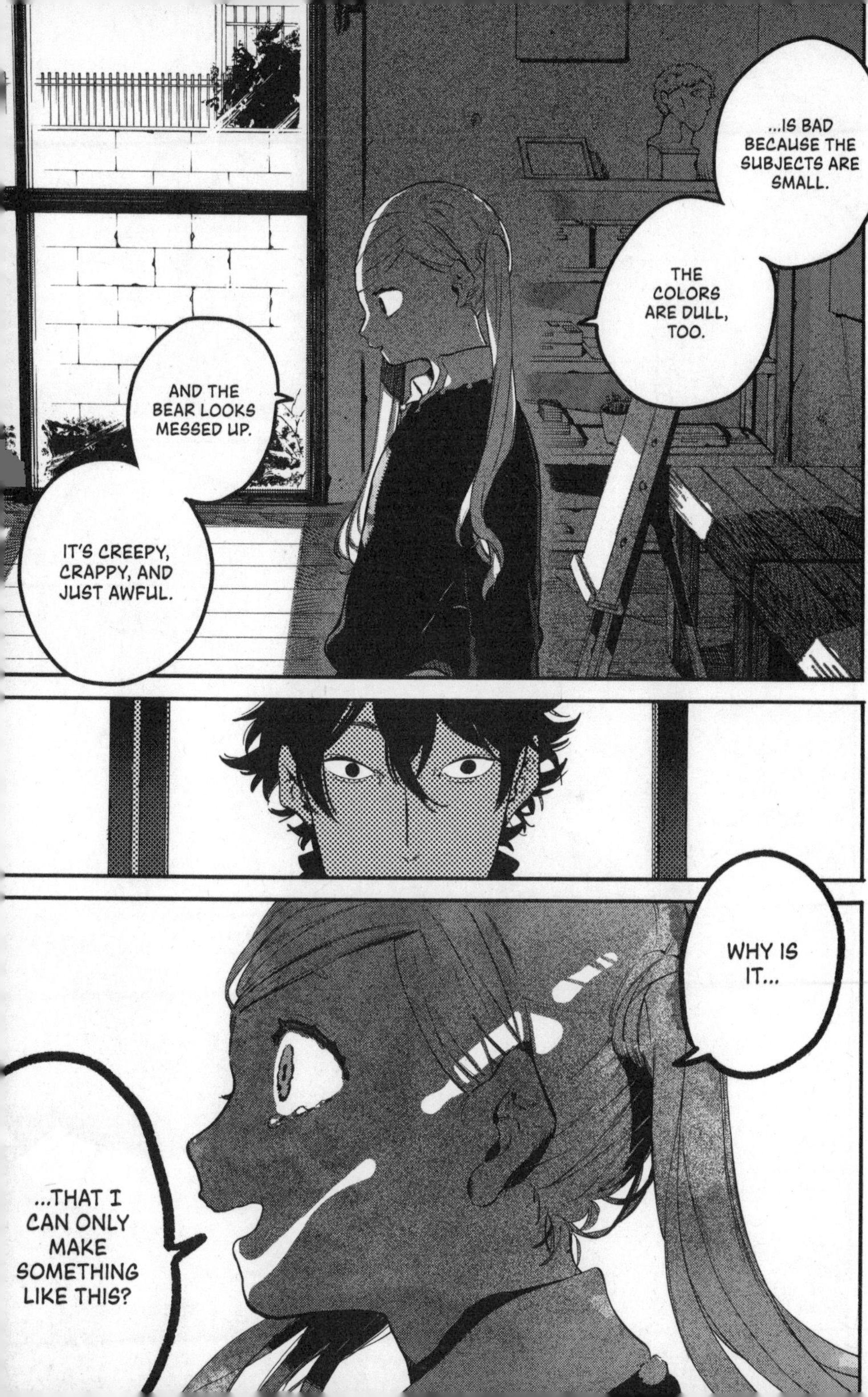
...IS BAD BECAUSE THE SUBJECTS ARE SMALL.
THE COLORS ARE DULL, TOO.
AND THE BEAR LOOKS MESSED UP.
IT'S CREEPY, CRAPPY, AND JUST AWFUL.
WHY IS IT...
...THAT I CAN ONLY MAKE SOMETHING LIKE THIS?

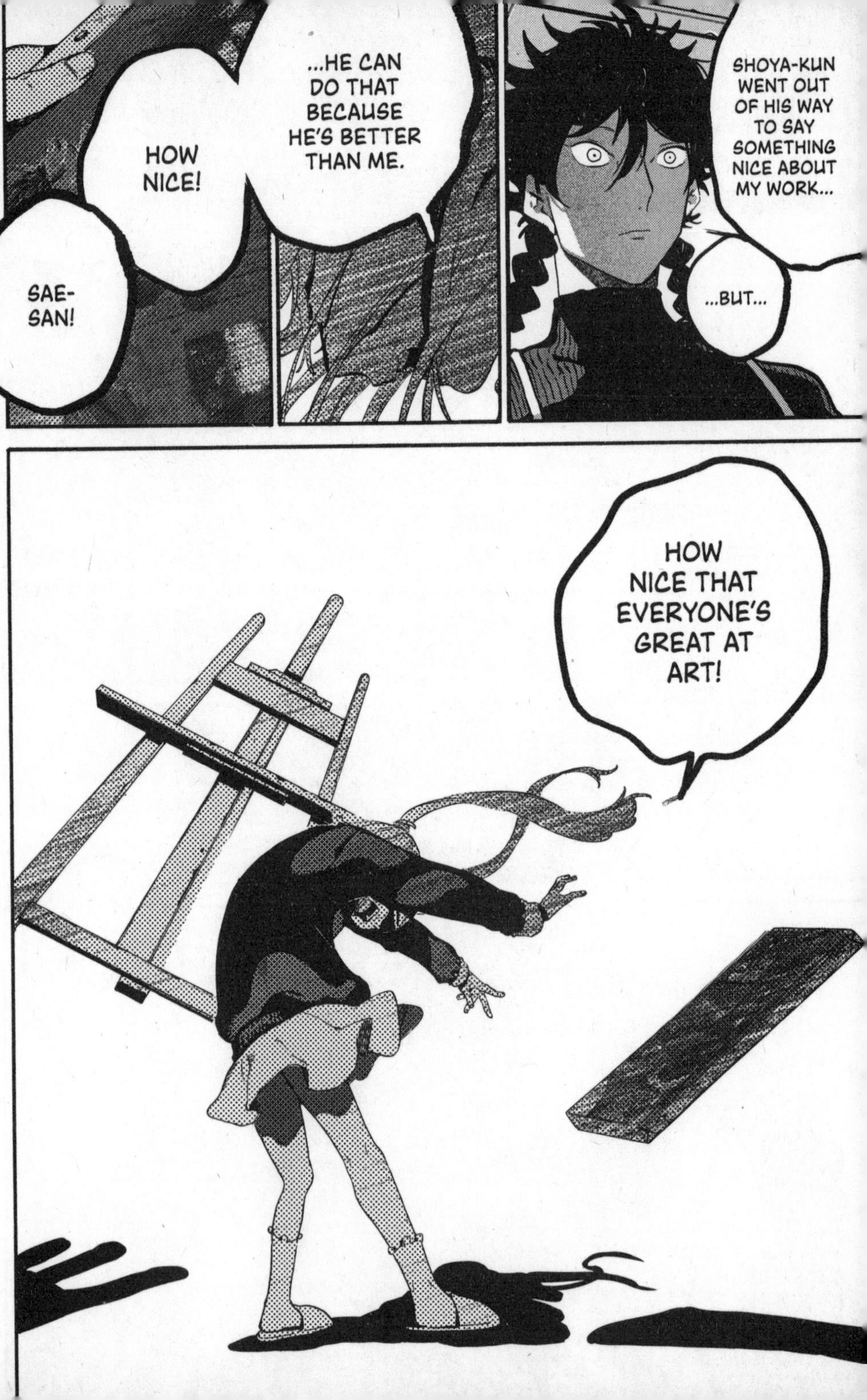
SHOYA-KUN WENT OUT OF HIS WAY TO SAY SOMETHING NICE ABOUT MY WORK...
...BUT...
...HE CAN DO THAT BECAUSE HE'S BETTER THAN ME.
HOW NICE!
SAE-SAN!
HOW NICE THAT EVERYONE'S GREAT AT ART!

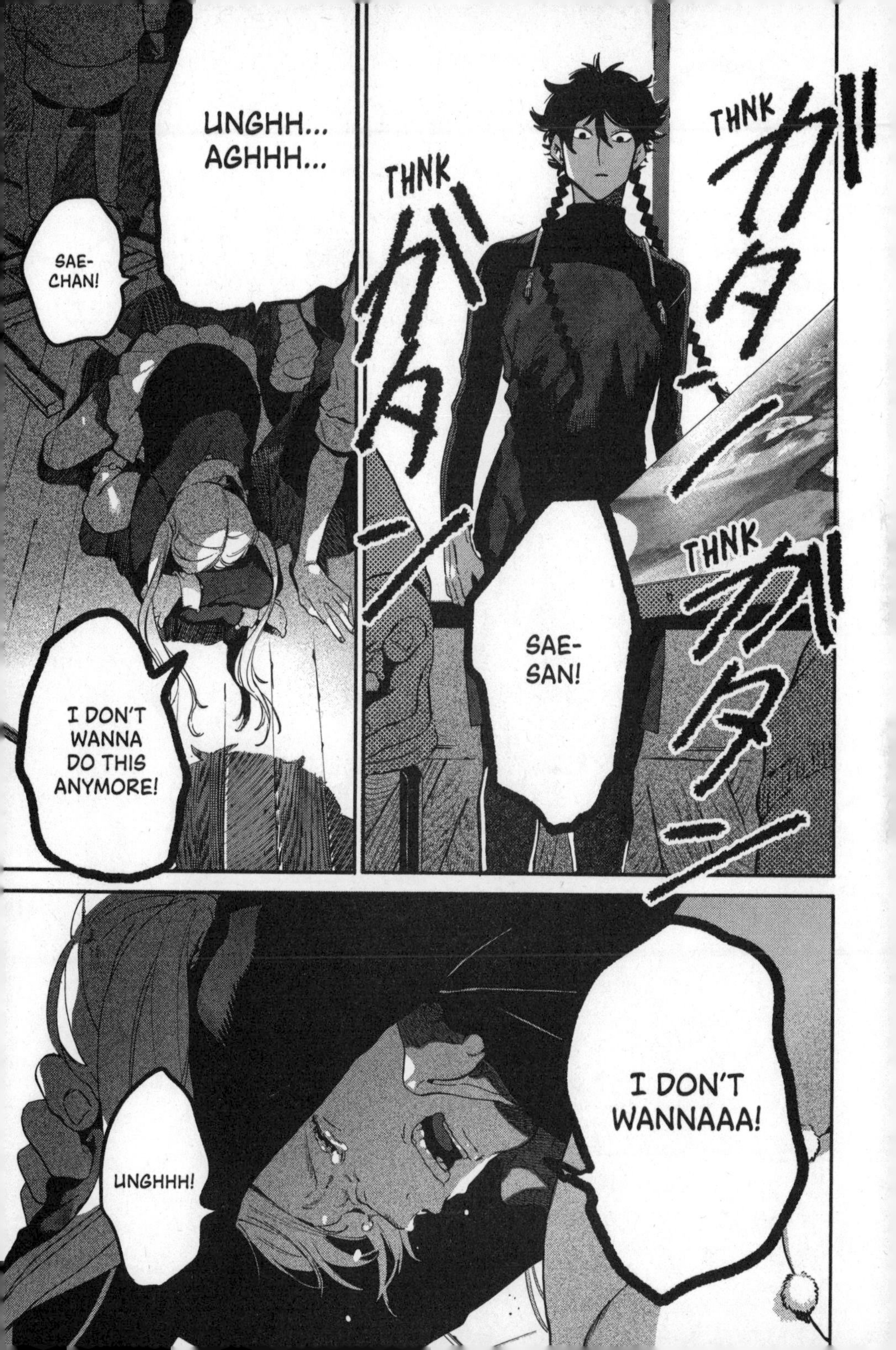
THNK
THNK
THNK
SAE-SAN!
UNGHH... AGHHH...
SAE-CHAN!
I DON'T WANNA DO THIS ANYMORE!
I DON'T WANNAAA!
UNGHHH!

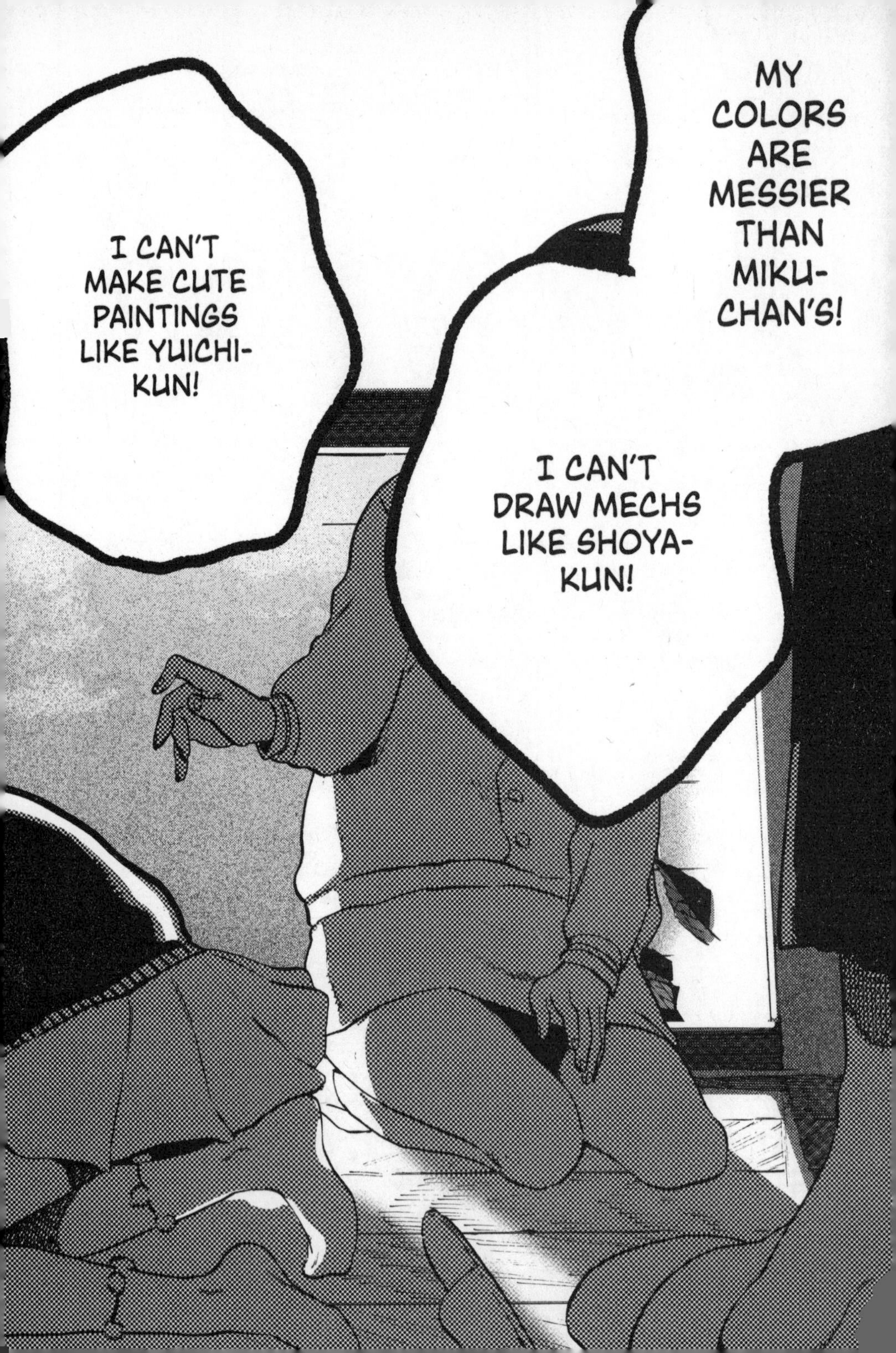
MY COLORS ARE MESSIER THAN MIKU-CHAN'S!
I CAN'T DRAW MECHS LIKE SHOYA-KUN!
I CAN'T MAKE CUTE PAINTINGS LIKE YUICHI-KUN!

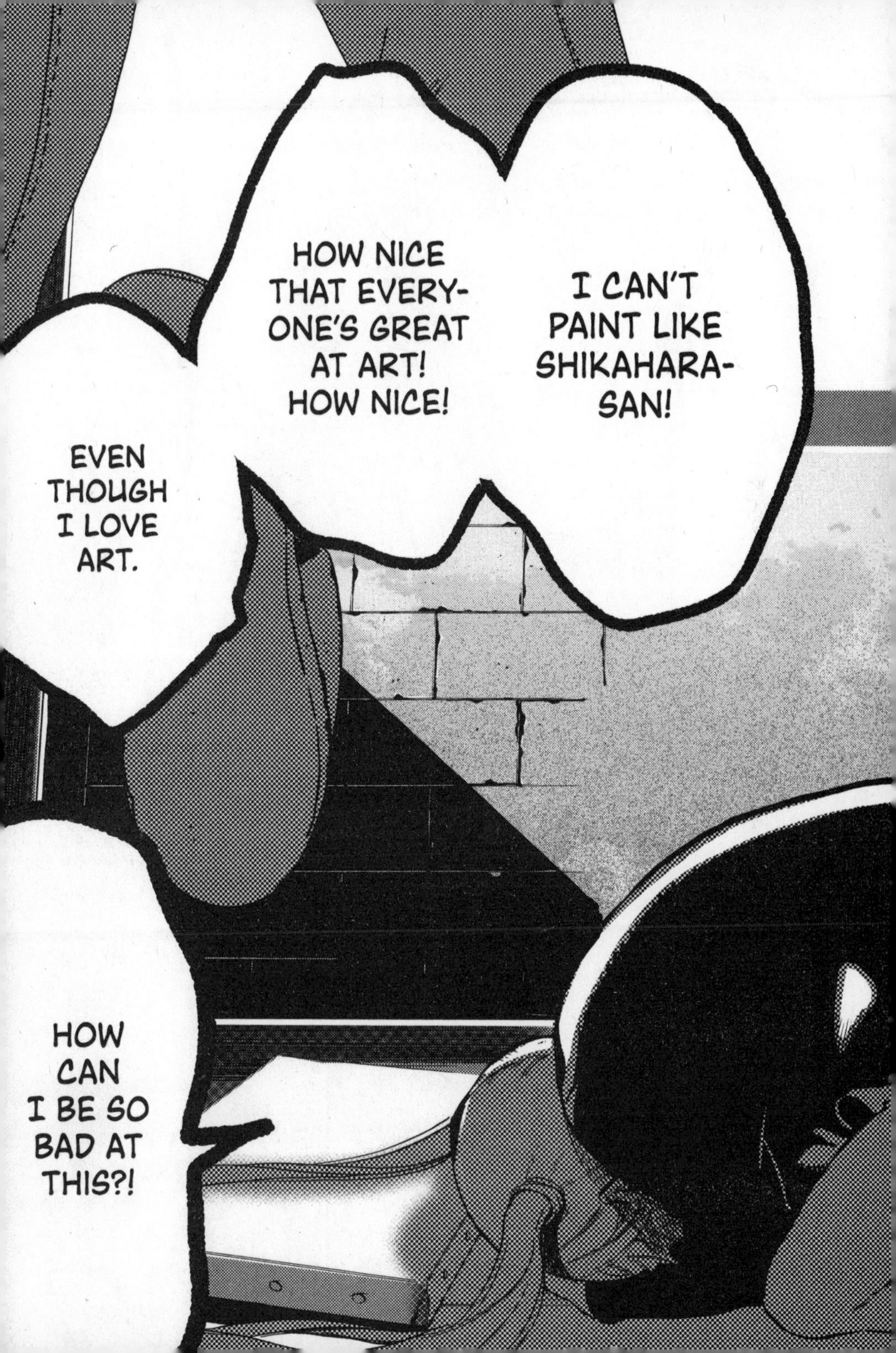
I CAN'T PAINT LIKE SHIKAHARA-SAN!
HOW NICE THAT EVERYONE'S GREAT AT ART! HOW NICE!
EVEN THOUGH I LOVE ART.
HOW CAN I BE SO BAD AT THIS?!

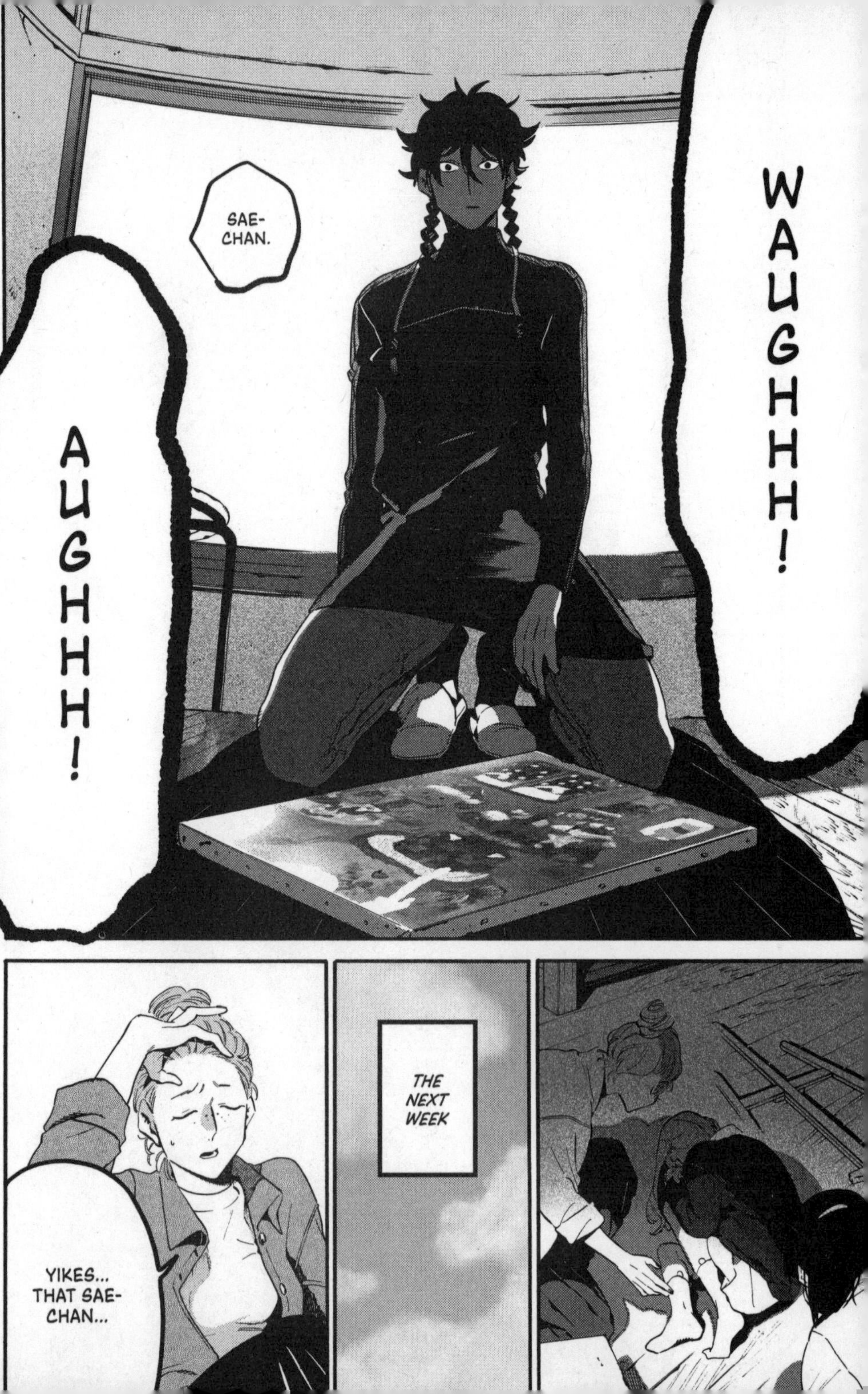
WAUGHHH!
SAE-CHAN.
AUGHHH!
THE NEXT WEEK
YIKES... THAT SAE-CHAN...

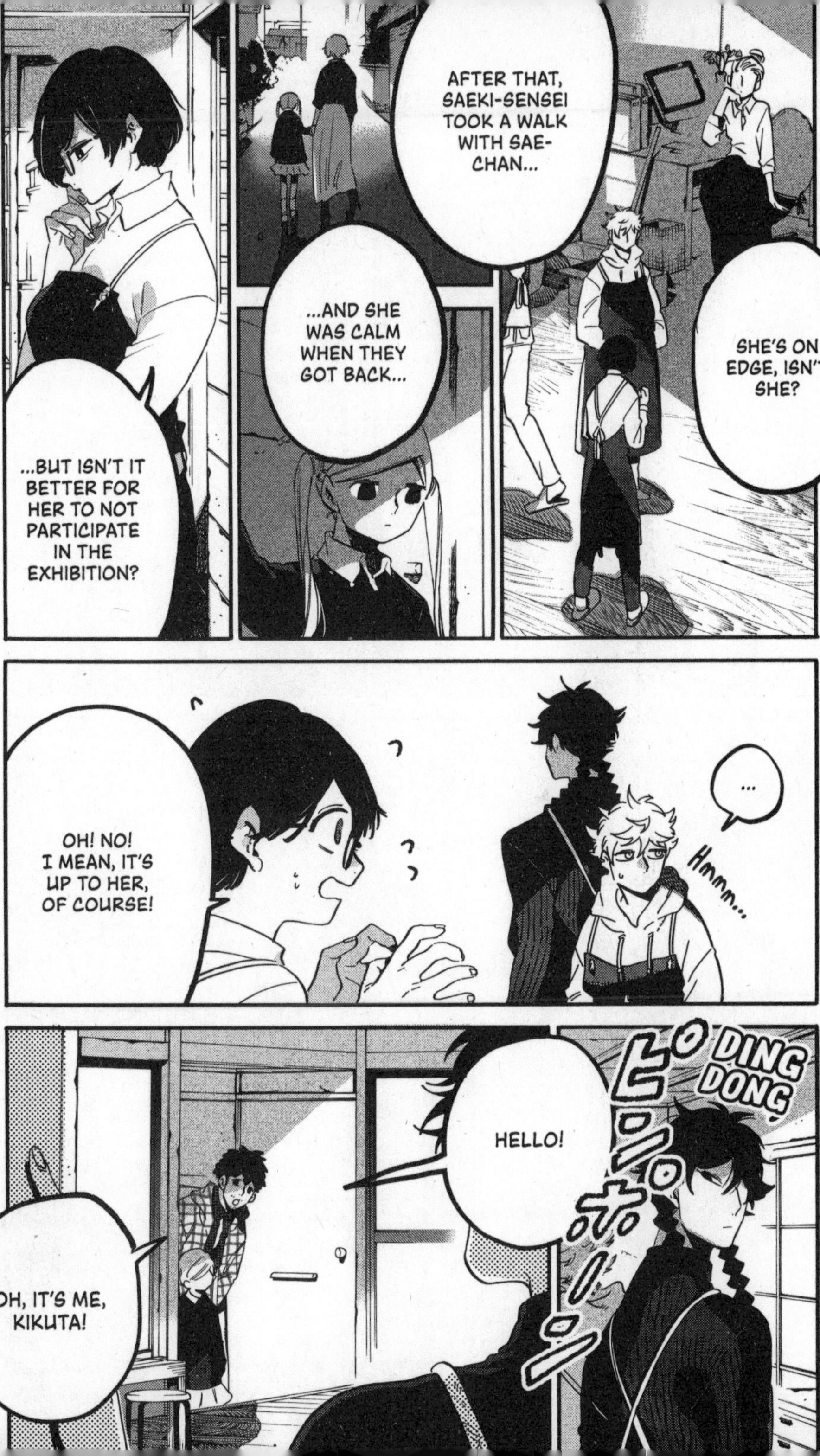
SHE'S ON EDGE, ISN'T SHE?
AFTER THAT, SAEKI-SENSEI TOOK A WALK WITH SAE-CHAN...
...AND SHE WAS CALM WHEN THEY GOT BACK...
...BUT ISN'T IT BETTER FOR HER TO NOT PARTICIPATE IN THE EXHIBITION?
...
Hmmm...
OH! NO! I MEAN, IT'S UP TO HER, OF COURSE!
DING DONG
HELLO!
OH, IT'S ME, KIKUTA!

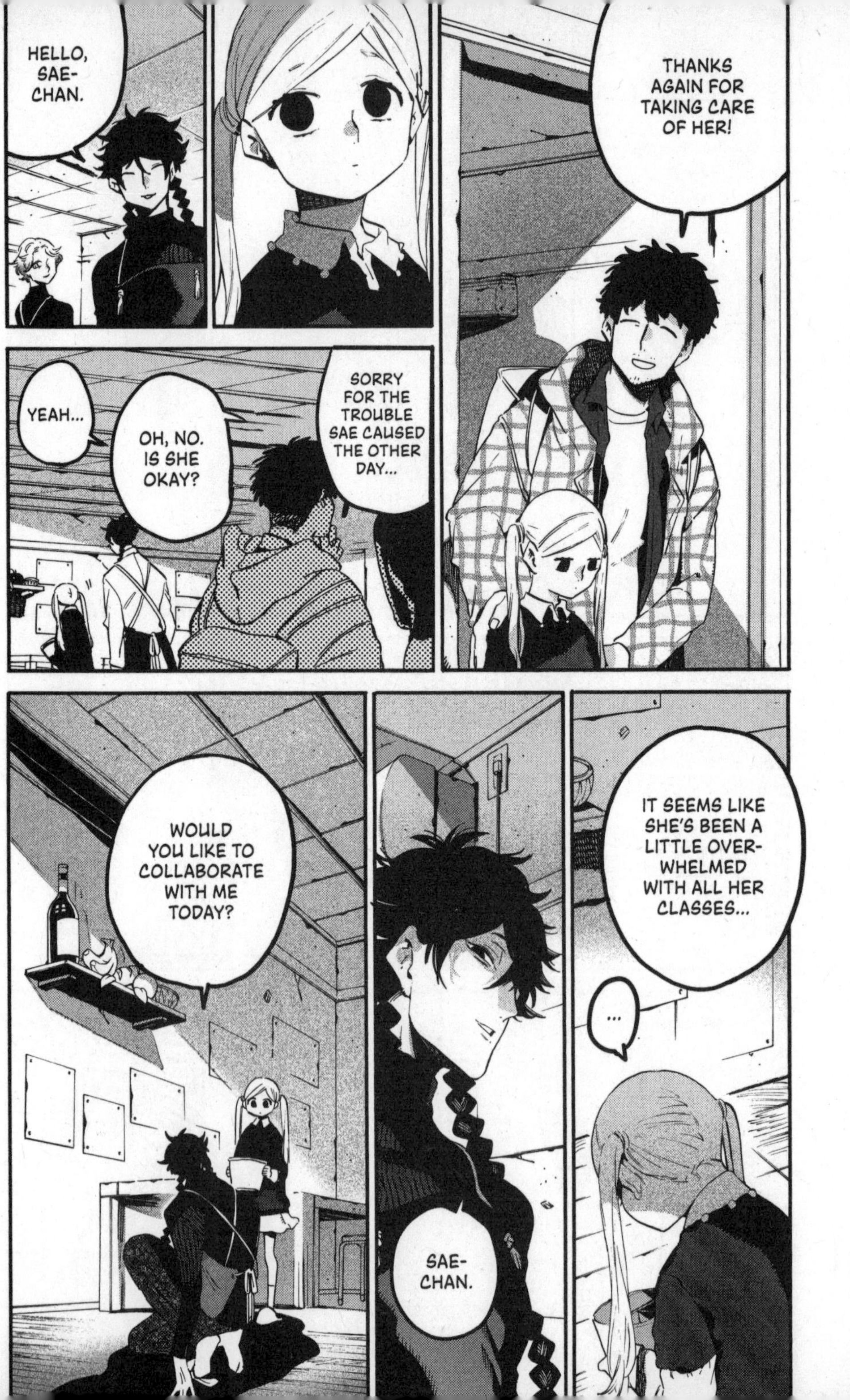
THANKS AGAIN FOR TAKING CARE OF HER!
HELLO, SAE-CHAN.
SORRY FOR THE TROUBLE SAE CAUSED THE OTHER DAY...
OH, NO. IS SHE OKAY?
YEAH...
IT SEEMS LIKE SHE'S BEEN A LITTLE OVER-WHELMED WITH ALL HER CLASSES...
...
SAE-CHAN.
WOULD YOU LIKE TO COLLABORATE WITH ME TODAY?

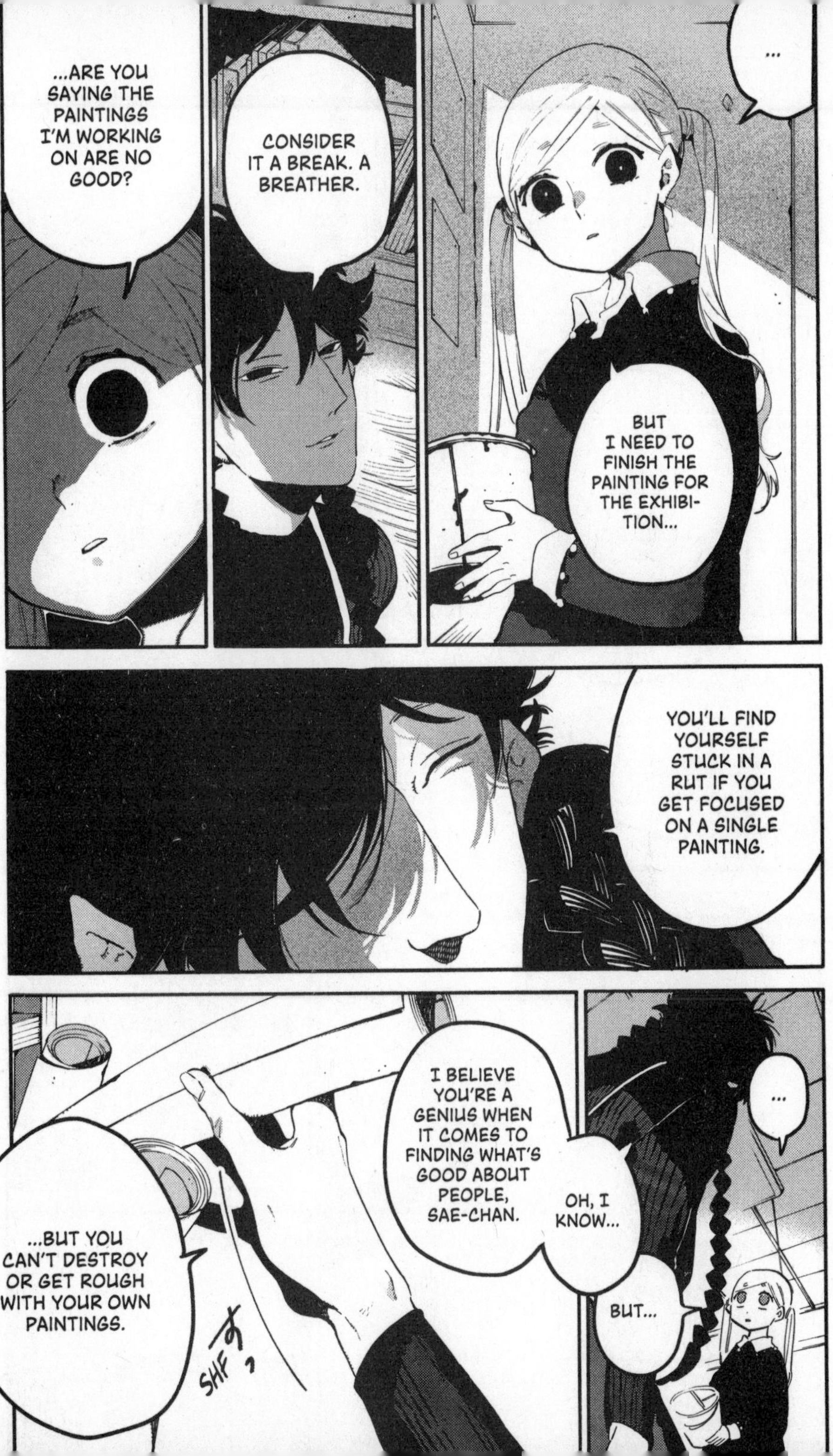
...
BUT I NEED TO FINISH THE PAINTING FOR THE EXHIBI-TION...
CONSIDER IT A BREAK. A BREATHER.
...ARE YOU SAYING THE PAINTINGS I'M WORKING ON ARE NO GOOD?
YOU'LL FIND YOURSELF STUCK IN A RUT IF YOU GET FOCUSED ON A SINGLE PAINTING.
...
I BELIEVE YOU'RE A GENIUS WHEN IT COMES TO FINDING WHAT'S GOOD ABOUT PEOPLE, SAE-CHAN.
OH, I KNOW...
BUT...
...BUT YOU CAN'T DESTROY OR GET ROUGH WITH YOUR OWN PAINTINGS.
SHF

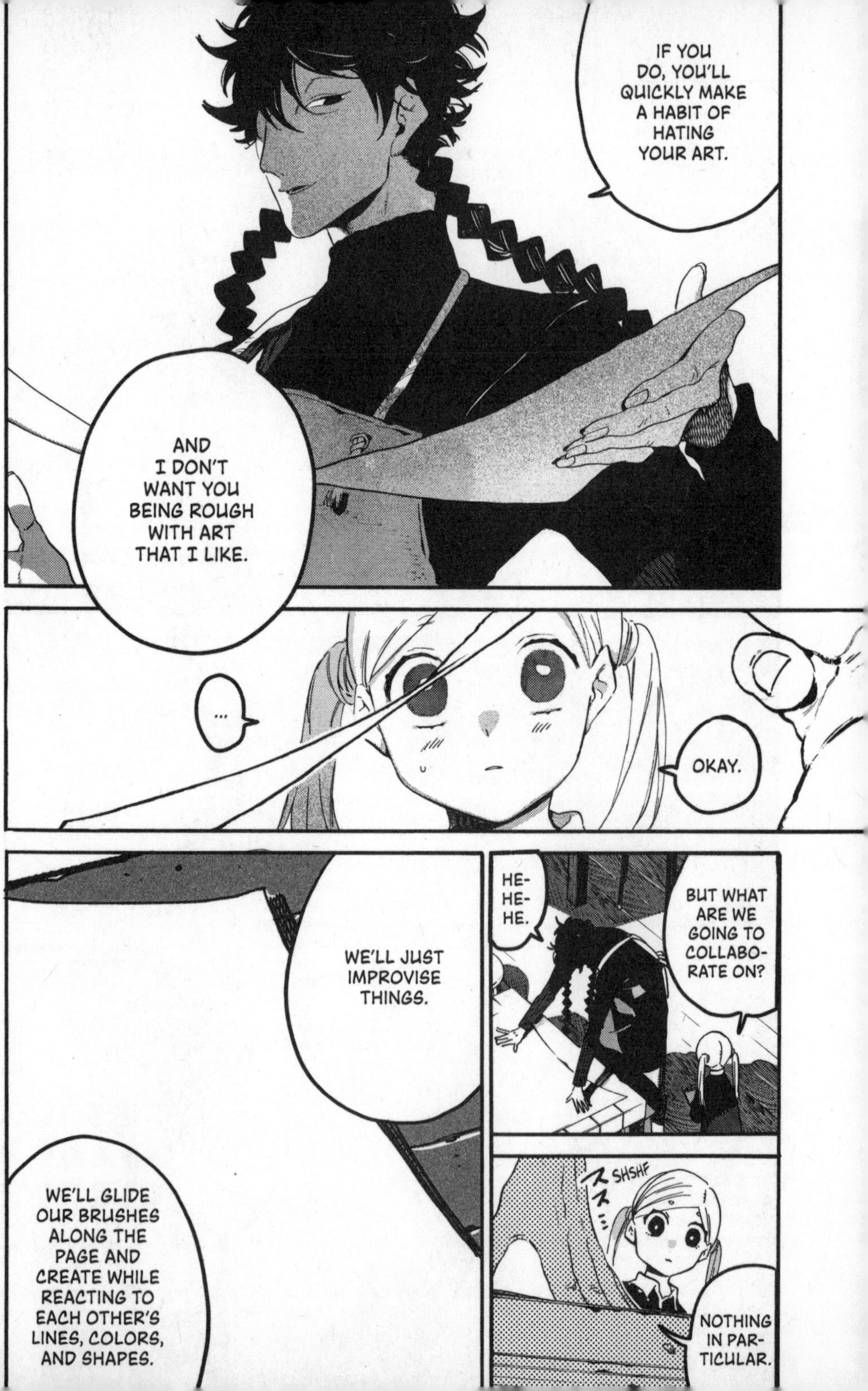
IF YOU DO, YOU'LL QUICKLY MAKE A HABIT OF HATING YOUR ART.
AND I DON'T WANT YOU BEING ROUGH WITH ART THAT I LIKE.
OKAY.
...
BUT WHAT ARE WE GOING TO COLLABO-RATE ON?
HE-HE-HE.
SHSHF
NOTHING IN PAR-TICULAR.
WE'LL JUST IMPROVISE THINGS.
WE'LL GLIDE OUR BRUSHES ALONG THE PAGE AND CREATE WHILE REACTING TO EACH OTHER'S LINES, COLORS, AND SHAPES.

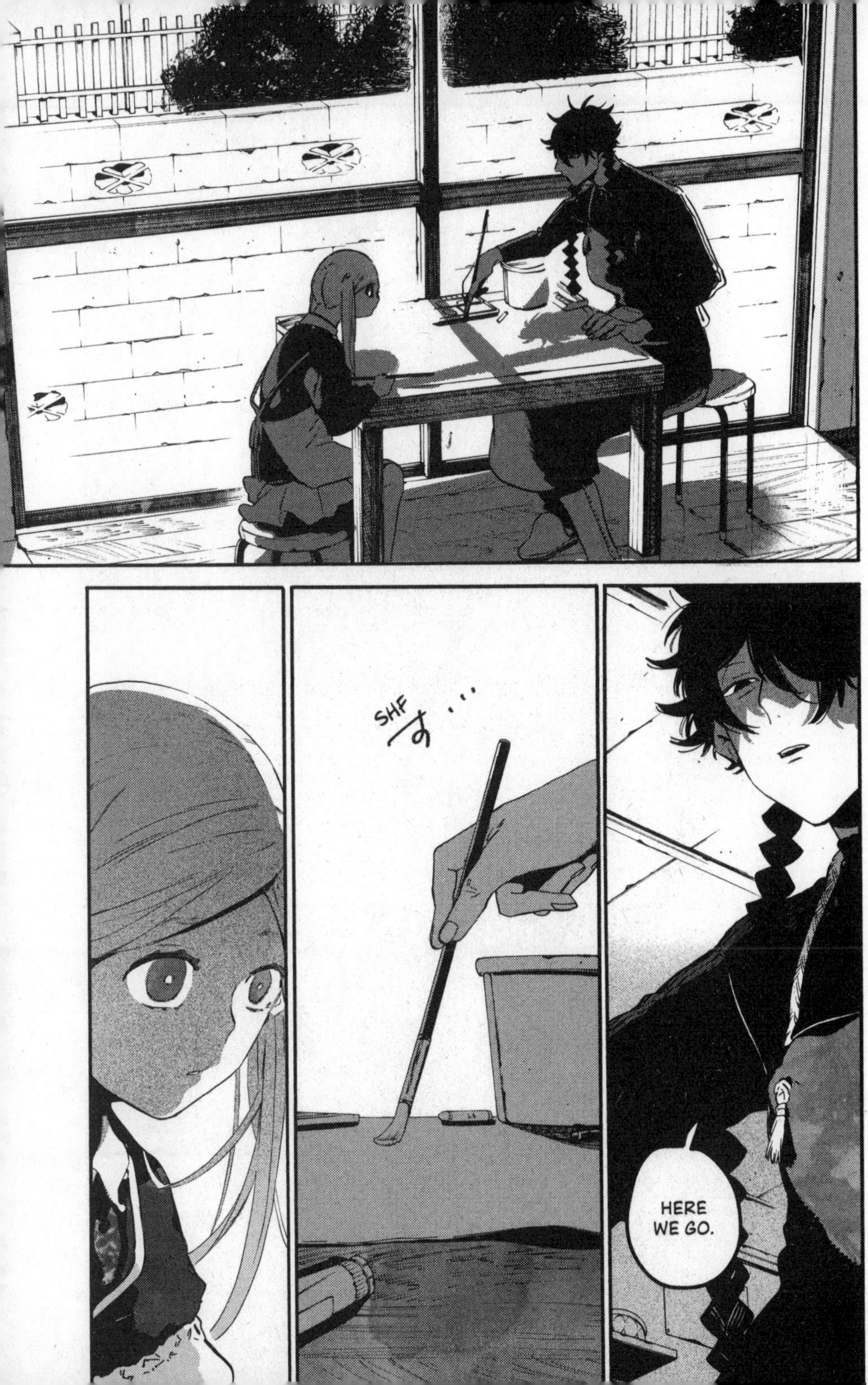
HERE WE GO.
SHF す...

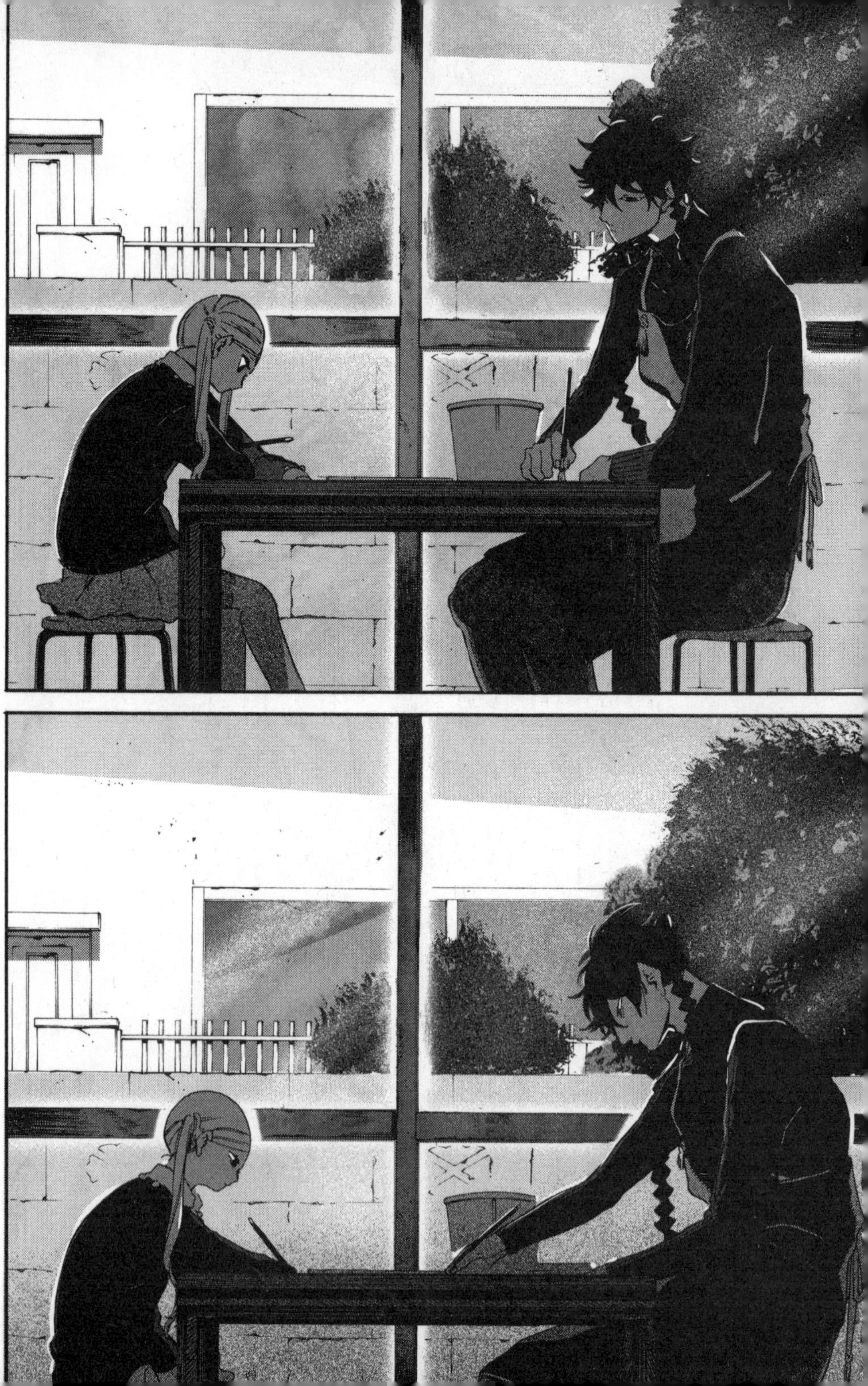

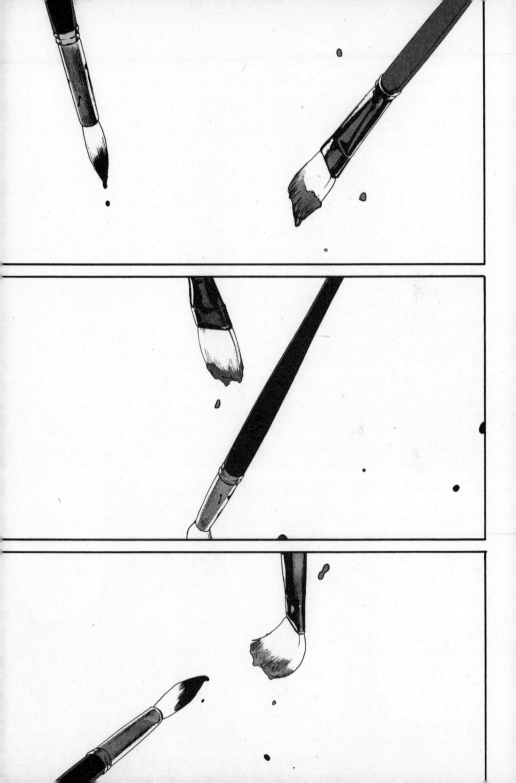

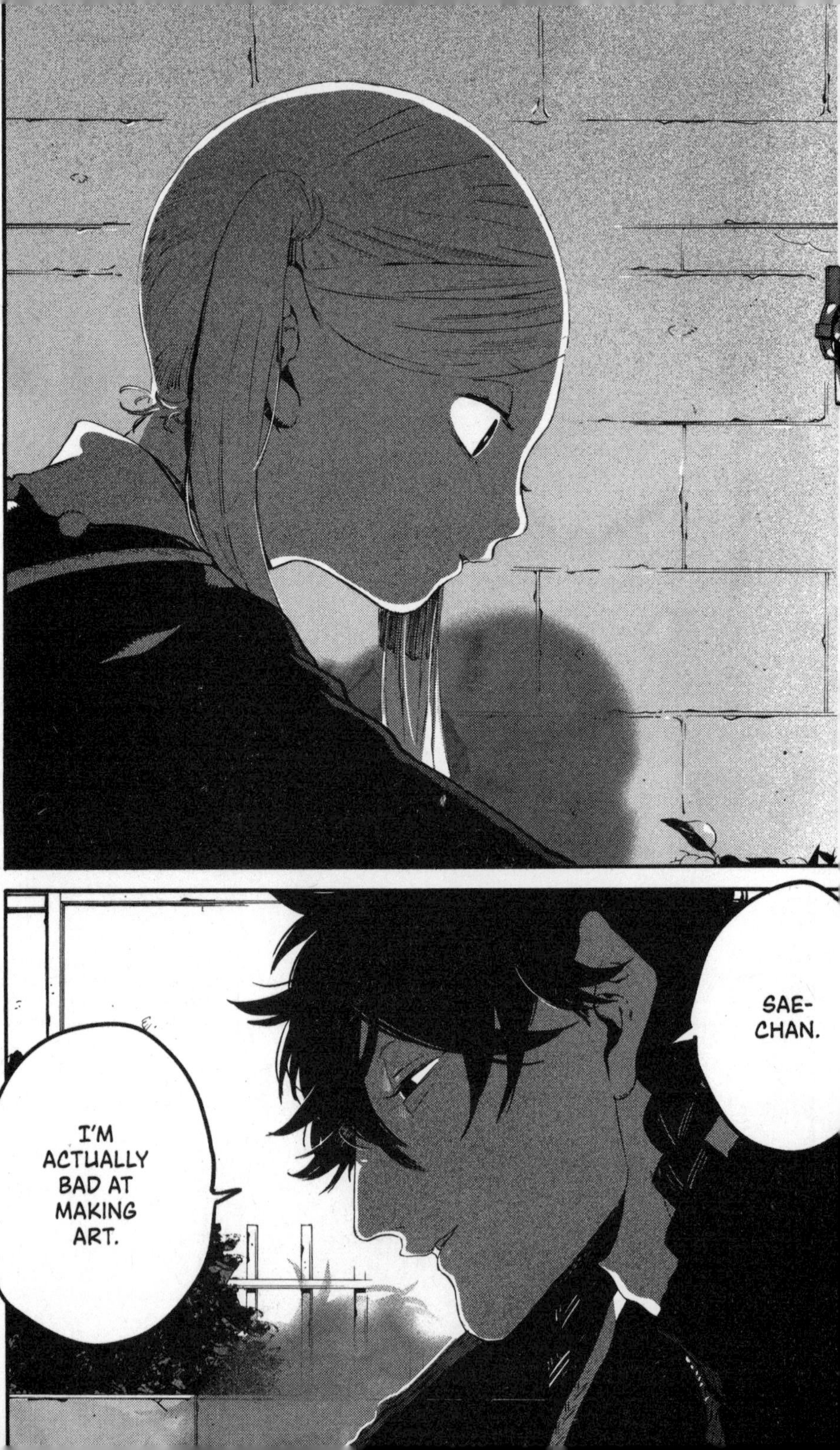
SAE-CHAN.
I'M ACTUALLY BAD AT MAKING ART.

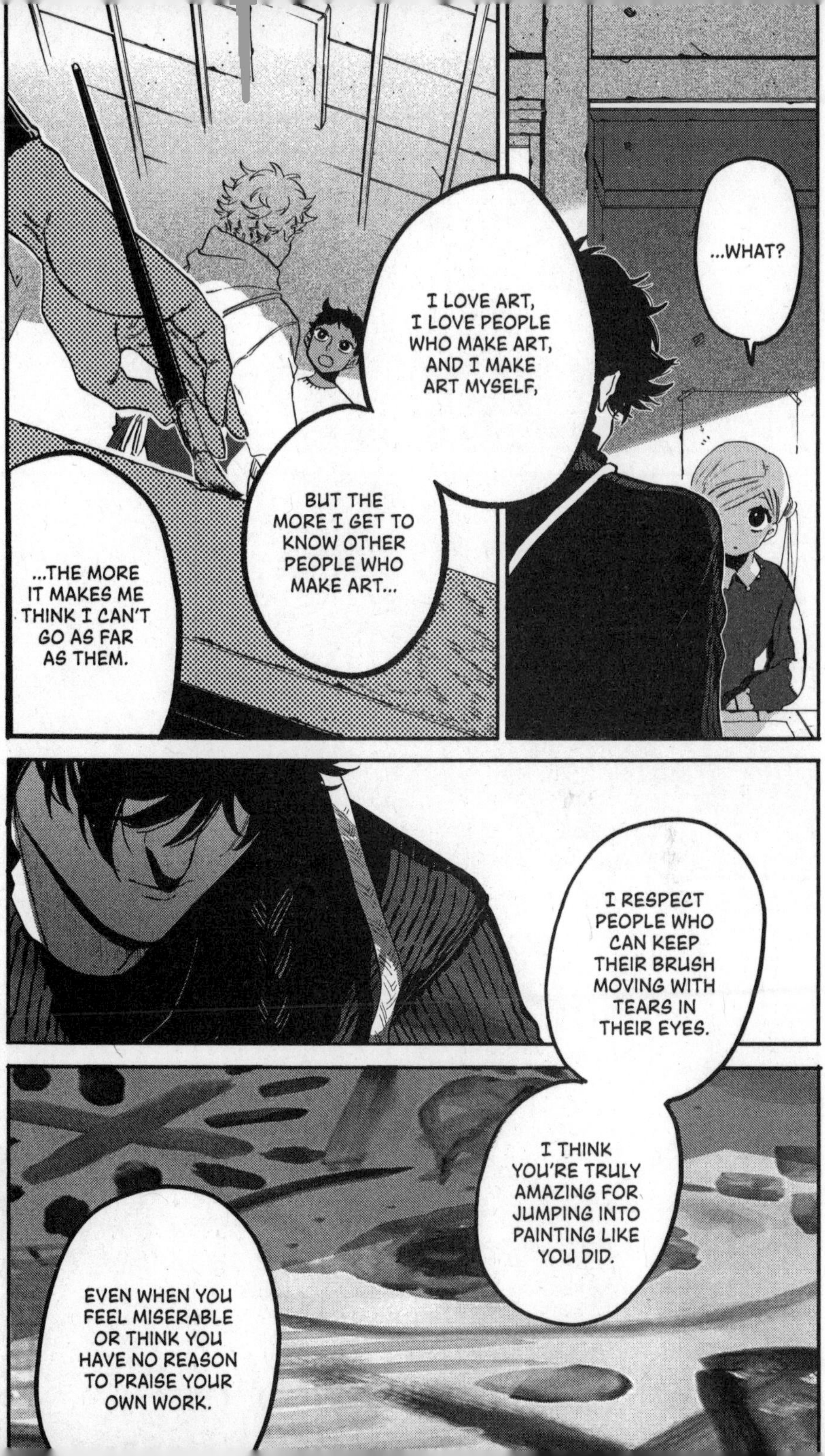
...WHAT?
I LOVE ART, I LOVE PEOPLE WHO MAKE ART, AND I MAKE ART MYSELF,
BUT THE MORE I GET TO KNOW OTHER PEOPLE WHO MAKE ART...
...THE MORE IT MAKES ME THINK I CAN'T GO AS FAR AS THEM.
I RESPECT PEOPLE WHO CAN KEEP THEIR BRUSH MOVING WITH TEARS IN THEIR EYES.
I THINK YOU'RE TRULY AMAZING FOR JUMPING INTO PAINTING LIKE YOU DID.
EVEN WHEN YOU FEEL MISERABLE OR THINK YOU HAVE NO REASON TO PRAISE YOUR OWN WORK.

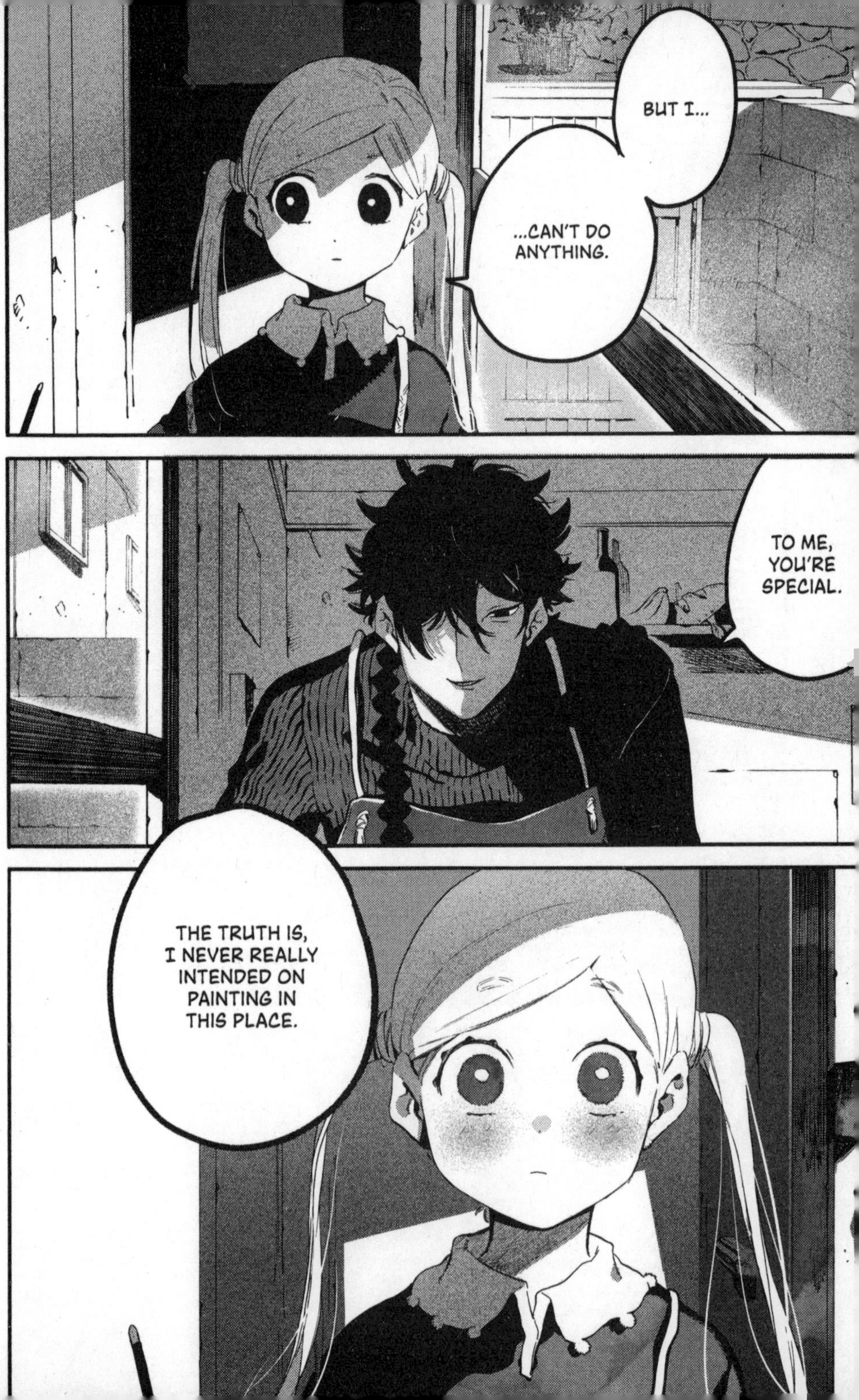
BUT I...
...CAN'T DO ANYTHING.
TO ME, YOU'RE SPECIAL.
THE TRUTH IS, I NEVER REALLY INTENDED ON PAINTING IN THIS PLACE.

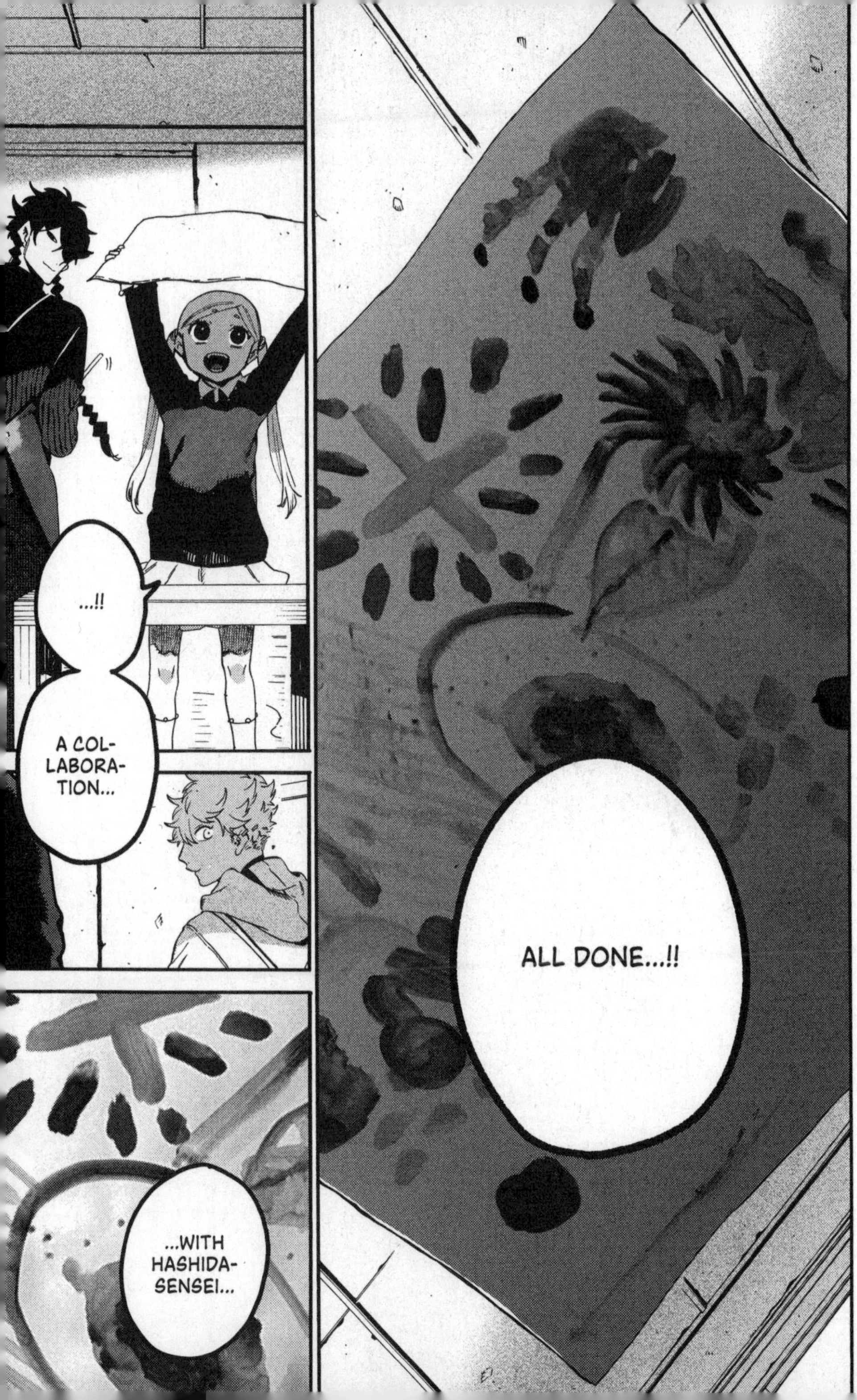
ALL DONE...!!
...!!
A COL-LABORA-TION...
...WITH HASHIDA-SENSEI...

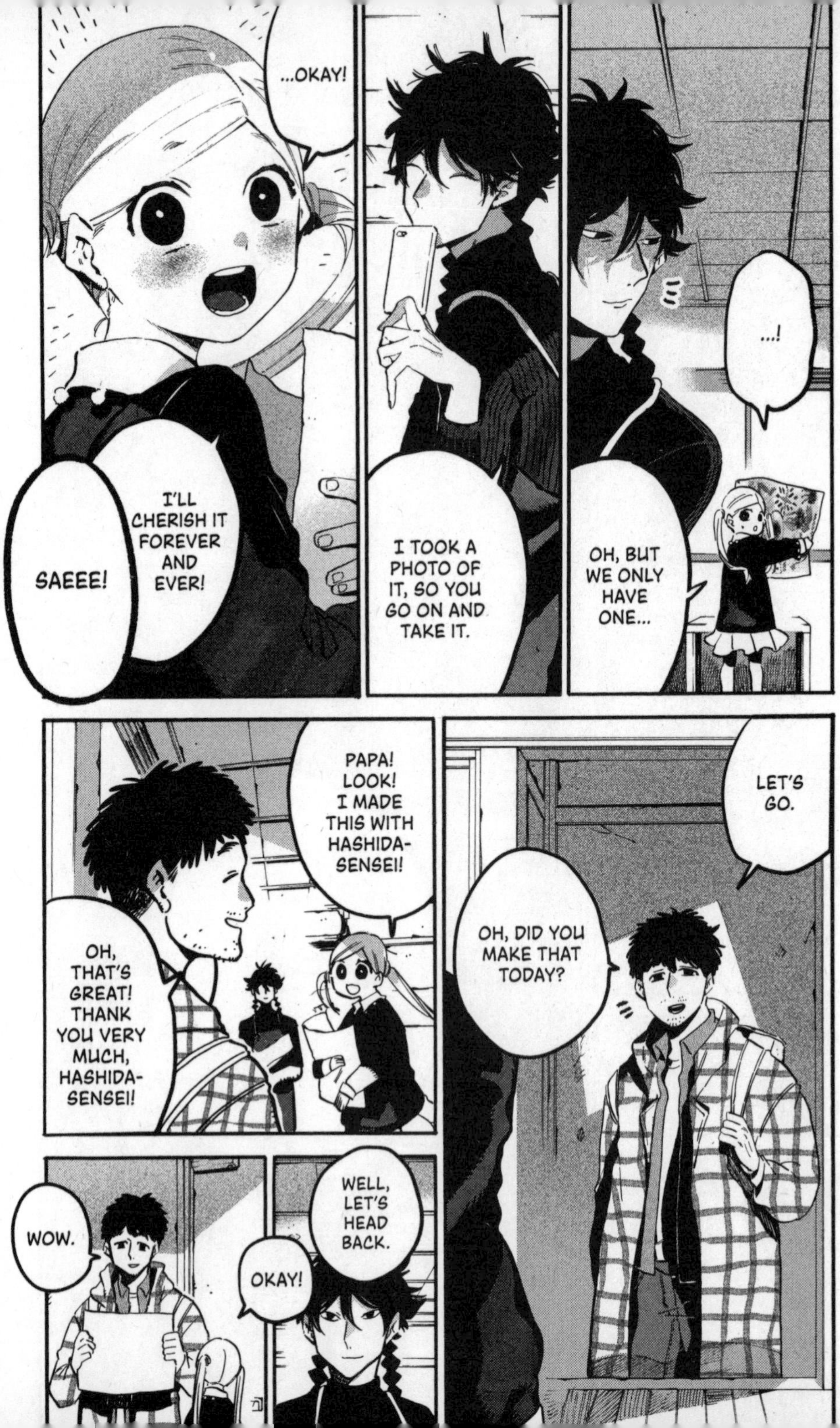
...!
OH, BUT WE ONLY HAVE ONE...
I TOOK A PHOTO OF IT, SO YOU GO ON AND TAKE IT.
...OKAY!
I'LL CHERISH IT FOREVER AND EVER!
SAEEE!
LET'S GO.
OH, DID YOU MAKE THAT TODAY?
PAPA! LOOK! I MADE THIS WITH HASHIDA-SENSEI!
OH, THAT'S GREAT! THANK YOU VERY MUCH, HASHIDA-SENSEI!
WELL, LET'S HEAD BACK.
OKAY!
WOW.

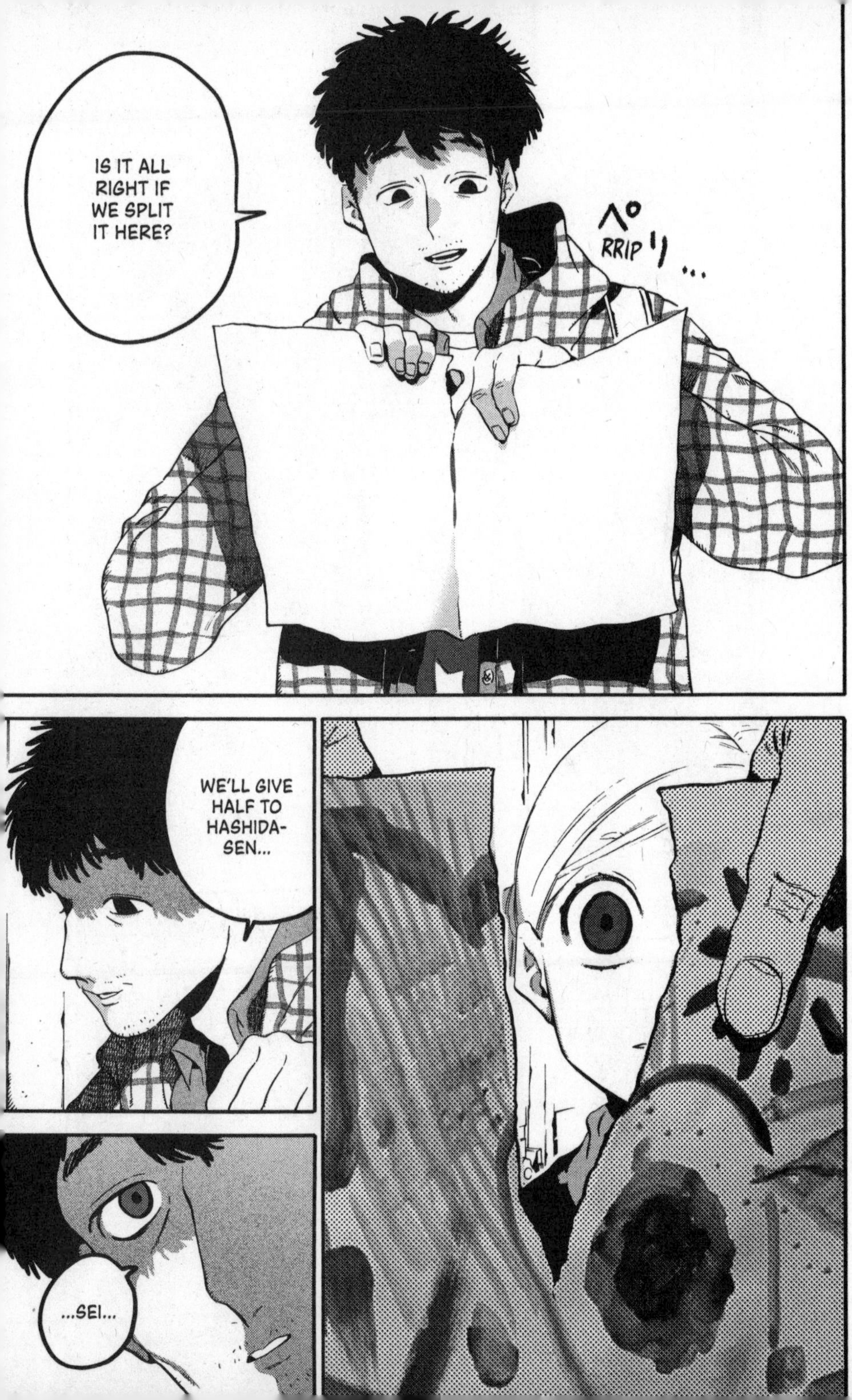
IS IT ALL RIGHT IF WE SPLIT IT HERE?
ぺ RRIP り...
WE'LL GIVE HALF TO HASHIDA-SEN...
...SEI...

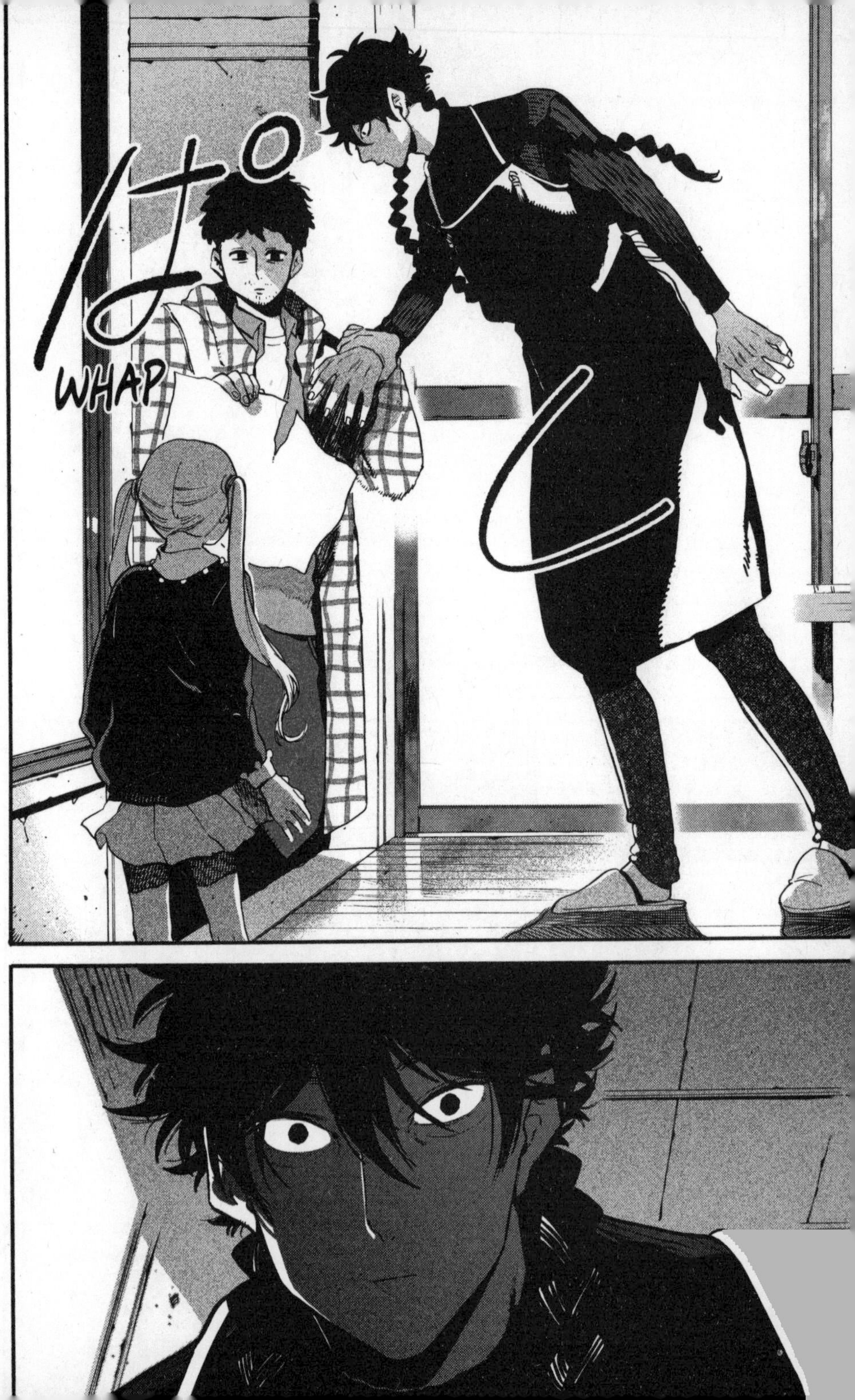
WHAP

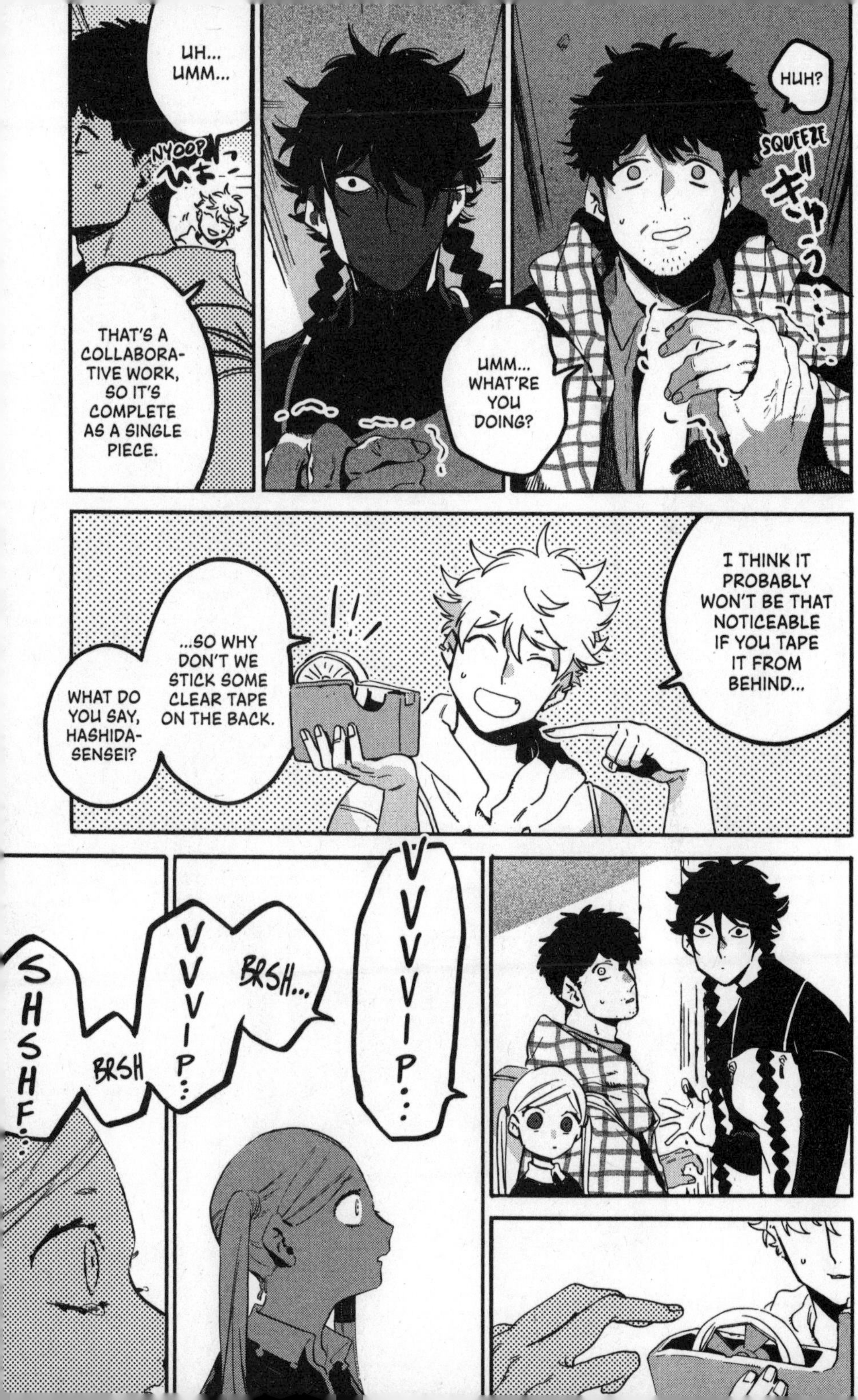
HUH?
SQUEEZE
UMM... WHAT'RE YOU DOING?
UH... UMM...
NYOOP
THAT'S A COLLABORATIVE WORK, SO IT'S COMPLETE AS A SINGLE PIECE.
I THINK IT PROBABLY WON'T BE THAT NOTICEABLE IF YOU TAPE IT FROM BEHIND...
...SO WHY DON'T WE STICK SOME CLEAR TAPE ON THE BACK.
WHAT DO YOU SAY, HASHIDA-SENSEI?
VVVVIP...
VVVIP...
BRSH...
BRSH
SHSHF...

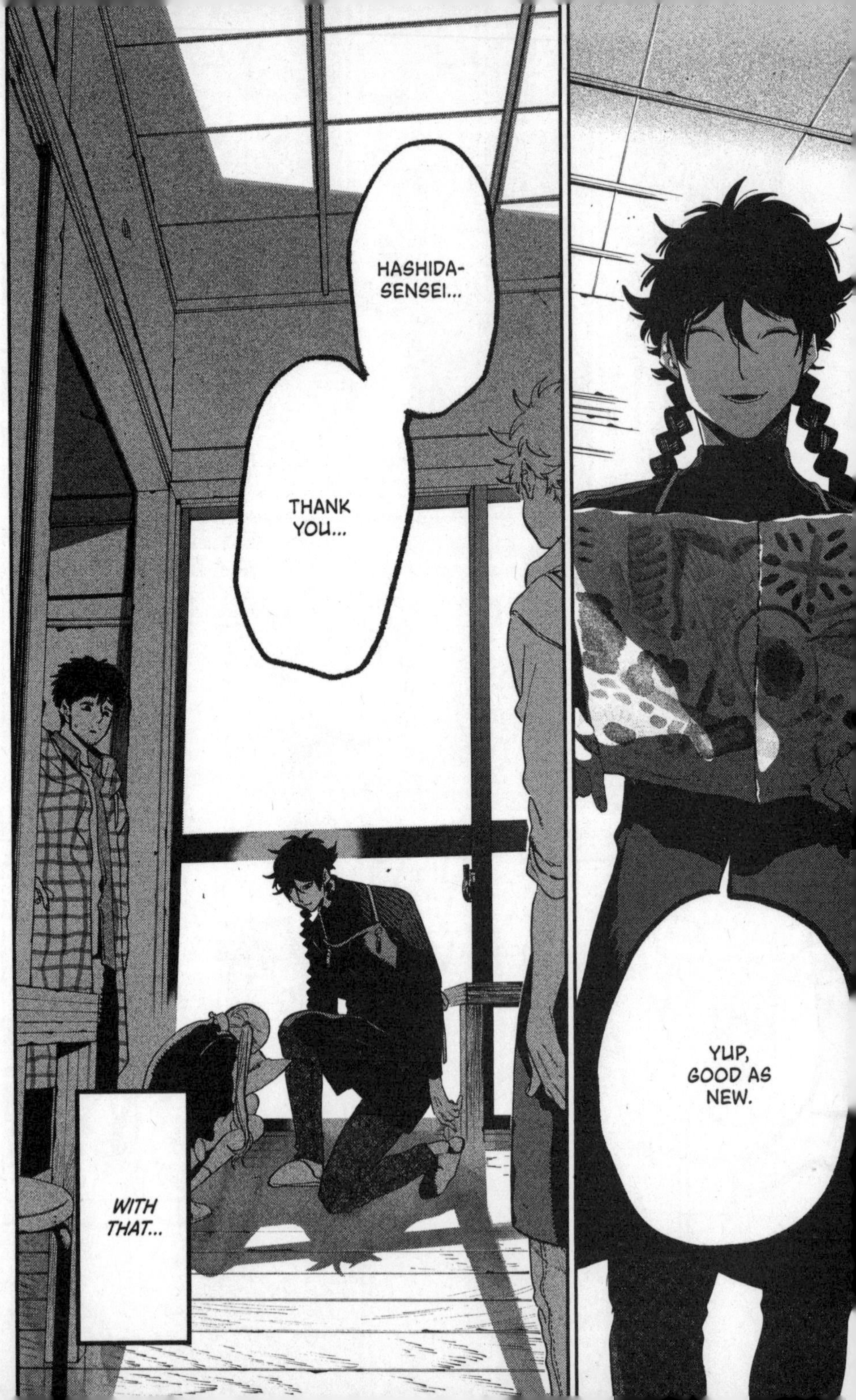
YUP, GOOD AS NEW.
HASHIDA-SENSEI...
THANK YOU...
WITH THAT...

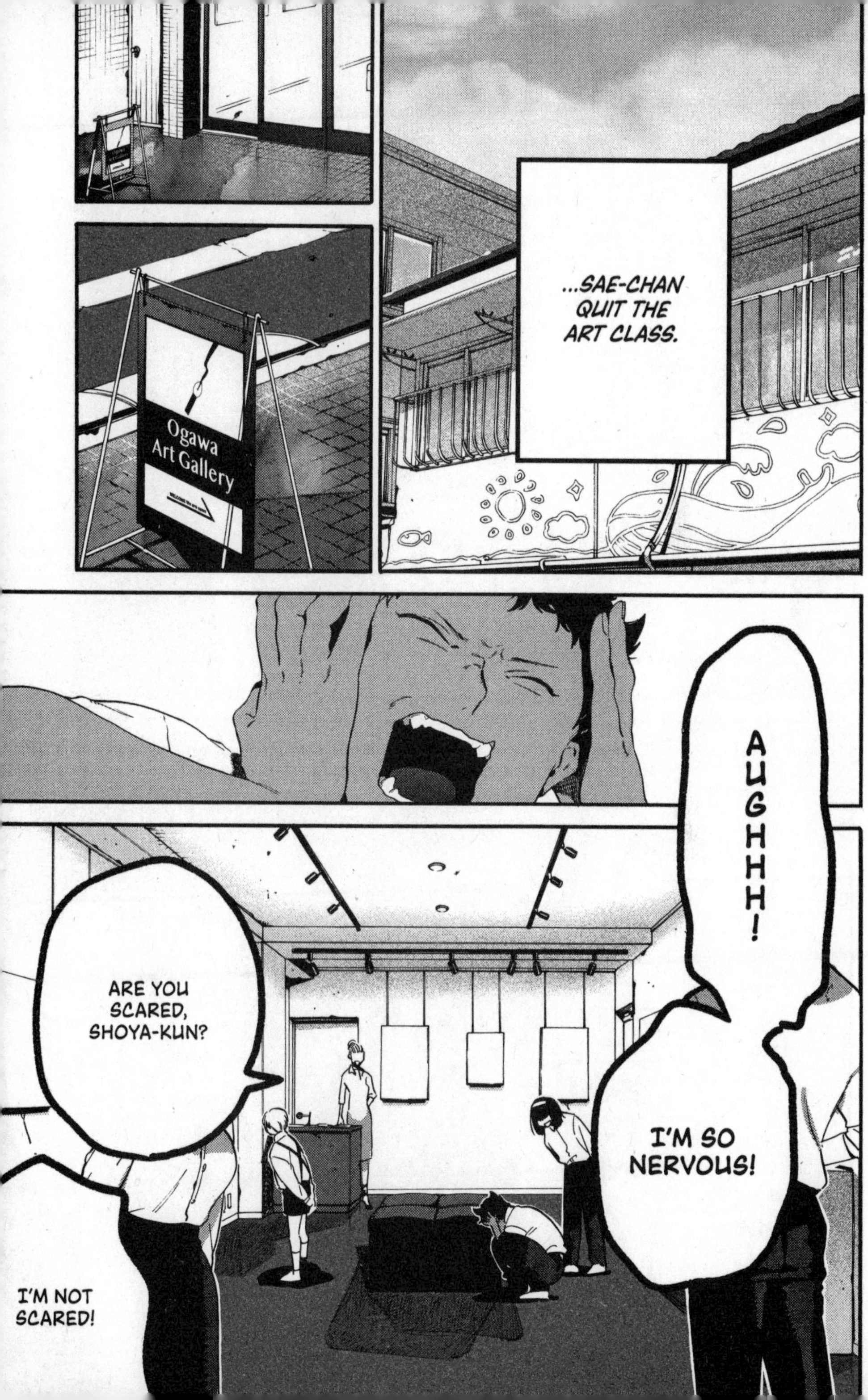
...SAE-CHAN QUIT THE ART CLASS.
Ogawa Art Gallery
AUGHHH!
I'M SO NERVOUS!
ARE YOU SCARED, SHOYA-KUN?
I'M NOT SCARED!

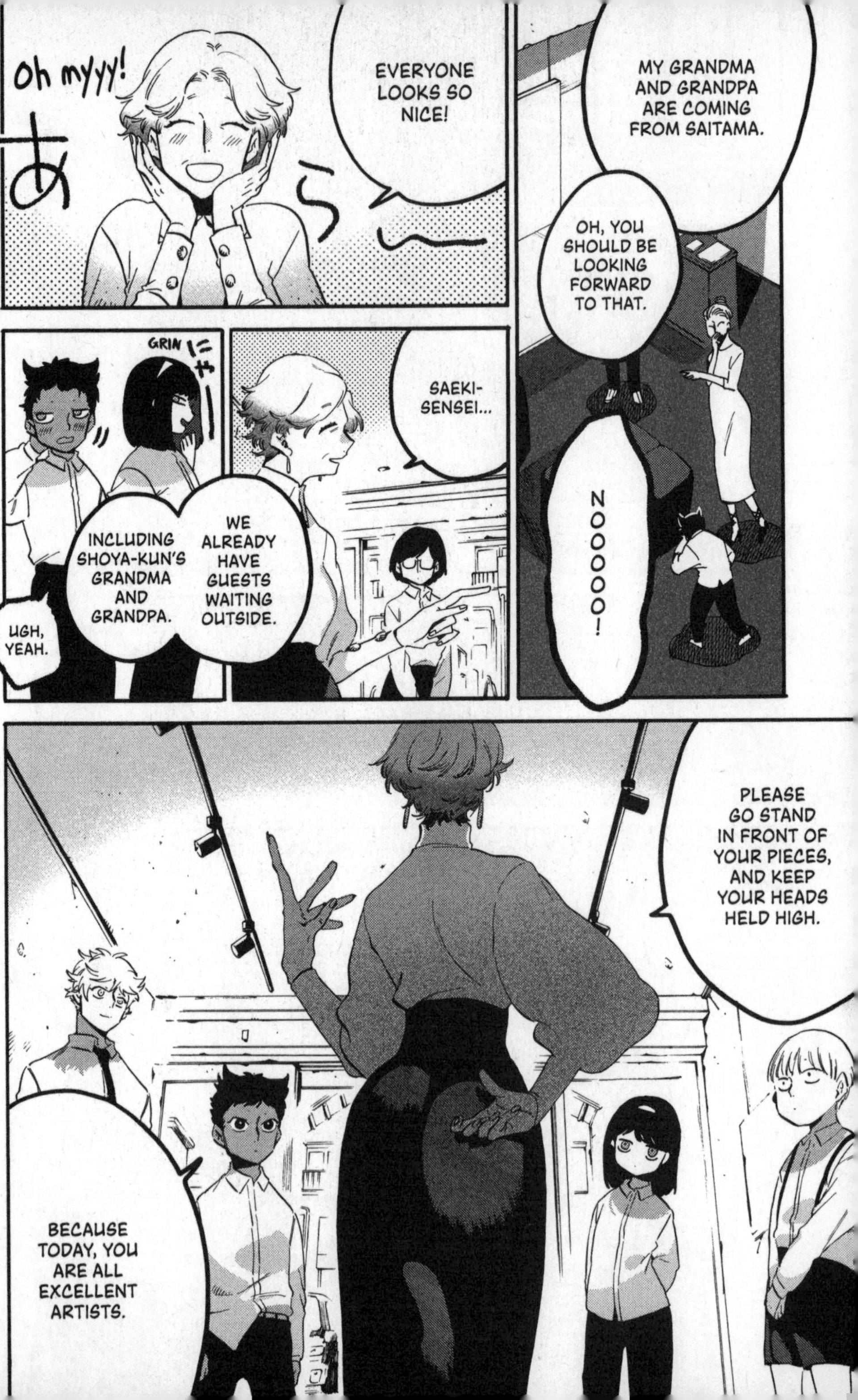
MY GRANDMA AND GRANDPA ARE COMING FROM SAITAMA.
OH, YOU SHOULD BE LOOKING FORWARD TO THAT.
NOOOOO!
EVERYONE LOOKS SO NICE!
Oh myyy!
あら〜
SAEKI-SENSEI...
WE ALREADY HAVE GUESTS WAITING OUTSIDE.
INCLUDING SHOYA-KUN'S GRANDMA AND GRANDPA.
GRIN
にや〜
UGH, YEAH.
PLEASE GO STAND IN FRONT OF YOUR PIECES, AND KEEP YOUR HEADS HELD HIGH.
BECAUSE TODAY, YOU ARE ALL EXCELLENT ARTISTS.

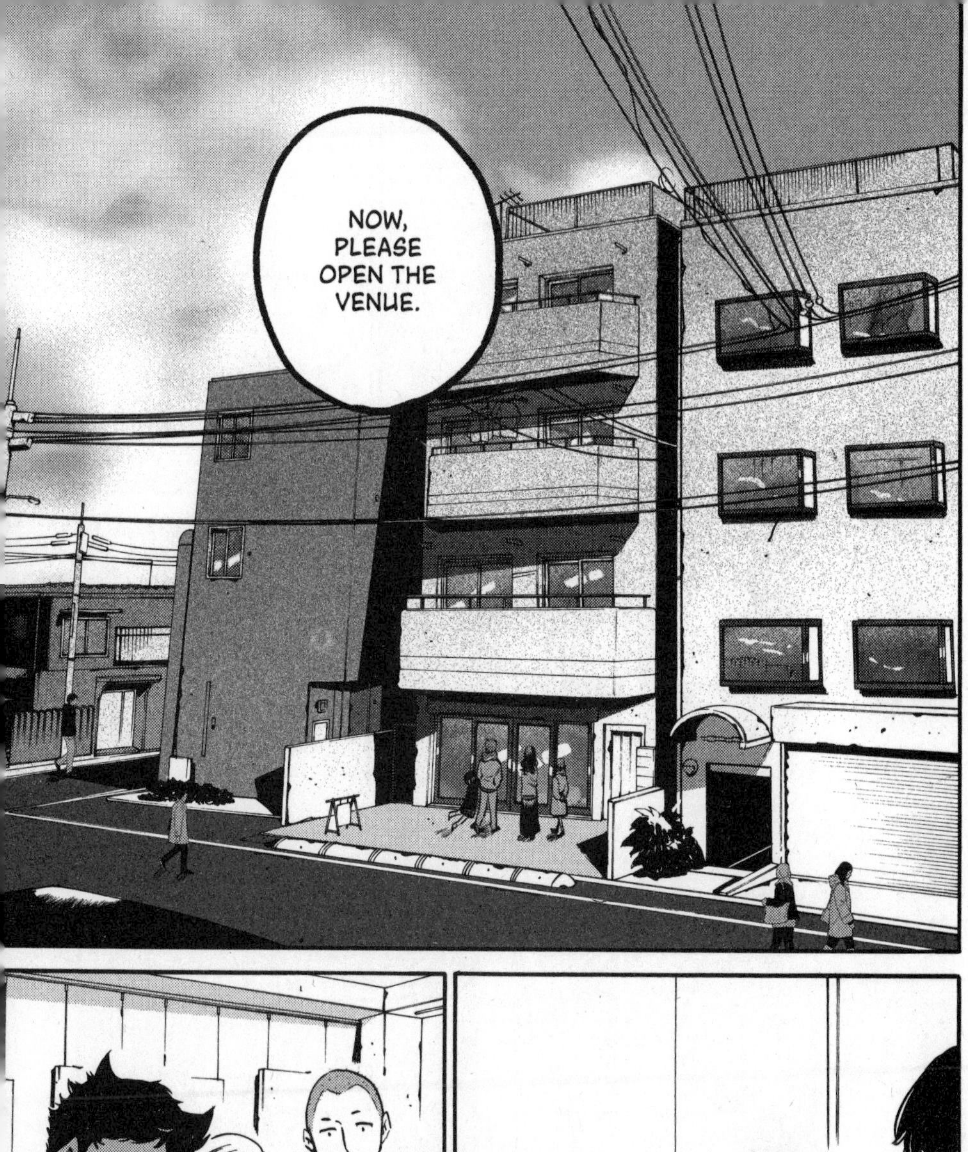
NOW, PLEASE OPEN THE VENUE.
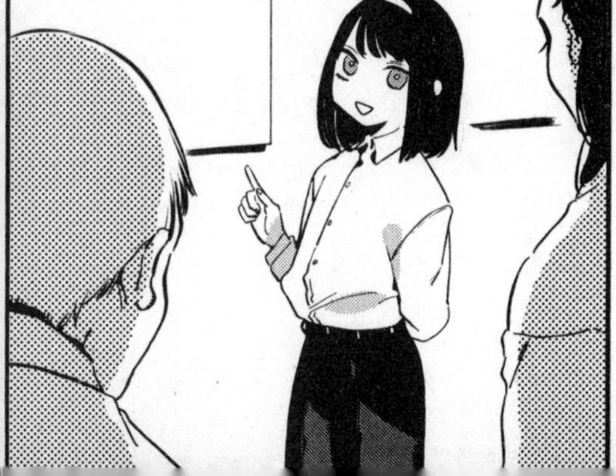
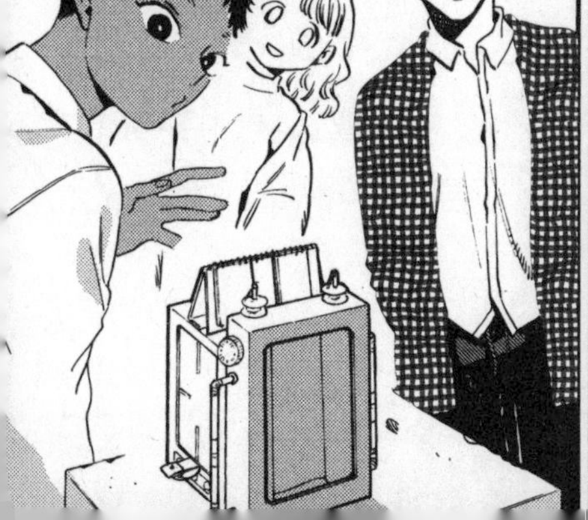

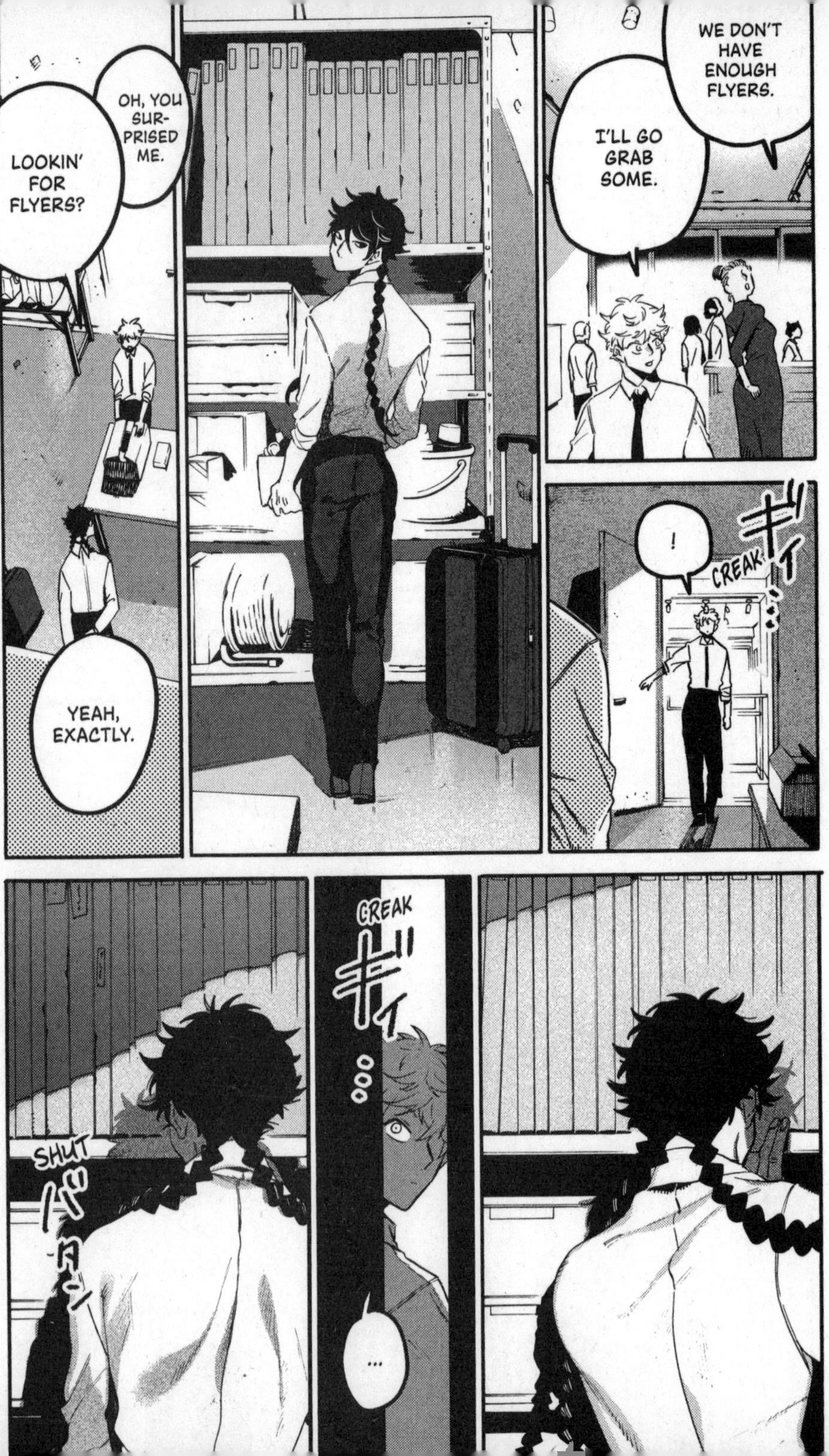
WE DON'T HAVE ENOUGH FLYERS.
I'LL GO GRAB SOME.
!
CREAK
OH, YOU SURPRISED ME.
LOOKIN' FOR FLYERS?
YEAH, EXACTLY.
CREAK
...
SHUT

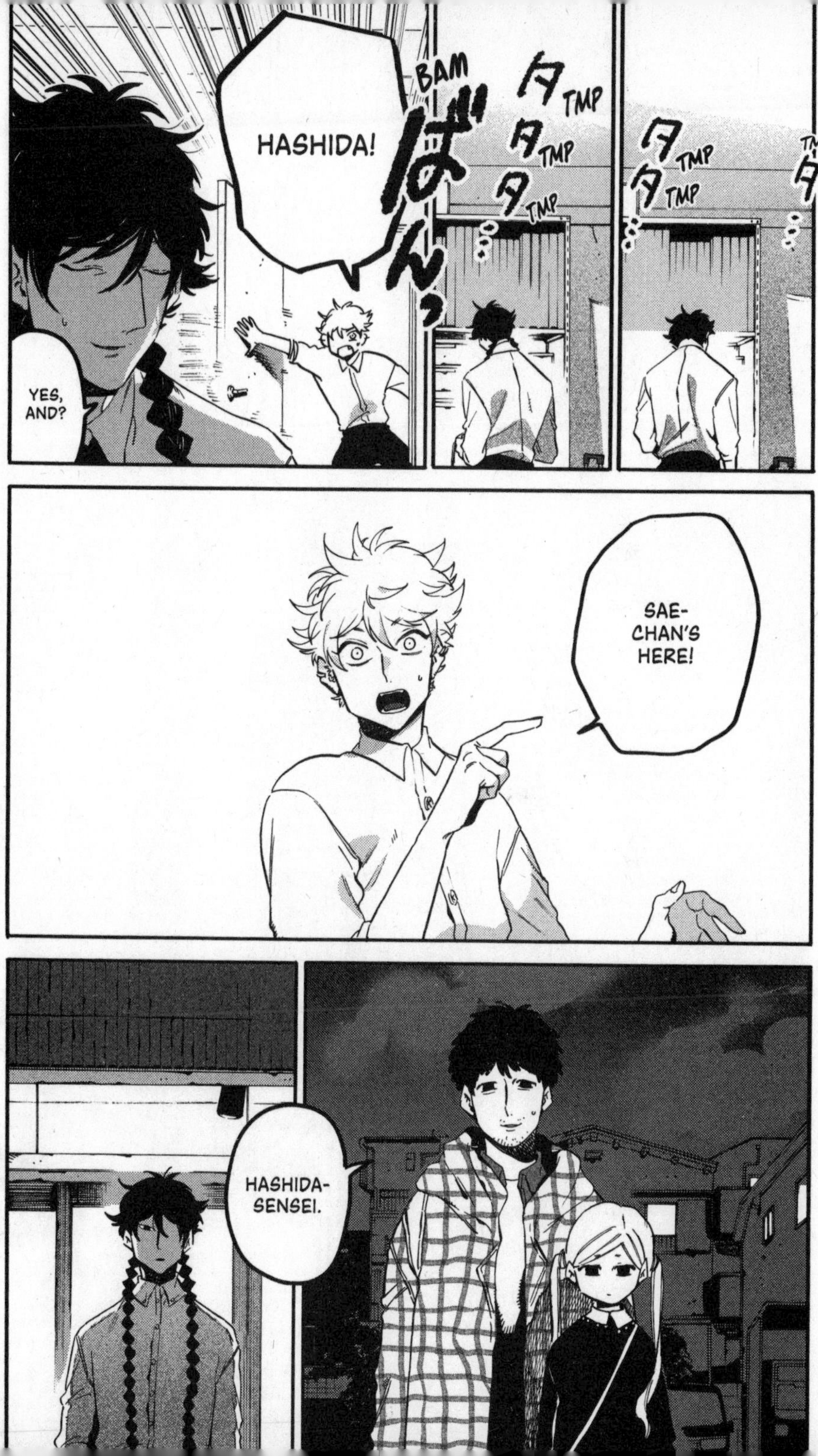

TMP タ
タ TMP タ TMP
タ TMP タ TMP タ TMP
BAM ばんっ
HASHIDA!
YES, AND?
SAE-CHAN'S HERE!
HASHIDA-SENSEI.

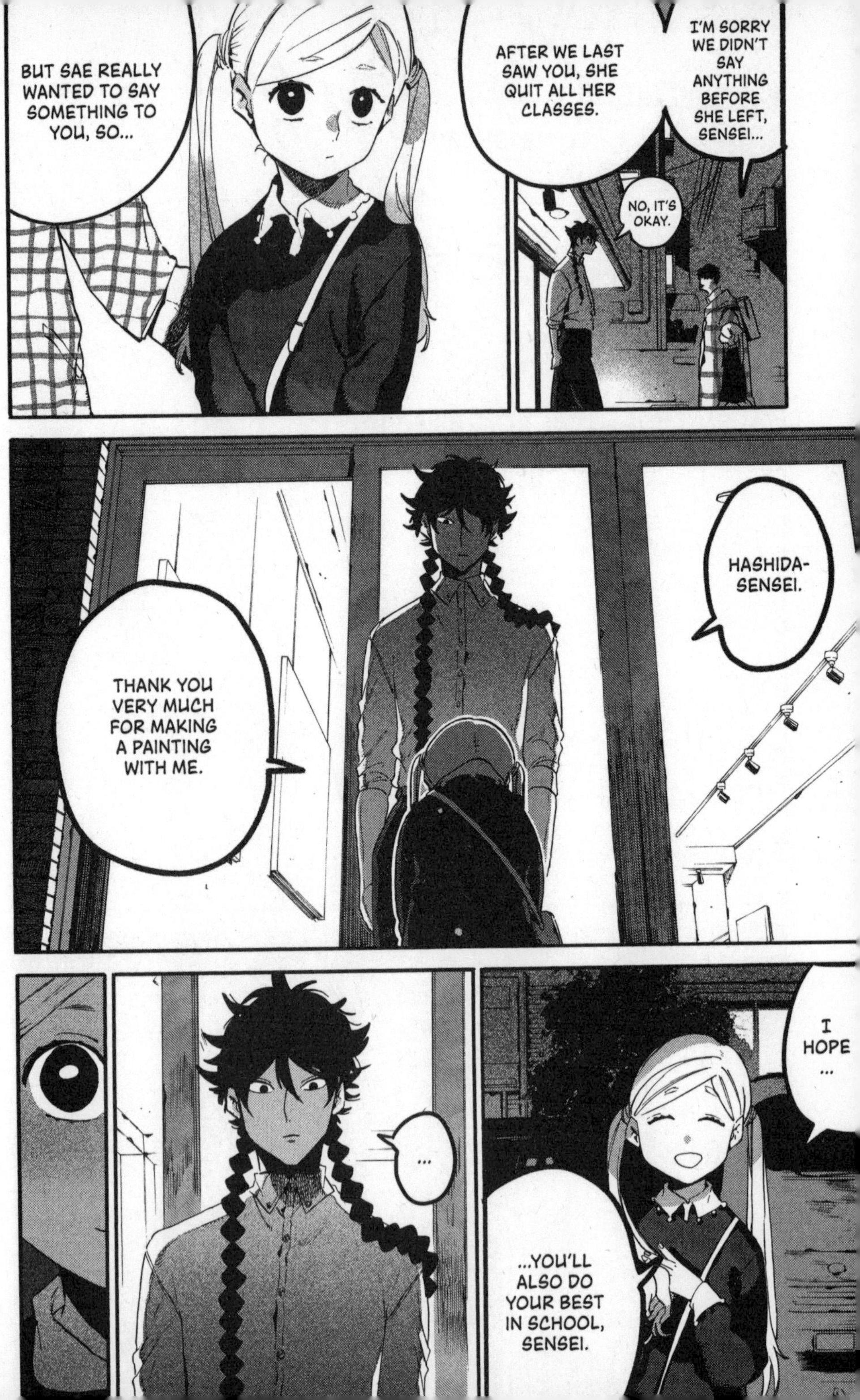
I'M SORRY WE DIDN'T SAY ANYTHING BEFORE SHE LEFT, SENSEI...
AFTER WE LAST SAW YOU, SHE QUIT ALL HER CLASSES.
NO, IT'S OKAY.
BUT SAE REALLY WANTED TO SAY SOMETHING TO YOU, SO...
HASHIDA-SENSEI.
THANK YOU VERY MUCH FOR MAKING A PAINTING WITH ME.
I HOPE...
...YOU'LL ALSO DO YOUR BEST IN SCHOOL, SENSEI.
...

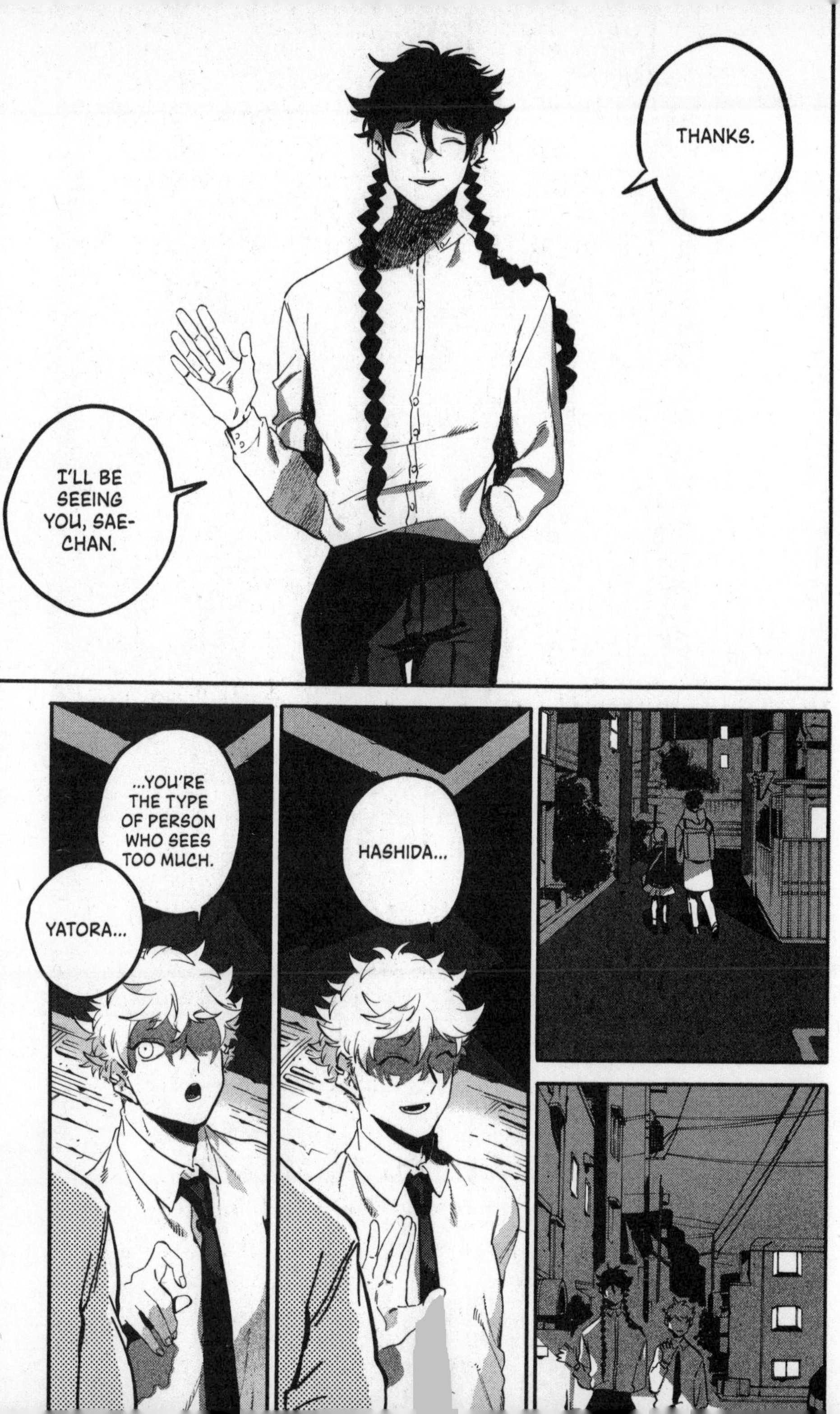
THANKS.
I'LL BE SEEING YOU, SAE-CHAN.
HASHIDA...
...YOU'RE THE TYPE OF PERSON WHO SEES TOO MUCH.
YATORA...

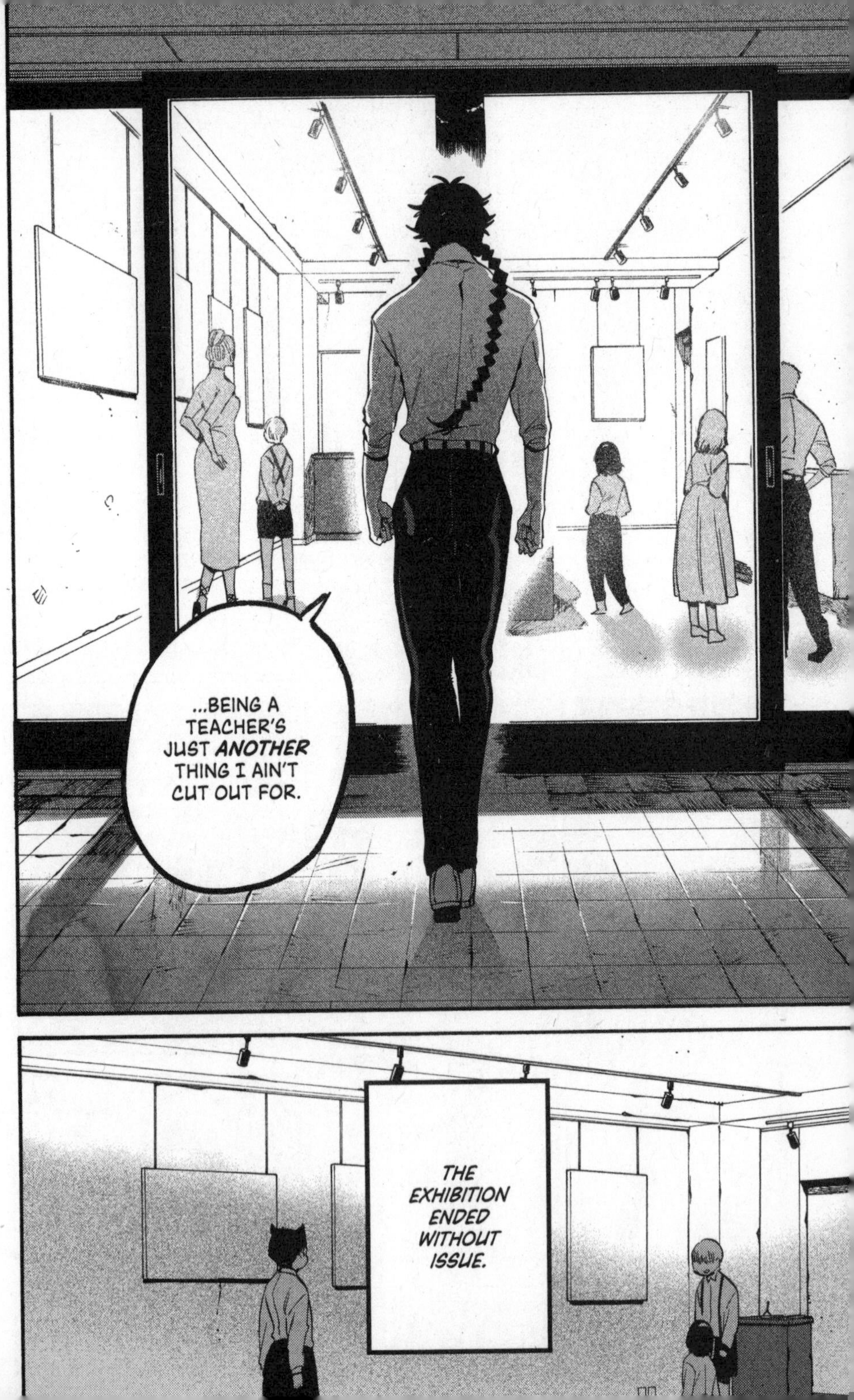
...BEING A TEACHER'S JUST ANOTHER THING I AIN'T CUT OUT FOR.
THE EXHIBITION ENDED WITHOUT ISSUE.

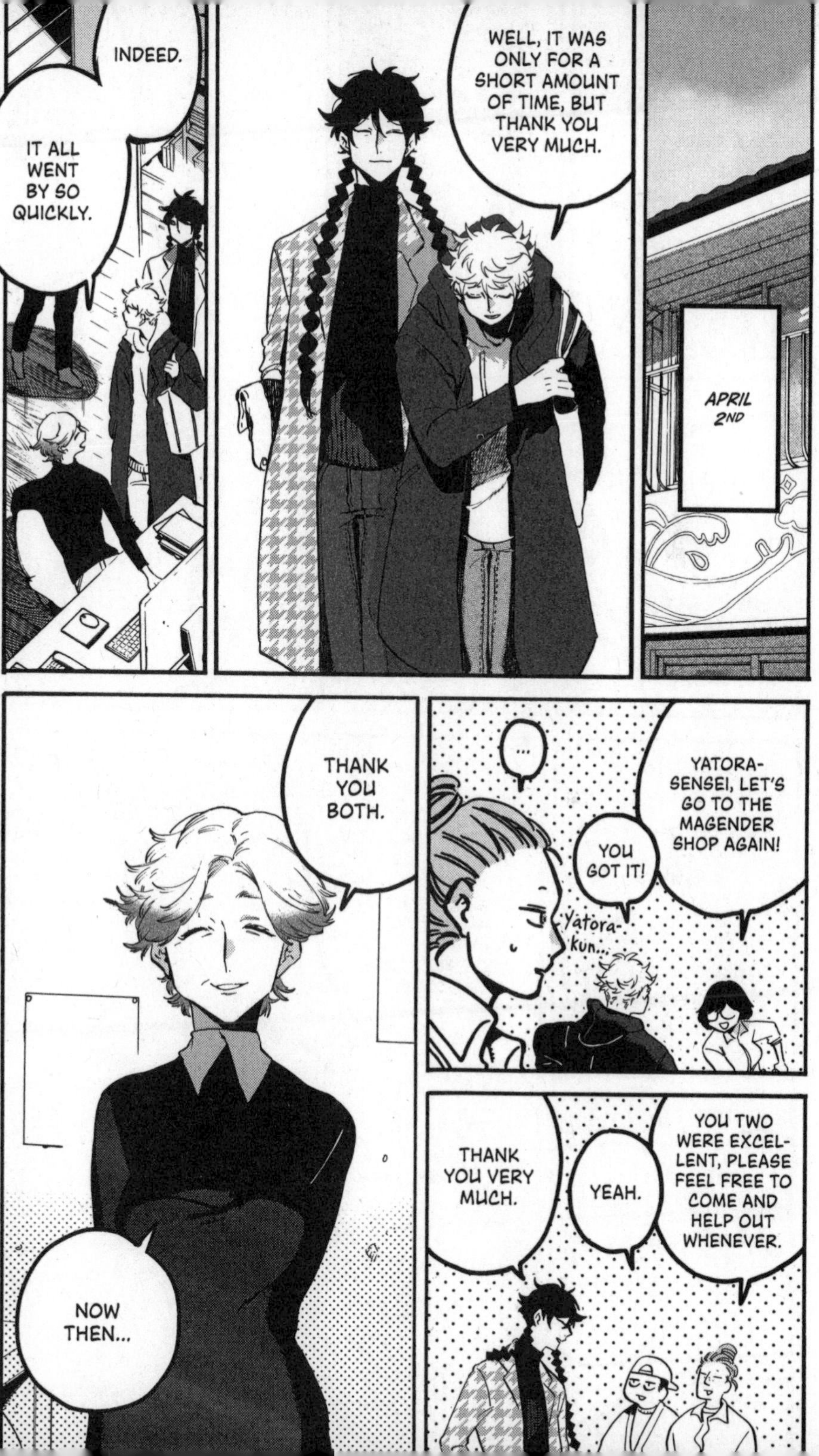
APRIL 2ND
WELL, IT WAS ONLY FOR A SHORT AMOUNT OF TIME, BUT THANK YOU VERY MUCH.
INDEED.
IT ALL WENT BY SO QUICKLY.
YATORA-SENSEI, LET'S GO TO THE MAGENDER SHOP AGAIN!
YOU GOT IT!
...
Yatora-kun...
YOU TWO WERE EXCEL-LENT, PLEASE FEEL FREE TO COME AND HELP OUT WHENEVER.
YEAH.
THANK YOU VERY MUCH.
THANK YOU BOTH.
NOW THEN...

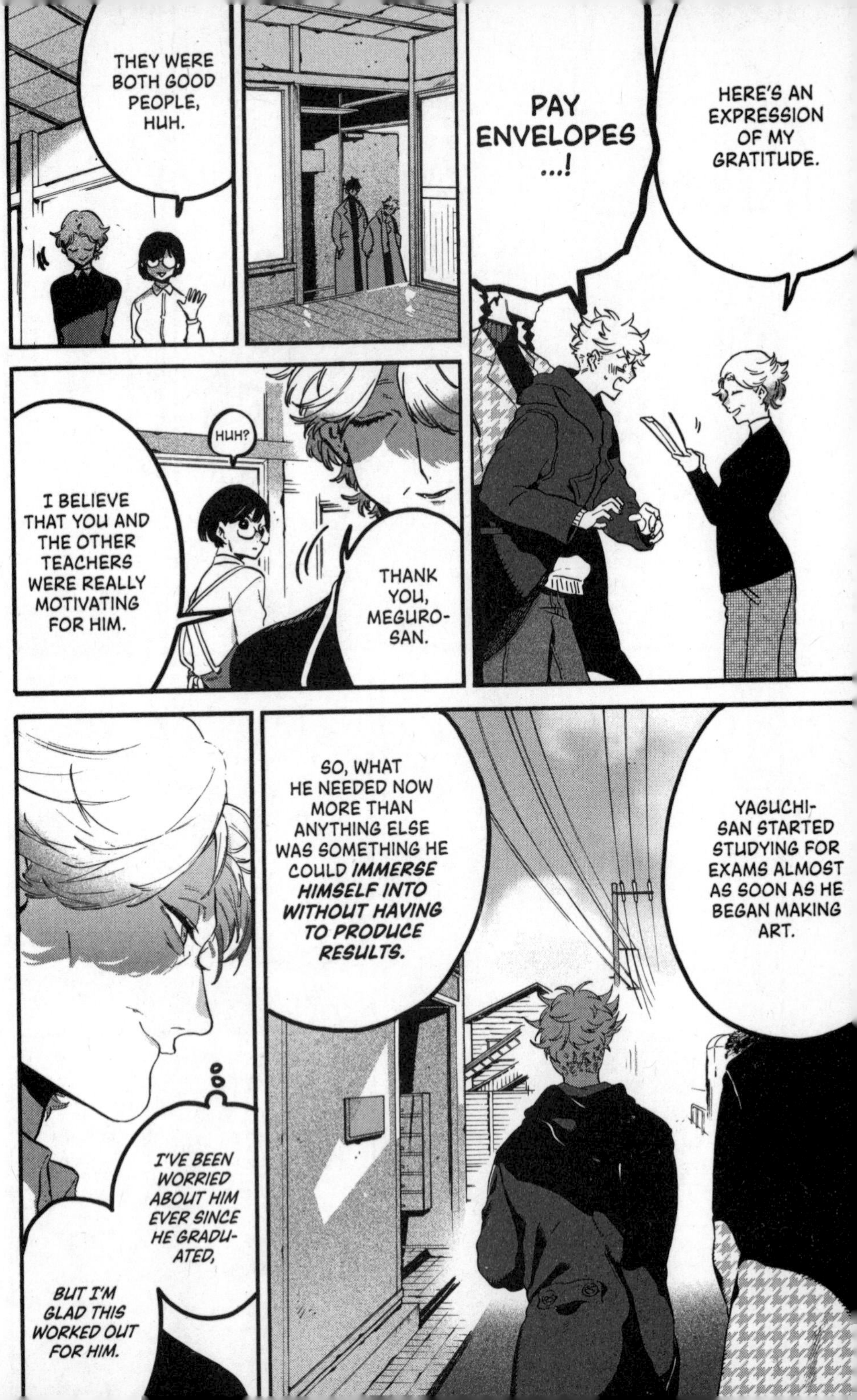
HERE'S AN EXPRESSION OF MY GRATITUDE.
PAY ENVELOPES ...!
THEY WERE BOTH GOOD PEOPLE, HUH.
THANK YOU, MEGURO-SAN.
HUH?
I BELIEVE THAT YOU AND THE OTHER TEACHERS WERE REALLY MOTIVATING FOR HIM.
YAGUCHI-SAN STARTED STUDYING FOR EXAMS ALMOST AS SOON AS HE BEGAN MAKING ART.
SO, WHAT HE NEEDED NOW MORE THAN ANYTHING ELSE WAS SOMETHING HE COULD *IMMERSE HIMSELF INTO WITHOUT HAVING TO PRODUCE RESULTS.*
I'VE BEEN WORRIED ABOUT HIM EVER SINCE HE GRADUATED,
BUT I'M GLAD THIS WORKED OUT FOR HIM.

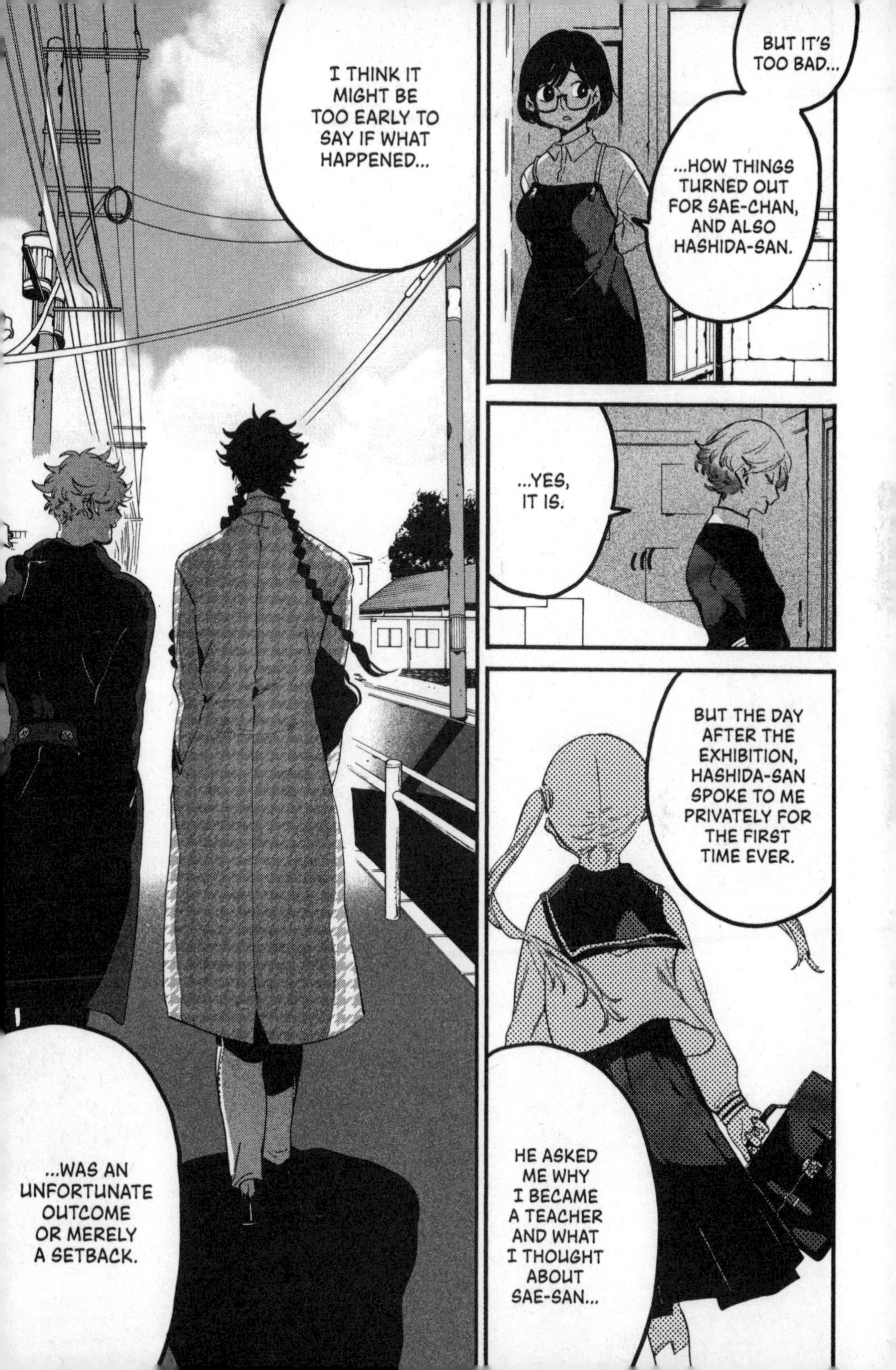
BUT IT'S TOO BAD...
...HOW THINGS TURNED OUT FOR SAE-CHAN, AND ALSO HASHIDA-SAN.
...YES, IT IS.
BUT THE DAY AFTER THE EXHIBITION, HASHIDA-SAN SPOKE TO ME PRIVATELY FOR THE FIRST TIME EVER.
HE ASKED ME WHY I BECAME A TEACHER AND WHAT I THOUGHT ABOUT SAE-SAN...
I THINK IT MIGHT BE TOO EARLY TO SAY IF WHAT HAPPENED...
...WAS AN UNFORTUNATE OUTCOME OR MERELY A SETBACK.

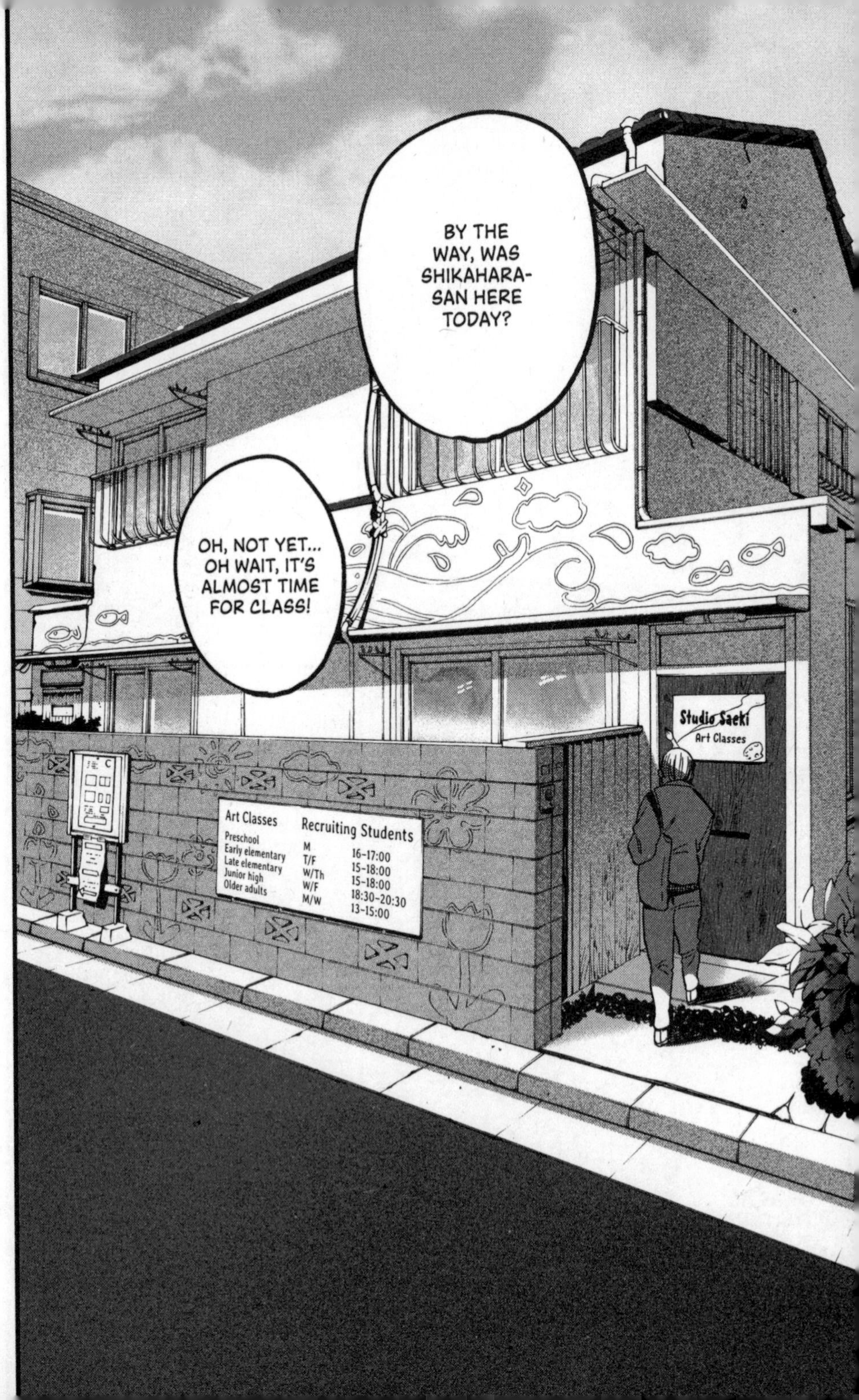
BY THE WAY, WAS SHIKAHARA-SAN HERE TODAY?
OH, NOT YET... OH WAIT, IT'S ALMOST TIME FOR CLASS!
Studio Saeki
Art Classes
Art Classes
Preschool
Early elementary
Late elementary
Junior high
Older adults
Recruiting Students
M 16-17:00
T/F 15-18:00
W/Th 15-18:00
W/F 18:30-20:30
M/W 13-15:00

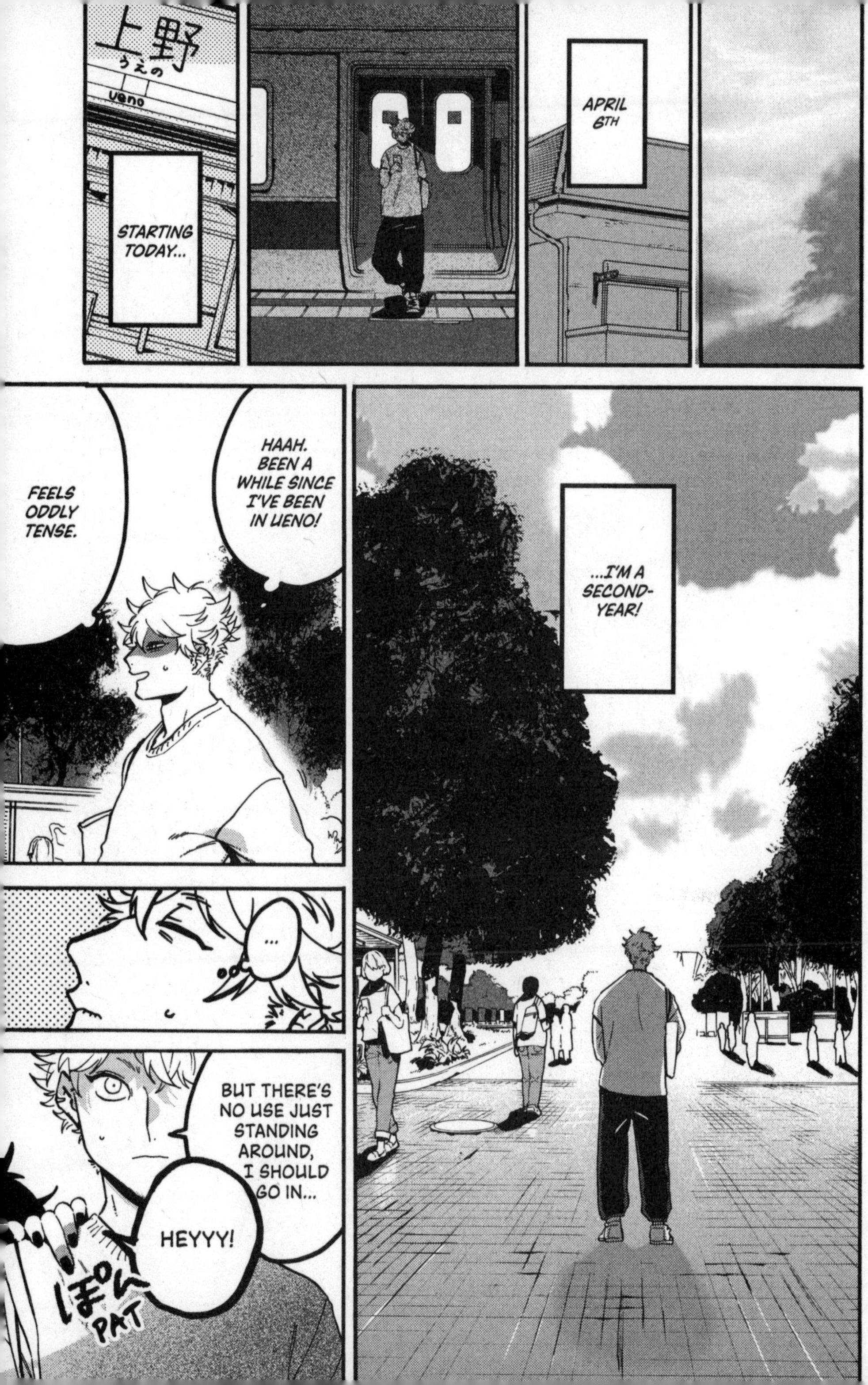

APRIL 6TH
上野
うえの
ueno
STARTING TODAY...
...I'M A SECOND-YEAR!
HAAH. BEEN A WHILE SINCE I'VE BEEN IN UENO!
FEELS ODDLY TENSE.
...
BUT THERE'S NO USE JUST STANDING AROUND, I SHOULD GO IN...
HEYYY!
ぽん
PAT

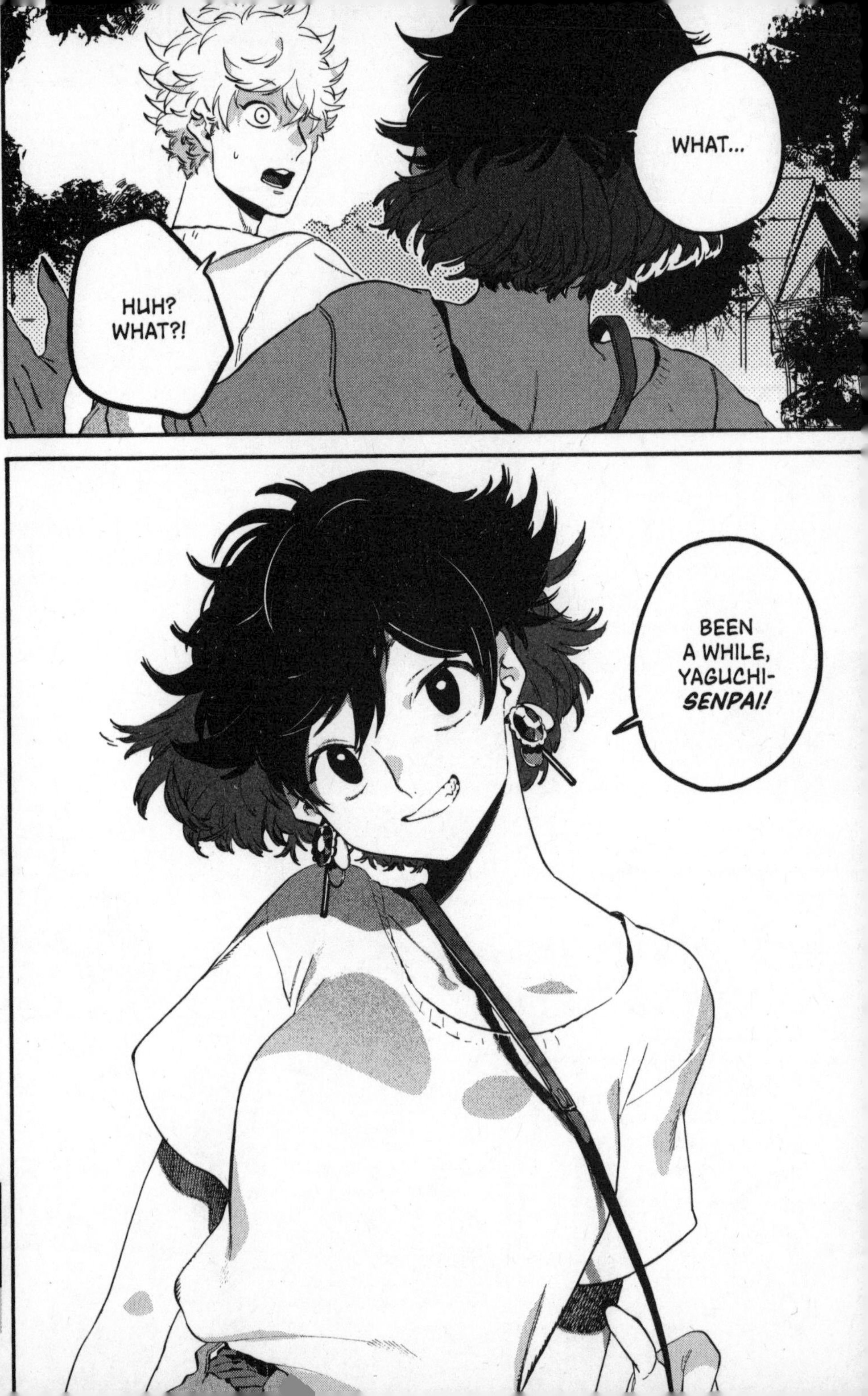
WHAT...
HUH? WHAT?!
BEEN A WHILE, YAGUCHI-*SENPAI!*

STROKE 47 END

DING DONG
ピンポーン!
Extra
COMING!
...OH?
COME ON IN.
SO, HOW'S JUNIOR HIGH?

Special Thanks

Blue Period was created with the support of many people!

Thank you so very much!

Wo-sakana-sama
Thank you for working on the designs and setting for Magender, despite my sudden request! Both Magender and Kento-kun are really cool and awesome...! I was also delighted to get so many recommendations on tokusatsu. I'm probably going to ask a lot of you from now on—I so appreciate your help!

Research cooperation: Kenji Matsuda-sama, The Hakone Open-Air Museum, BCF-sama—thank you very much!

Blue Period is now an anime!!
Check it out!

THE ART CLASS KIDS (1)

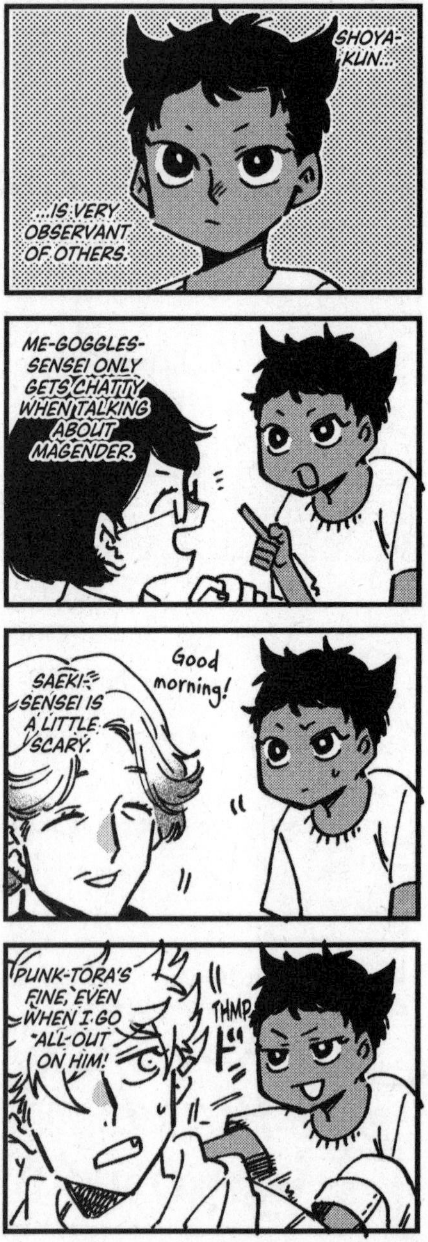
SHOYA-KUN...
...IS VERY OBSERVANT OF OTHERS.
ME-GOGGLES-SENSEI ONLY GETS CHATTY WHEN TALKING ABOUT MAGENDER.
Good morning!
SAEKI-SENSEI IS A LITTLE SCARY.
THMP
PUNK-TORA'S FINE, EVEN WHEN I GO ALL-OUT ON HIM!

THE ART CLASS KIDS (2)

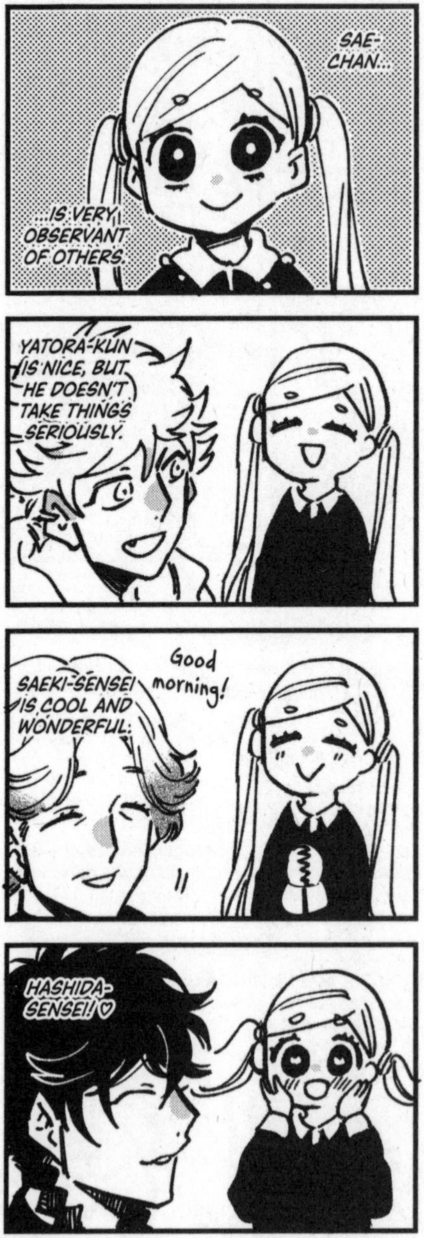
SAE-CHAN...
...IS VERY OBSERVANT OF OTHERS.
YATORA-KUN IS NICE, BUT HE DOESN'T TAKE THINGS SERIOUSLY.
Good morning!
SAEKI-SENSEI IS COOL AND WONDERFUL.
HASHIDA-SENSEI! ♡

THE ART CLASS TEACHERS (1)

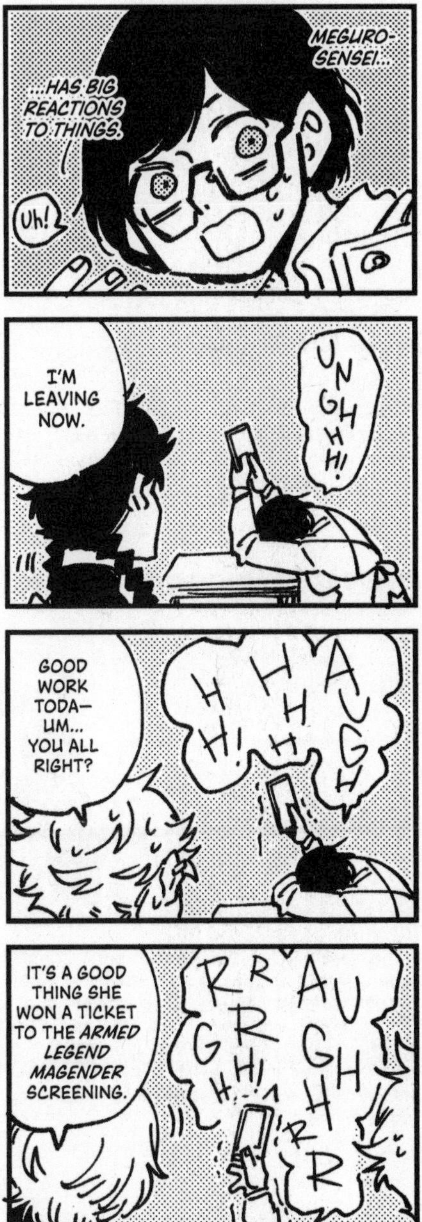
MEGURO-SENSEI...
...HAS BIG REACTIONS TO THINGS.
Uh!
UNGHHHH!
I'M LEAVING NOW.
AUGHH
HHHH
HH!
GOOD WORK TODA— UM... YOU ALL RIGHT?
RRAUGH
GRGHH
HH!
RRR
IT'S A GOOD THING SHE WON A TICKET TO THE *ARMED LEGEND MAGENDER* SCREENING.

THE ART CLASS TEACHERS (2)

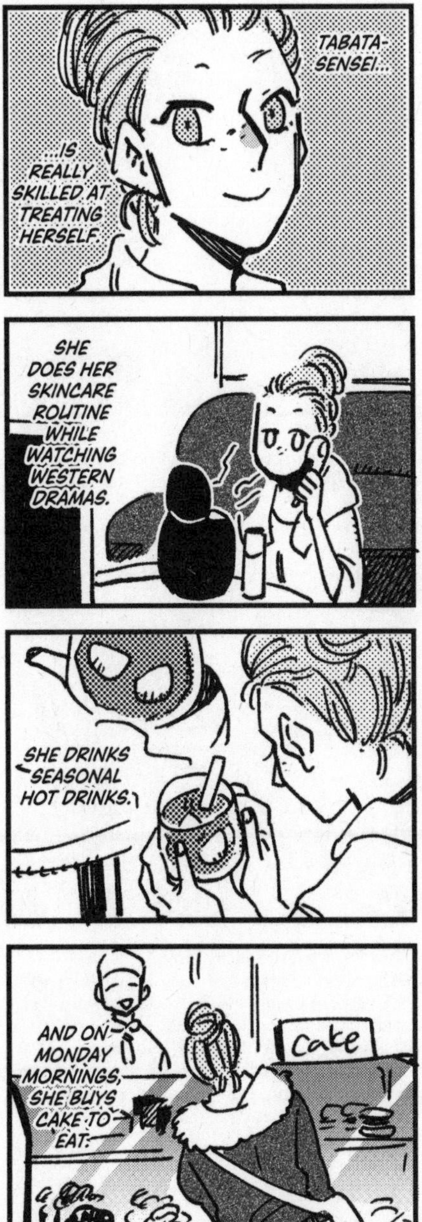
TABATA-SENSEI...
...IS REALLY SKILLED AT TREATING HERSELF.
SHE DOES HER SKINCARE ROUTINE WHILE WATCHING WESTERN DRAMAS.
SHE DRINKS SEASONAL HOT DRINKS.
cake
AND ON MONDAY MORNINGS, SHE BUYS CAKE TO EAT.

TRANSLATION NOTES

MY STUDIO EMPLOYS A TOTAL OF FIVE PEOPLE. THERE ARE FOUR INSTRUCTORS—MYSELF INCLUDED—TEACHING THE FOUR COURSES HERE, PLUS ONE ASSISTANT TEACHER.
Wakashi Course (3-5 years)
Inada Course (6-10 years)
Warasa Course (11-15 years)
Buri Course (For older adults)
CLASSES ARE AN HOUR LONG, START WITH A 15-MINUTE EXPLANATION OF THE ASSIGNMENT, AND END WITH PRESENTATIONS FOR 15 MINUTES.
Explanation
Production
Presentation

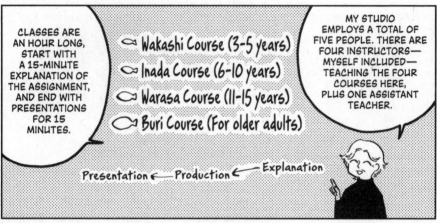

***Wakashi*, *inada*, *warasa*, and *buri*, page 12**
The names for Saeki-sensei's art courses are the names for Japanese yellowtail fish at different stages in their life. *Wakashi* is used for fish that are 5 to 15 cm long, *inada* is from 15 to 40 cm, *warasa* is from 40 to 60 cm, and *buri* is for fish that are over 60 cm.

Picasso's name is long?!
Picasso's name is extremely long. His full name is Pablo Diego José Francisco de Paula Juan Nepomuceno María de los Remedios Crispín Crispiniano de la Santísima Trinidad Ruiz
This type of long name partly comes from the Christian tradition of naming children after saints when they are baptized. In other words, it's like...
Jugemu Jugemu Goko-no Surikire Kaijarisu
no Suigyomatsu Unraimatsu Furaimatsu
tokoro-ni Sumutokoro Yaburakoji-no Burakoji
Paipopaipo Paipo-no Shuringan Shuringan-no
Gurindai Gurindai-no Ponpokopii-no Ponpokona-
...

Jugemu, page 21
In this scene, the book Yatora's reading compares Picasso's extraordinarily long name to the equally long name of someone whose name starts with Jugemu. This extra-long Japanese name is from a famous rakugo (a type of traditional storytelling performance) of the same name. The basic plot involves a new father who seeks the advice of a Buddhist priest to help him and his wife figure out a name for their child. The priest gives several suggestions, but the father is unable to choose one, so he chooses all of them. The performance of this story involves repeating the over 100-syllable long name several times, making it entertaining and great practice for young rakugo performers.

Some guy who was giving out pad thai, page 22
This is referring to the contemporary artist, Rirkrit Tiravanija. He's best known for a series of exhibitions where his piece was the act of cooking pad thai and distributing it to gallery visitors.

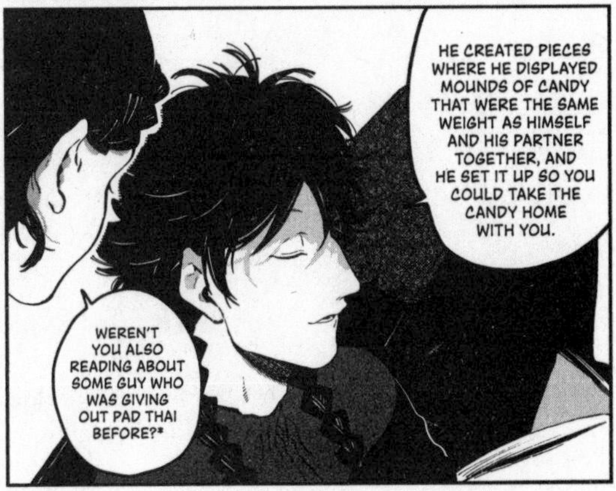
HE CREATED PIECES WHERE HE DISPLAYED MOUNDS OF CANDY THAT WERE THE SAME WEIGHT AS HIMSELF AND HIS PARTNER TOGETHER, AND HE SET IT UP SO YOU COULD TAKE THE CANDY HOME WITH YOU.
WEREN'T YOU ALSO READING ABOUT SOME GUY WHO WAS GIVING OUT PAD THAI BEFORE?*

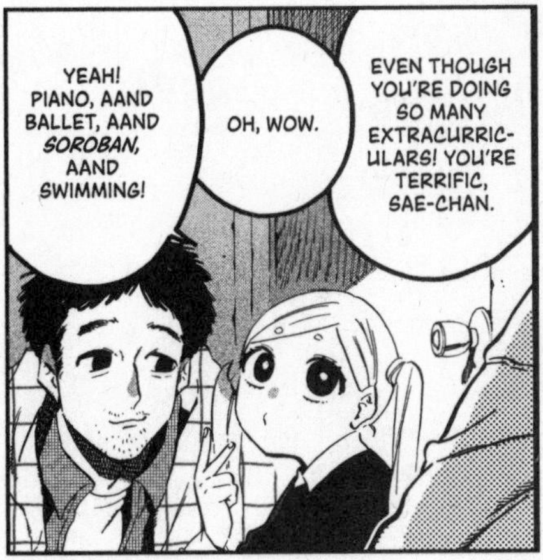
EVEN THOUGH YOU'RE DOING SO MANY EXTRACURRIC-ULARS! YOU'RE TERRIFIC, SAE-CHAN.
OH, WOW.
YEAH! PIANO, AAND BALLET, AAND *SOROBAN*, AAND SWIMMING!

Soroban, page 70
Soroban is a Japanese version of the abacus. Though ancient calculating tools like the abacus are rarely used in the United States, the soroban is a familiar sight in Japanese preschools and primary schools, where it is often used to teach basic arithmetic.

Pay envelopes, page 118
People in Japan don't use checks as a form of payment, so paychecks are uncommon. When automated, salaries are paid monthly through bank transfers or direct deposit. For smaller operations, it's traditional to receive cash in a long manila envelope. Cash is also much more of the norm in Japan compared to places like the United States, but credit cards are seeing more widespread use in recent years.

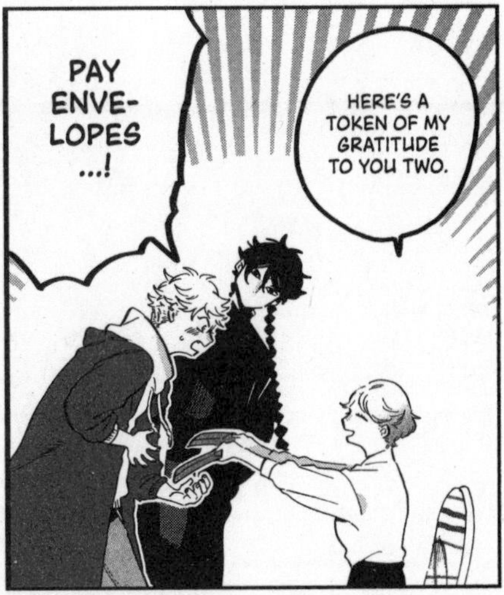
HERE'S A TOKEN OF MY GRATITUDE TO YOU TWO.
PAY ENVE-LOPES ...!

A Kodansha Comics Trade Paperback Original
Blue Period 11 copyright © 2021 Tsubasa Yamaguchi
English translation copyright © 2022 Tsubasa Yamaguchi

Published in the United States by Kodansha Comics, an imprint of Kodansha USA Publishing, LLC, New York.

Publication rights for this English edition arranged through Kodansha Ltd., Tokyo.

First published in Japan in 2021 by Kodansha Ltd., Tokyo.

ISBN 978-1-64651-566-0

Printed in the United States of America.

www.kodansha.us

9 8 7 6 5 4 3 2 1
Translation: Ajani Oloye
Lettering: Lys Blakeslee
Editing: Haruko Hashimoto
Kodansha Comics edition cover design by Matthew Akuginow

Publisher: Kiichiro Sugawara

Director of publishing services: Ben Applegate
Director of publishing operations: Dave Barrett
Associate director of publishing operations: Stephen Pakula
Publishing services managing editors: Madison Salters, Alanna Ruse, with Grace Chen
Production manager: Emi Lotto
Logo and character art ©Kodansha USA Publishing, LLC